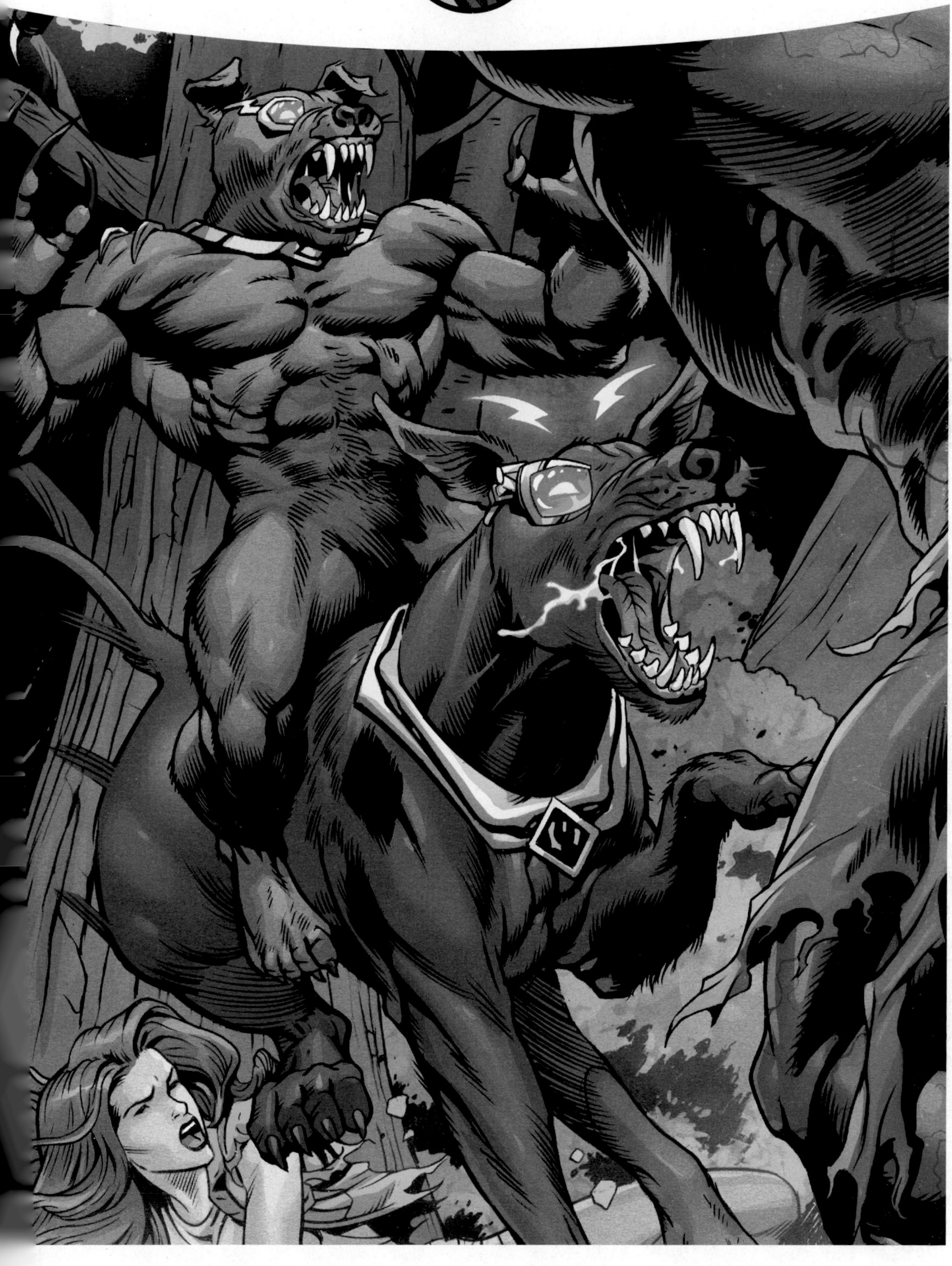

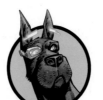

SCOOBY APOCALYPSE

VOL.3

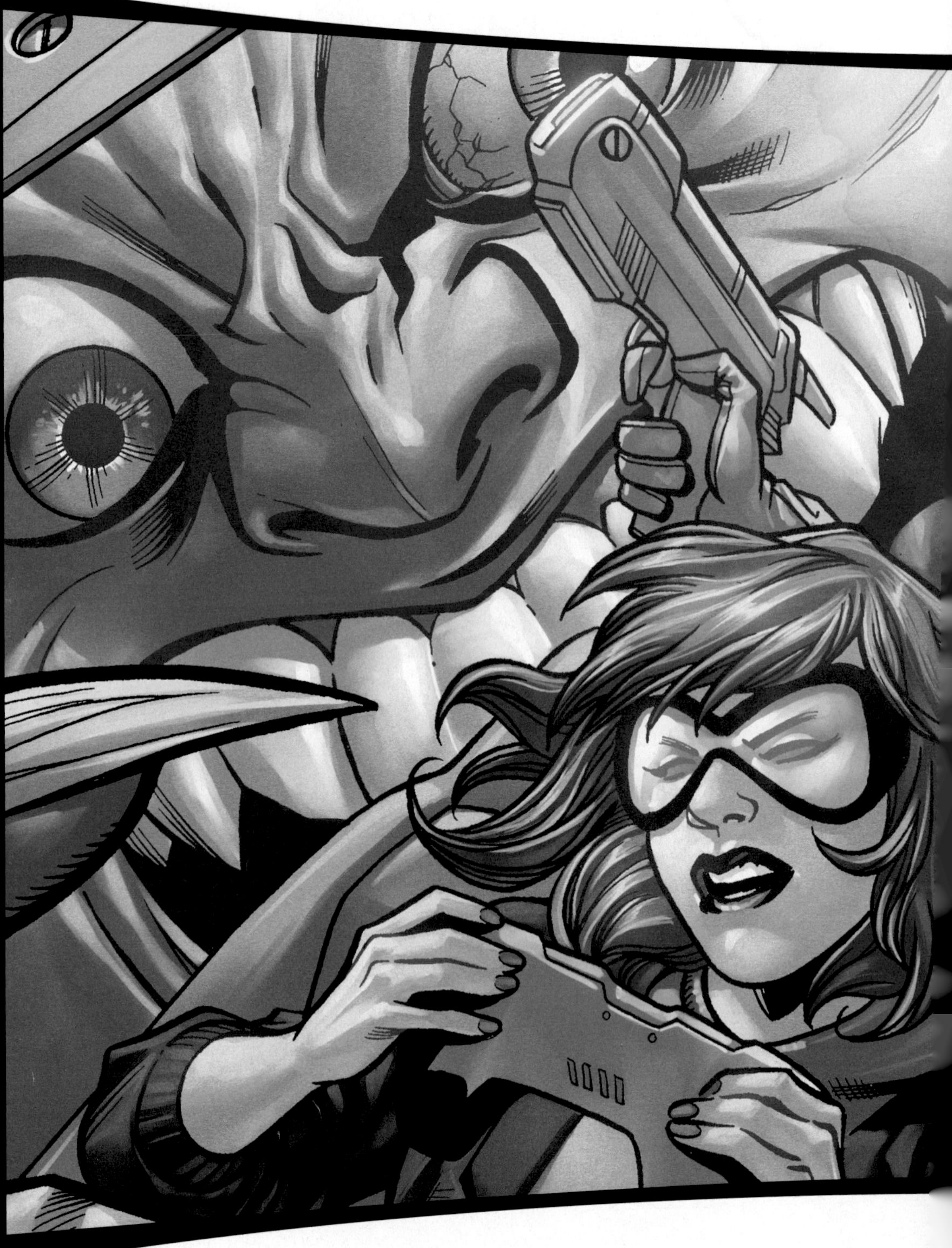

SCOOBY APOCALYPSE

VOL.

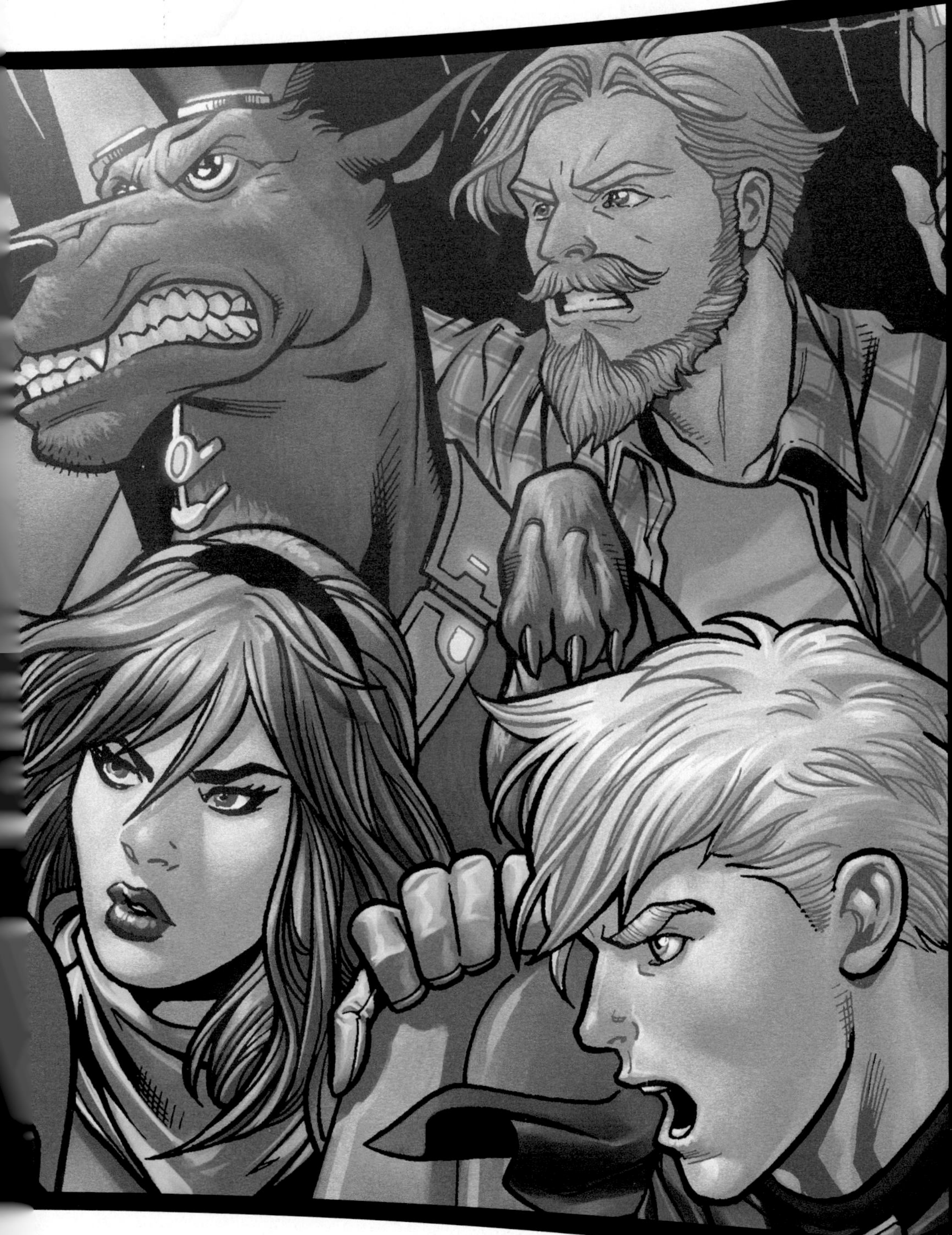

KEITH GIFFEN J.M. DeMATTEIS writers
DALE EAGLESHAM JAN DUURSEMA TOM DERENICK
RON WAGNER ANDY OWENS
TOM MANDRAKE SEAN PARSONS RICK LEONARDI
HOWARD PORTER DAN GREEN BEN CALDWELL artists
HI-FI JEREMY LAWSON colorists **TRAVIS LANHAM** letterer
NICK BRADSHAW and TOMEU MOREY collection cover artists
Based on a concept by **JIM LEE**

MARIE JAVINS Editor – Original Series BRITTANY HOLZHERR Associate Editor – Original Series DIEGO LOPEZ Assistant Editor – Original Series
JEB WOODARD Group Editor – Collected Editions ERIKA ROTHBERG Editor – Collected Edition
STEVE COOK Design Director – Books SHANNON STEWART Publication Design

BOB HARRAS Senior VP – Editor-in-Chief, DC Comics
PAT McCALLUM Executive Editor, DC Comics

DIANE NELSON President DAN DiDIO Publisher JIM LEE Publisher GEOFF JOHNS President & Chief Creative Officer
AMIT DESAI Executive VP – Business & Marketing Strategy, Direct to Consumer & Global Franchise Management
SAM ADES Senior VP & General Manager, Digital Services BOBBIE CHASE VP & Executive Editor, Young Reader & Talent Development
MARK CHIARELLO Senior VP – Art, Design & Collected Editions JOHN CUNNINGHAM Senior VP – Sales & Trade Marketing
ANNE DePIES Senior VP – Business Strategy, Finance & Administration DON FALLETTI VP – Manufacturing Operations
LAWRENCE GANEM VP – Editorial Administration & Talent Relations ALISON GILL Senior VP – Manufacturing & Operations
HANK KANALZ Senior VP – Editorial Strategy & Administration JAY KOGAN VP – Legal Affairs JACK MAHAN VP – Business Affairs
NICK J. NAPOLITANO VP – Manufacturing Administration EDDIE SCANNELL VP – Consumer Marketing
COURTNEY SIMMONS Senior VP – Publicity & Communications JIM (SKI) SOKOLOWSKI VP – Comic Book Specialty Sales & Trade Marketing
NANCY SPEARS VP – Mass, Book, Digital Sales & Trade Marketing MICHELE R. WELLS VP – Content Strategy

SCOOBY APOCALYPSE VOLUME 3

DC Comics, 2900 West Alameda Ave., Burbank, CA 91505
Printed by LSC Communications, Kendallville, IN, USA. 1/5/18. First Printing.
ISBN: 978-1-4012-7748-2

Library of Congress Cataloging-in-Publication Data is available

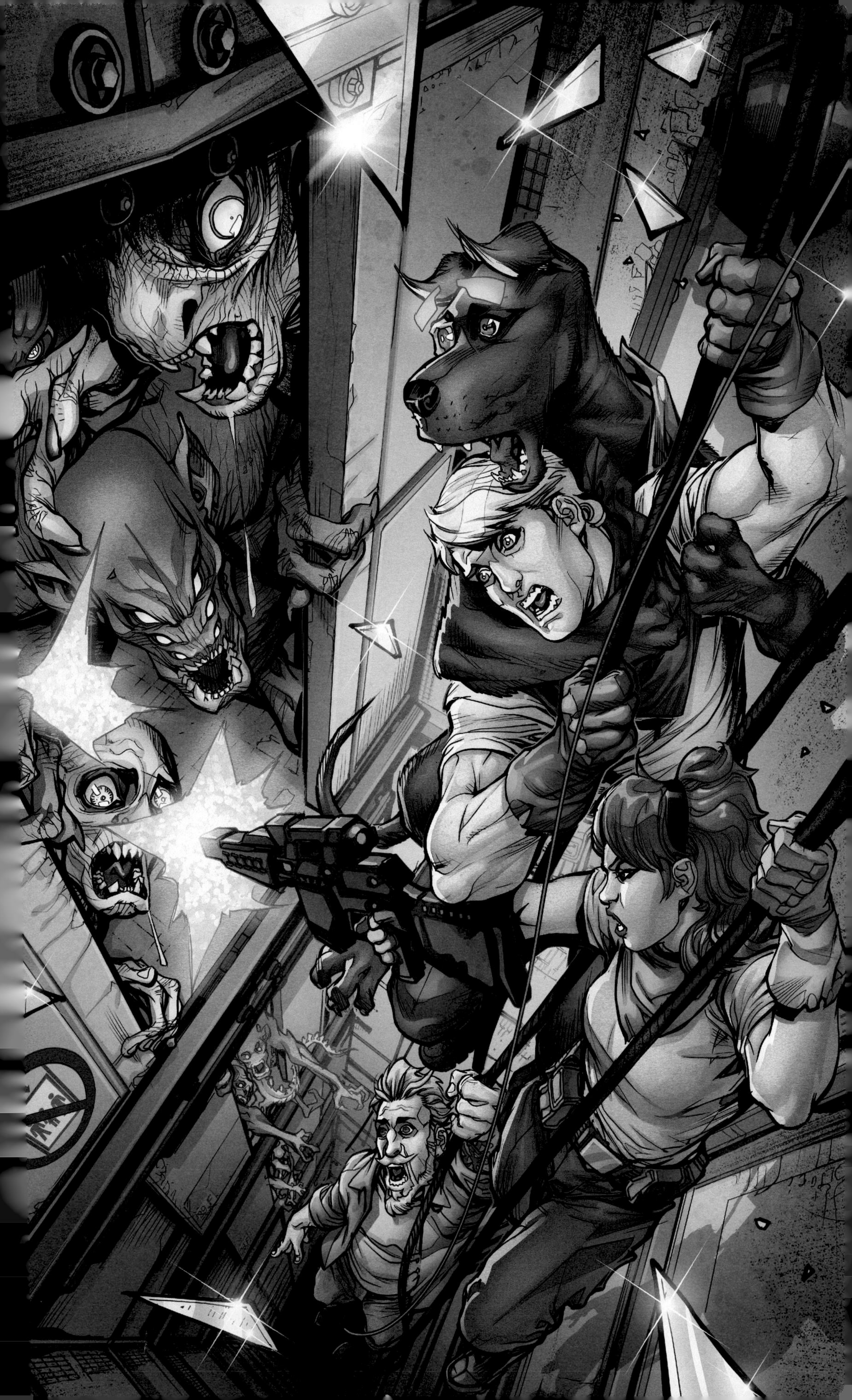

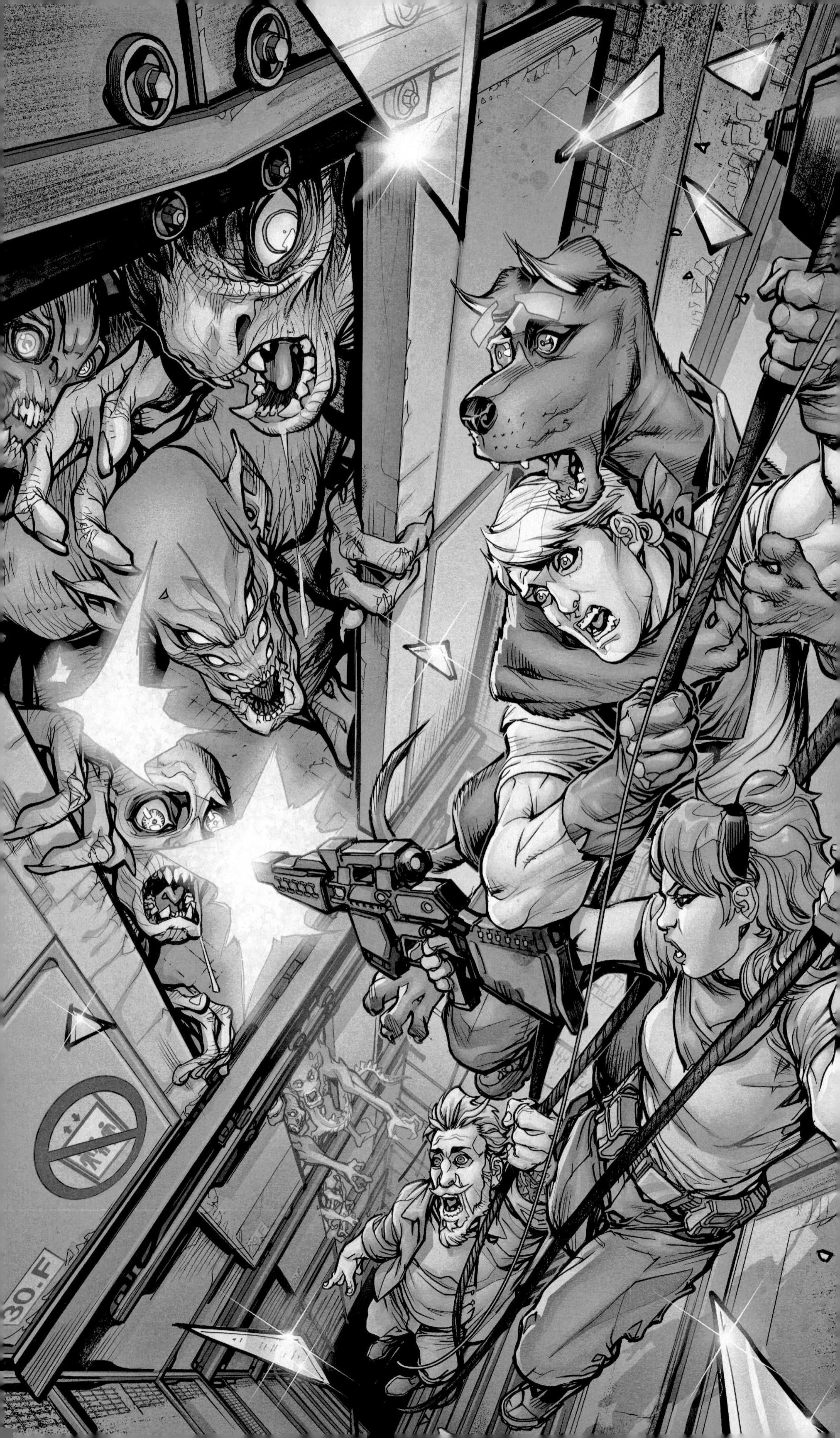
30.F

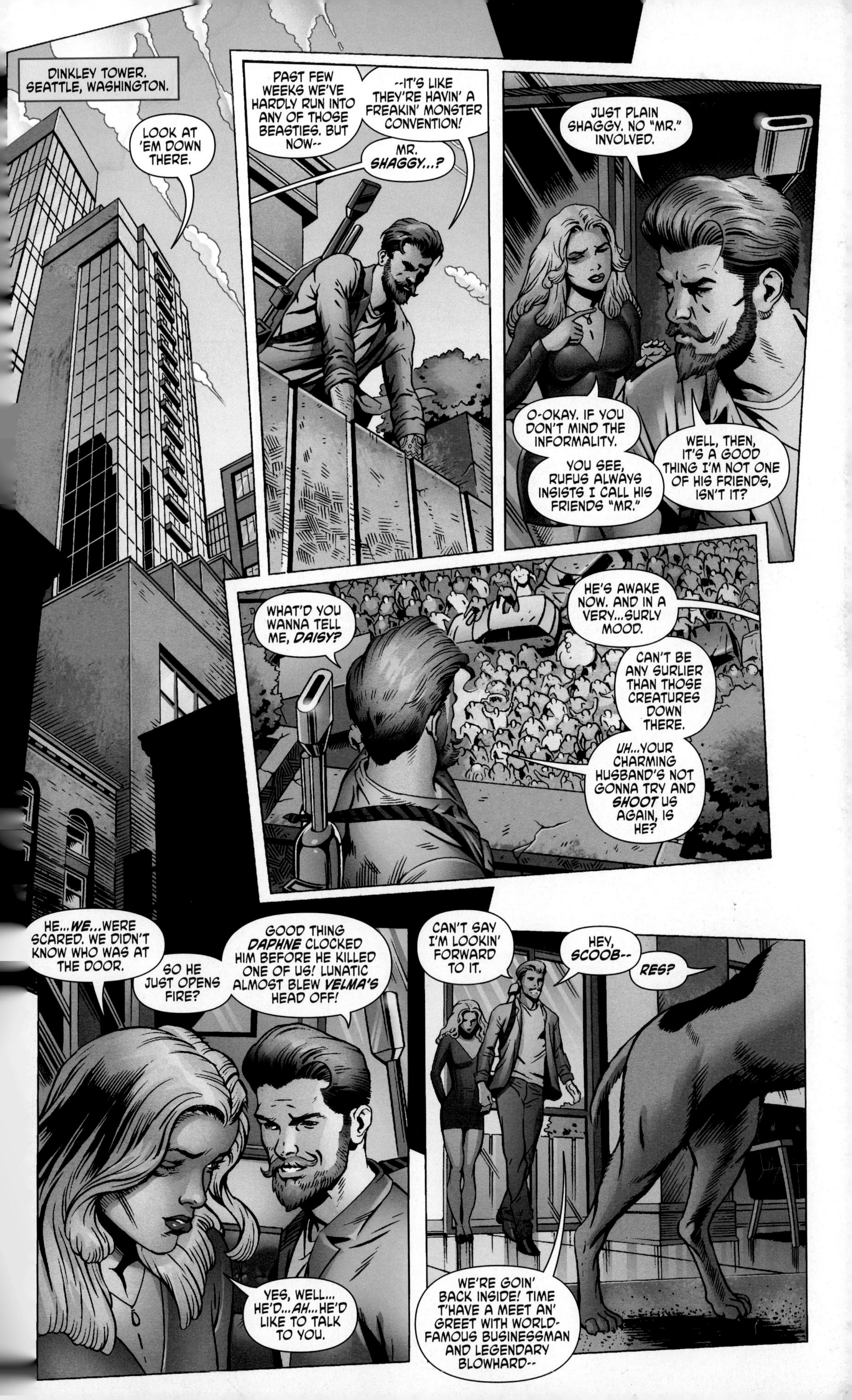

DINKLEY TOWER. SEATTLE, WASHINGTON.
LOOK AT 'EM DOWN THERE.
PAST FEW WEEKS WE'VE HARDLY RUN INTO ANY OF THOSE BEASTIES. BUT NOW--
--IT'S LIKE THEY'RE HAVIN' A FREAKIN' MONSTER CONVENTION!
MR. SHAGGY...?
JUST PLAIN SHAGGY. NO "MR." INVOLVED.
O-OKAY. IF YOU DON'T MIND THE INFORMALITY.
YOU SEE, RUFUS ALWAYS INSISTS I CALL HIS FRIENDS "MR."
WELL, THEN, IT'S A GOOD THING I'M NOT ONE OF HIS FRIENDS, ISN'T IT?
WHAT'D YOU WANNA TELL ME, DAISY?
HE'S AWAKE NOW. AND IN A VERY...SURLY MOOD.
CAN'T BE ANY SURLIER THAN THOSE CREATURES DOWN THERE.
UH...YOUR CHARMING HUSBAND'S NOT GONNA TRY AND SHOOT US AGAIN, IS HE?
HE...WE...WERE SCARED. WE DIDN'T KNOW WHO WAS AT THE DOOR.
SO HE JUST OPENS FIRE?
GOOD THING DAPHNE CLOCKED HIM BEFORE HE KILLED ONE OF US! LUNATIC ALMOST BLEW VELMA'S HEAD OFF!
YES, WELL... HE'D...AH...HE'D LIKE TO TALK TO YOU.
CAN'T SAY I'M LOOKIN' FORWARD TO IT.
HEY, SCOOB--
RES?
WE'RE GOIN' BACK INSIDE! TIME T'HAVE A MEET AN' GREET WITH WORLD-FAMOUS BUSINESSMAN AND LEGENDARY BLOWHARD--

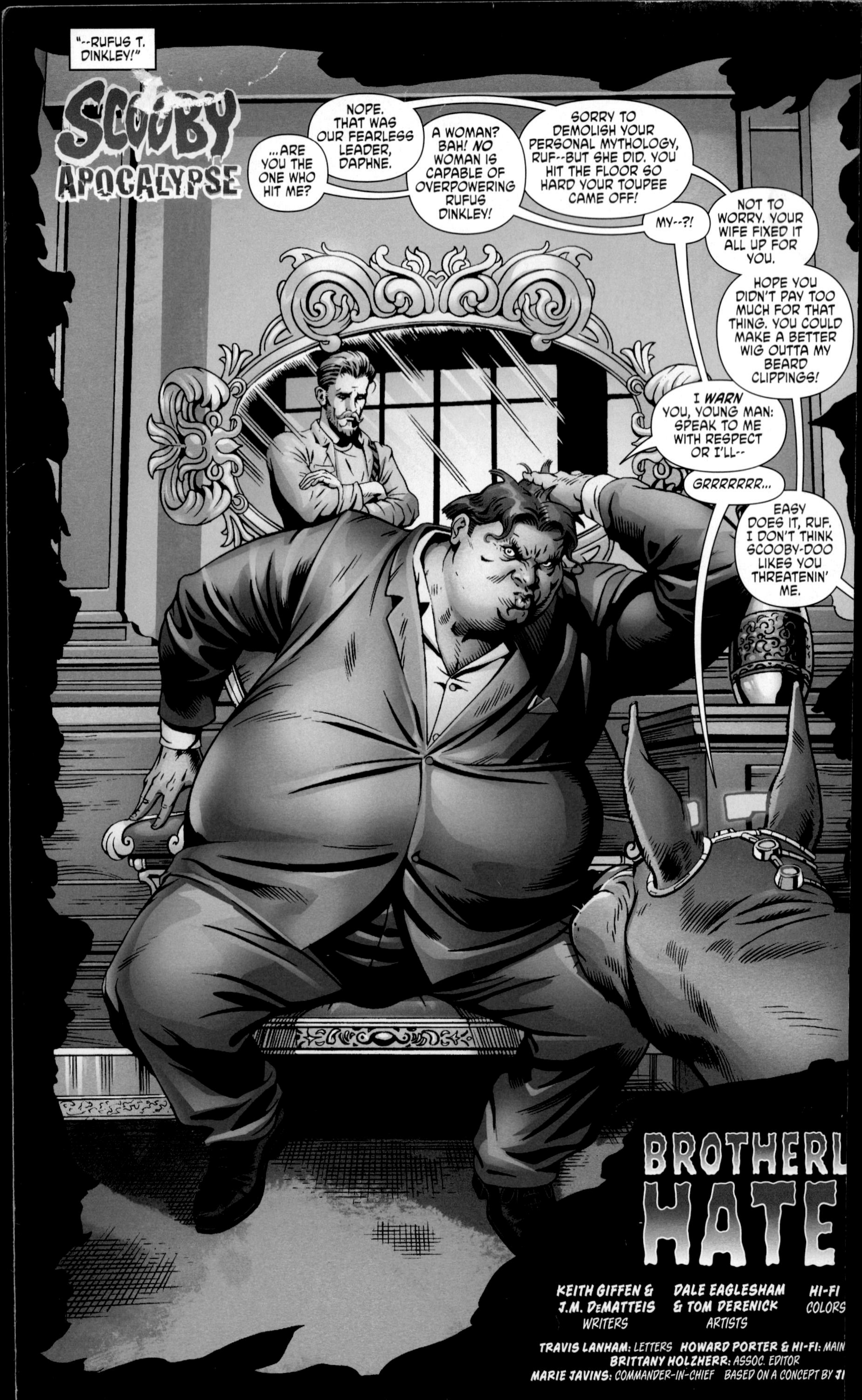
"--RUFUS T. DINKLEY!"
SCOOBY APOCALYPSE
...ARE YOU THE ONE WHO HIT ME?
NOPE. THAT WAS OUR FEARLESS LEADER, DAPHNE.
A WOMAN? BAH! NO WOMAN IS CAPABLE OF OVERPOWERING RUFUS DINKLEY!
SORRY TO DEMOLISH YOUR PERSONAL MYTHOLOGY, RUF--BUT SHE DID. YOU HIT THE FLOOR SO HARD YOUR TOUPEE CAME OFF!
MY--?!
NOT TO WORRY. YOUR WIFE FIXED IT ALL UP FOR YOU.
HOPE YOU DIDN'T PAY TOO MUCH FOR THAT THING. YOU COULD MAKE A BETTER WIG OUTTA MY BEARD CLIPPINGS!
I WARN YOU, YOUNG MAN: SPEAK TO ME WITH RESPECT OR I'LL--
GRRRRRRR...
EASY DOES IT, RUF. I DON'T THINK SCOOBY-DOO LIKES YOU THREATENIN' ME.
BROTHERL
HATE
KEITH GIFFEN & J.M. DeMATTEIS WRITERS
DALE EAGLESHAM & TOM DERENICK ARTISTS
HI-FI COLORS
TRAVIS LANHAM: LETTERS HOWARD PORTER & HI-FI: MAIN
BRITTANY HOLZHERR: ASSOC. EDITOR
MARIE JAVINS: COMMANDER-IN-CHIEF BASED ON A CONCEPT BY JI

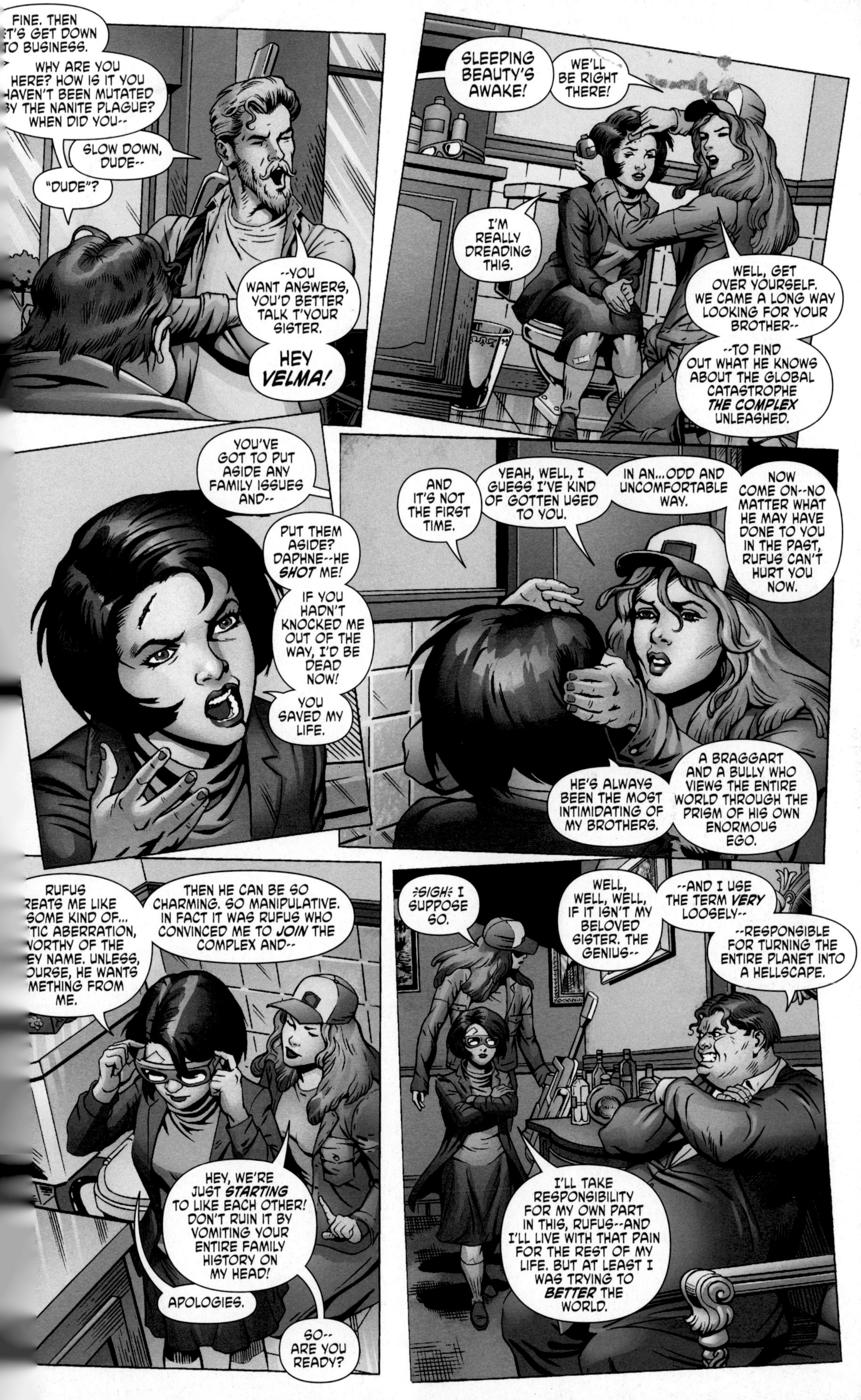

FINE. THEN ET'S GET DOWN TO BUSINESS.
WHY ARE YOU HERE? HOW IS IT YOU HAVEN'T BEEN MUTATED BY THE NANITE PLAGUE? WHEN DID YOU--
SLOW DOWN, DUDE--
"DUDE"?
--YOU WANT ANSWERS, YOU'D BETTER TALK T'YOUR SISTER.
HEY *VELMA!*
SLEEPING BEAUTY'S AWAKE!
WE'LL BE RIGHT THERE!
I'M REALLY DREADING THIS.
WELL, GET OVER YOURSELF. WE CAME A LONG WAY LOOKING FOR YOUR BROTHER--
--TO FIND OUT WHAT HE KNOWS ABOUT THE GLOBAL CATASTROPHE *THE COMPLEX* UNLEASHED.
YOU'VE GOT TO PUT ASIDE ANY FAMILY ISSUES AND--
PUT THEM ASIDE? DAPHNE--HE *SHOT* ME!
IF YOU HADN'T KNOCKED ME OUT OF THE WAY, I'D BE DEAD NOW!
YOU SAVED MY LIFE.
AND IT'S NOT THE FIRST TIME.
YEAH, WELL, I GUESS I'VE KIND OF GOTTEN USED TO YOU.
IN AN...ODD AND UNCOMFORTABLE WAY.
NOW COME ON--NO MATTER WHAT HE MAY HAVE DONE TO YOU IN THE PAST, RUFUS CAN'T HURT YOU NOW.
HE'S ALWAYS BEEN THE MOST INTIMIDATING OF MY BROTHERS.
A BRAGGART AND A BULLY WHO VIEWS THE ENTIRE WORLD THROUGH THE PRISM OF HIS OWN ENORMOUS EGO.
RUFUS REATS ME LIKE SOME KIND OF... TIC ABERRATION, WORTHY OF THE EY NAME. UNLESS, OURSE, HE WANTS METHING FROM ME.
THEN HE CAN BE SO CHARMING. SO MANIPULATIVE. IN FACT IT WAS RUFUS WHO CONVINCED ME TO *JOIN* THE COMPLEX AND--
HEY, WE'RE JUST *STARTING* TO LIKE EACH OTHER! DON'T RUIN IT BY VOMITING YOUR ENTIRE FAMILY HISTORY ON MY HEAD!
APOLOGIES.
SO--ARE YOU READY?
SIGH I SUPPOSE SO.
WELL, WELL, WELL, IF IT ISN'T MY BELOVED SISTER. THE GENIUS--
--AND I USE THE TERM *VERY* LOOSELY--
--RESPONSIBLE FOR TURNING THE ENTIRE PLANET INTO A HELLSCAPE.
I'LL TAKE RESPONSIBILITY FOR MY OWN PART IN THIS, RUFUS--AND I'LL LIVE WITH THAT PAIN FOR THE REST OF MY LIFE. BUT AT LEAST I WAS TRYING TO *BETTER* THE WORLD.

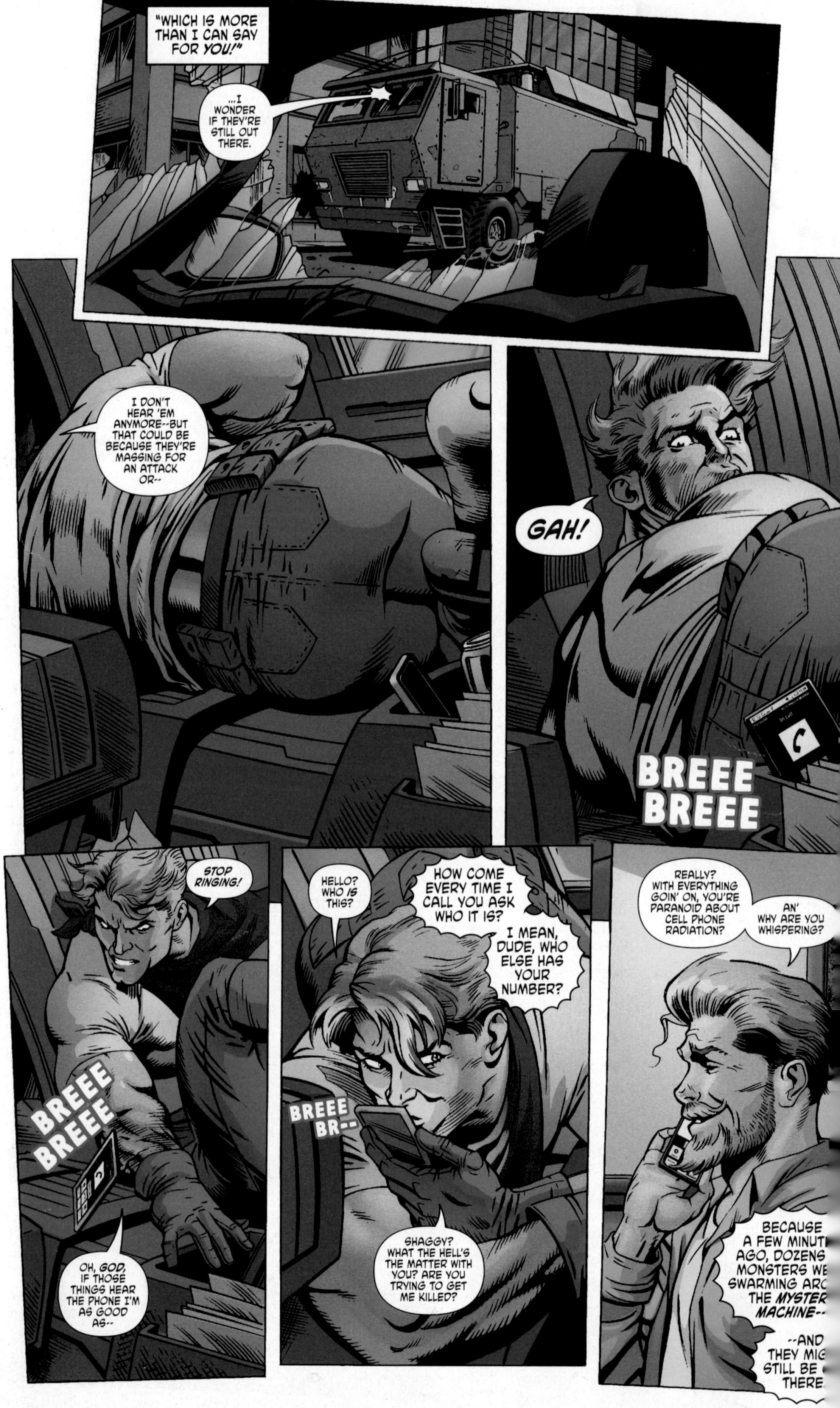
"WHICH IS MORE THAN I CAN SAY FOR YOU!"
...I WONDER IF THEY'RE STILL OUT THERE.
I DON'T HEAR 'EM ANYMORE--BUT THAT COULD BE BECAUSE THEY'RE MASSING FOR AN ATTACK OR--
GAH!
BREEE BREEE
STOP RINGING!
BREEE BREEE
OH, GOD, IF THOSE THINGS HEAR THE PHONE I'M AS GOOD AS--
HELLO? WHO IS THIS?
HOW COME EVERY TIME I CALL YOU ASK WHO IT IS?
I MEAN, DUDE, WHO ELSE HAS YOUR NUMBER?
BREEE BR--
SHAGGY? WHAT THE HELL'S THE MATTER WITH YOU? ARE YOU TRYING TO GET ME KILLED?
REALLY? WITH EVERYTHING GOIN' ON, YOU'RE PARANOID ABOUT CELL PHONE RADIATION?
AN' WHY ARE YOU WHISPERING?
BECAUSE A FEW MINUT AGO, DOZENS MONSTERS WE SWARMING ARO THE MYSTER MACHINE--
--AND THEY MIG STILL BE THERE

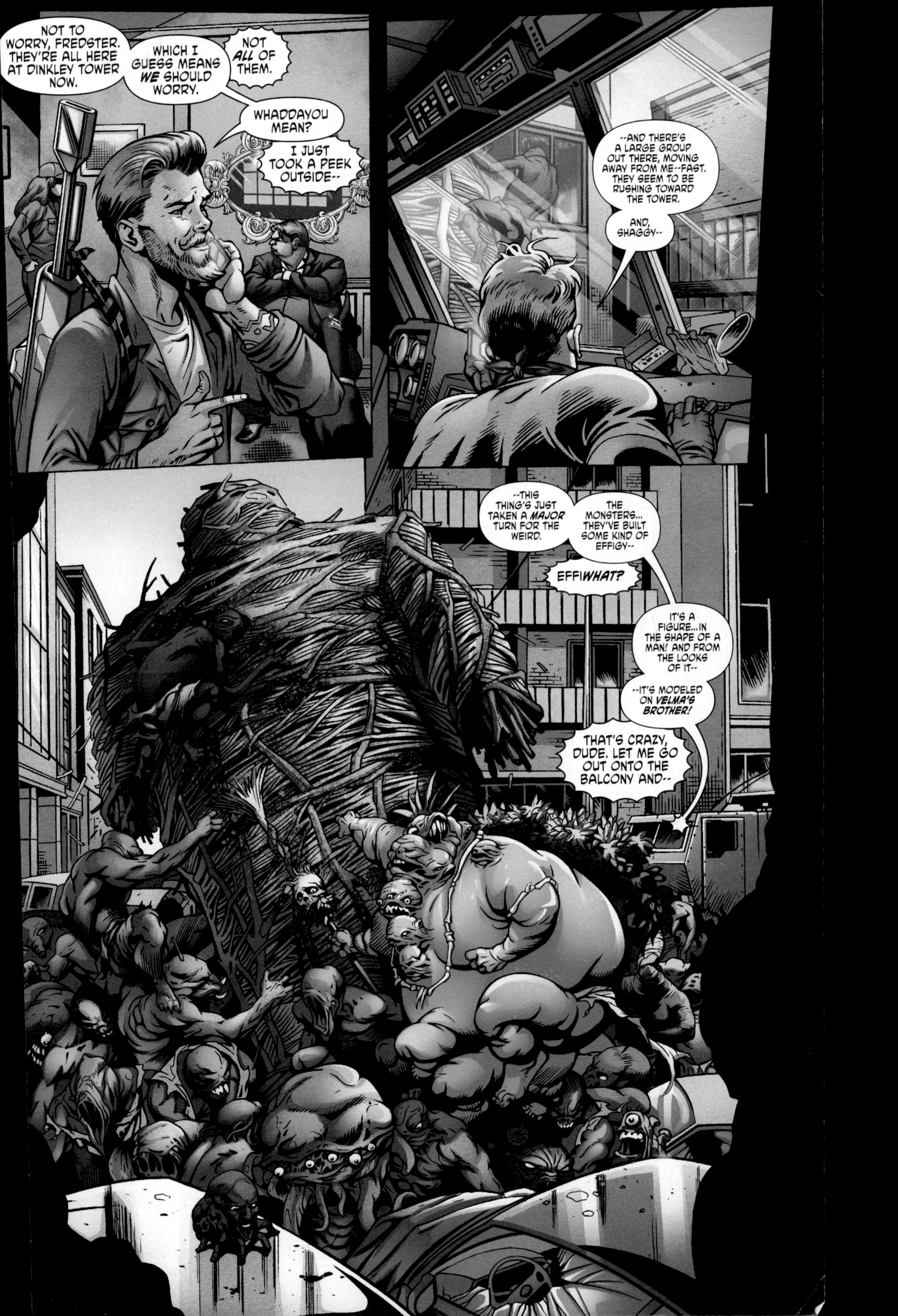
NOT TO WORRY, FREDSTER. THEY'RE ALL HERE AT DINKLEY TOWER NOW.
WHICH I GUESS MEANS *WE* SHOULD WORRY.
NOT *ALL* OF THEM.
WHADDAYOU MEAN?
I JUST TOOK A PEEK OUTSIDE--
--AND THERE'S A LARGE GROUP OUT THERE, MOVING AWAY FROM ME--FAST. THEY SEEM TO BE RUSHING TOWARD THE TOWER.
AND, SHAGGY--
--THIS THING'S JUST TAKEN A *MAJOR* TURN FOR THE WEIRD.
THE MONSTERS... THEY'VE BUILT SOME KIND OF EFFIGY--
EFFI*WHAT?*
IT'S A FIGURE...IN THE SHAPE OF A MAN! AND FROM THE LOOKS OF IT--
--IT'S MODELED ON *VELMA'S BROTHER!*
THAT'S CRAZY, DUDE. LET ME GO OUT ONTO THE BALCONY AND--

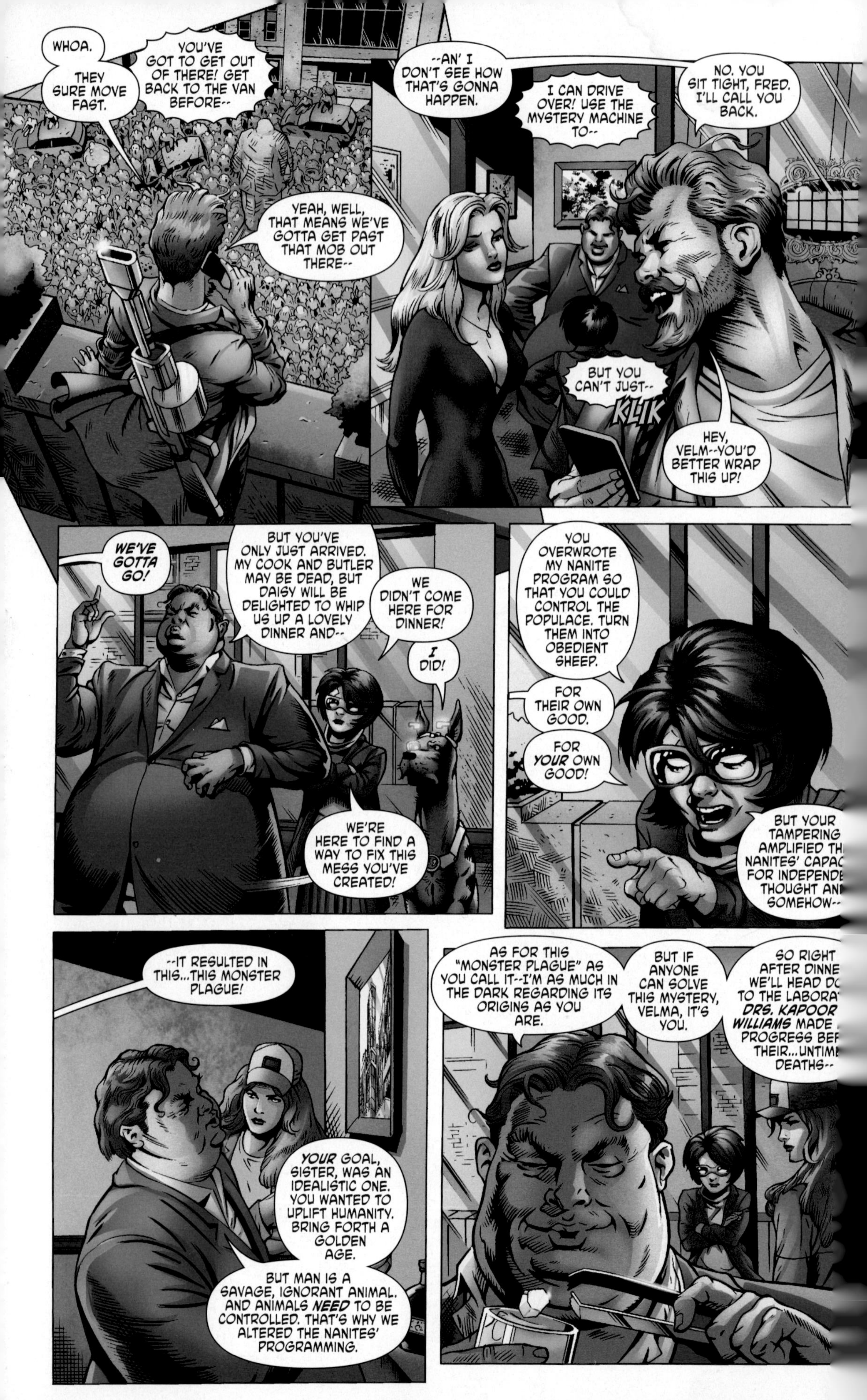
WHOA.
THEY SURE MOVE FAST.
YOU'VE GOT TO GET OUT OF THERE! GET BACK TO THE VAN BEFORE--
YEAH, WELL, THAT MEANS WE'VE GOTTA GET PAST THAT MOB OUT THERE--
--AN' I DON'T SEE HOW THAT'S GONNA HAPPEN.
I CAN DRIVE OVER! USE THE MYSTERY MACHINE TO--
NO. YOU SIT TIGHT, FRED. I'LL CALL YOU BACK.
BUT YOU CAN'T JUST--
KLIK
HEY, VELM--YOU'D BETTER WRAP THIS UP!
WE'VE GOTTA GO!
BUT YOU'VE ONLY JUST ARRIVED. MY COOK AND BUTLER MAY BE DEAD, BUT DAISY WILL BE DELIGHTED TO WHIP US UP A LOVELY DINNER AND--
WE DIDN'T COME HERE FOR DINNER!
I DID!
WE'RE HERE TO FIND A WAY TO FIX THIS MESS YOU'VE CREATED!
YOU OVERWROTE MY NANITE PROGRAM SO THAT YOU COULD CONTROL THE POPULACE. TURN THEM INTO OBEDIENT SHEEP.
FOR THEIR OWN GOOD.
FOR YOUR OWN GOOD!
BUT YOUR TAMPERING AMPLIFIED THE NANITES' CAPAC FOR INDEPENDE THOUGHT AN SOMEHOW--
--IT RESULTED IN THIS...THIS MONSTER PLAGUE!
YOUR GOAL, SISTER, WAS AN IDEALISTIC ONE. YOU WANTED TO UPLIFT HUMANITY. BRING FORTH A GOLDEN AGE.
BUT MAN IS A SAVAGE, IGNORANT ANIMAL. AND ANIMALS NEED TO BE CONTROLLED. THAT'S WHY WE ALTERED THE NANITES' PROGRAMMING.
AS FOR THIS "MONSTER PLAGUE" AS YOU CALL IT--I'M AS MUCH IN THE DARK REGARDING ITS ORIGINS AS YOU ARE.
BUT IF ANYONE CAN SOLVE THIS MYSTERY, VELMA, IT'S YOU.
SO RIGHT AFTER DINNE WE'LL HEAD DO TO THE LABORA DRS. KAPOOR WILLIAMS MADE PROGRESS BEF THEIR...UNTIME DEATHS--

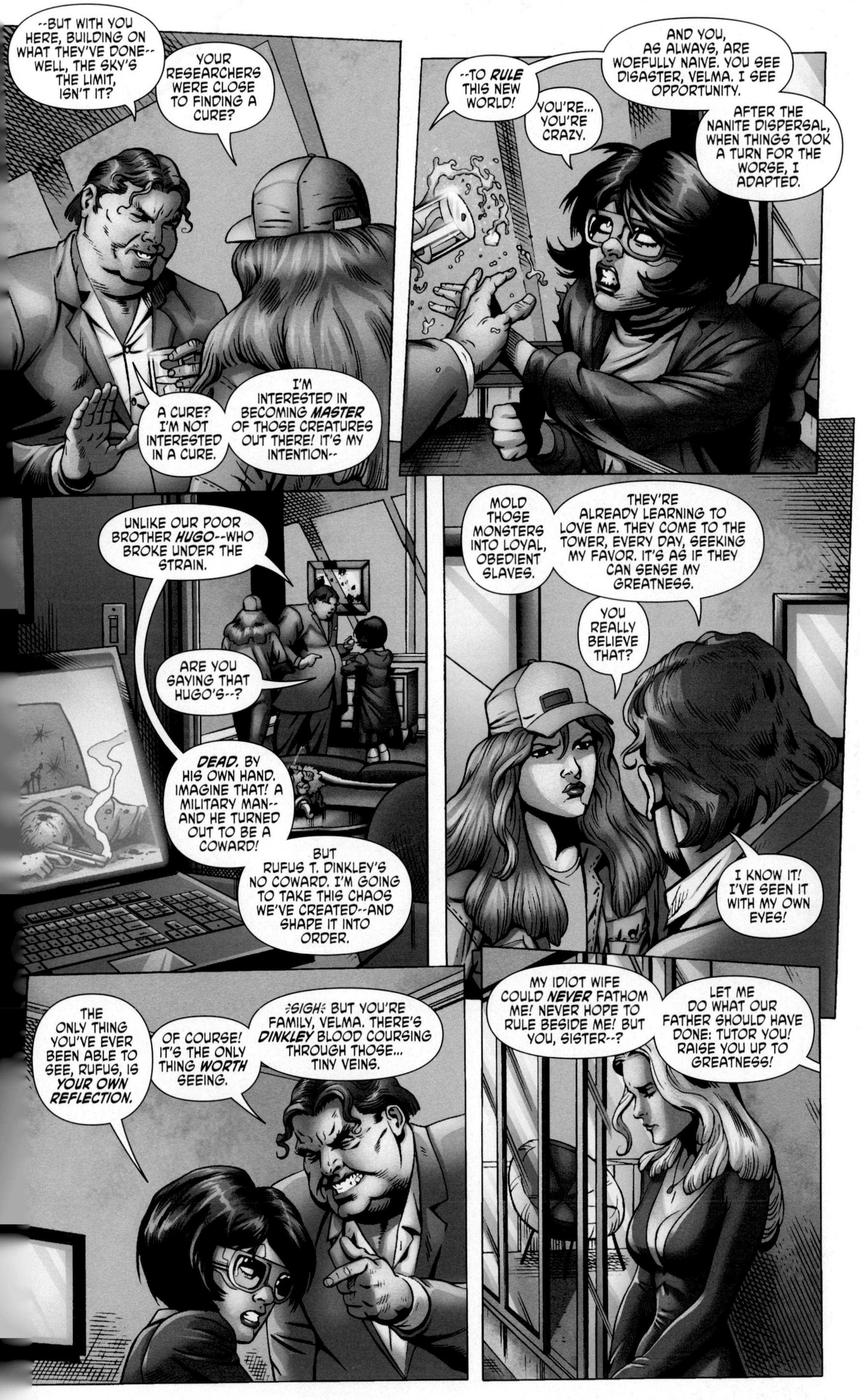
--BUT WITH YOU HERE, BUILDING ON WHAT THEY'VE DONE--WELL, THE SKY'S THE LIMIT, ISN'T IT?
YOUR RESEARCHERS WERE CLOSE TO FINDING A CURE?
A CURE? I'M NOT INTERESTED IN A CURE.
I'M INTERESTED IN BECOMING MASTER OF THOSE CREATURES OUT THERE! IT'S MY INTENTION--
--TO RULE THIS NEW WORLD!
YOU'RE... YOU'RE CRAZY.
AND YOU, AS ALWAYS, ARE WOEFULLY NAIVE. YOU SEE DISASTER, VELMA. I SEE OPPORTUNITY.
AFTER THE NANITE DISPERSAL, WHEN THINGS TOOK A TURN FOR THE WORSE, I ADAPTED.
UNLIKE OUR POOR BROTHER HUGO--WHO BROKE UNDER THE STRAIN.
ARE YOU SAYING THAT HUGO'S--?
DEAD. BY HIS OWN HAND. IMAGINE THAT! A MILITARY MAN--AND HE TURNED OUT TO BE A COWARD!
BUT RUFUS T. DINKLEY'S NO COWARD. I'M GOING TO TAKE THIS CHAOS WE'VE CREATED--AND SHAPE IT INTO ORDER.
MOLD THOSE MONSTERS INTO LOYAL, OBEDIENT SLAVES.
THEY'RE ALREADY LEARNING TO LOVE ME. THEY COME TO THE TOWER, EVERY DAY, SEEKING MY FAVOR. IT'S AS IF THEY CAN SENSE MY GREATNESS.
YOU REALLY BELIEVE THAT?
I KNOW IT! I'VE SEEN IT WITH MY OWN EYES!
THE ONLY THING YOU'VE EVER BEEN ABLE TO SEE, RUFUS, IS YOUR OWN REFLECTION.
OF COURSE! IT'S THE ONLY THING WORTH SEEING.
SIGH BUT YOU'RE FAMILY, VELMA. THERE'S DINKLEY BLOOD COURSING THROUGH THOSE... TINY VEINS.
MY IDIOT WIFE COULD NEVER FATHOM ME! NEVER HOPE TO RULE BESIDE ME! BUT YOU, SISTER--?
LET ME DO WHAT OUR FATHER SHOULD HAVE DONE: TUTOR YOU! RAISE YOU UP TO GREATNESS!

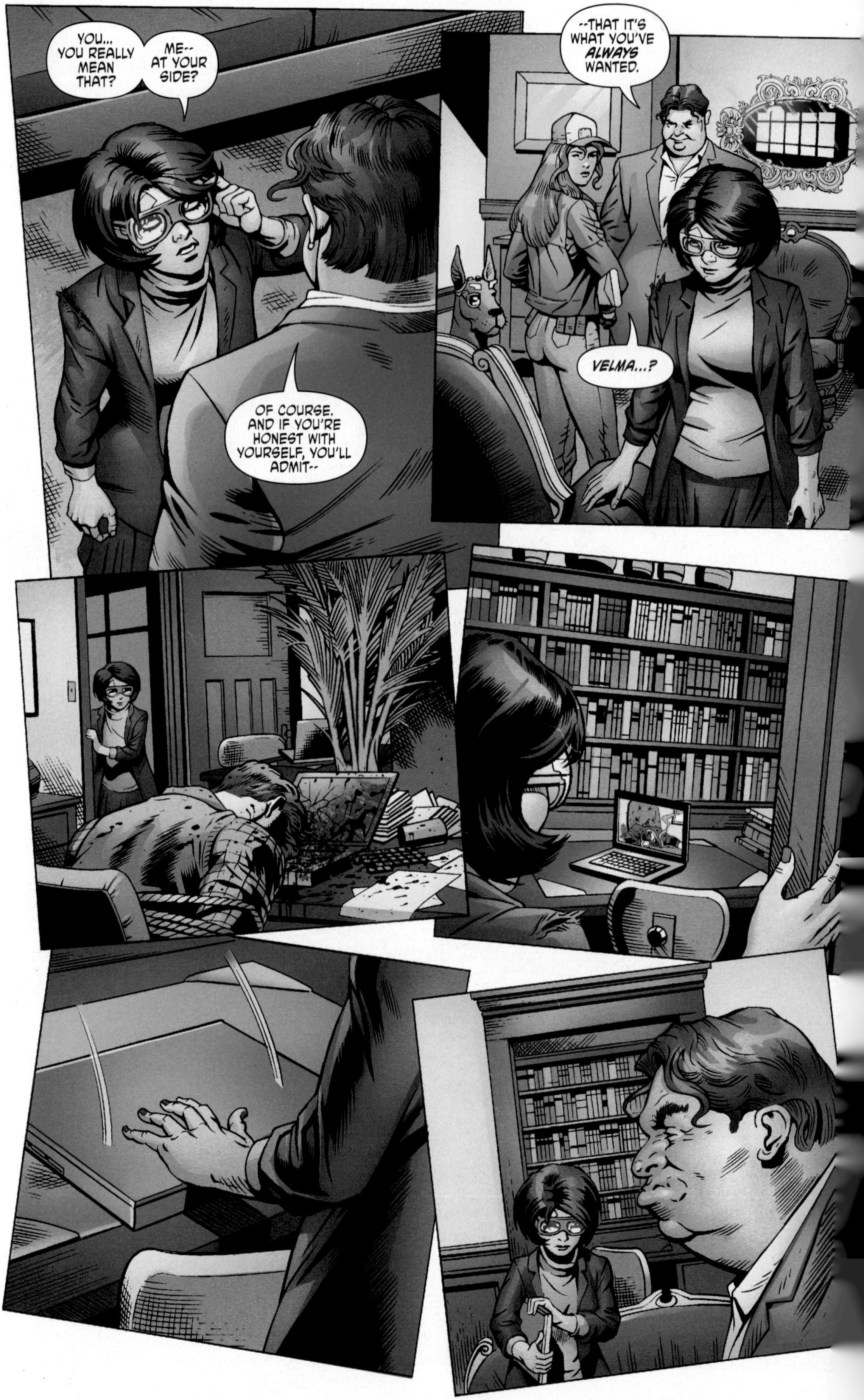
YOU... YOU REALLY MEAN THAT?
ME-- AT YOUR SIDE?
OF COURSE. AND IF YOU'RE HONEST WITH YOURSELF, YOU'LL ADMIT--
--THAT IT'S WHAT YOU'VE *ALWAYS* WANTED.
VELMA...?

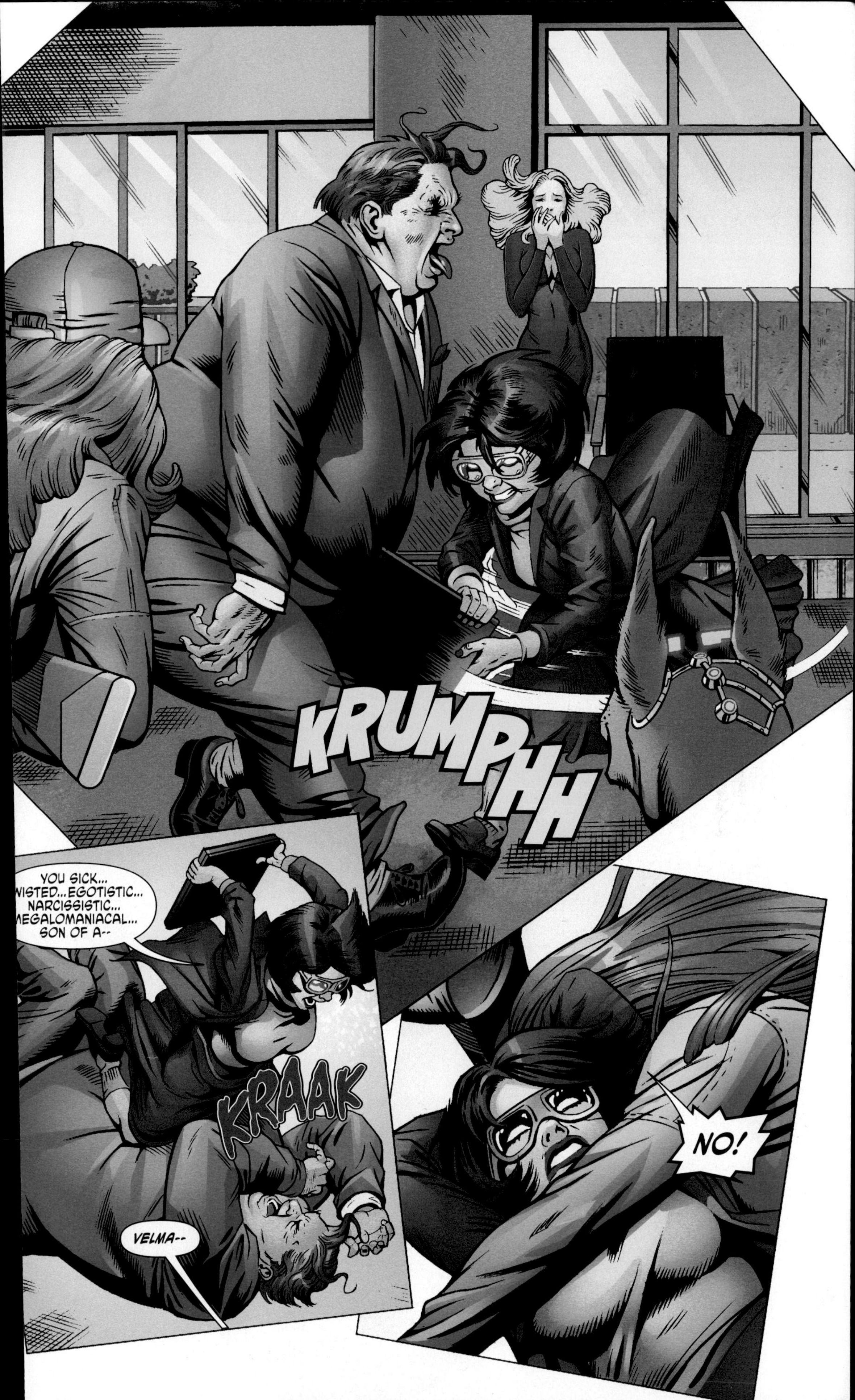
KRUMPHH
YOU SICK... TWISTED...EGOTISTIC... NARCISSISTIC... MEGALOMANIACAL... SON OF A--
KRAAK
VELMA--
NO!

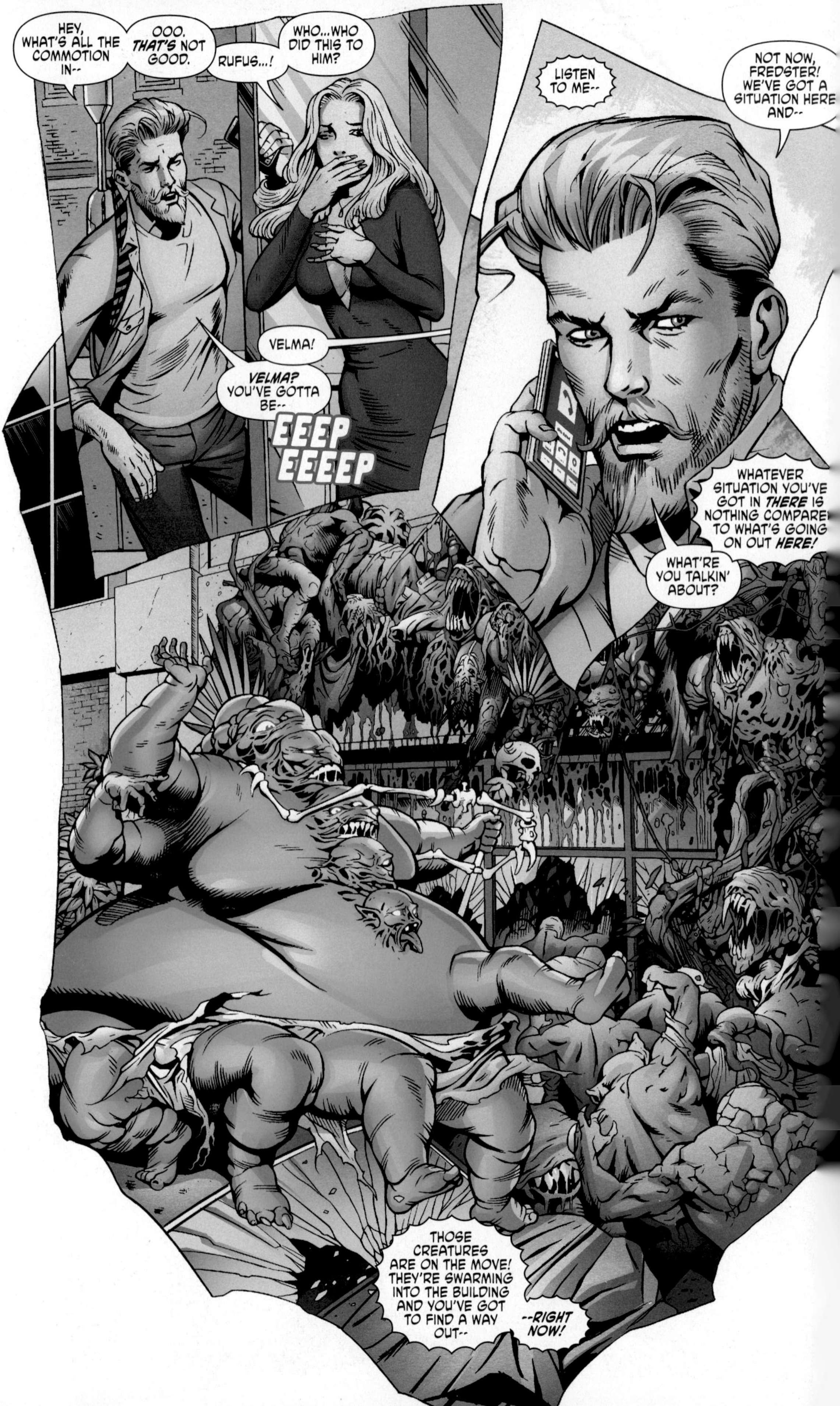

HEY, WHAT'S ALL THE COMMOTION IN--
OOO. *THAT'S* NOT GOOD.
RUFUS...!
WHO...WHO DID THIS TO HIM?
VELMA!
VELMA? YOU'VE GOTTA BE--
EEEP EEEEP
LISTEN TO ME--
NOT NOW, FREDSTER! WE'VE GOT A SITUATION HERE AND--
WHATEVER SITUATION YOU'VE GOT IN *THERE* IS NOTHING COMPARE TO WHAT'S GOING ON OUT *HERE!*
WHAT'RE YOU TALKIN' ABOUT?
THOSE CREATURES ARE ON THE MOVE! THEY'RE SWARMING INTO THE BUILDING AND YOU'VE GOT TO FIND A WAY OUT--
--*RIGHT NOW!*

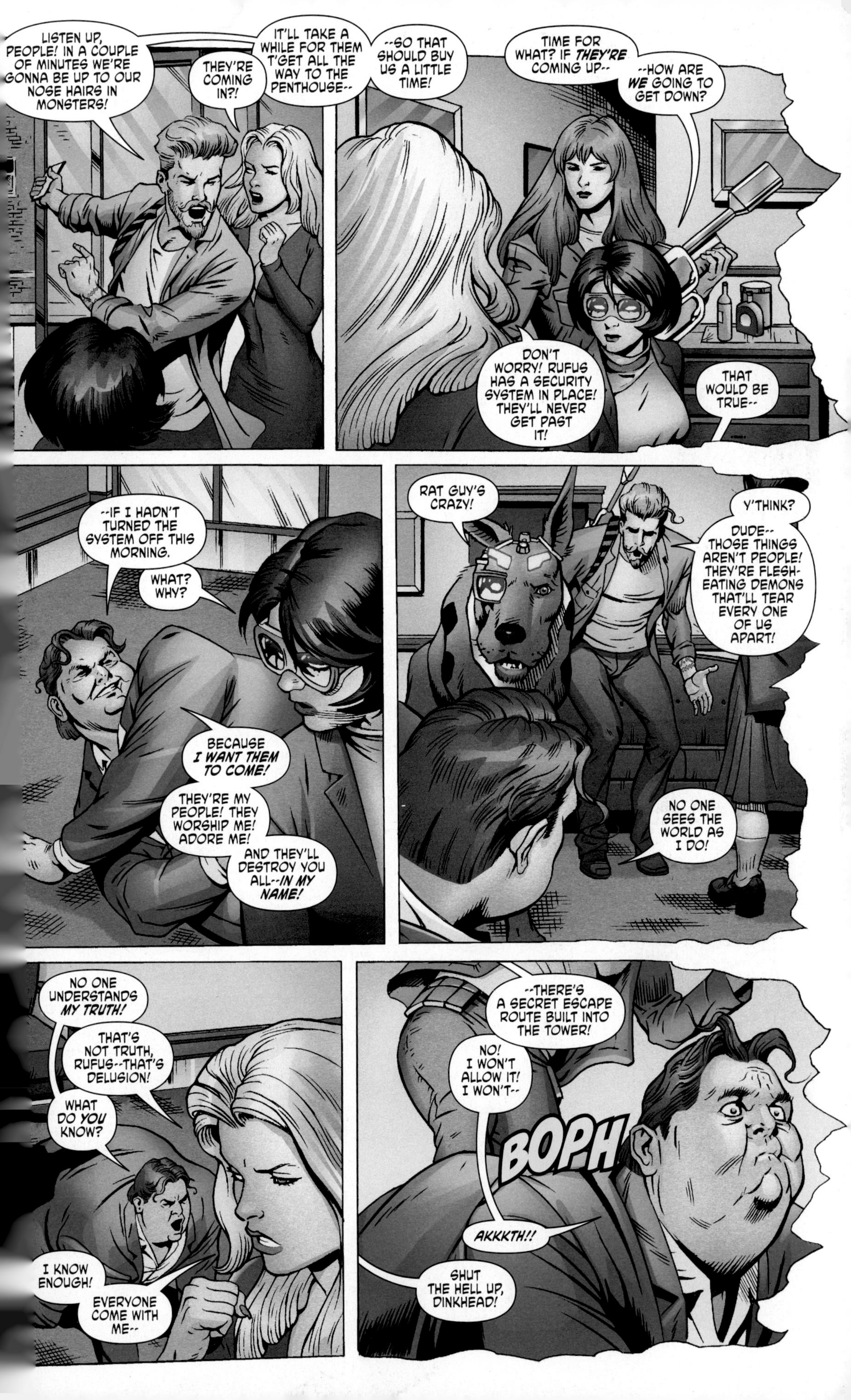
LISTEN UP, PEOPLE! IN A COUPLE OF MINUTES WE'RE GONNA BE UP TO OUR NOSE HAIRS IN MONSTERS!
THEY'RE COMING IN?!
IT'LL TAKE A WHILE FOR THEM T'GET ALL THE WAY TO THE PENTHOUSE--
--SO THAT SHOULD BUY US A LITTLE TIME!
TIME FOR WHAT? IF THEY'RE COMING UP--
--HOW ARE WE GOING TO GET DOWN?
DON'T WORRY! RUFUS HAS A SECURITY SYSTEM IN PLACE! THEY'LL NEVER GET PAST IT!
THAT WOULD BE TRUE--
--IF I HADN'T TURNED THE SYSTEM OFF THIS MORNING.
WHAT? WHY?
BECAUSE I WANT THEM TO COME!
THEY'RE MY PEOPLE! THEY WORSHIP ME! ADORE ME!
AND THEY'LL DESTROY YOU ALL--IN MY NAME!
RAT GUY'S CRAZY!
Y'THINK?
DUDE-- THOSE THINGS AREN'T PEOPLE! THEY'RE FLESH-EATING DEMONS THAT'LL TEAR EVERY ONE OF US APART!
NO ONE SEES THE WORLD AS I DO!
NO ONE UNDERSTANDS MY TRUTH!
THAT'S NOT TRUTH, RUFUS--THAT'S DELUSION!
WHAT DO YOU KNOW?
I KNOW ENOUGH!
EVERYONE COME WITH ME--
--THERE'S A SECRET ESCAPE ROUTE BUILT INTO THE TOWER!
NO! I WON'T ALLOW IT! I WON'T--
BOPH
AKKKTH!!
SHUT THE HELL UP, DINKHEAD!

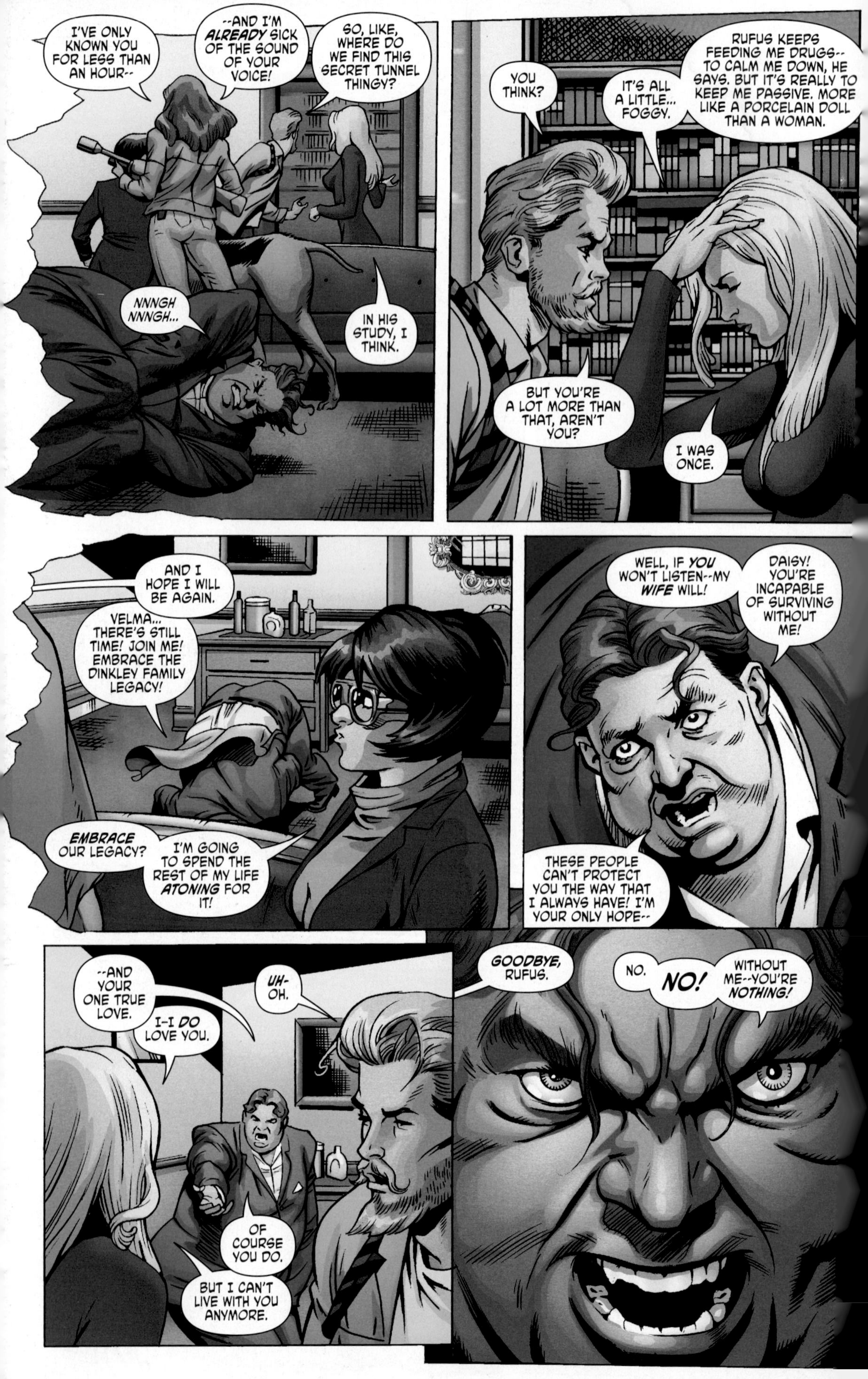

I'VE ONLY KNOWN YOU FOR LESS THAN AN HOUR--
--AND I'M ALREADY SICK OF THE SOUND OF YOUR VOICE!
SO, LIKE, WHERE DO WE FIND THIS SECRET TUNNEL THINGY?
NNNGH NNNGH...
IN HIS STUDY, I THINK.
YOU THINK?
IT'S ALL A LITTLE... FOGGY.
RUFUS KEEPS FEEDING ME DRUGS-- TO CALM ME DOWN, HE SAYS. BUT IT'S REALLY TO KEEP ME PASSIVE. MORE LIKE A PORCELAIN DOLL THAN A WOMAN.
BUT YOU'RE A LOT MORE THAN THAT, AREN'T YOU?
I WAS ONCE.
AND I HOPE I WILL BE AGAIN.
VELMA... THERE'S STILL TIME! JOIN ME! EMBRACE THE DINKLEY FAMILY LEGACY!
EMBRACE OUR LEGACY?
I'M GOING TO SPEND THE REST OF MY LIFE ATONING FOR IT!
WELL, IF YOU WON'T LISTEN--MY WIFE WILL!
DAISY! YOU'RE INCAPABLE OF SURVIVING WITHOUT ME!
THESE PEOPLE CAN'T PROTECT YOU THE WAY THAT I ALWAYS HAVE! I'M YOUR ONLY HOPE--
--AND YOUR ONE TRUE LOVE.
I-I DO LOVE YOU.
UH-OH.
OF COURSE YOU DO.
BUT I CAN'T LIVE WITH YOU ANYMORE.
GOODBYE, RUFUS.
NO.
NO!
WITHOUT ME--YOU'RE NOTHING!

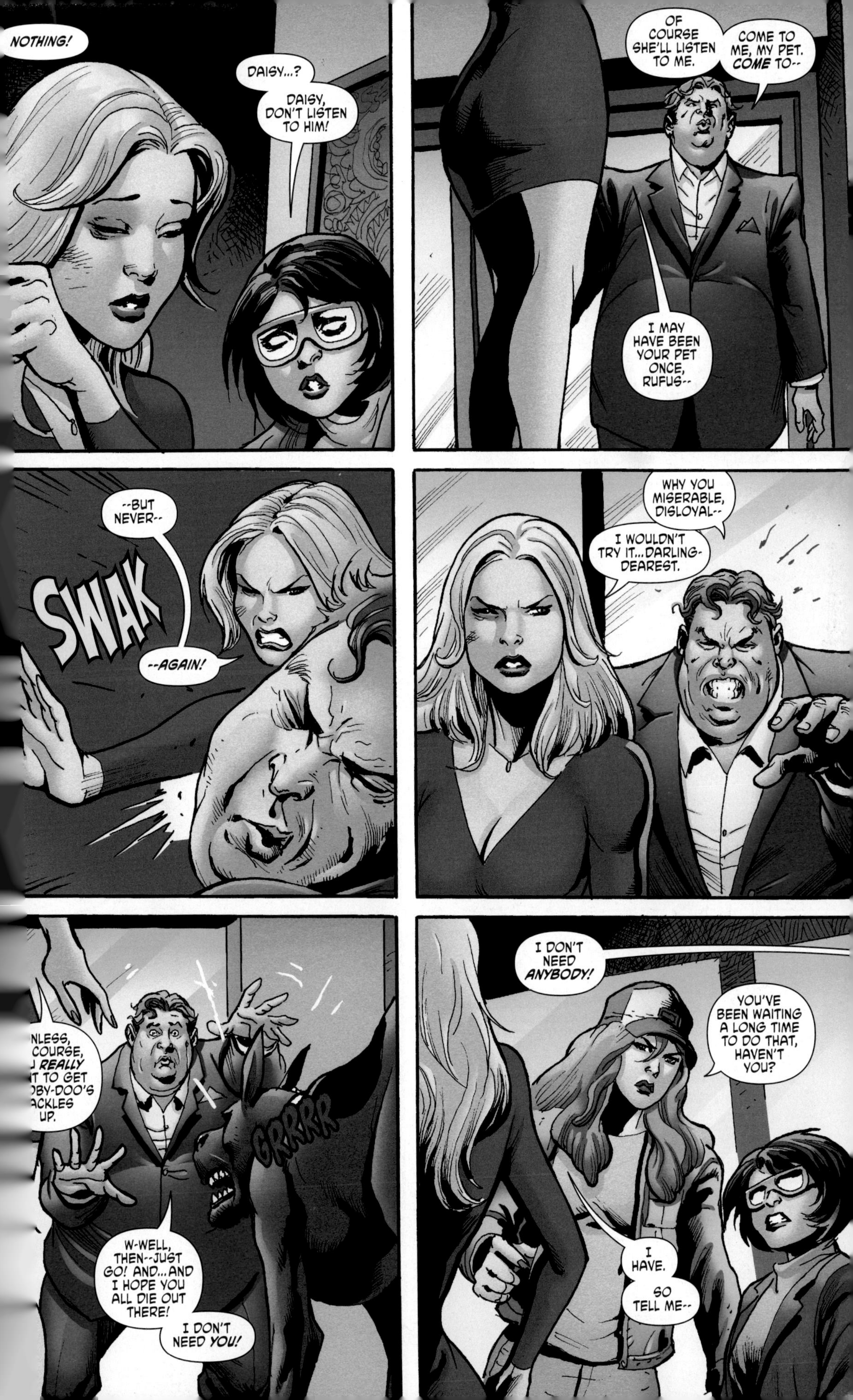
NOTHING!
DAISY...?
DAISY, DON'T LISTEN TO HIM!
OF COURSE SHE'LL LISTEN TO ME.
COME TO ME, MY PET. COME TO--
I MAY HAVE BEEN YOUR PET ONCE, RUFUS--
--BUT NEVER--
SWAK
--AGAIN!
WHY YOU MISERABLE, DISLOYAL--
I WOULDN'T TRY IT...DARLING-DEAREST.
NLESS, COURSE, REALLY T TO GET OBY-DOO'S ACKLES UP.
CRRRR
W-WELL, THEN--JUST GO! AND...AND I HOPE YOU ALL DIE OUT THERE!
I DON'T NEED YOU!
I DON'T NEED ANYBODY!
YOU'VE BEEN WAITING A LONG TIME TO DO THAT, HAVEN'T YOU?
I HAVE.
SO TELL ME--

--WHY DIDN'T I ENJOY IT?

BECAUSE YOU'RE NOTHING LIKE HIM.

RAR YOU OKAY?

I WILL BE-- ONCE WE'RE FREE OF THIS PLACE.

NOW I THINK THE SWITCH IS SOMEWHERE AROUND--

KLIK

YES... *THERE* IT IS!

THANKS, DAISY. YOU JUST SAVED OUR LIVES.

YOU'RE A HELLUVA WOMAN, Y'KNOW THAT?

ONLY FAIR--SINCE *YOU* JUST SAVED MINE.

AND YOU...ARE A HELLUVA MAN.

AND SCOOBY'S A HELLUVA DOG! NOW WILL YOU TWO STOP FLIRTING AND GET YOUR ASSES DOWN THOSE STAIRS!

WE'RE NOT FLIRTING!

ARE WE?

YOU CAN WORK THAT OUT LATER.

NOW CALL FRED! WE NEED THE MYSTERY MACHINE ASAP!

HELLO, FRED...?

WHAT DO YOU *MEAN* "WHO IS THIS?" IT'S SHAGGY!

S-H-A-G-G--

TELL THAT NITWIT TO STO[P] JOKING AND D[RIVE] THE VAN TO T[HE] FRONT OF T[HE] BUILDING--*RIG[HT]* NOW!

DAPHNE SAYS THAT--

OH, YOU HEARD HER? YEAH--

"--SHE *DOES* LIKE T'YELL, DOESN'T SHE?"

FOOLS! THEY THINK THEY CAN ESCAPE FROM RUFUS T. DINKLEY!

BUT NOW THAT MY TRUE BELIEVERS HAVE ARRIVED--THERE'S NO ESCAPE FOR ANYONE WHO'S DISLOYAL TO ME.

WAIT! WHAT ARE YOU DOING?

S-STAY BACK! *STAY BACK!* STAY--

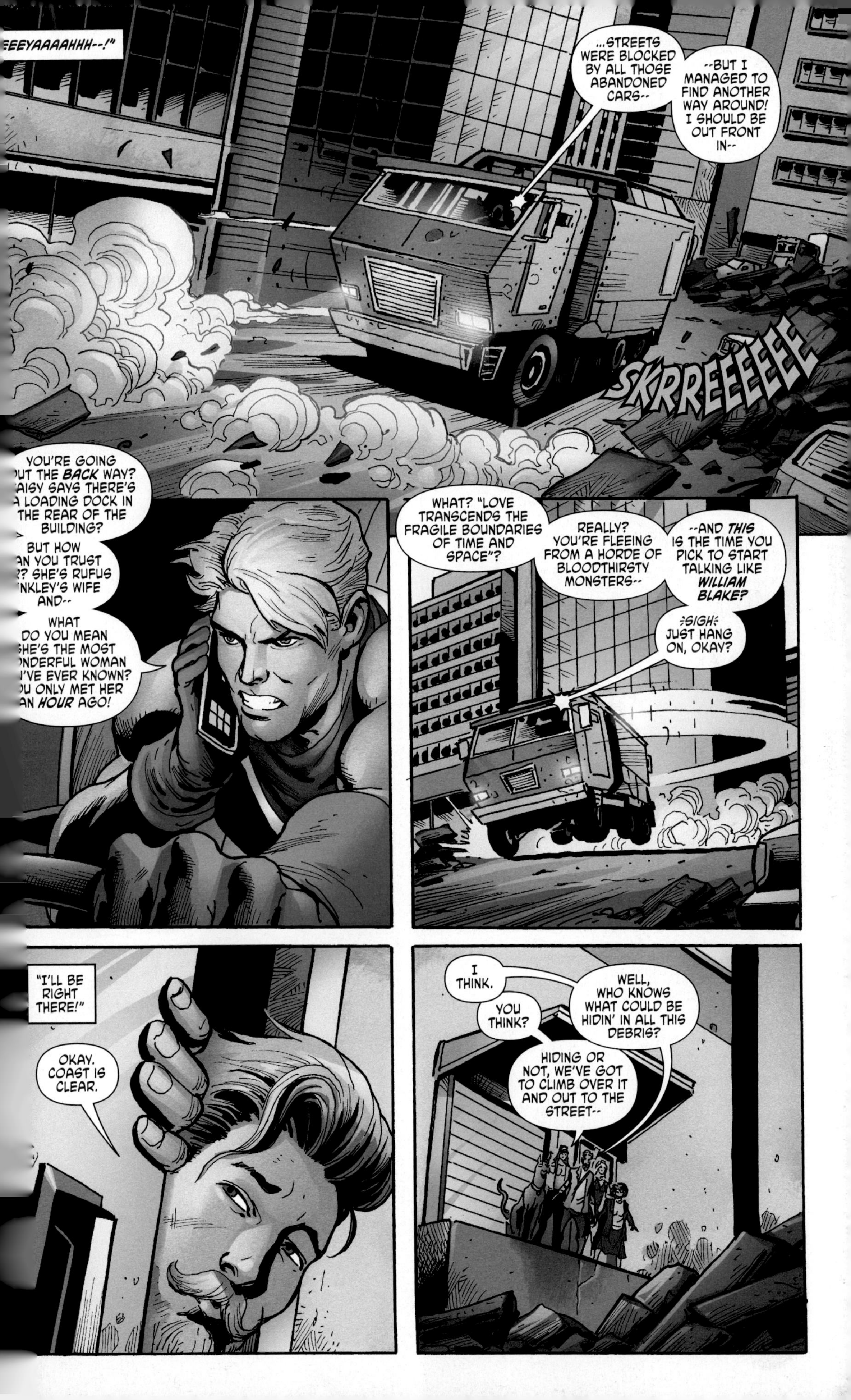
EEEYAAAAHHH--!"
...STREETS WERE BLOCKED BY ALL THOSE ABANDONED CARS--
--BUT I MANAGED TO FIND ANOTHER WAY AROUND! I SHOULD BE OUT FRONT IN--
SKRREEEEEE
YOU'RE GOING UT THE BACK WAY? AISY SAYS THERE'S A LOADING DOCK IN THE REAR OF THE BUILDING?
BUT HOW AN YOU TRUST R? SHE'S RUFUS NKLEY'S WIFE AND--
WHAT DO YOU MEAN SHE'S THE MOST ONDERFUL WOMAN U'VE EVER KNOWN? OU ONLY MET HER AN HOUR AGO!
WHAT? "LOVE TRANSCENDS THE FRAGILE BOUNDARIES OF TIME AND SPACE"?
REALLY? YOU'RE FLEEING FROM A HORDE OF BLOODTHIRSTY MONSTERS--
--AND THIS IS THE TIME YOU PICK TO START TALKING LIKE WILLIAM BLAKE?
SIGH JUST HANG ON, OKAY?
"I'LL BE RIGHT THERE!"
OKAY. COAST IS CLEAR.
I THINK.
YOU THINK?
WELL, WHO KNOWS WHAT COULD BE HIDIN' IN ALL THIS DEBRIS?
HIDING OR NOT, WE'VE GOT TO CLIMB OVER IT AND OUT TO THE STREET--

--SO FRED CAN HAVE A CLEAR PATH TO US!

I...I'M SORRY, DAISY.

FOR WHAT?

HOWEVER TERRIBLE A MAN MY BROTHER WAS...HE WAS STILL A HUMAN BEING. AND HE DESERVES TO BE MOURNED.

YES.

YES, HE DOES.

C'MON, YOU TWO!

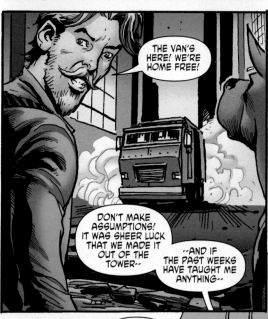

THE VAN'S HERE! WE'RE HOME FREE!

DON'T MAKE ASSUMPTIONS! IT WAS SHEER LUCK THAT WE MADE IT OUT OF THE TOWER--

--AND IF THE PAST WEEKS HAVE TAUGHT ME ANYTHING--

--IT'S THAT LUCK DOESN'T LAST!

WELL, DON'T JUST STAND THERE WITH YOUR MOUTHS HANGING OPEN--

MOVE IT!

I'D TELL YOU THAT HER BARK IS WORSE THAN HER BITE--BUT THAT WOULDN'T BE TRUE.

WHY DO YOU PUT UP WITH HER?

SAME REASON SHE PUTS UP WITH ME. WE'RE FRIENDS.

GOOD WORK, FREDSTER!

WHO'RE YOU?

NOW DON'T START THAT AGAIN!

GET IN THE VAN, ABBOTT-- SO COSTELLO CAN DRIVE US OUT OF HERE!

DO YOU... DO YOU THINK THERE'S A CHANCE RUFUS GOT AWAY FROM THEM?

NO.

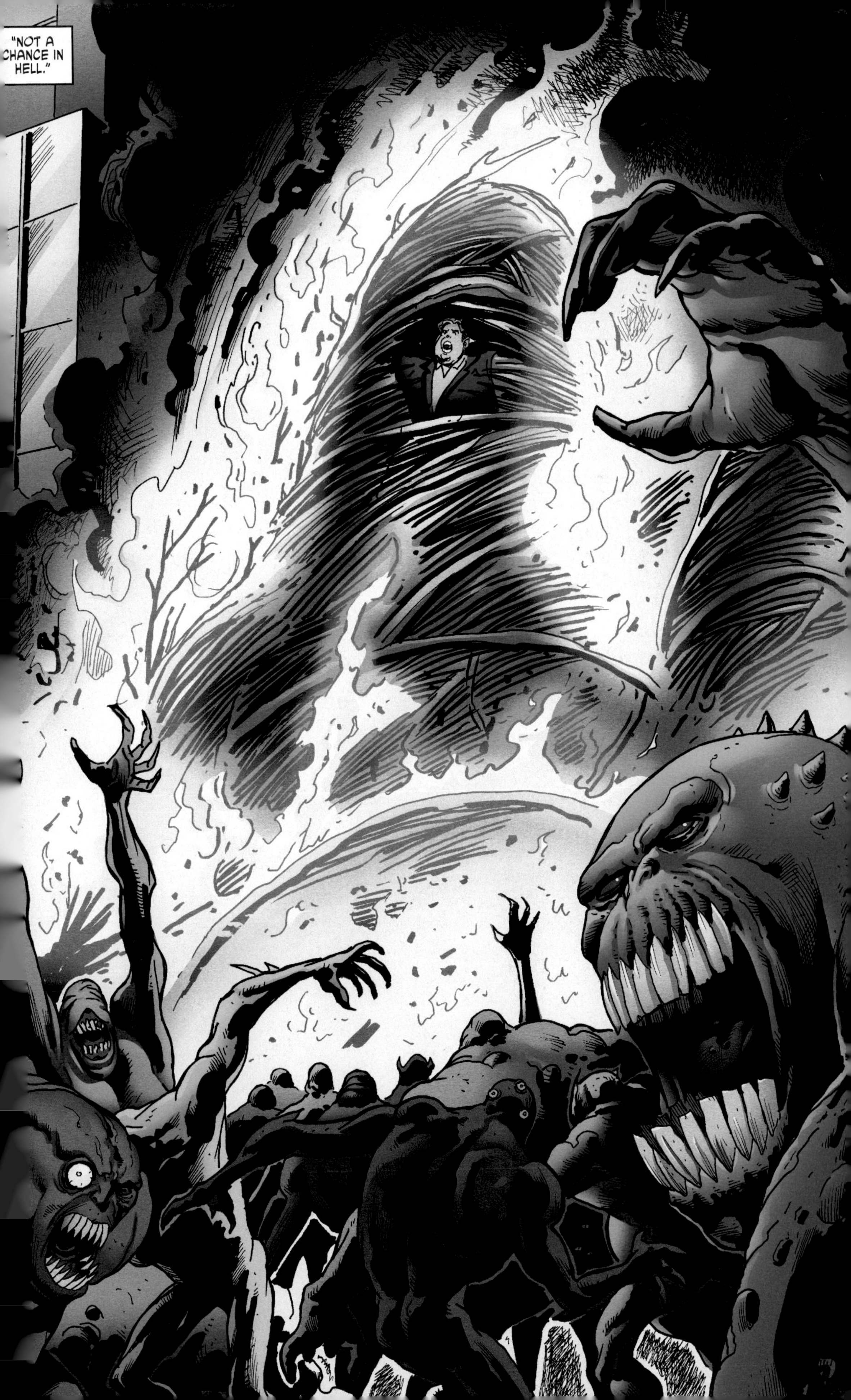
"NOT A CHANCE IN HELL."

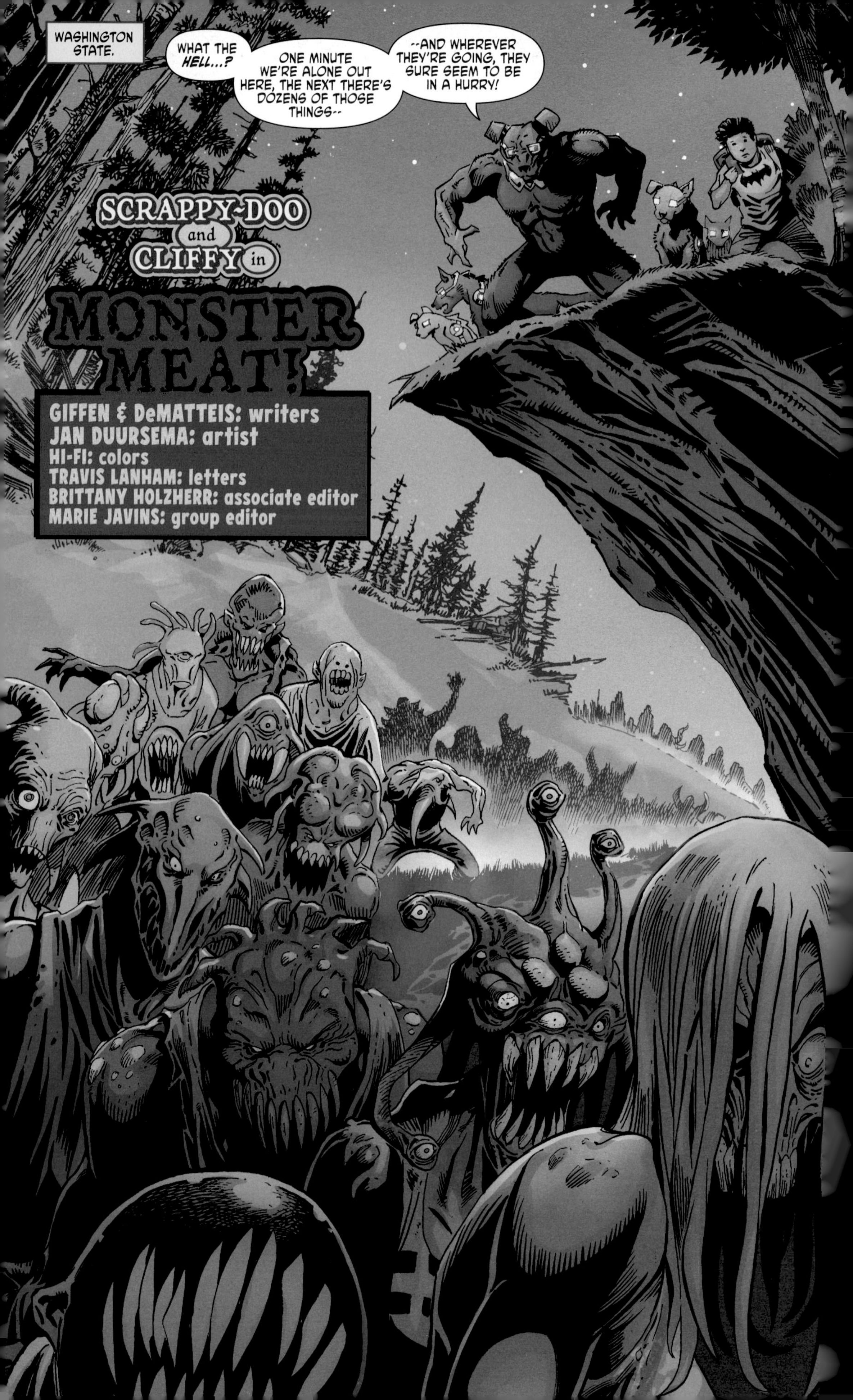

WASHINGTON STATE.
WHAT THE *HELL...?*
ONE MINUTE WE'RE ALONE OUT HERE, THE NEXT THERE'S DOZENS OF THOSE THINGS--
--AND WHEREVER THEY'RE GOING, THEY SURE SEEM TO BE IN A HURRY!
SCRAPPY-DOO and CLIFFY in
MONSTER MEAT!
GIFFEN & DeMATTEIS: writers
JAN DUURSEMA: artist
HI-FI: colors
TRAVIS LANHAM: letters
BRITTANY HOLZHERR: associate editor
MARIE JAVINS: group editor

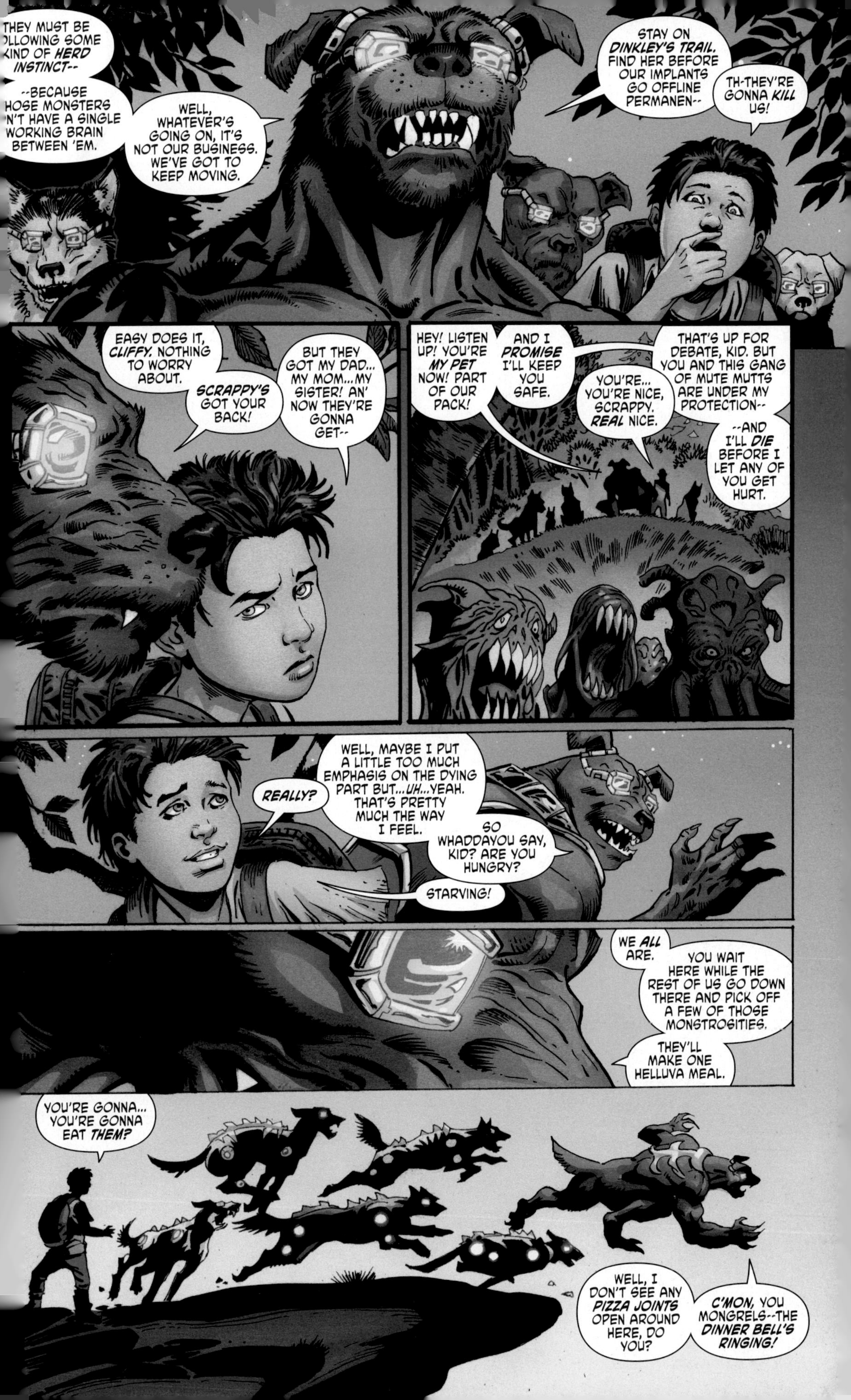
THEY MUST BE
OLLOWING SOME
KIND OF HERD
INSTINCT--
--BECAUSE
HOSE MONSTERS
N'T HAVE A SINGLE
WORKING BRAIN
BETWEEN 'EM.
WELL, WHATEVER'S GOING ON, IT'S NOT OUR BUSINESS. WE'VE GOT TO KEEP MOVING.
STAY ON DINKLEY'S TRAIL. FIND HER BEFORE OUR IMPLANTS GO OFFLINE PERMANEN--
TH-THEY'RE GONNA KILL US!
EASY DOES IT, CLIFFY. NOTHING TO WORRY ABOUT.
SCRAPPY'S GOT YOUR BACK!
BUT THEY GOT MY DAD... MY MOM...MY SISTER! AN' NOW THEY'RE GONNA GET--
HEY! LISTEN UP! YOU'RE MY PET NOW! PART OF OUR PACK!
AND I PROMISE I'LL KEEP YOU SAFE.
YOU'RE... YOU'RE NICE, SCRAPPY. REAL NICE.
THAT'S UP FOR DEBATE, KID. BUT YOU AND THIS GANG OF MUTE MUTTS ARE UNDER MY PROTECTION--
--AND I'LL DIE BEFORE I LET ANY OF YOU GET HURT.
REALLY?
WELL, MAYBE I PUT A LITTLE TOO MUCH EMPHASIS ON THE DYING PART BUT...UH...YEAH. THAT'S PRETTY MUCH THE WAY I FEEL.
SO WHADDAYOU SAY, KID? ARE YOU HUNGRY?
STARVING!
WE ALL ARE.
YOU WAIT HERE WHILE THE REST OF US GO DOWN THERE AND PICK OFF A FEW OF THOSE MONSTROSITIES.
THEY'LL MAKE ONE HELLUVA MEAL.
YOU'RE GONNA... YOU'RE GONNA EAT THEM?
WELL, I DON'T SEE ANY PIZZA JOINTS OPEN AROUND HERE, DO YOU?
C'MON, YOU MONGRELS--THE DINNER BELL'S RINGING!

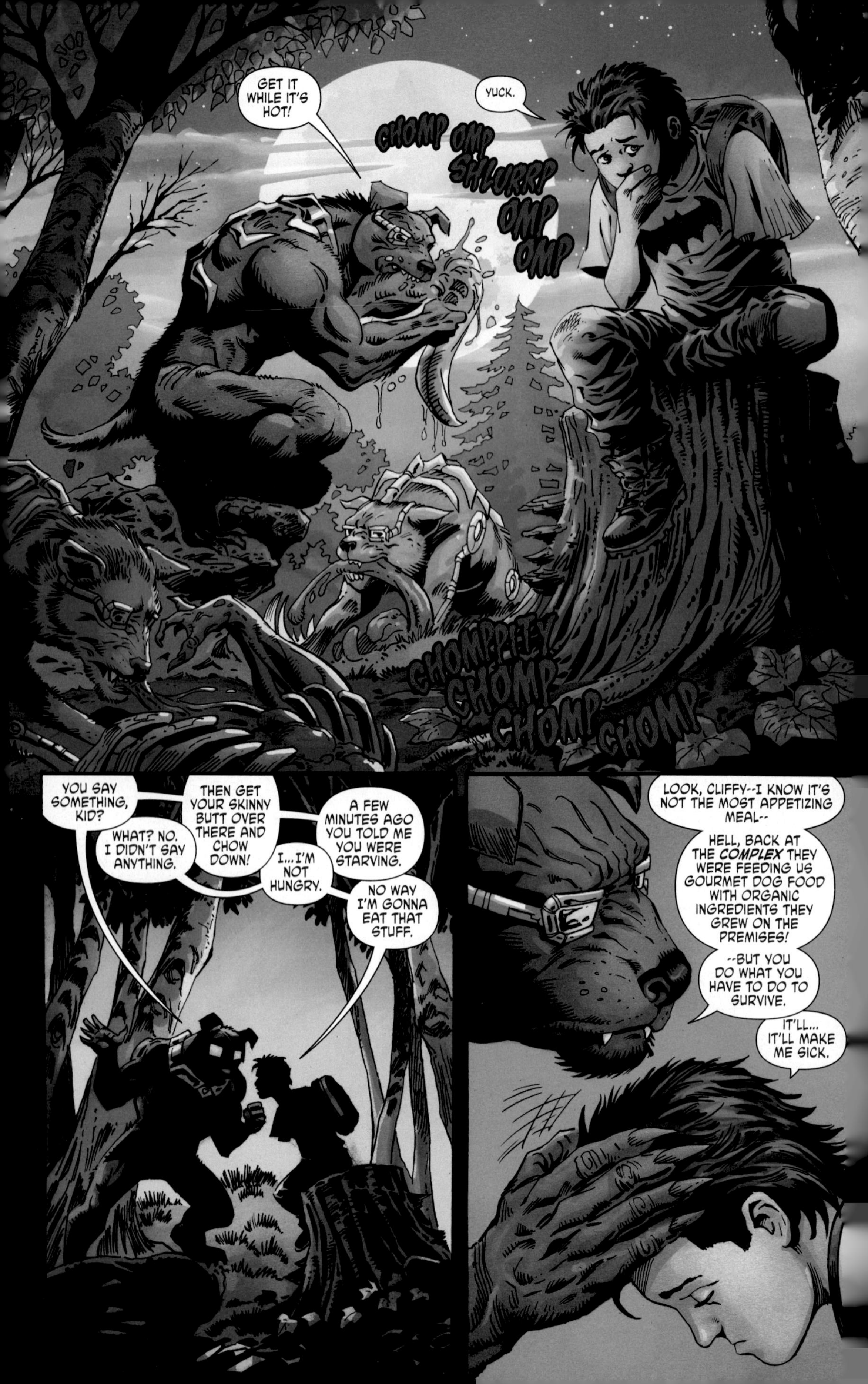
GET IT WHILE IT'S HOT!
YUCK.
CHOMP OMP SHLURRP OMP OMP
CHOMPPITY CHOMP CHOMP CHOMP
YOU SAY SOMETHING, KID?
WHAT? NO. I DIDN'T SAY ANYTHING.
THEN GET YOUR SKINNY BUTT OVER THERE AND CHOW DOWN!
I...I'M NOT HUNGRY.
A FEW MINUTES AGO YOU TOLD ME YOU WERE STARVING.
NO WAY I'M GONNA EAT THAT STUFF.
LOOK, CLIFFY--I KNOW IT'S NOT THE MOST APPETIZING MEAL--
HELL, BACK AT THE COMPLEX THEY WERE FEEDING US GOURMET DOG FOOD WITH ORGANIC INGREDIENTS THEY GREW ON THE PREMISES!
--BUT YOU DO WHAT YOU HAVE TO DO TO SURVIVE.
IT'LL... IT'LL MAKE ME SICK.

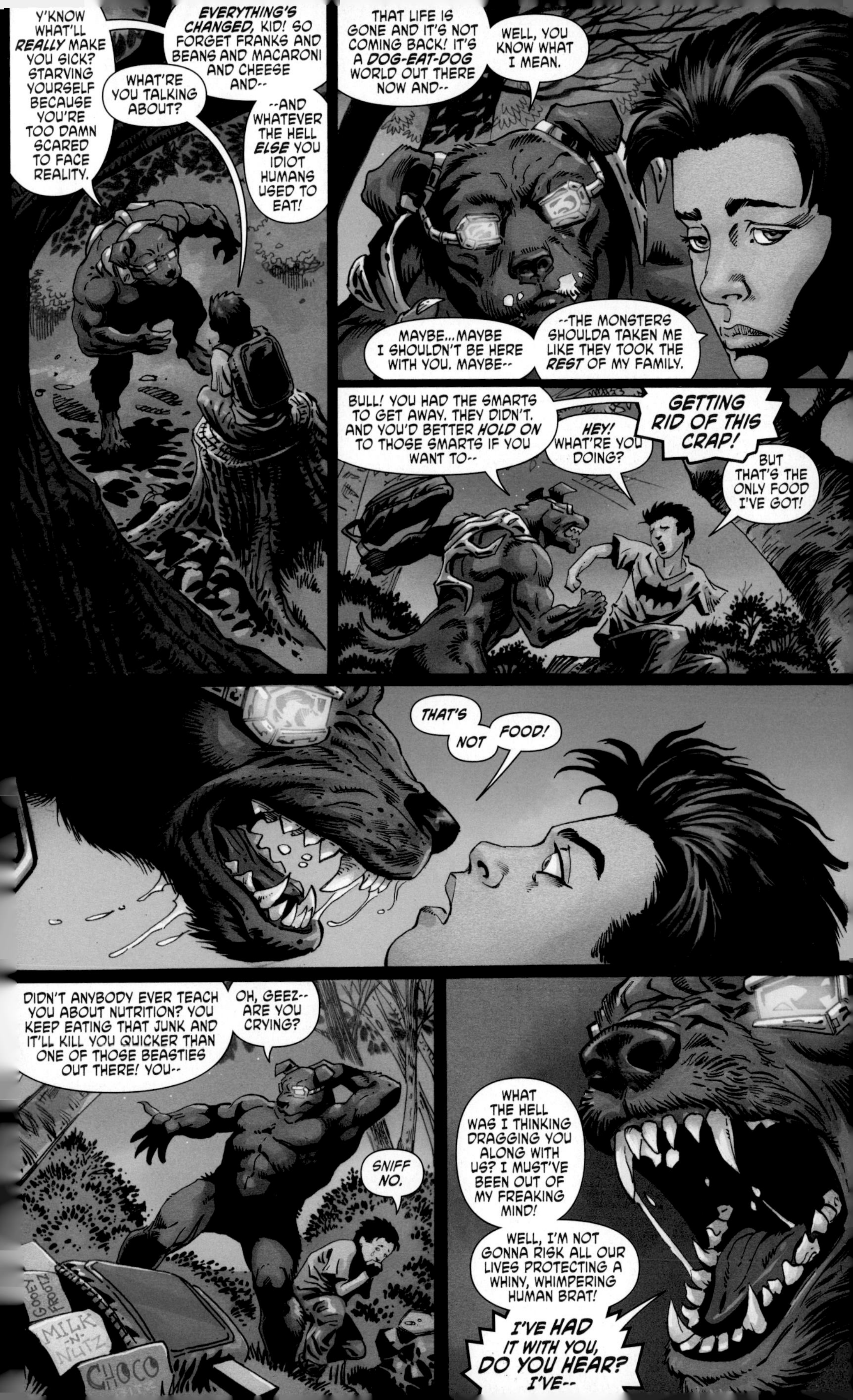
Y'KNOW WHAT'LL REALLY MAKE YOU SICK? STARVING YOURSELF BECAUSE YOU'RE TOO DAMN SCARED TO FACE REALITY.
WHAT'RE YOU TALKING ABOUT?
EVERYTHING'S CHANGED, KID! SO FORGET FRANKS AND BEANS AND MACARONI AND CHEESE AND--
--AND WHATEVER THE HELL ELSE YOU IDIOT HUMANS USED TO EAT!
THAT LIFE IS GONE AND IT'S NOT COMING BACK! IT'S A DOG-EAT-DOG WORLD OUT THERE NOW AND--
WELL, YOU KNOW WHAT I MEAN.
MAYBE...MAYBE I SHOULDN'T BE HERE WITH YOU. MAYBE--
--THE MONSTERS SHOULDA TAKEN ME LIKE THEY TOOK THE REST OF MY FAMILY.
BULL! YOU HAD THE SMARTS TO GET AWAY. THEY DIDN'T. AND YOU'D BETTER HOLD ON TO THOSE SMARTS IF YOU WANT TO--
HEY! WHAT'RE YOU DOING?
GETTING RID OF THIS CRAP!
BUT THAT'S THE ONLY FOOD I'VE GOT!
THAT'S NOT FOOD!
DIDN'T ANYBODY EVER TEACH YOU ABOUT NUTRITION? YOU KEEP EATING THAT JUNK AND IT'LL KILL YOU QUICKER THAN ONE OF THOSE BEASTIES OUT THERE! YOU--
OH, GEEZ-- ARE YOU CRYING?
SNIFF NO.
GOOEY FROOTZ
MILK -N- NUTZ
CHOCO
WHAT THE HELL WAS I THINKING DRAGGING YOU ALONG WITH US? I MUST'VE BEEN OUT OF MY FREAKING MIND!
WELL, I'M NOT GONNA RISK ALL OUR LIVES PROTECTING A WHINY, WHIMPERING HUMAN BRAT!
I'VE HAD IT WITH YOU, DO YOU HEAR? I'VE--

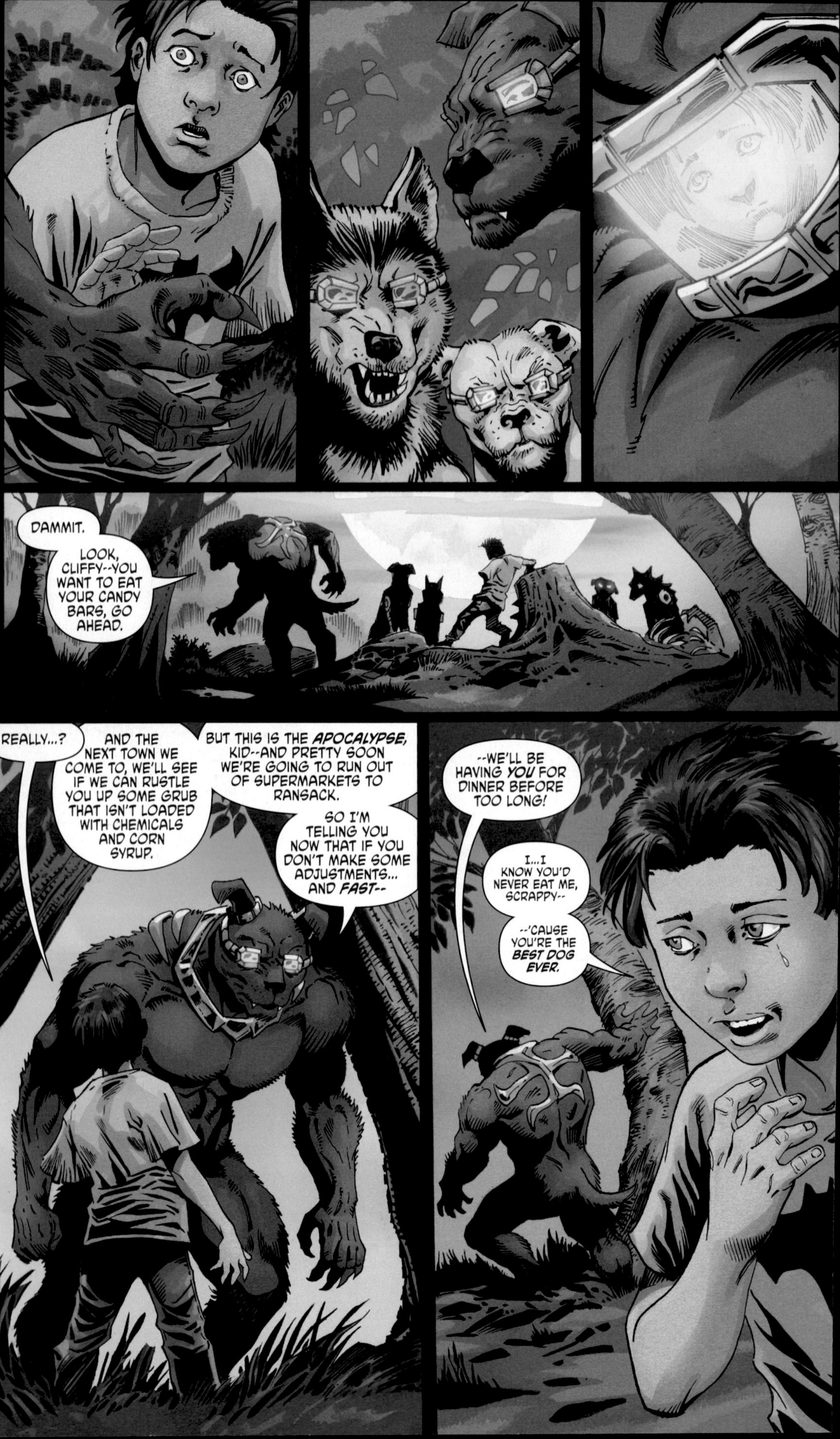
DAMMIT.
LOOK, CLIFFY--YOU WANT TO EAT YOUR CANDY BARS, GO AHEAD.
REALLY...?
AND THE NEXT TOWN WE COME TO, WE'LL SEE IF WE CAN RUSTLE YOU UP SOME GRUB THAT ISN'T LOADED WITH CHEMICALS AND CORN SYRUP.
BUT THIS IS THE *APOCALYPSE,* KID--AND PRETTY SOON WE'RE GOING TO RUN OUT OF SUPERMARKETS TO RANSACK.
SO I'M TELLING YOU NOW THAT IF YOU DON'T MAKE SOME ADJUSTMENTS... AND *FAST*--
--WE'LL BE HAVING *YOU* FOR DINNER BEFORE TOO LONG!
I...I KNOW YOU'D NEVER EAT ME, SCRAPPY--
--'CAUSE YOU'RE THE *BEST DOG EVER.*

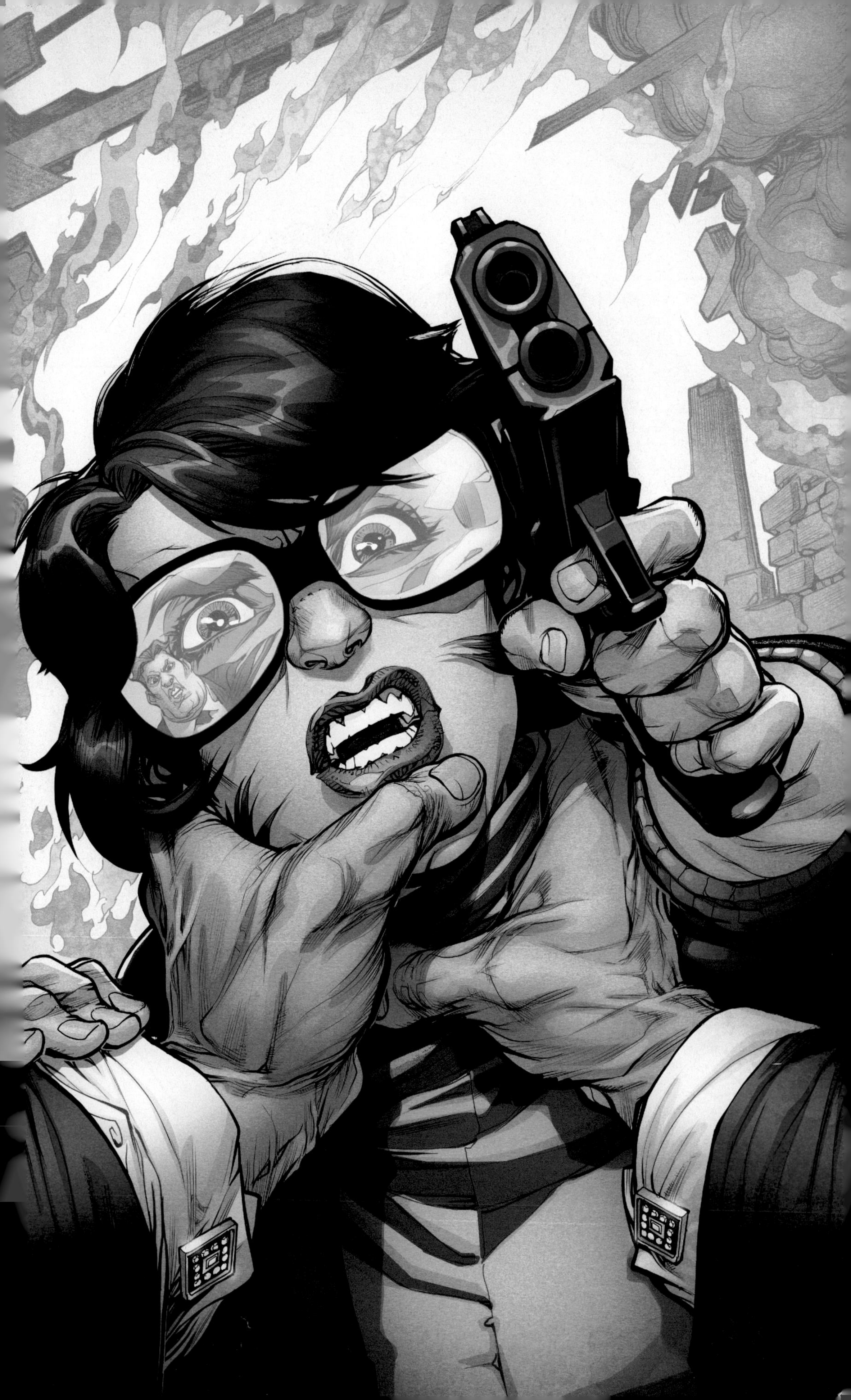

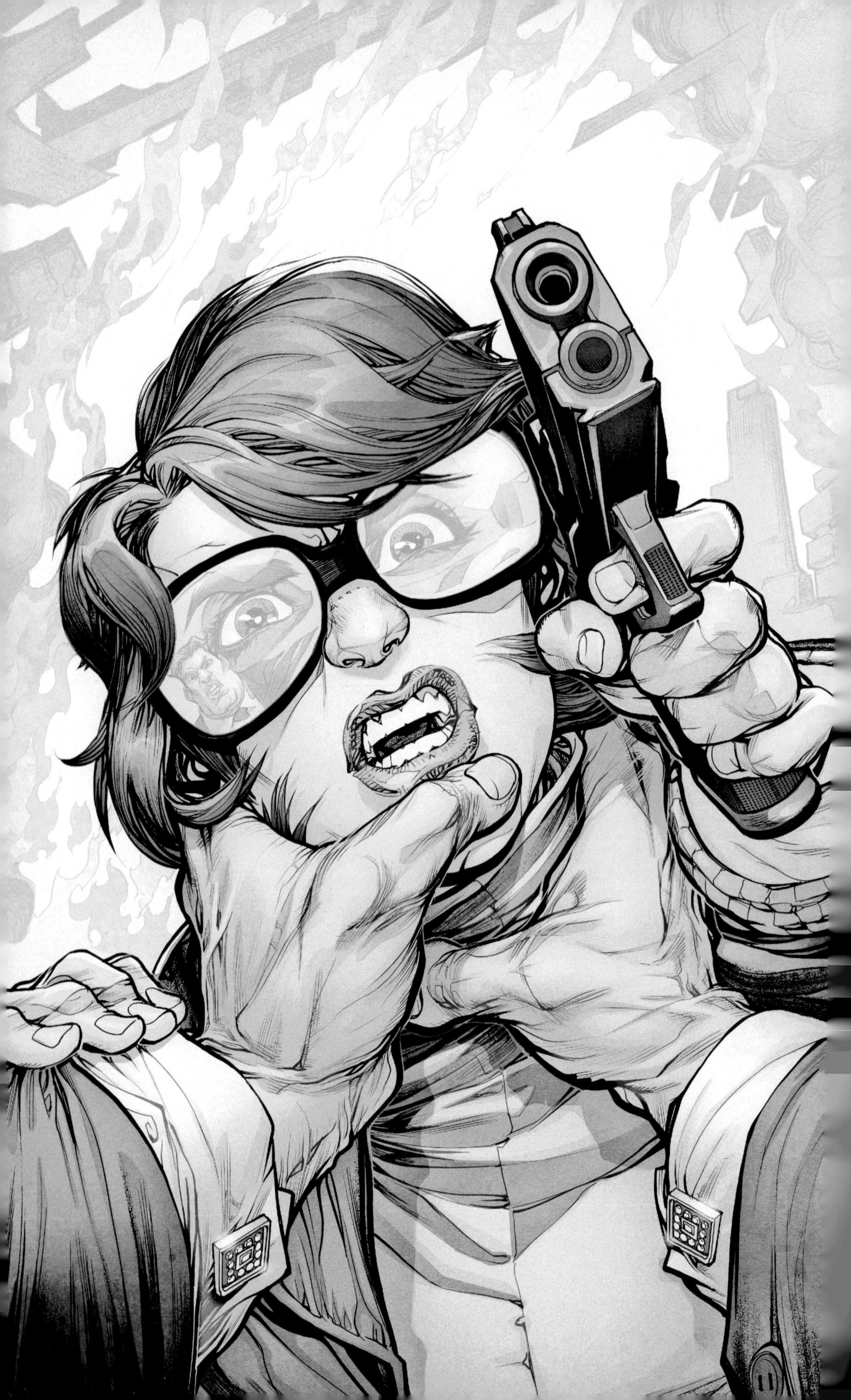

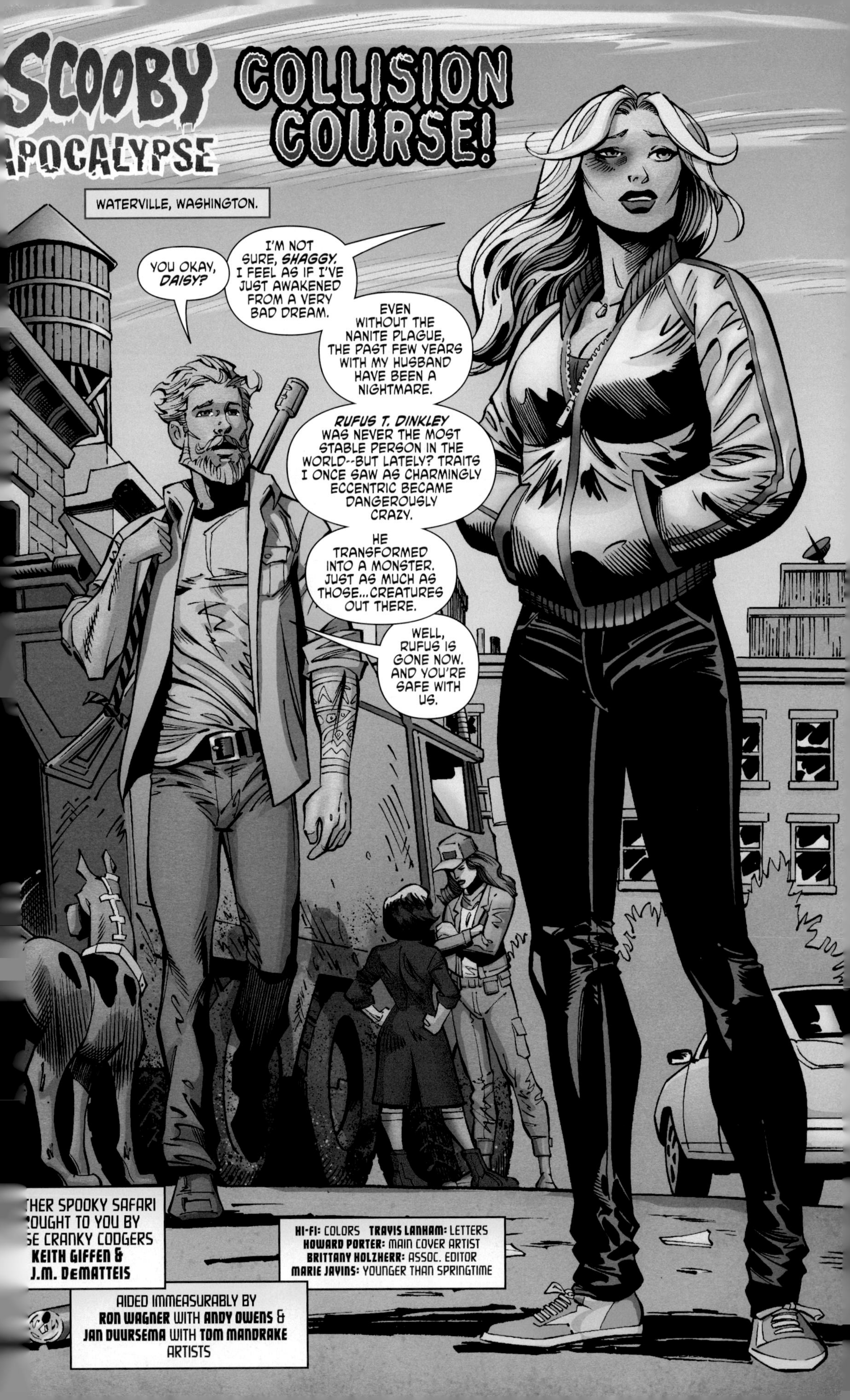
SCOOBY APOCALYPSE
COLLISION COURSE!
WATERVILLE, WASHINGTON.
YOU OKAY, DAISY?
I'M NOT SURE, SHAGGY. I FEEL AS IF I'VE JUST AWAKENED FROM A VERY BAD DREAM.
EVEN WITHOUT THE NANITE PLAGUE, THE PAST FEW YEARS WITH MY HUSBAND HAVE BEEN A NIGHTMARE.
RUFUS T. DINKLEY WAS NEVER THE MOST STABLE PERSON IN THE WORLD--BUT LATELY? TRAITS I ONCE SAW AS CHARMINGLY ECCENTRIC BECAME DANGEROUSLY CRAZY.
HE TRANSFORMED INTO A MONSTER. JUST AS MUCH AS THOSE...CREATURES OUT THERE.
WELL, RUFUS IS GONE NOW. AND YOU'RE SAFE WITH US.
THER SPOOKY SAFARI ROUGHT TO YOU BY SE CRANKY CODGERS KEITH GIFFEN & J.M. DeMATTEIS
HI-FI: COLORS TRAVIS LANHAM: LETTERS
HOWARD PORTER: MAIN COVER ARTIST
BRITTANY HOLZHERR: ASSOC. EDITOR
MARIE JAVINS: YOUNGER THAN SPRINGTIME
AIDED IMMEASURABLY BY RON WAGNER WITH ANDY OWENS & JAN DUURSEMA WITH TOM MANDRAKE ARTISTS

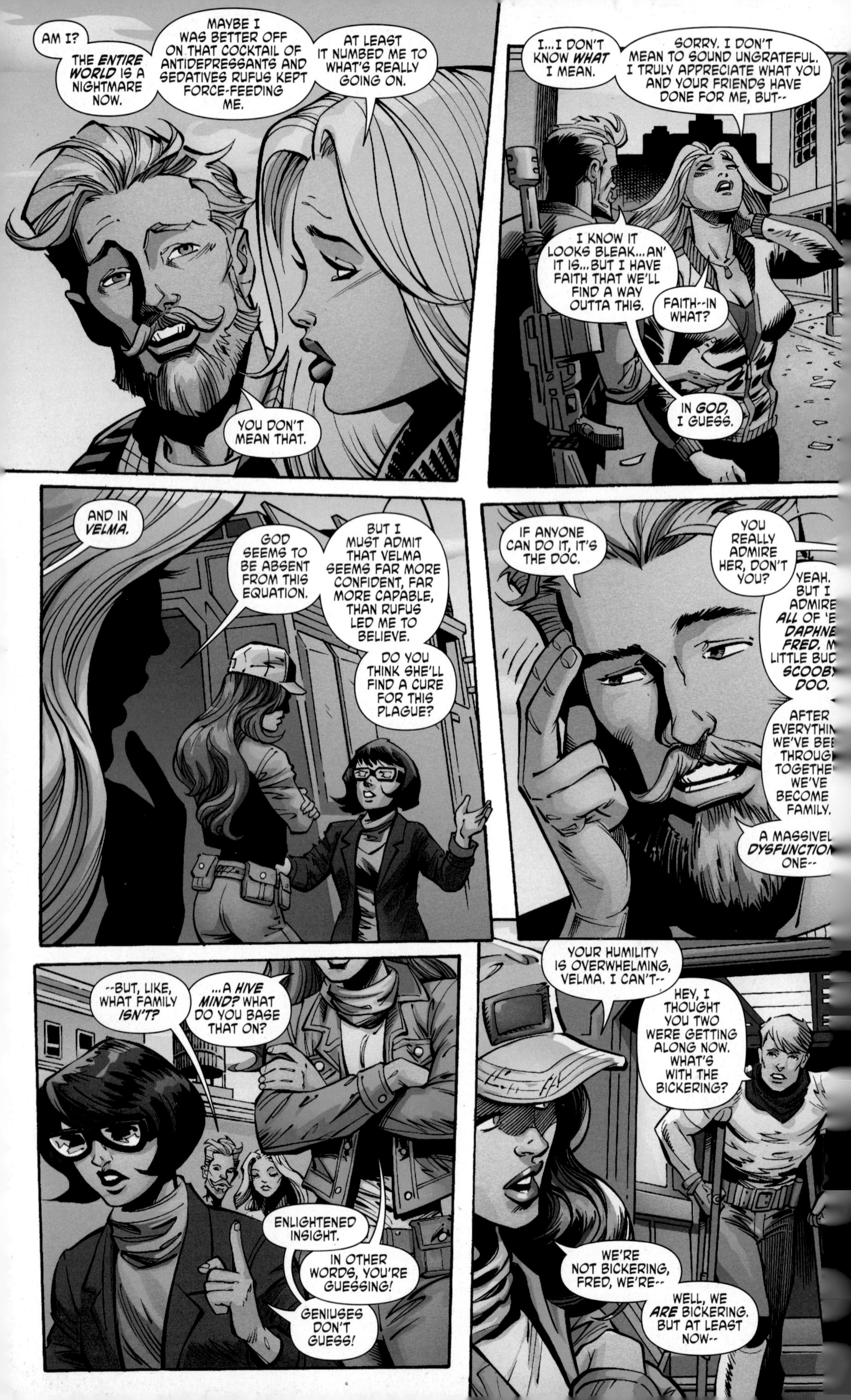
AM I?
THE ENTIRE WORLD IS A NIGHTMARE NOW.
MAYBE I WAS BETTER OFF ON THAT COCKTAIL OF ANTIDEPRESSANTS AND SEDATIVES RUFUS KEPT FORCE-FEEDING ME.
AT LEAST IT NUMBED ME TO WHAT'S REALLY GOING ON.
YOU DON'T MEAN THAT.
I...I DON'T KNOW WHAT I MEAN.
SORRY. I DON'T MEAN TO SOUND UNGRATEFUL. I TRULY APPRECIATE WHAT YOU AND YOUR FRIENDS HAVE DONE FOR ME, BUT--
I KNOW IT LOOKS BLEAK...AN' IT IS...BUT I HAVE FAITH THAT WE'LL FIND A WAY OUTTA THIS.
FAITH--IN WHAT?
IN GOD, I GUESS.
AND IN VELMA.
GOD SEEMS TO BE ABSENT FROM THIS EQUATION.
BUT I MUST ADMIT THAT VELMA SEEMS FAR MORE CONFIDENT, FAR MORE CAPABLE, THAN RUFUS LED ME TO BELIEVE.
DO YOU THINK SHE'LL FIND A CURE FOR THIS PLAGUE?
IF ANYONE CAN DO IT, IT'S THE DOC.
YOU REALLY ADMIRE HER, DON'T YOU?
YEAH. BUT I ADMIRE ALL OF 'E DAPHNE FRED. M LITTLE BUD SCOOBY DOO.
AFTER EVERYTHIN WE'VE BEE THROUG TOGETHE WE'VE BECOME FAMILY.
A MASSIVEL DYSFUNCTION ONE--
--BUT, LIKE, WHAT FAMILY ISN'T?
...A HIVE MIND? WHAT DO YOU BASE THAT ON?
ENLIGHTENED INSIGHT.
IN OTHER WORDS, YOU'RE GUESSING!
GENIUSES DON'T GUESS!
YOUR HUMILITY IS OVERWHELMING, VELMA. I CAN'T--
HEY, I THOUGHT YOU TWO WERE GETTING ALONG NOW. WHAT'S WITH THE BICKERING?
WE'RE NOT BICKERING, FRED, WE'RE--
WELL, WE ARE BICKERING. BUT AT LEAST NOW--

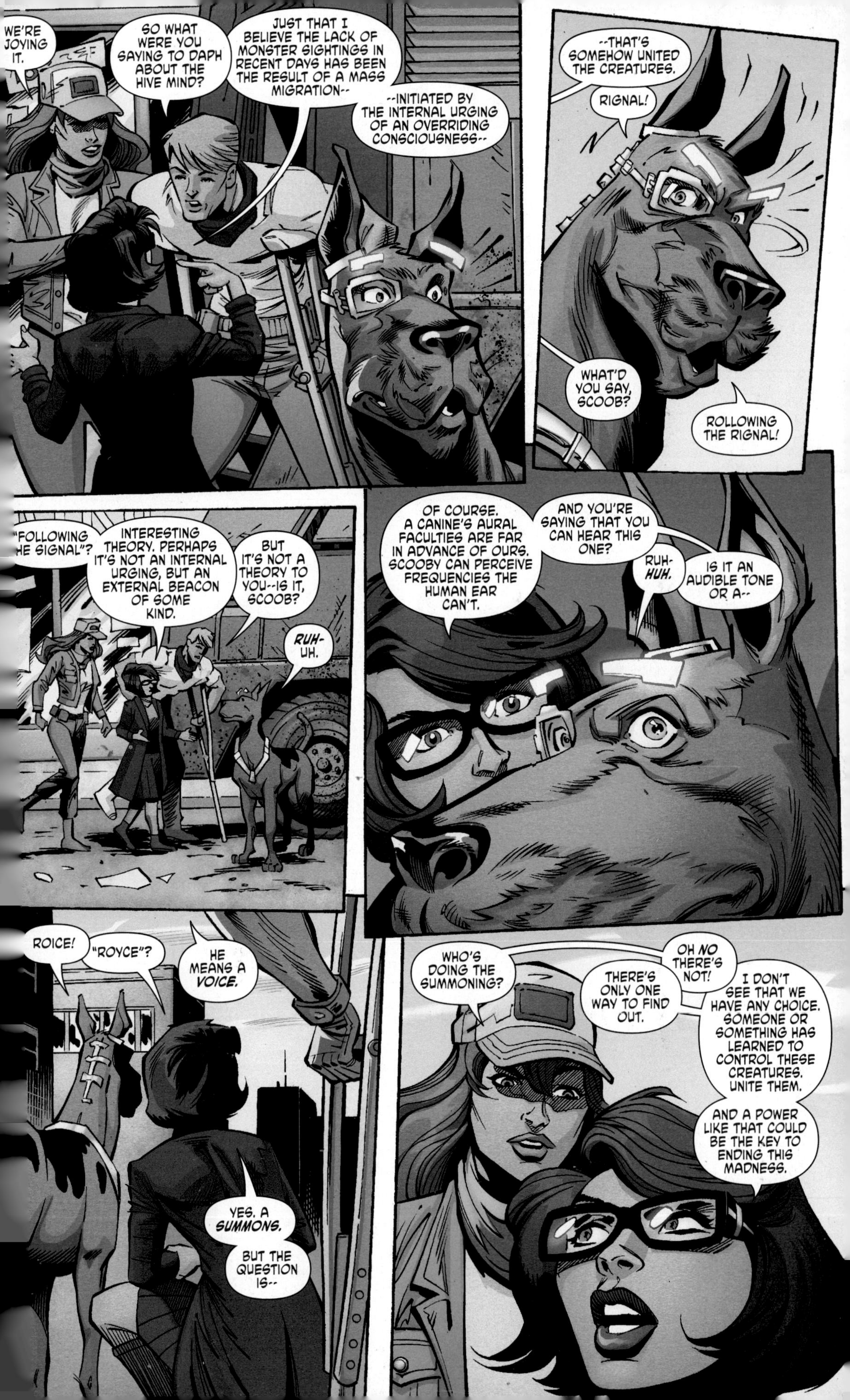
WE'RE JOYING IT.
SO WHAT WERE YOU SAYING TO DAPH ABOUT THE HIVE MIND?
JUST THAT I BELIEVE THE LACK OF MONSTER SIGHTINGS IN RECENT DAYS HAS BEEN THE RESULT OF A MASS MIGRATION--
--INITIATED BY THE INTERNAL URGING OF AN OVERRIDING CONSCIOUSNESS--
--THAT'S SOMEHOW UNITED THE CREATURES.
RIGNAL!
WHAT'D YOU SAY, SCOOB?
ROLLOWING THE RIGNAL!
"FOLLOWING THE SIGNAL"?
INTERESTING THEORY. PERHAPS IT'S NOT AN INTERNAL URGING, BUT AN EXTERNAL BEACON OF SOME KIND.
BUT IT'S NOT A THEORY TO YOU--IS IT, SCOOB?
RUH-UH.
OF COURSE. A CANINE'S AURAL FACULTIES ARE FAR IN ADVANCE OF OURS. SCOOBY CAN PERCEIVE FREQUENCIES THE HUMAN EAR CAN'T.
AND YOU'RE SAYING THAT YOU CAN HEAR THIS ONE?
RUH-HUH.
IS IT AN AUDIBLE TONE OR A--
ROICE!
"ROYCE"?
HE MEANS A VOICE.
YES. A SUMMONS.
BUT THE QUESTION IS--
WHO'S DOING THE SUMMONING?
OH NO THERE'S NOT!
THERE'S ONLY ONE WAY TO FIND OUT.
I DON'T SEE THAT WE HAVE ANY CHOICE. SOMEONE OR SOMETHING HAS LEARNED TO CONTROL THESE CREATURES. UNITE THEM.
AND A POWER LIKE THAT COULD BE THE KEY TO ENDING THIS MADNESS.

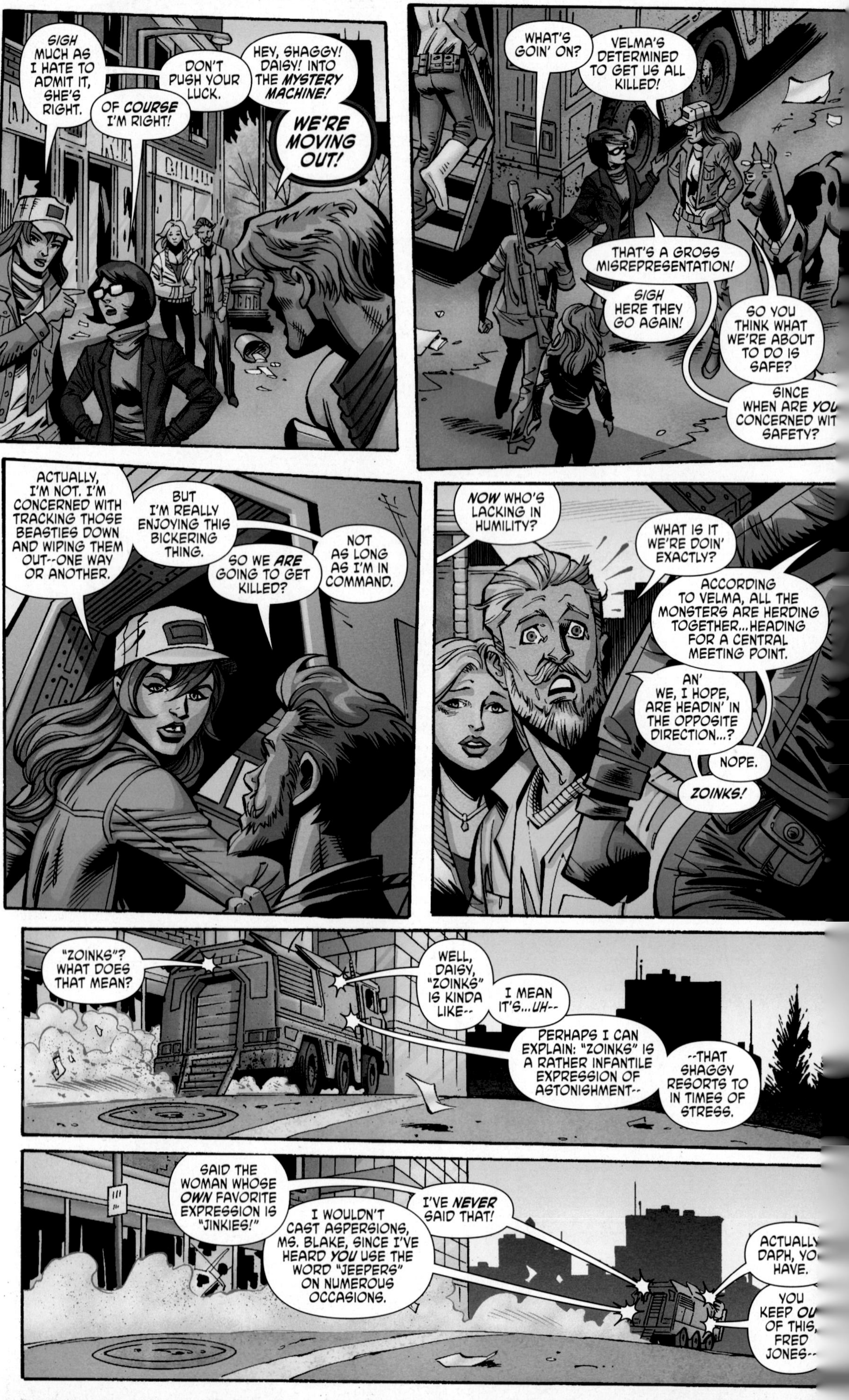
SIGH
MUCH AS I HATE TO ADMIT IT, SHE'S RIGHT.
DON'T PUSH YOUR LUCK.
OF COURSE I'M RIGHT!
HEY, SHAGGY! DAISY! INTO THE MYSTERY MACHINE!
WE'RE MOVING OUT!
WHAT'S GOIN' ON?
VELMA'S DETERMINED TO GET US ALL KILLED!
THAT'S A GROSS MISREPRESENTATION!
SIGH
HERE THEY GO AGAIN!
SO YOU THINK WHAT WE'RE ABOUT TO DO IS SAFE?
SINCE WHEN ARE YOU CONCERNED WIT SAFETY?
ACTUALLY, I'M NOT. I'M CONCERNED WITH TRACKING THOSE BEASTIES DOWN AND WIPING THEM OUT--ONE WAY OR ANOTHER.
BUT I'M REALLY ENJOYING THIS BICKERING THING.
SO WE ARE GOING TO GET KILLED?
NOT AS LONG AS I'M IN COMMAND.
NOW WHO'S LACKING IN HUMILITY?
WHAT IS IT WE'RE DOIN' EXACTLY?
ACCORDING TO VELMA, ALL THE MONSTERS ARE HERDING TOGETHER...HEADING FOR A CENTRAL MEETING POINT.
AN' WE, I HOPE, ARE HEADIN' IN THE OPPOSITE DIRECTION...?
NOPE.
ZOINKS!
"ZOINKS"? WHAT DOES THAT MEAN?
WELL, DAISY, "ZOINKS" IS KINDA LIKE--
I MEAN IT'S...UH--
PERHAPS I CAN EXPLAIN: "ZOINKS" IS A RATHER INFANTILE EXPRESSION OF ASTONISHMENT--
--THAT SHAGGY RESORTS TO IN TIMES OF STRESS.
SAID THE WOMAN WHOSE OWN FAVORITE EXPRESSION IS "JINKIES!"
I WOULDN'T CAST ASPERSIONS, MS. BLAKE, SINCE I'VE HEARD YOU USE THE WORD "JEEPERS" ON NUMEROUS OCCASIONS.
I'VE NEVER SAID THAT!
ACTUALLY DAPH, YO HAVE.
YOU KEEP OU OF THIS, FRED JONES--

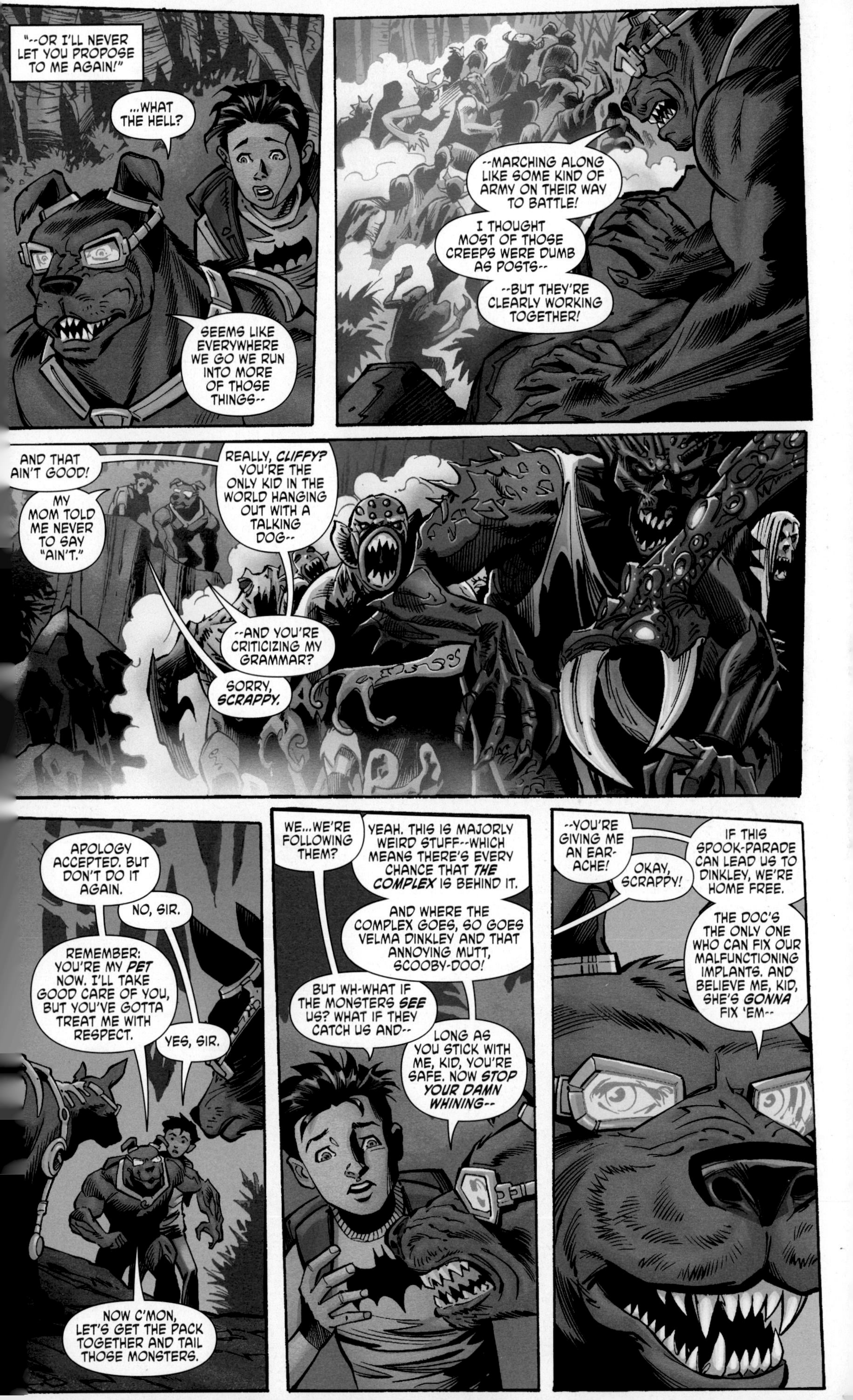
"--OR I'LL NEVER LET YOU PROPOSE TO ME AGAIN!"
...WHAT THE HELL?
SEEMS LIKE EVERYWHERE WE GO WE RUN INTO MORE OF THOSE THINGS--
--MARCHING ALONG LIKE SOME KIND OF ARMY ON THEIR WAY TO BATTLE!
I THOUGHT MOST OF THOSE CREEPS WERE DUMB AS POSTS--
--BUT THEY'RE CLEARLY WORKING TOGETHER!
AND THAT AIN'T GOOD!
MY MOM TOLD ME NEVER TO SAY "AIN'T."
REALLY, CLIFFY? YOU'RE THE ONLY KID IN THE WORLD HANGING OUT WITH A TALKING DOG--
--AND YOU'RE CRITICIZING MY GRAMMAR?
SORRY, SCRAPPY.
APOLOGY ACCEPTED. BUT DON'T DO IT AGAIN.
NO, SIR.
REMEMBER: YOU'RE MY PET NOW. I'LL TAKE GOOD CARE OF YOU, BUT YOU'VE GOTTA TREAT ME WITH RESPECT.
YES, SIR.
NOW C'MON, LET'S GET THE PACK TOGETHER AND TAIL THOSE MONSTERS.
WE...WE'RE FOLLOWING THEM?
YEAH. THIS IS MAJORLY WEIRD STUFF--WHICH MEANS THERE'S EVERY CHANCE THAT THE COMPLEX IS BEHIND IT.
AND WHERE THE COMPLEX GOES, SO GOES VELMA DINKLEY AND THAT ANNOYING MUTT, SCOOBY-DOO!
BUT WH-WHAT IF THE MONSTERS SEE US? WHAT IF THEY CATCH US AND--
LONG AS YOU STICK WITH ME, KID, YOU'RE SAFE. NOW STOP YOUR DAMN WHINING--
--YOU'RE GIVING ME AN EAR-ACHE!
OKAY, SCRAPPY!
IF THIS SPOOK-PARADE CAN LEAD US TO DINKLEY, WE'RE HOME FREE.
THE DOC'S THE ONLY ONE WHO CAN FIX OUR MALFUNCTIONING IMPLANTS. AND BELIEVE ME, KID, SHE'S GONNA FIX 'EM--

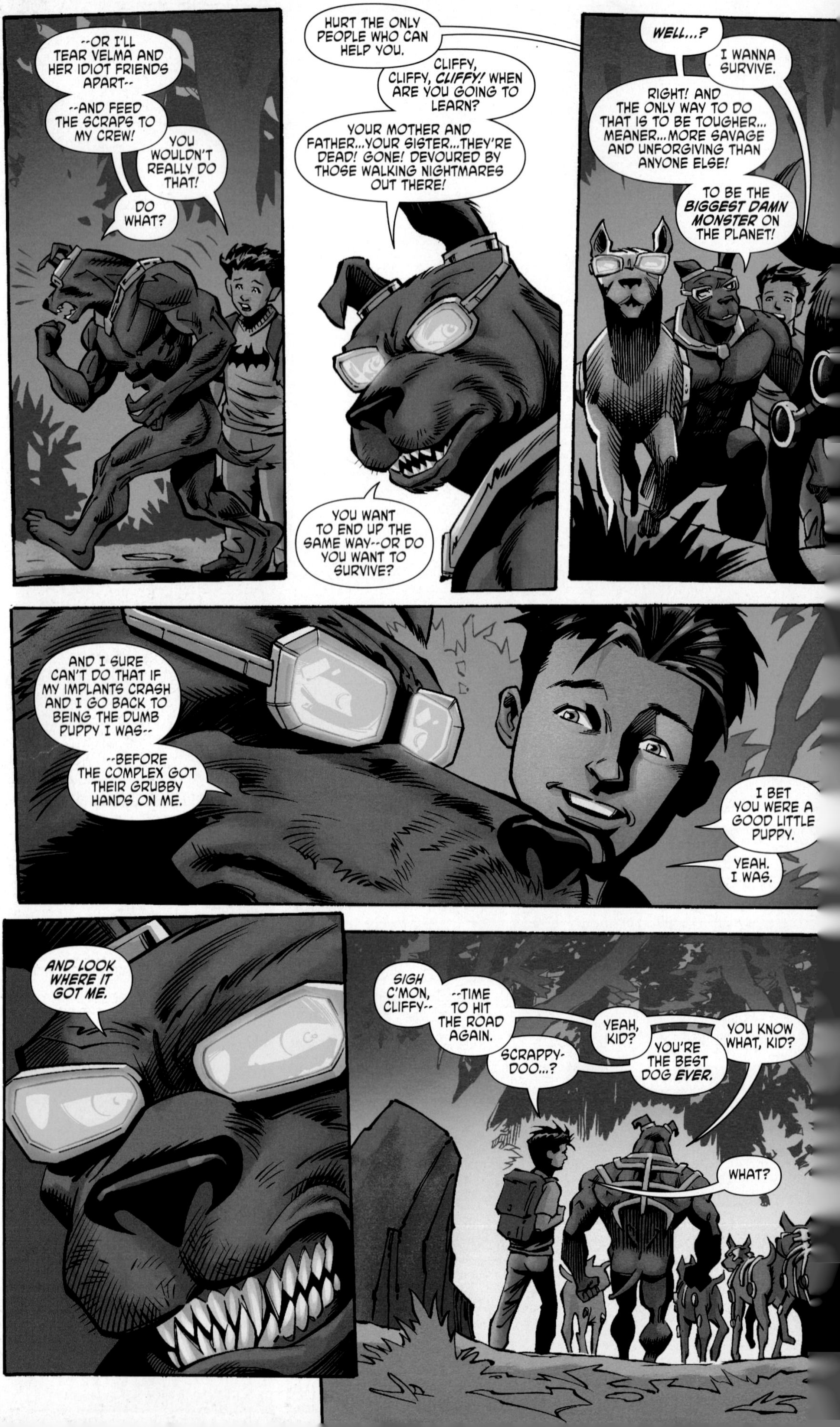
--OR I'LL TEAR VELMA AND HER IDIOT FRIENDS APART--
--AND FEED THE SCRAPS TO MY CREW!
YOU WOULDN'T REALLY DO THAT!
DO WHAT?
HURT THE ONLY PEOPLE WHO CAN HELP YOU.
CLIFFY, CLIFFY, CLIFFY! WHEN ARE YOU GOING TO LEARN?
YOUR MOTHER AND FATHER...YOUR SISTER...THEY'RE DEAD! GONE! DEVOURED BY THOSE WALKING NIGHTMARES OUT THERE!
YOU WANT TO END UP THE SAME WAY--OR DO YOU WANT TO SURVIVE?
WELL...?
I WANNA SURVIVE.
RIGHT! AND THE ONLY WAY TO DO THAT IS TO BE TOUGHER... MEANER...MORE SAVAGE AND UNFORGIVING THAN ANYONE ELSE!
TO BE THE BIGGEST DAMN MONSTER ON THE PLANET!
AND I SURE CAN'T DO THAT IF MY IMPLANTS CRASH AND I GO BACK TO BEING THE DUMB PUPPY I WAS--
--BEFORE THE COMPLEX GOT THEIR GRUBBY HANDS ON ME.
I BET YOU WERE A GOOD LITTLE PUPPY.
YEAH. I WAS.
AND LOOK WHERE IT GOT ME.
SIGH C'MON, CLIFFY--
--TIME TO HIT THE ROAD AGAIN.
SCRAPPY-DOO...?
YEAH, KID?
YOU KNOW WHAT, KID?
WHAT?
YOU'RE THE BEST DOG EVER.

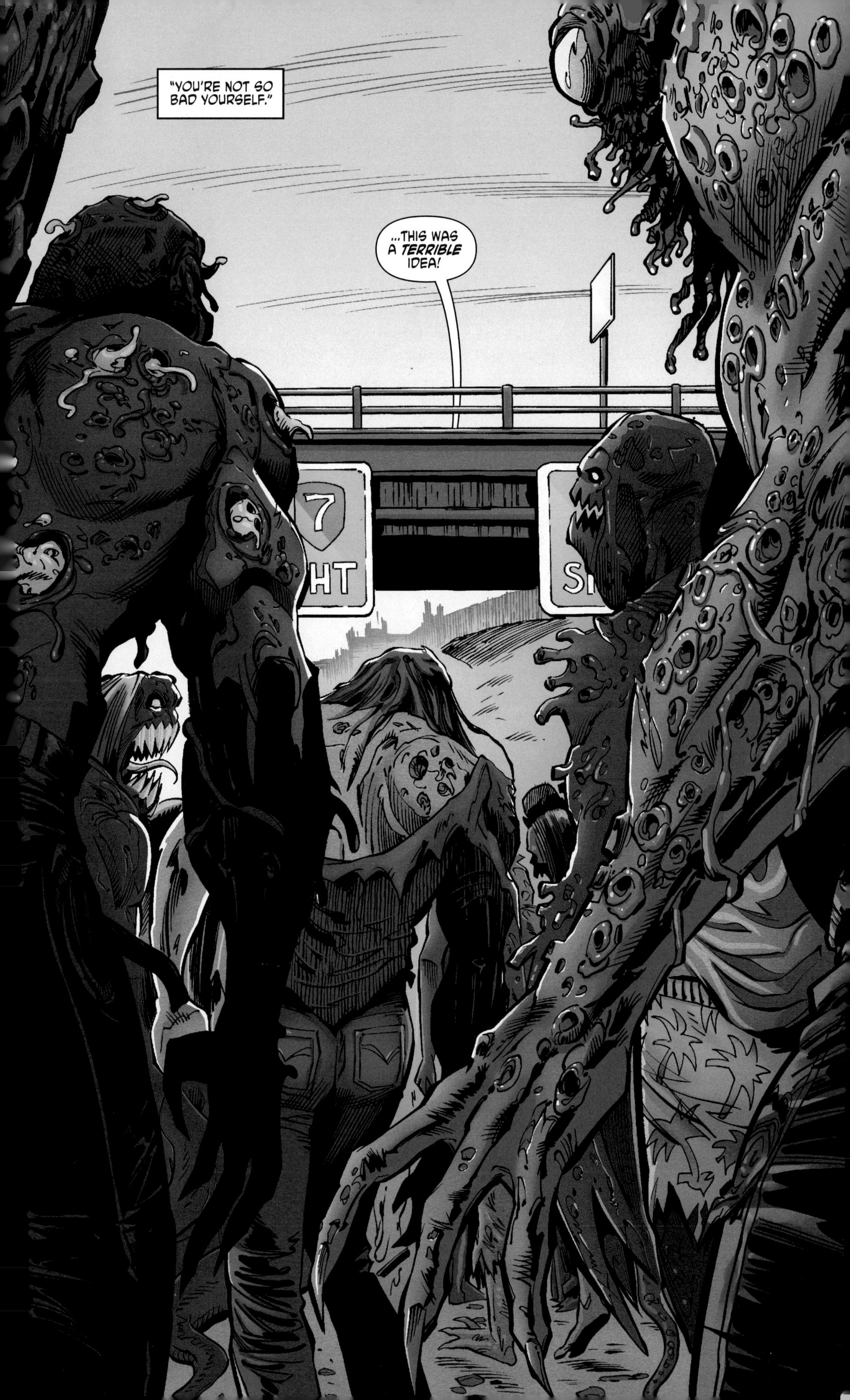
"YOU'RE NOT SO BAD YOURSELF."
...THIS WAS A *TERRIBLE* IDEA!
7
HT

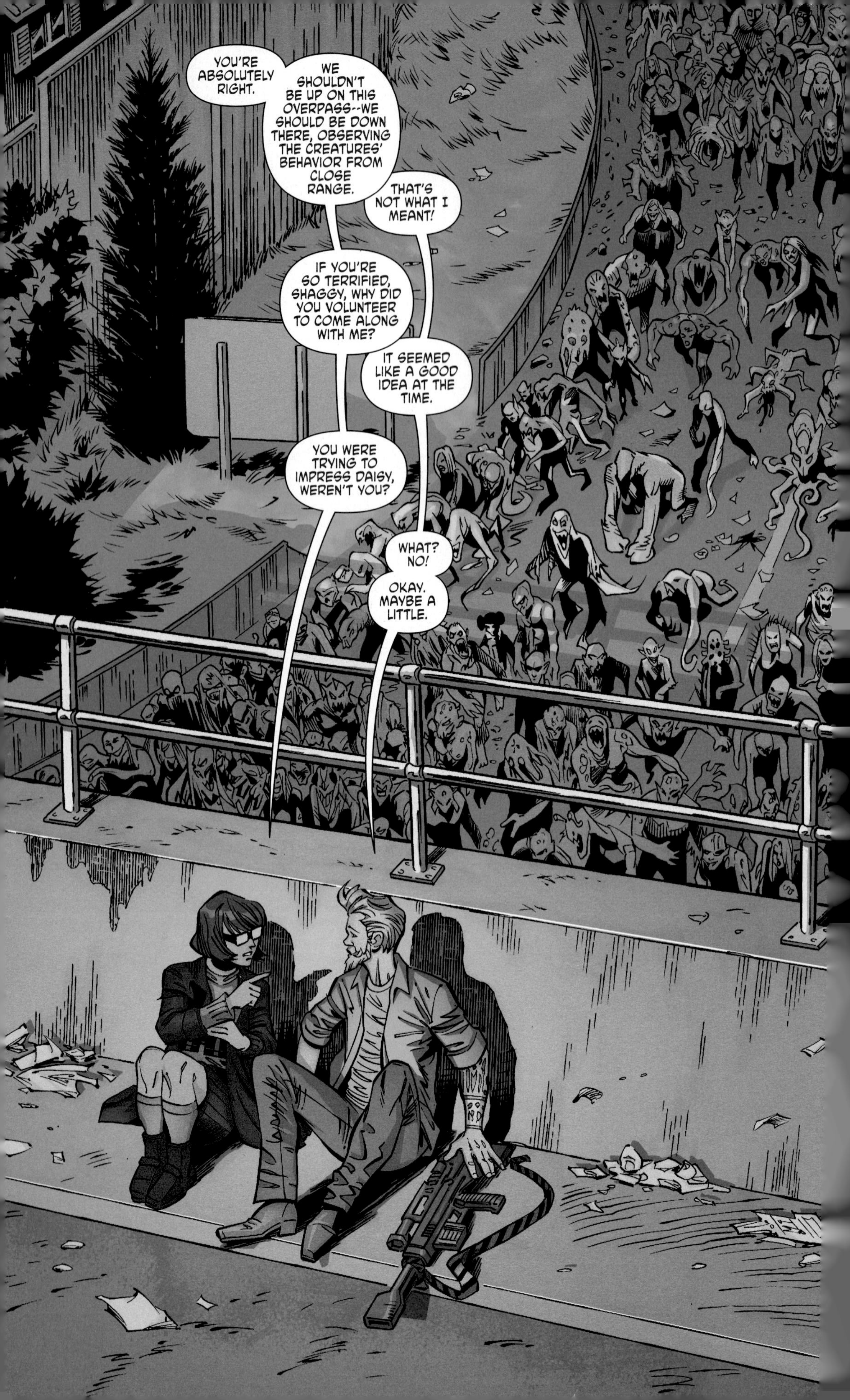
YOU'RE ABSOLUTELY RIGHT.
WE SHOULDN'T BE UP ON THIS OVERPASS--WE SHOULD BE DOWN THERE, OBSERVING THE CREATURES' BEHAVIOR FROM CLOSE RANGE.
THAT'S NOT WHAT I MEANT!
IF YOU'RE SO TERRIFIED, SHAGGY, WHY DID YOU VOLUNTEER TO COME ALONG WITH ME?
IT SEEMED LIKE A GOOD IDEA AT THE TIME.
YOU WERE TRYING TO IMPRESS DAISY, WEREN'T YOU?
WHAT? NO!
OKAY. MAYBE A LITTLE.

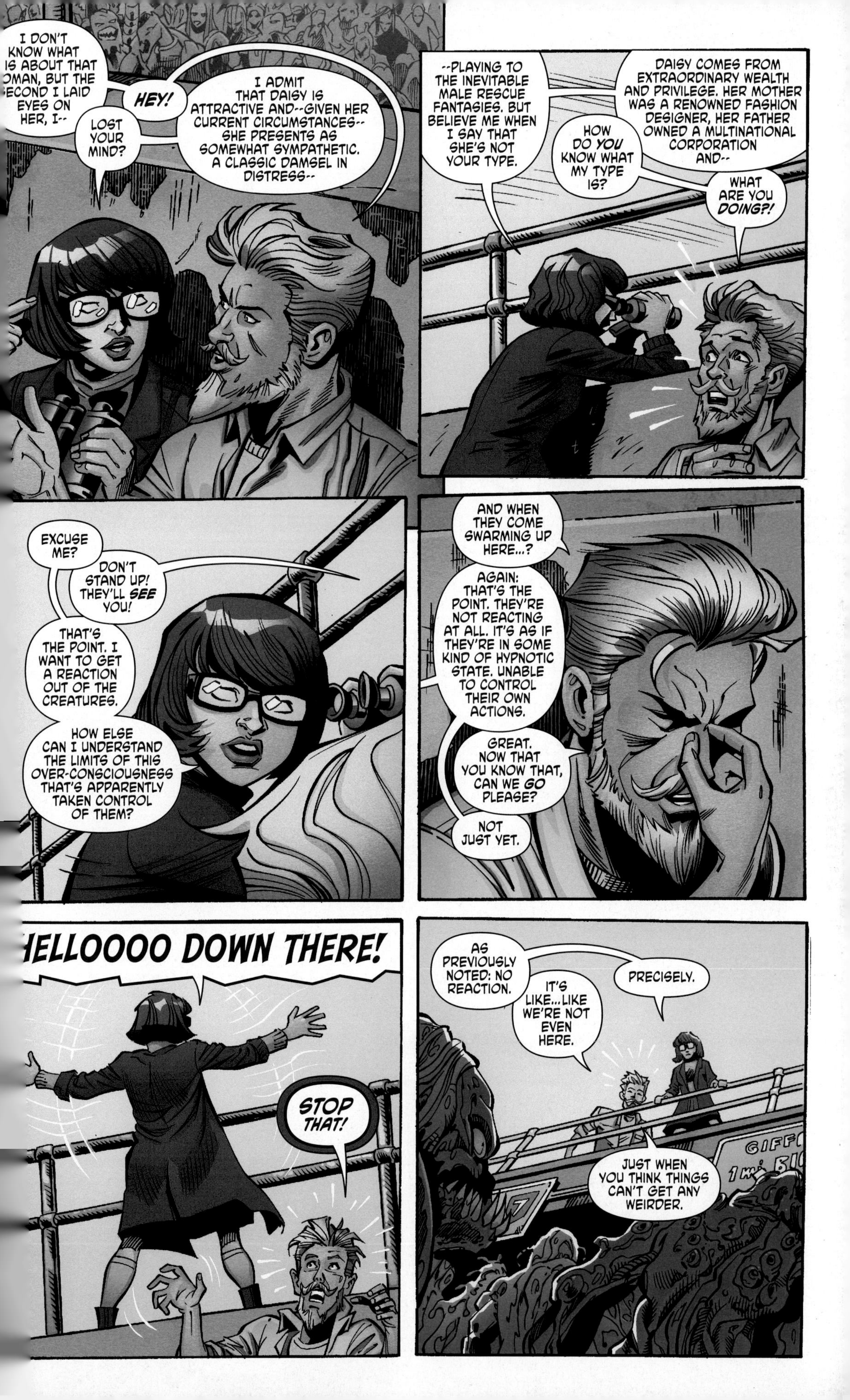

I DON'T KNOW WHAT IS ABOUT THAT OMAN, BUT THE SECOND I LAID EYES ON HER, I--
HEY!
LOST YOUR MIND?
I ADMIT THAT DAISY IS ATTRACTIVE AND--GIVEN HER CURRENT CIRCUMSTANCES--SHE PRESENTS AS SOMEWHAT SYMPATHETIC. A CLASSIC DAMSEL IN DISTRESS--
--PLAYING TO THE INEVITABLE MALE RESCUE FANTASIES. BUT BELIEVE ME WHEN I SAY THAT SHE'S NOT YOUR TYPE.
HOW DO YOU KNOW WHAT MY TYPE IS?
DAISY COMES FROM EXTRAORDINARY WEALTH AND PRIVILEGE. HER MOTHER WAS A RENOWNED FASHION DESIGNER, HER FATHER OWNED A MULTINATIONAL CORPORATION AND--
WHAT ARE YOU DOING?!
EXCUSE ME?
DON'T STAND UP! THEY'LL SEE YOU!
THAT'S THE POINT. I WANT TO GET A REACTION OUT OF THE CREATURES.
HOW ELSE CAN I UNDERSTAND THE LIMITS OF THIS OVER-CONSCIOUSNESS THAT'S APPARENTLY TAKEN CONTROL OF THEM?
AND WHEN THEY COME SWARMING UP HERE...?
AGAIN: THAT'S THE POINT. THEY'RE NOT REACTING AT ALL. IT'S AS IF THEY'RE IN SOME KIND OF HYPNOTIC STATE. UNABLE TO CONTROL THEIR OWN ACTIONS.
GREAT. NOW THAT YOU KNOW THAT, CAN WE GO PLEASE?
NOT JUST YET.
HELLOOOO DOWN THERE!
STOP THAT!
AS PREVIOUSLY NOTED: NO REACTION.
IT'S LIKE...LIKE WE'RE NOT EVEN HERE.
PRECISELY.
JUST WHEN YOU THINK THINGS CAN'T GET ANY WEIRDER.

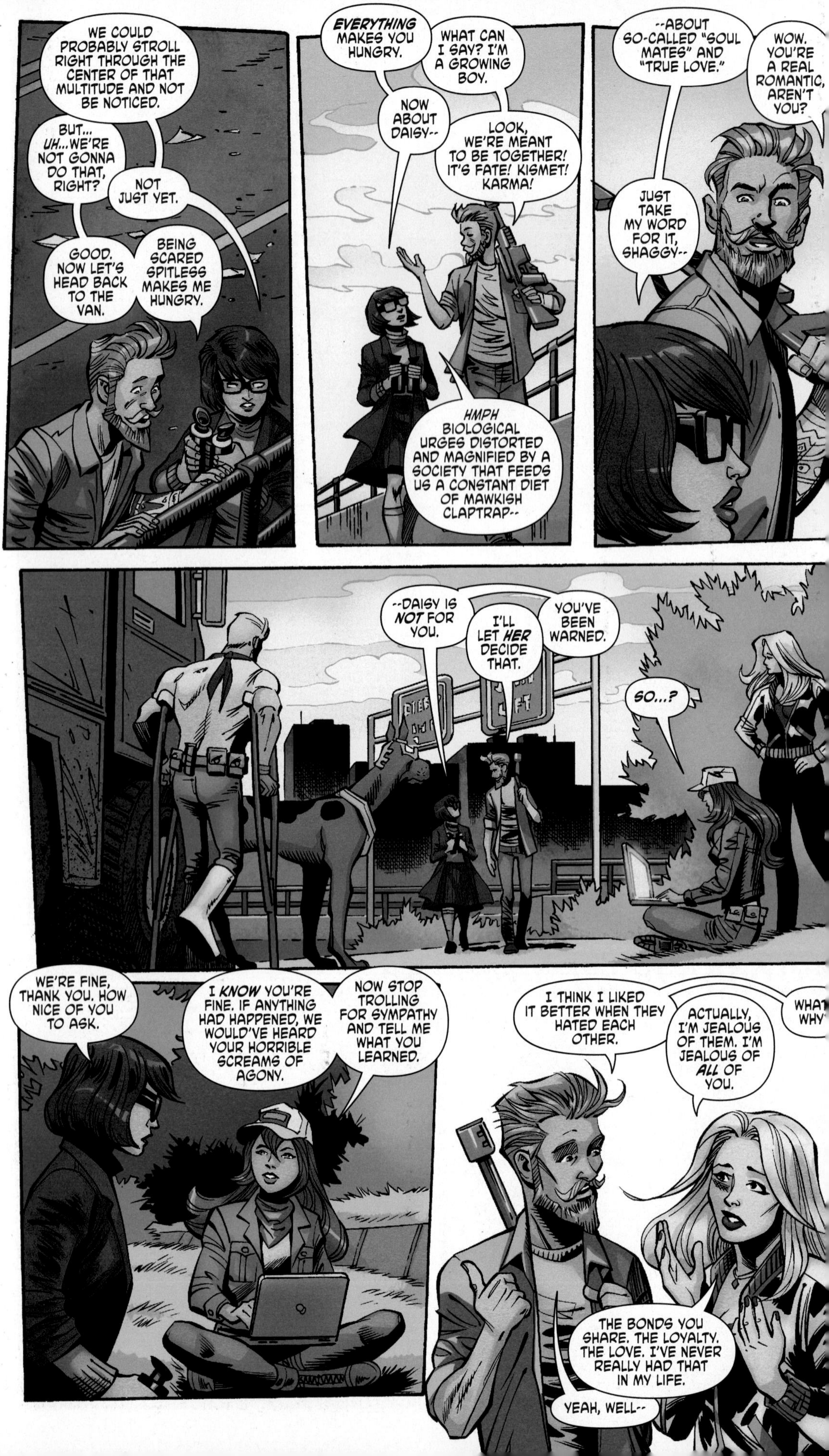
WE COULD PROBABLY STROLL RIGHT THROUGH THE CENTER OF THAT MULTITUDE AND NOT BE NOTICED.
BUT... *UH*...WE'RE NOT GONNA DO THAT, RIGHT?
NOT JUST YET.
GOOD. NOW LET'S HEAD BACK TO THE VAN.
BEING SCARED SPITLESS MAKES ME HUNGRY.
EVERYTHING MAKES YOU HUNGRY.
WHAT CAN I SAY? I'M A GROWING BOY.
NOW ABOUT DAISY--
LOOK, WE'RE MEANT TO BE TOGETHER! IT'S FATE! KISMET! KARMA!
HMPH BIOLOGICAL URGES DISTORTED AND MAGNIFIED BY A SOCIETY THAT FEEDS US A CONSTANT DIET OF MAWKISH CLAPTRAP--
--ABOUT SO-CALLED "SOUL MATES" AND "TRUE LOVE."
WOW. YOU'RE A REAL ROMANTIC, AREN'T YOU?
JUST TAKE MY WORD FOR IT, SHAGGY--
--DAISY IS *NOT* FOR YOU.
I'LL LET *HER* DECIDE THAT.
YOU'VE BEEN WARNED.
SO...?
WE'RE FINE, THANK YOU. HOW NICE OF YOU TO ASK.
I *KNOW* YOU'RE FINE. IF ANYTHING HAD HAPPENED, WE WOULD'VE HEARD YOUR HORRIBLE SCREAMS OF AGONY.
NOW STOP TROLLING FOR SYMPATHY AND TELL ME WHAT YOU LEARNED.
I THINK I LIKED IT BETTER WHEN THEY HATED EACH OTHER.
WHAT
WHY
ACTUALLY, I'M JEALOUS OF THEM. I'M JEALOUS OF *ALL* OF YOU.
THE BONDS YOU SHARE. THE LOYALTY. THE LOVE. I'VE NEVER REALLY HAD THAT IN MY LIFE.
YEAH, WELL--

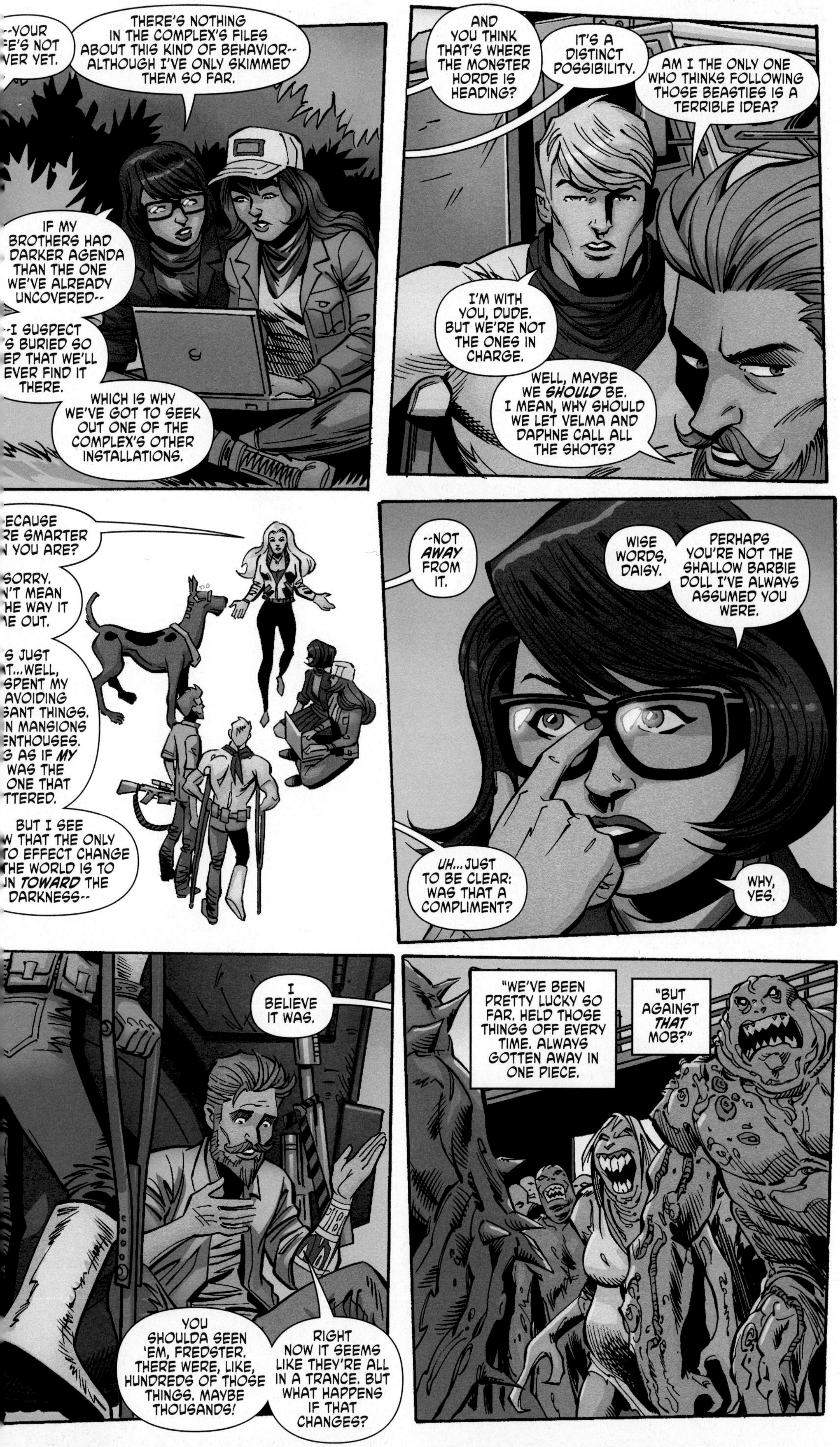
--YOUR
FE'S NOT
VER YET.
THERE'S NOTHING IN THE COMPLEX'S FILES ABOUT THIS KIND OF BEHAVIOR-- ALTHOUGH I'VE ONLY SKIMMED THEM SO FAR.
IF MY BROTHERS HAD DARKER AGENDA THAN THE ONE WE'VE ALREADY UNCOVERED--
--I SUSPECT 'S BURIED SO EP THAT WE'LL EVER FIND IT THERE.
WHICH IS WHY WE'VE GOT TO SEEK OUT ONE OF THE COMPLEX'S OTHER INSTALLATIONS.
AND YOU THINK THAT'S WHERE THE MONSTER HORDE IS HEADING?
IT'S A DISTINCT POSSIBILITY.
AM I THE ONLY ONE WHO THINKS FOLLOWING THOSE BEASTIES IS A TERRIBLE IDEA?
I'M WITH YOU, DUDE. BUT WE'RE NOT THE ONES IN CHARGE.
WELL, MAYBE WE SHOULD BE. I MEAN, WHY SHOULD WE LET VELMA AND DAPHNE CALL ALL THE SHOTS?
ECAUSE RE SMARTER N YOU ARE?
SORRY. N'T MEAN HE WAY IT E OUT.
S JUST T...WELL, SPENT MY AVOIDING SANT THINGS. N MANSIONS ENTHOUSES. G AS IF MY WAS THE ONE THAT TTERED.
BUT I SEE W THAT THE ONLY TO EFFECT CHANGE THE WORLD IS TO N TOWARD THE DARKNESS--
--NOT AWAY FROM IT.
WISE WORDS, DAISY.
PERHAPS YOU'RE NOT THE SHALLOW BARBIE DOLL I'VE ALWAYS ASSUMED YOU WERE.
UH... JUST TO BE CLEAR: WAS THAT A COMPLIMENT?
WHY, YES.
I BELIEVE IT WAS.
YOU SHOULDA SEEN 'EM, FREDSTER. THERE WERE, LIKE, HUNDREDS OF THOSE THINGS. MAYBE THOUSANDS!
RIGHT NOW IT SEEMS LIKE THEY'RE ALL IN A TRANCE. BUT WHAT HAPPENS IF THAT CHANGES?
"WE'VE BEEN PRETTY LUCKY SO FAR. HELD THOSE THINGS OFF EVERY TIME. ALWAYS GOTTEN AWAY IN ONE PIECE.
"BUT AGAINST THAT MOB?"

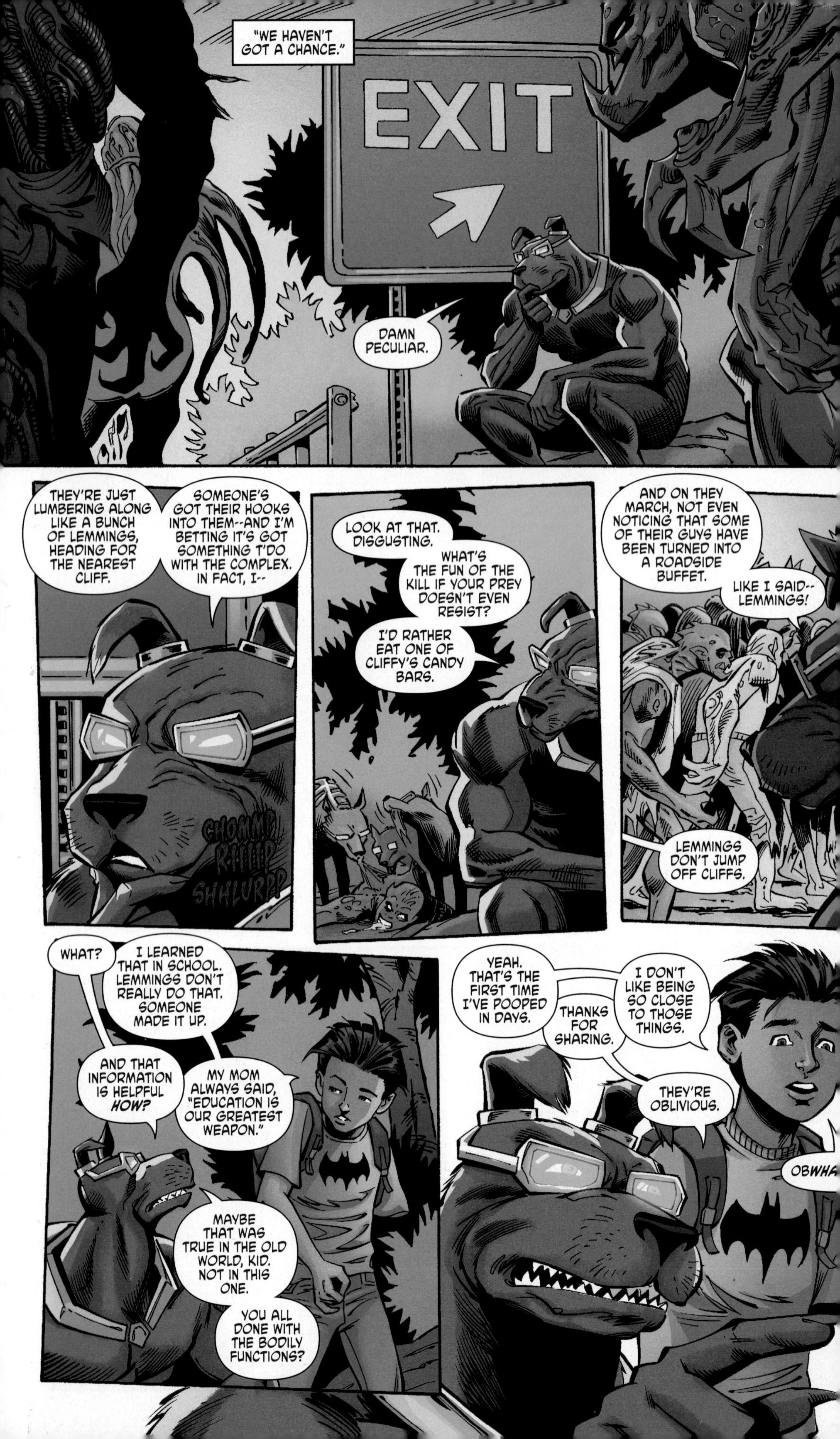
"WE HAVEN'T GOT A CHANCE."
EXIT
DAMN PECULIAR.
THEY'RE JUST LUMBERING ALONG LIKE A BUNCH OF LEMMINGS, HEADING FOR THE NEAREST CLIFF.
SOMEONE'S GOT THEIR HOOKS INTO THEM--AND I'M BETTING IT'S GOT SOMETHING T'DO WITH THE COMPLEX. IN FACT, I--
CHOMMP
SHHLURPP
LOOK AT THAT. DISGUSTING.
WHAT'S THE FUN OF THE KILL IF YOUR PREY DOESN'T EVEN RESIST?
I'D RATHER EAT ONE OF CLIFFY'S CANDY BARS.
AND ON THEY MARCH, NOT EVEN NOTICING THAT SOME OF THEIR GUYS HAVE BEEN TURNED INTO A ROADSIDE BUFFET.
LIKE I SAID-- LEMMINGS!
LEMMINGS DON'T JUMP OFF CLIFFS.
WHAT?
I LEARNED THAT IN SCHOOL. LEMMINGS DON'T REALLY DO THAT. SOMEONE MADE IT UP.
AND THAT INFORMATION IS HELPFUL *HOW?*
MY MOM ALWAYS SAID, "EDUCATION IS OUR GREATEST WEAPON."
MAYBE THAT WAS TRUE IN THE OLD WORLD, KID. NOT IN THIS ONE.
YOU ALL DONE WITH THE BODILY FUNCTIONS?
YEAH. THAT'S THE FIRST TIME I'VE POOPED IN DAYS.
THANKS FOR SHARING.
I DON'T LIKE BEING SO CLOSE TO THOSE THINGS.
THEY'RE OBLIVIOUS.
OBWHA

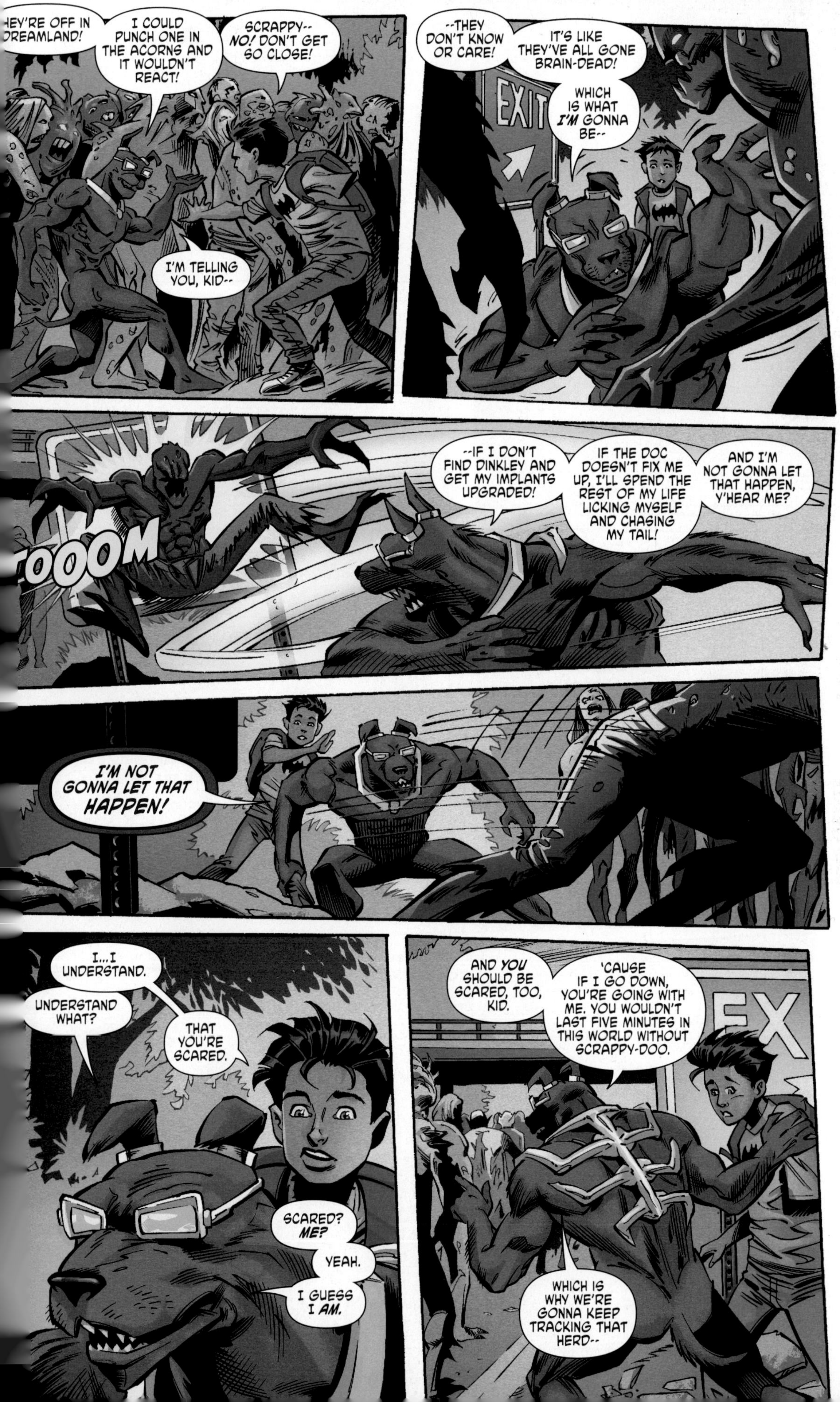
HEY'RE OFF IN DREAMLAND!
I COULD PUNCH ONE IN THE ACORNS AND IT WOULDN'T REACT!
SCRAPPY-- NO! DON'T GET SO CLOSE!
I'M TELLING YOU, KID--
--THEY DON'T KNOW OR CARE!
IT'S LIKE THEY'VE ALL GONE BRAIN-DEAD!
WHICH IS WHAT I'M GONNA BE--
EXIT
--IF I DON'T FIND DINKLEY AND GET MY IMPLANTS UPGRADED!
IF THE DOC DOESN'T FIX ME UP, I'LL SPEND THE REST OF MY LIFE LICKING MYSELF AND CHASING MY TAIL!
AND I'M NOT GONNA LET THAT HAPPEN, Y'HEAR ME?
TOOOM
I'M NOT GONNA LET THAT HAPPEN!
I...I UNDERSTAND.
UNDERSTAND WHAT?
THAT YOU'RE SCARED.
SCARED? ME?
YEAH.
I GUESS I AM.
AND YOU SHOULD BE SCARED, TOO, KID.
'CAUSE IF I GO DOWN, YOU'RE GOING WITH ME. YOU WOULDN'T LAST FIVE MINUTES IN THIS WORLD WITHOUT SCRAPPY-DOO.
EX
WHICH IS WHY WE'RE GONNA KEEP TRACKING THAT HERD--

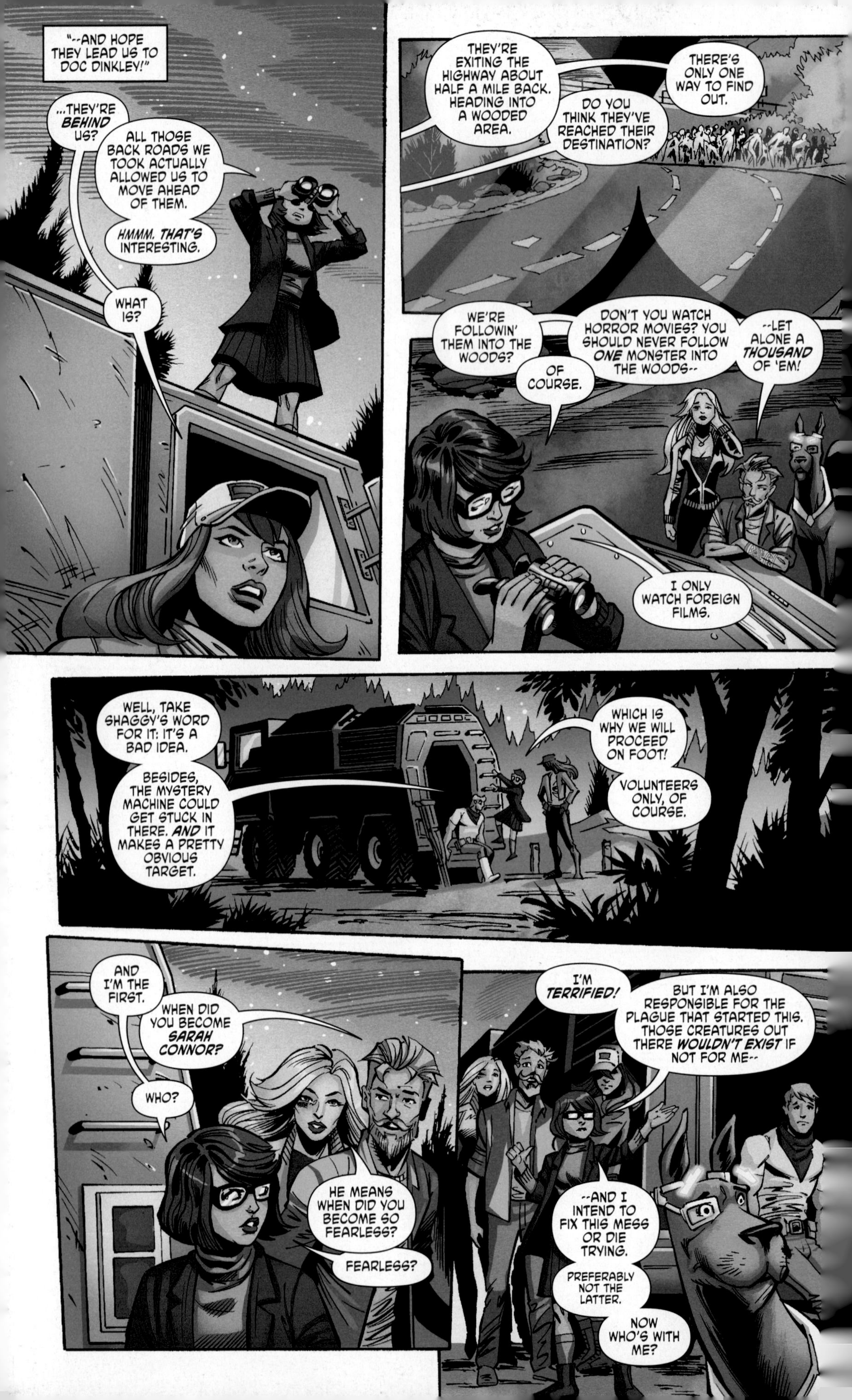
"--AND HOPE THEY LEAD US TO DOC DINKLEY!"
...THEY'RE *BEHIND* US?
ALL THOSE BACK ROADS WE TOOK ACTUALLY ALLOWED US TO MOVE AHEAD OF THEM.
HMMM. THAT'S INTERESTING.
WHAT IS?
THEY'RE EXITING THE HIGHWAY ABOUT HALF A MILE BACK. HEADING INTO A WOODED AREA.
DO YOU THINK THEY'VE REACHED THEIR DESTINATION?
THERE'S ONLY ONE WAY TO FIND OUT.
WE'RE FOLLOWIN' THEM INTO THE WOODS?
OF COURSE.
DON'T YOU WATCH HORROR MOVIES? YOU SHOULD NEVER FOLLOW *ONE* MONSTER INTO THE WOODS--
--LET ALONE A *THOUSAND* OF 'EM!
I ONLY WATCH FOREIGN FILMS.
WELL, TAKE SHAGGY'S WORD FOR IT: IT'S A BAD IDEA.
BESIDES, THE MYSTERY MACHINE COULD GET STUCK IN THERE. *AND* IT MAKES A PRETTY OBVIOUS TARGET.
WHICH IS WHY WE WILL PROCEED ON FOOT!
VOLUNTEERS ONLY, OF COURSE.
AND I'M THE FIRST.
WHEN DID YOU BECOME *SARAH CONNOR?*
WHO?
HE MEANS WHEN DID YOU BECOME SO FEARLESS?
FEARLESS?
I'M *TERRIFIED!*
BUT I'M ALSO RESPONSIBLE FOR THE PLAGUE THAT STARTED THIS. THOSE CREATURES OUT THERE *WOULDN'T EXIST* IF NOT FOR ME--
--AND I INTEND TO FIX THIS MESS OR DIE TRYING.
PREFERABLY NOT THE LATTER.
NOW WHO'S WITH ME?

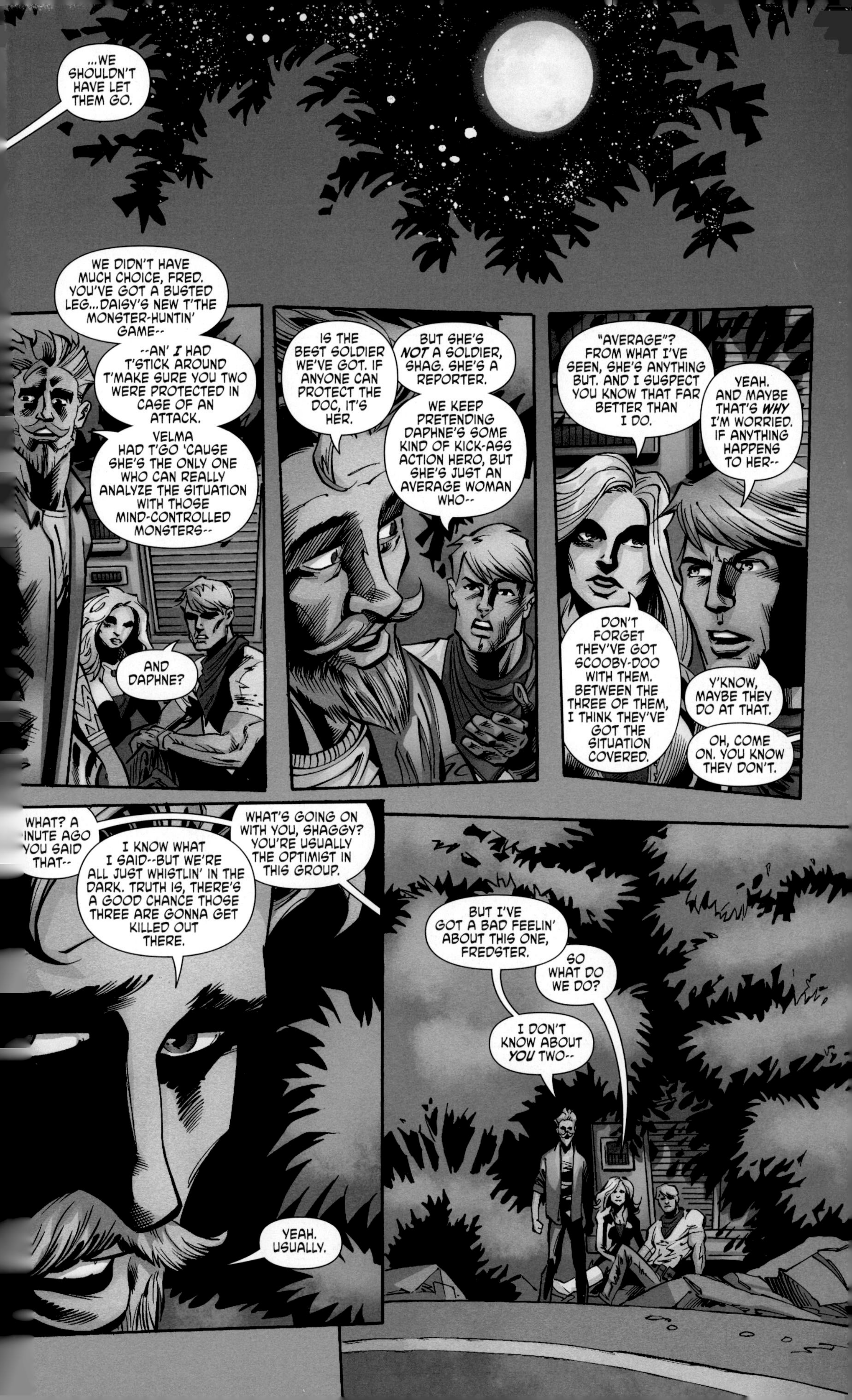
...WE SHOULDN'T HAVE LET THEM GO.
WE DIDN'T HAVE MUCH CHOICE, FRED. YOU'VE GOT A BUSTED LEG...DAISY'S NEW T'THE MONSTER-HUNTIN' GAME--
--AN' I HAD T'STICK AROUND T'MAKE SURE YOU TWO WERE PROTECTED IN CASE OF AN ATTACK.
VELMA HAD T'GO 'CAUSE SHE'S THE ONLY ONE WHO CAN REALLY ANALYZE THE SITUATION WITH THOSE MIND-CONTROLLED MONSTERS--
AND DAPHNE?
IS THE BEST SOLDIER WE'VE GOT. IF ANYONE CAN PROTECT THE DOC, IT'S HER.
BUT SHE'S NOT A SOLDIER, SHAG. SHE'S A REPORTER.
WE KEEP PRETENDING DAPHNE'S SOME KIND OF KICK-ASS ACTION HERO, BUT SHE'S JUST AN AVERAGE WOMAN WHO--
"AVERAGE"? FROM WHAT I'VE SEEN, SHE'S ANYTHING BUT. AND I SUSPECT YOU KNOW THAT FAR BETTER THAN I DO.
YEAH. AND MAYBE THAT'S WHY I'M WORRIED. IF ANYTHING HAPPENS TO HER--
DON'T FORGET THEY'VE GOT SCOOBY-DOO WITH THEM. BETWEEN THE THREE OF THEM, I THINK THEY'VE GOT THE SITUATION COVERED.
Y'KNOW, MAYBE THEY DO AT THAT.
OH, COME ON. YOU KNOW THEY DON'T.
WHAT? A MINUTE AGO YOU SAID THAT--
I KNOW WHAT I SAID--BUT WE'RE ALL JUST WHISTLIN' IN THE DARK. TRUTH IS, THERE'S A GOOD CHANCE THOSE THREE ARE GONNA GET KILLED OUT THERE.
WHAT'S GOING ON WITH YOU, SHAGGY? YOU'RE USUALLY THE OPTIMIST IN THIS GROUP.
YEAH. USUALLY.
BUT I'VE GOT A BAD FEELIN' ABOUT THIS ONE, FREDSTER.
SO WHAT DO WE DO?
I DON'T KNOW ABOUT YOU TWO--

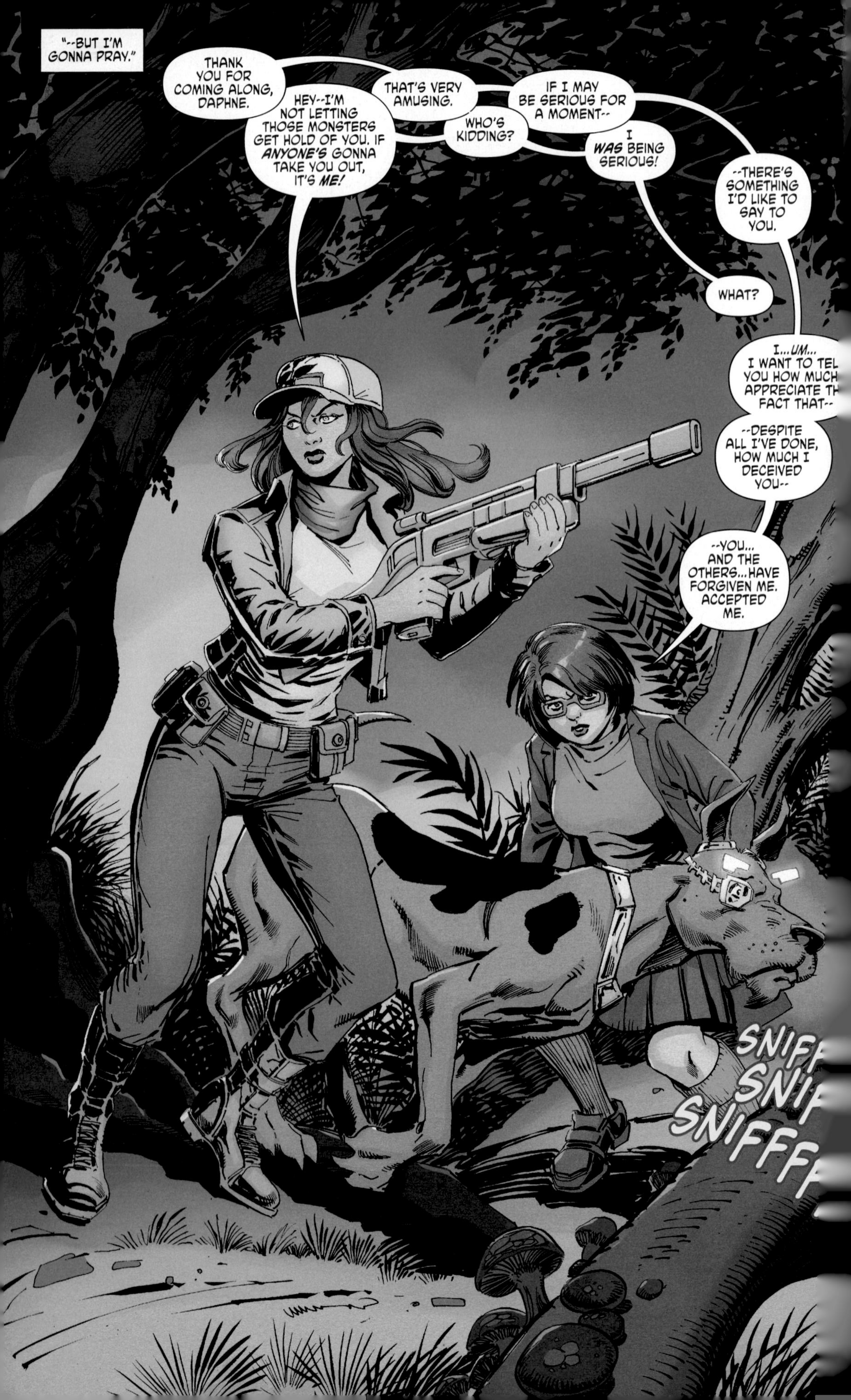
"--BUT I'M GONNA PRAY."
THANK YOU FOR COMING ALONG, DAPHNE.
HEY--I'M NOT LETTING THOSE MONSTERS GET HOLD OF YOU. IF *ANYONE'S* GONNA TAKE YOU OUT, IT'S *ME!*
THAT'S VERY AMUSING.
WHO'S KIDDING?
IF I MAY BE SERIOUS FOR A MOMENT--
I *WAS* BEING SERIOUS!
--THERE'S SOMETHING I'D LIKE TO SAY TO YOU.
WHAT?
I...*UM*... I WANT TO TEL YOU HOW MUCH APPRECIATE TH FACT THAT--
--DESPITE ALL I'VE DONE, HOW MUCH I DECEIVED YOU--
--YOU... AND THE OTHERS...HAVE FORGIVEN ME. ACCEPTED ME.
SNIFF SNIF SNIFFFF

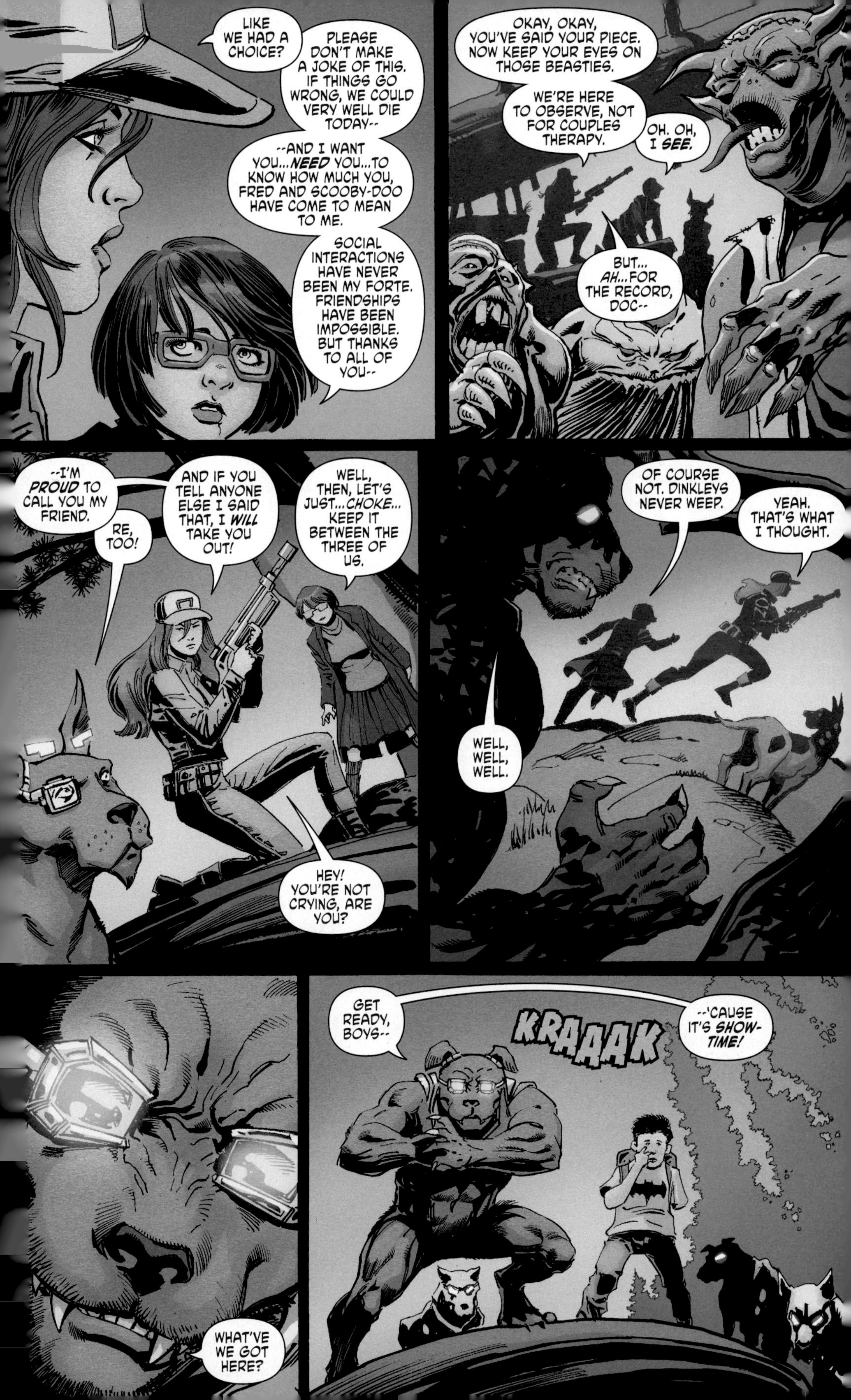
LIKE WE HAD A CHOICE?
PLEASE DON'T MAKE A JOKE OF THIS. IF THINGS GO WRONG, WE COULD VERY WELL DIE TODAY--
--AND I WANT YOU...NEED YOU...TO KNOW HOW MUCH YOU, FRED AND SCOOBY-DOO HAVE COME TO MEAN TO ME.
SOCIAL INTERACTIONS HAVE NEVER BEEN MY FORTE. FRIENDSHIPS HAVE BEEN IMPOSSIBLE. BUT THANKS TO ALL OF YOU--
OKAY, OKAY, YOU'VE SAID YOUR PIECE. NOW KEEP YOUR EYES ON THOSE BEASTIES.
WE'RE HERE TO OBSERVE, NOT FOR COUPLES THERAPY.
OH. OH, I SEE.
BUT... AH...FOR THE RECORD, DOC--
--I'M PROUD TO CALL YOU MY FRIEND.
RE, TOO!
AND IF YOU TELL ANYONE ELSE I SAID THAT, I WILL TAKE YOU OUT!
WELL, THEN, LET'S JUST...CHOKE... KEEP IT BETWEEN THE THREE OF US.
HEY! YOU'RE NOT CRYING, ARE YOU?
OF COURSE NOT. DINKLEYS NEVER WEEP.
YEAH. THAT'S WHAT I THOUGHT.
WELL, WELL, WELL.
WHAT'VE WE GOT HERE?
GET READY, BOYS--
KRAAAK
--'CAUSE IT'S SHOW-TIME!

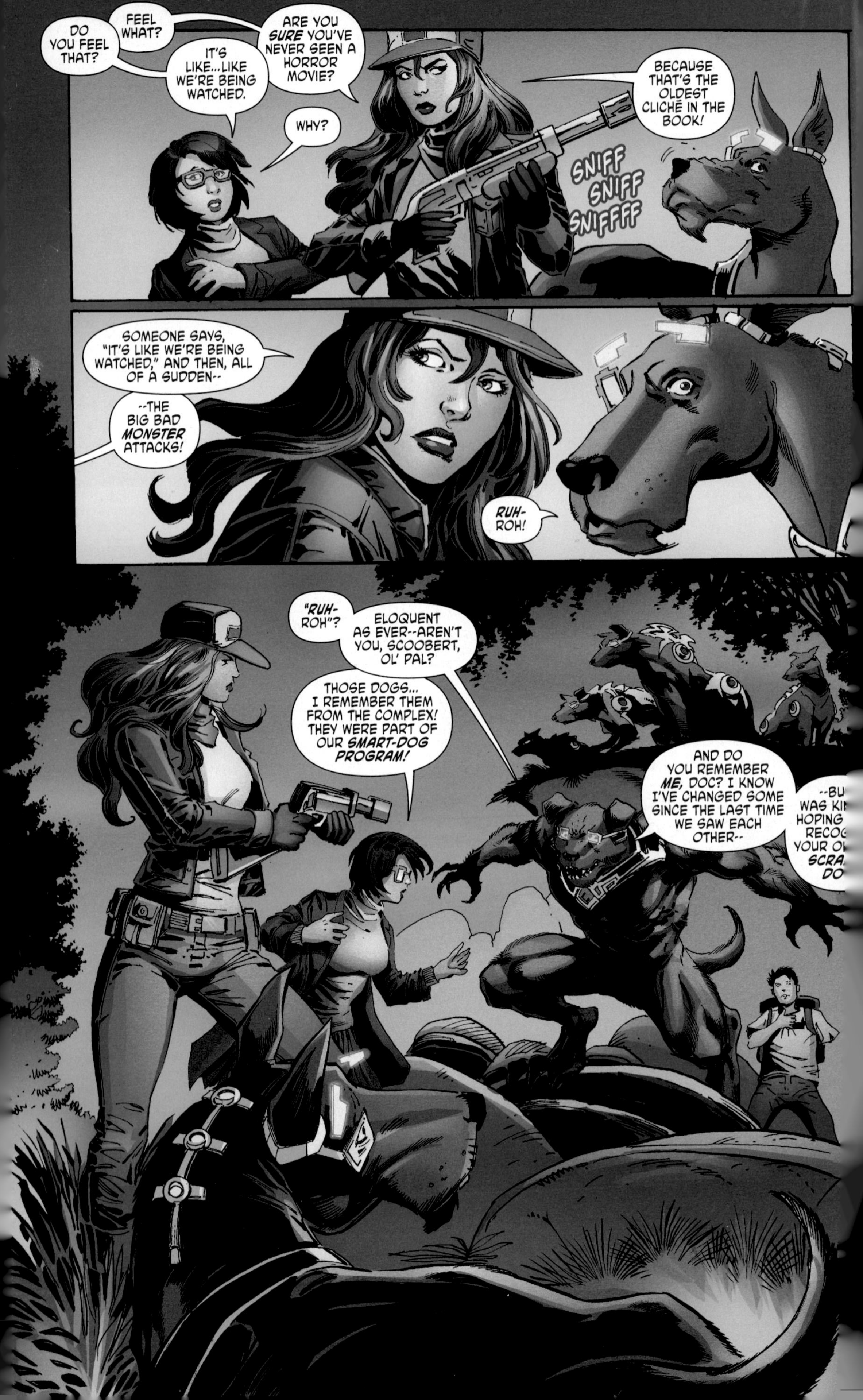
DO YOU FEEL THAT?
FEEL WHAT?
IT'S LIKE...LIKE WE'RE BEING WATCHED.
ARE YOU SURE YOU'VE NEVER SEEN A HORROR MOVIE?
WHY?
BECAUSE THAT'S THE OLDEST CLICHÉ IN THE BOOK!
SNIFF SNIFF SNIFFFF
SOMEONE SAYS, "IT'S LIKE WE'RE BEING WATCHED," AND THEN, ALL OF A SUDDEN--
--THE BIG BAD MONSTER ATTACKS!
RUH-ROH!
"RUH-ROH"?
ELOQUENT AS EVER--AREN'T YOU, SCOOBERT, OL' PAL?
THOSE DOGS... I REMEMBER THEM FROM THE COMPLEX! THEY WERE PART OF OUR SMART-DOG PROGRAM!
AND DO YOU REMEMBER ME, DOC? I KNOW I'VE CHANGED SOME SINCE THE LAST TIME WE SAW EACH OTHER--

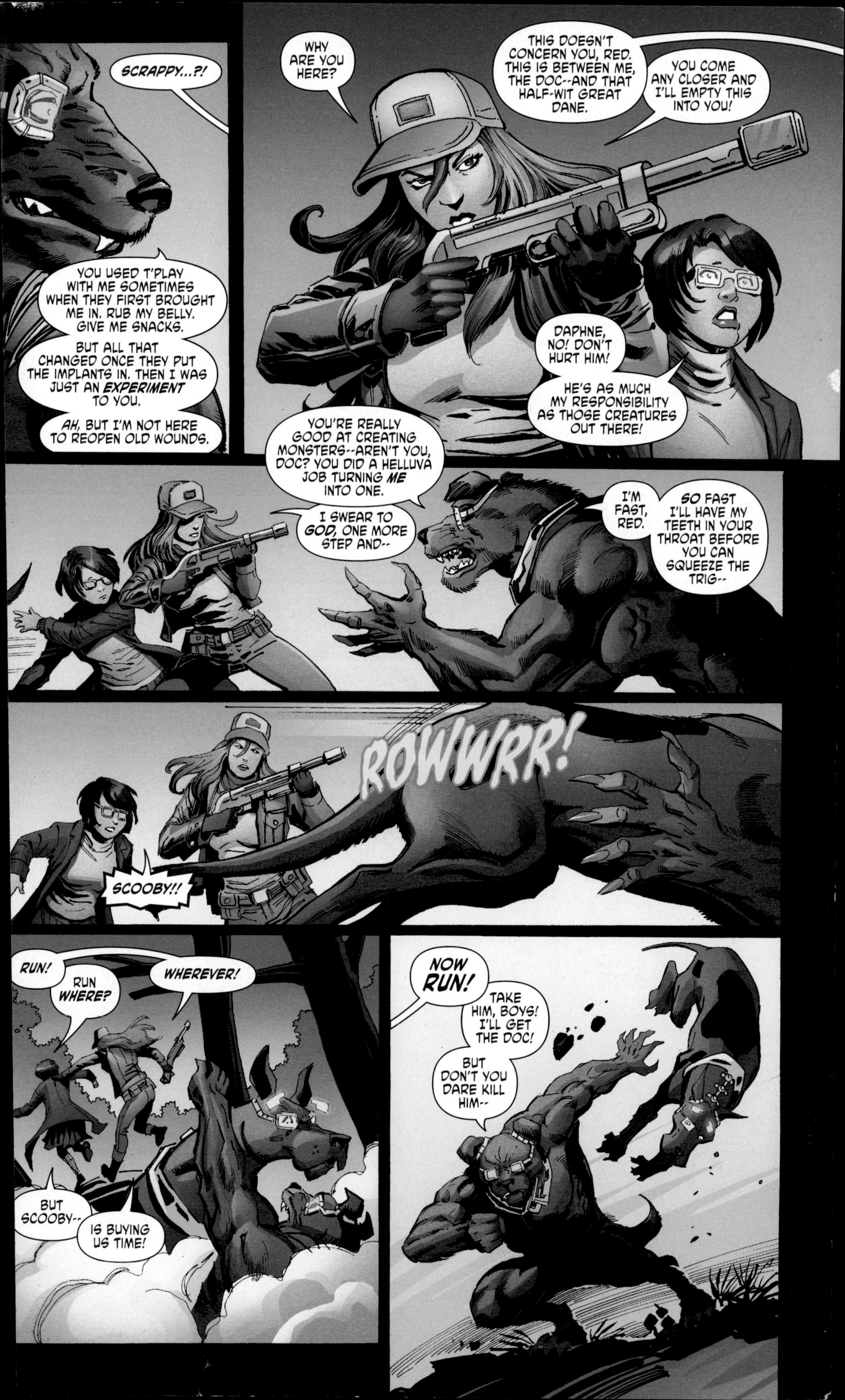
SCRAPPY...?!
WHY ARE YOU HERE?
THIS DOESN'T CONCERN YOU, RED. THIS IS BETWEEN ME, THE DOC--AND THAT HALF-WIT GREAT DANE.
YOU COME ANY CLOSER AND I'LL EMPTY THIS INTO YOU!
YOU USED T'PLAY WITH ME SOMETIMES WHEN THEY FIRST BROUGHT ME IN. RUB MY BELLY. GIVE ME SNACKS.
BUT ALL THAT CHANGED ONCE THEY PUT THE IMPLANTS IN. THEN I WAS JUST AN EXPERIMENT TO YOU.
AH, BUT I'M NOT HERE TO REOPEN OLD WOUNDS.
DAPHNE, NO! DON'T HURT HIM!
HE'S AS MUCH MY RESPONSIBILITY AS THOSE CREATURES OUT THERE!
YOU'RE REALLY GOOD AT CREATING MONSTERS--AREN'T YOU, DOC? YOU DID A HELLUVA JOB TURNING ME INTO ONE.
I SWEAR TO GOD, ONE MORE STEP AND--
I'M FAST, RED.
SO FAST I'LL HAVE MY TEETH IN YOUR THROAT BEFORE YOU CAN SQUEEZE THE TRIG--
ROWWRR!
SCOOBY!!
RUN!
RUN WHERE?
WHEREVER!
BUT SCOOBY--
IS BUYING US TIME!
NOW RUN!
TAKE HIM, BOYS! I'LL GET THE DOC!
BUT DON'T YOU DARE KILL HIM--

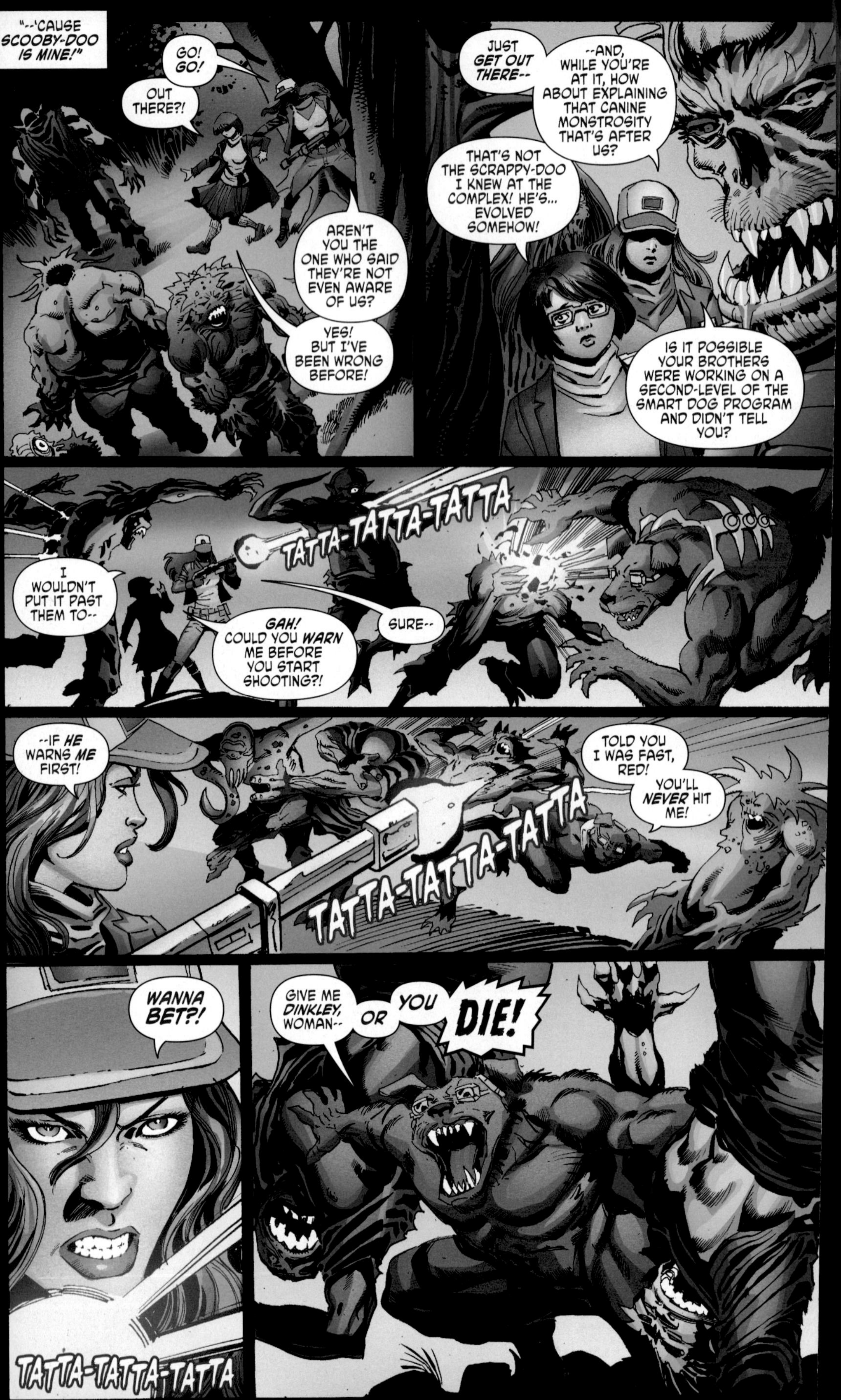
"--'CAUSE SCOOBY-DOO IS MINE!"
GO! GO!
OUT THERE?!
AREN'T YOU THE ONE WHO SAID THEY'RE NOT EVEN AWARE OF US?
YES! BUT I'VE BEEN WRONG BEFORE!
JUST GET OUT THERE--
--AND, WHILE YOU'RE AT IT, HOW ABOUT EXPLAINING THAT CANINE MONSTROSITY THAT'S AFTER US?
THAT'S NOT THE SCRAPPY-DOO I KNEW AT THE COMPLEX! HE'S... EVOLVED SOMEHOW!
IS IT POSSIBLE YOUR BROTHERS WERE WORKING ON A SECOND-LEVEL OF THE SMART DOG PROGRAM AND DIDN'T TELL YOU?
TATTA-TATTA-TATTA
I WOULDN'T PUT IT PAST THEM TO--
GAH! COULD YOU WARN ME BEFORE YOU START SHOOTING?!
SURE--
--IF HE WARNS ME FIRST!
TOLD YOU I WAS FAST, RED!
YOU'LL NEVER HIT ME!
TATTA-TATTA-TATTA
WANNA BET?!
GIVE ME DINKLEY, WOMAN--
OR
YOU
DIE!
TATTA-TATTA-TATTA

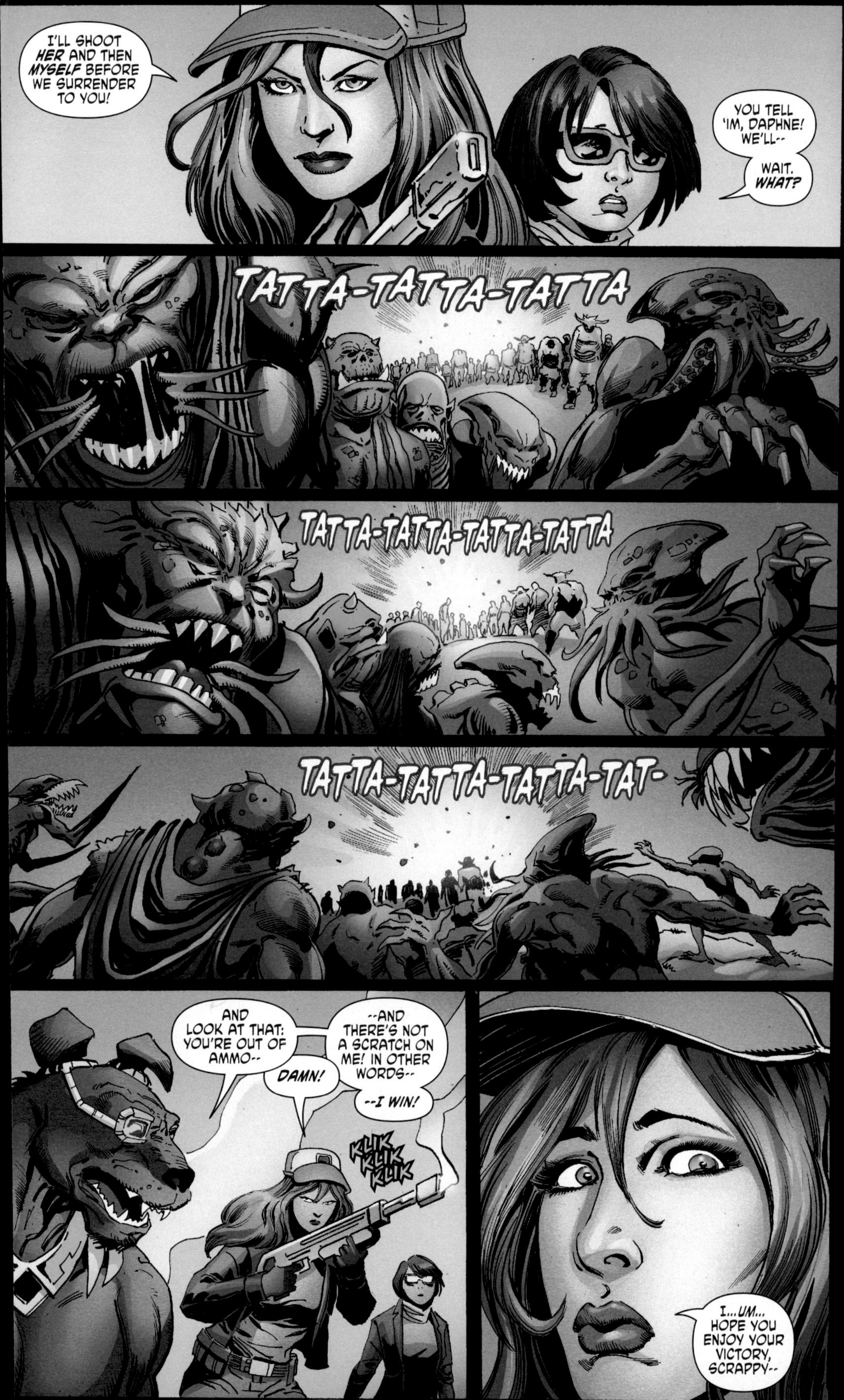
I'LL SHOOT HER AND THEN MYSELF BEFORE WE SURRENDER TO YOU!
YOU TELL 'IM, DAPHNE! WE'LL--
WAIT. WHAT?
TATTA-TATTA-TATTA-TATTA
TATTA-TATTA-TATTA-TATTA
TATTA-TATTA-TATTA-TAT-
AND LOOK AT THAT: YOU'RE OUT OF AMMO--
DAMN!
--AND THERE'S NOT A SCRATCH ON ME! IN OTHER WORDS--
--I WIN!
KLIK KLIK KLIK
I...UM... HOPE YOU ENJOY YOUR VICTORY, SCRAPPY--

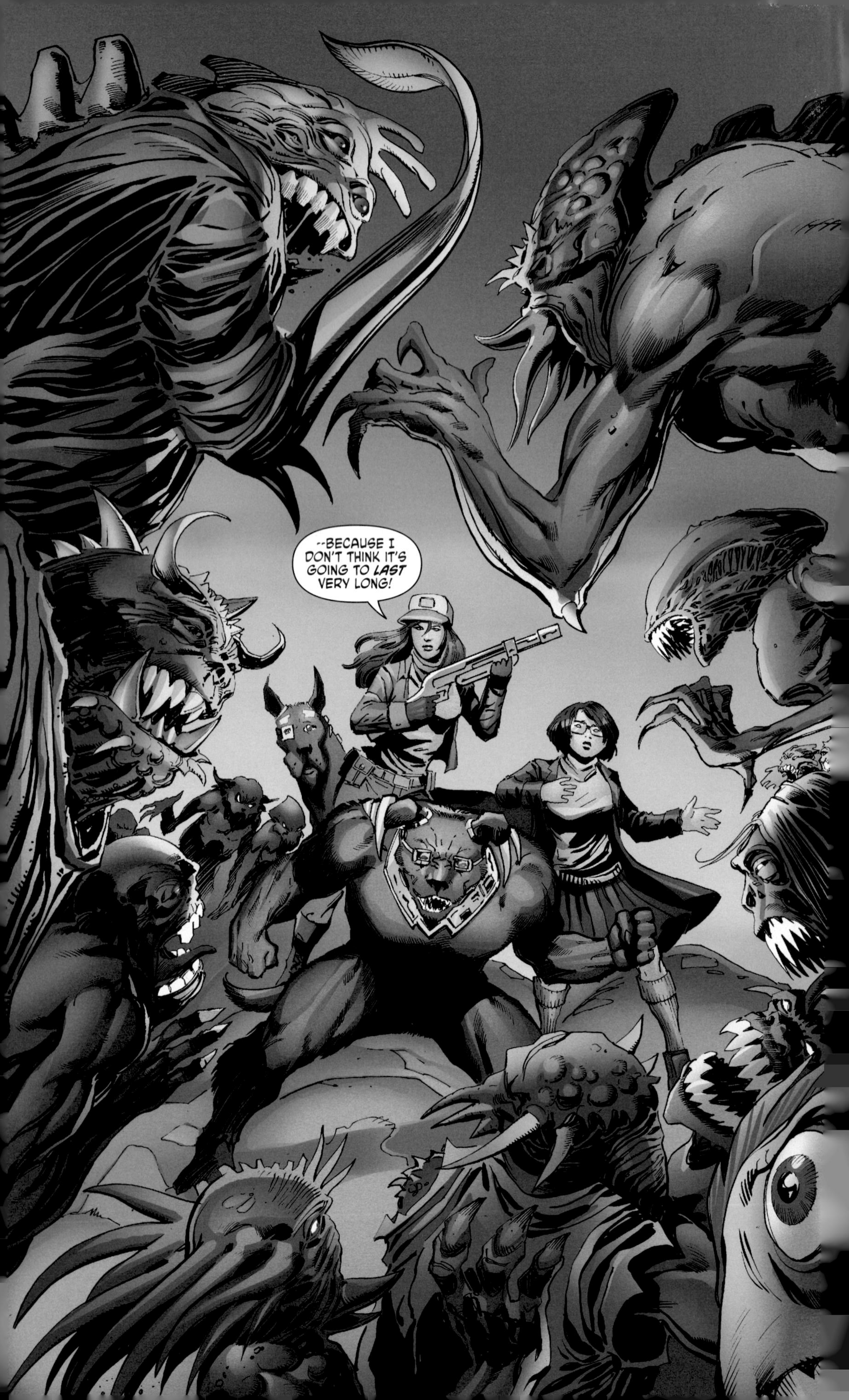
--BECAUSE I DON'T THINK IT'S GOING TO LAST VERY LONG!

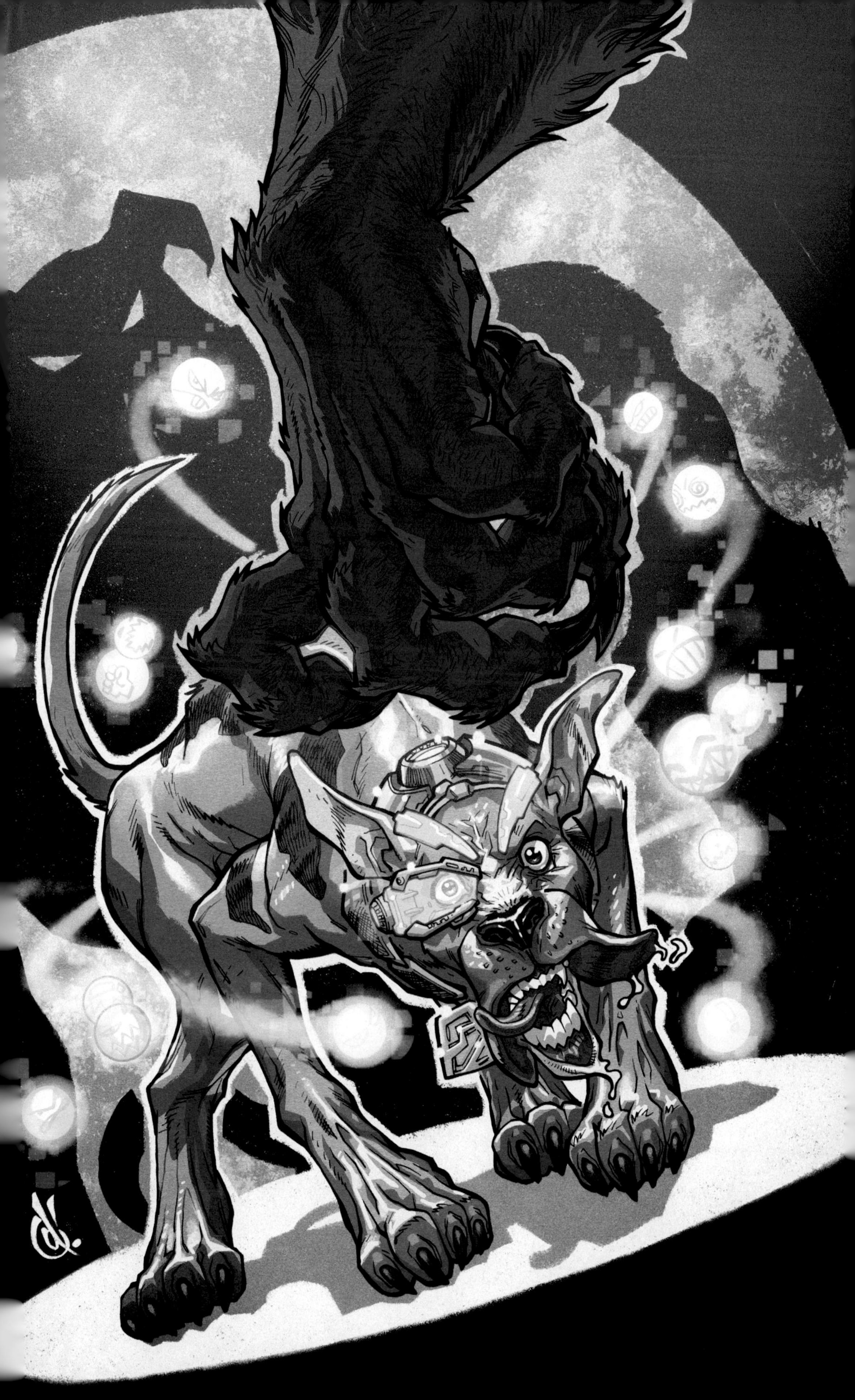

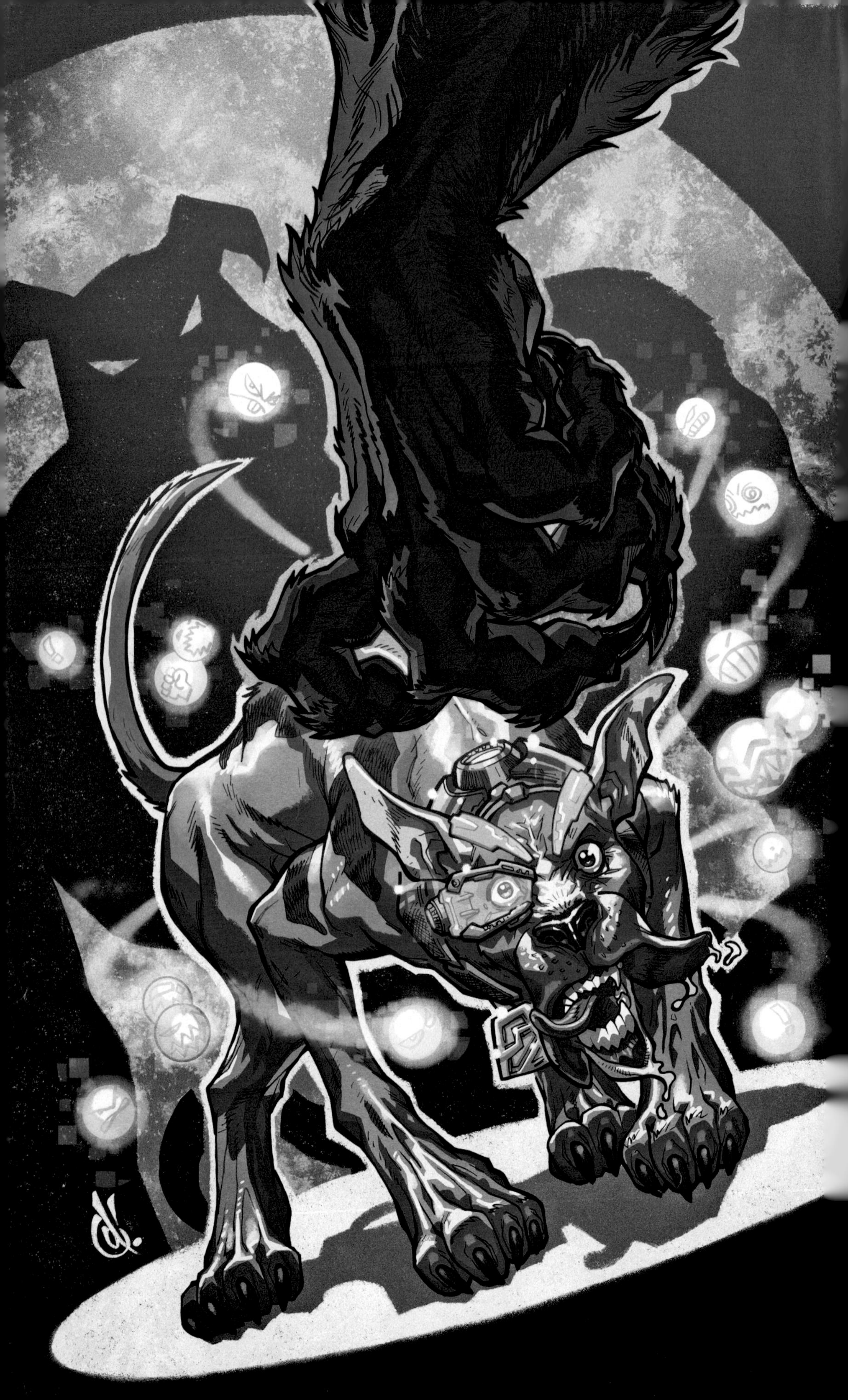

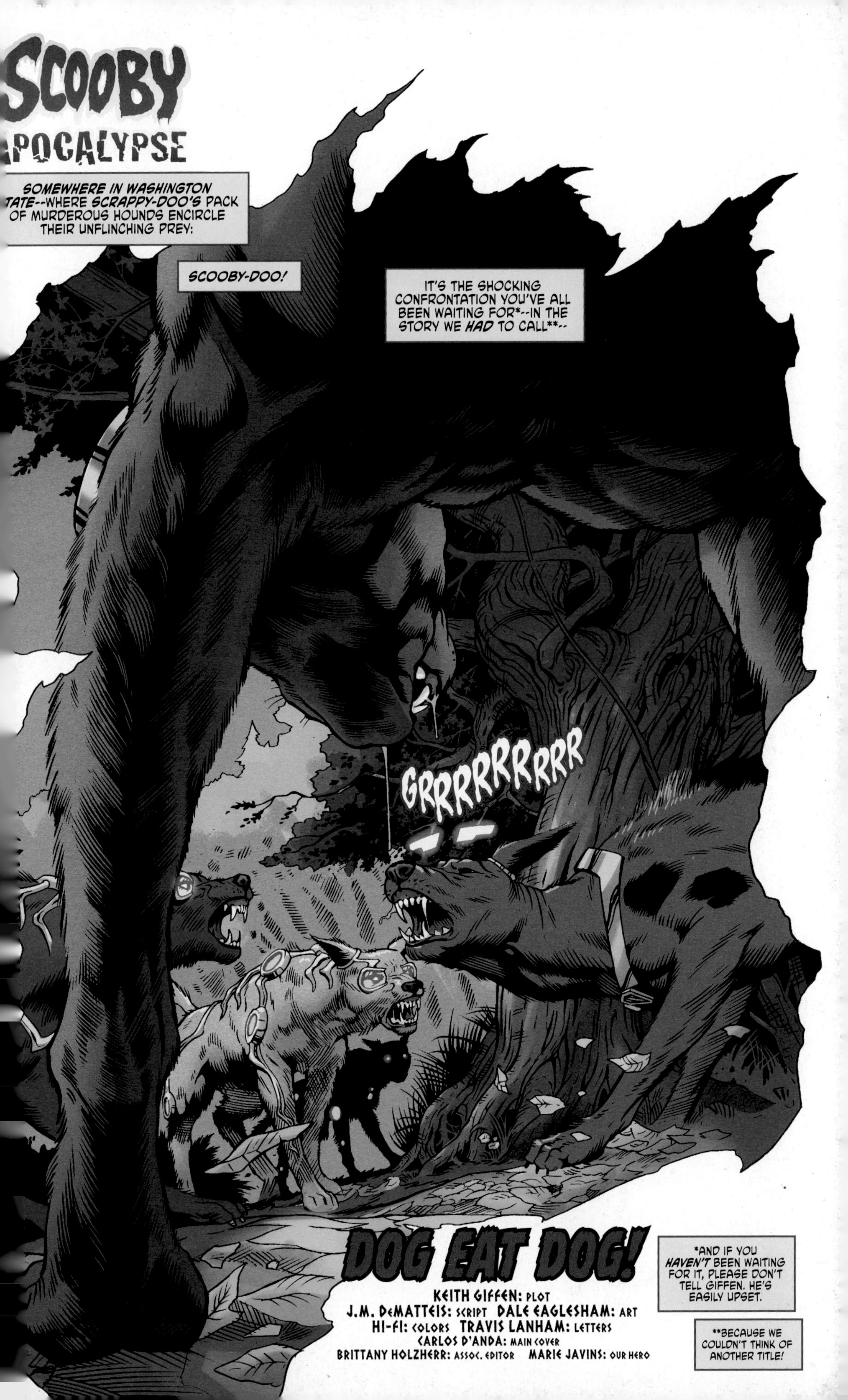
SCOOBY
POCALYPSE
SOMEWHERE IN WASHINGTON TATE--WHERE SCRAPPY-DOO'S PACK OF MURDEROUS HOUNDS ENCIRCLE THEIR UNFLINCHING PREY:
SCOOBY-DOO!
IT'S THE SHOCKING CONFRONTATION YOU'VE ALL BEEN WAITING FOR*--IN THE STORY WE HAD TO CALL**--
GRRRRRRRRR
DOG EAT DOG!
KEITH GIFFEN: PLOT
J.M. DeMATTEIS: SCRIPT DALE EAGLESHAM: ART
HI-FI: COLORS TRAVIS LANHAM: LETTERS
CARLOS D'ANDA: MAIN COVER
BRITTANY HOLZHERR: ASSOC. EDITOR MARIE JAVINS: OUR HERO
*AND IF YOU HAVEN'T BEEN WAITING FOR IT, PLEASE DON'T TELL GIFFEN. HE'S EASILY UPSET.
**BECAUSE WE COULDN'T THINK OF ANOTHER TITLE!

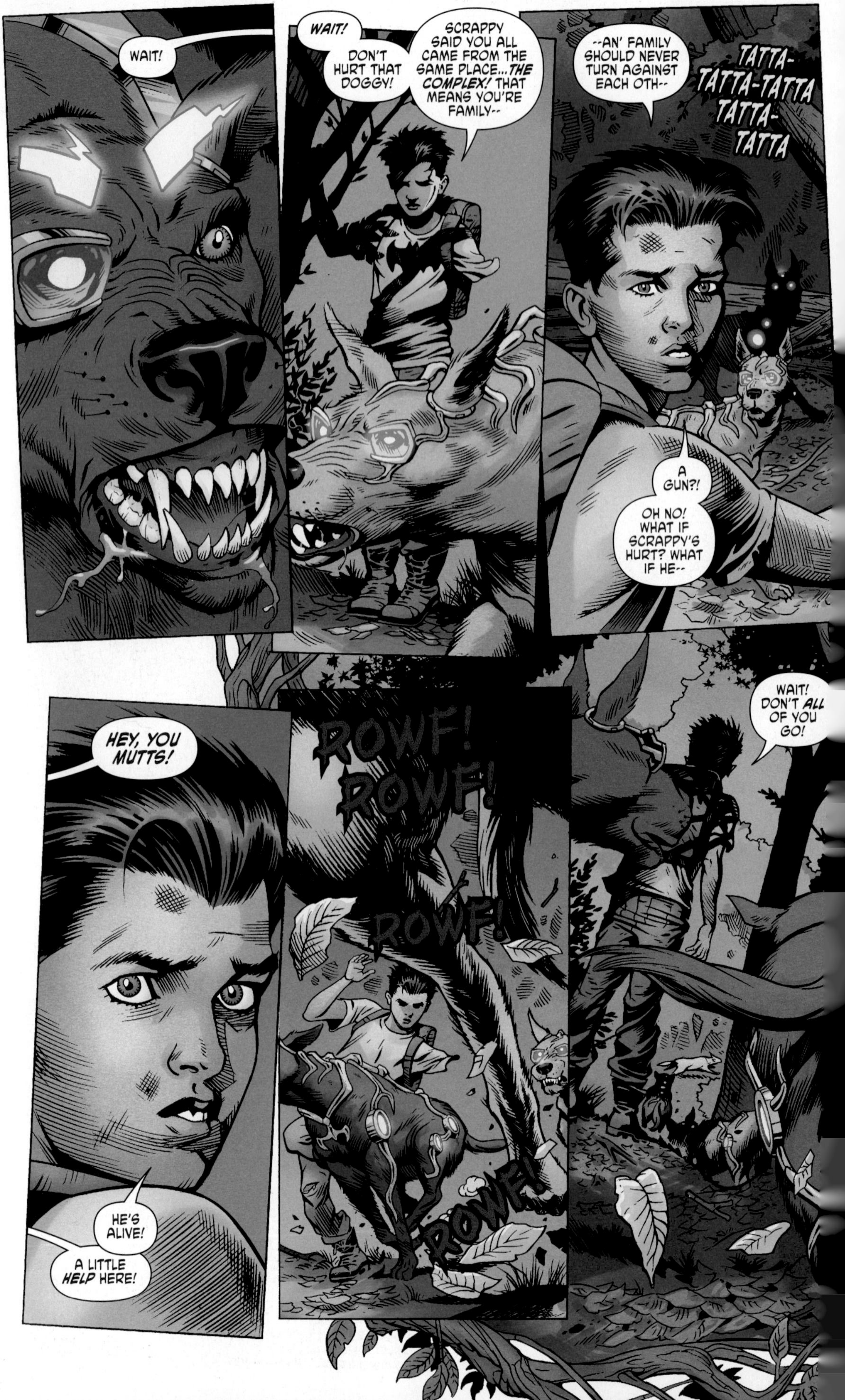
WAIT!
WAIT! DON'T HURT THAT DOGGY!
SCRAPPY SAID YOU ALL CAME FROM THE SAME PLACE...THE COMPLEX! THAT MEANS YOU'RE FAMILY--
--AN' FAMILY SHOULD NEVER TURN AGAINST EACH OTH--
TATTA-TATTA-TATTA TATTA-TATTA
A GUN?!
OH NO! WHAT IF SCRAPPY'S HURT? WHAT IF HE--
HEY, YOU MUTTS!
HE'S ALIVE!
A LITTLE HELP HERE!
ROWF! ROWF!
ROWF!
ROWF!
WAIT! DON'T ALL OF YOU GO!

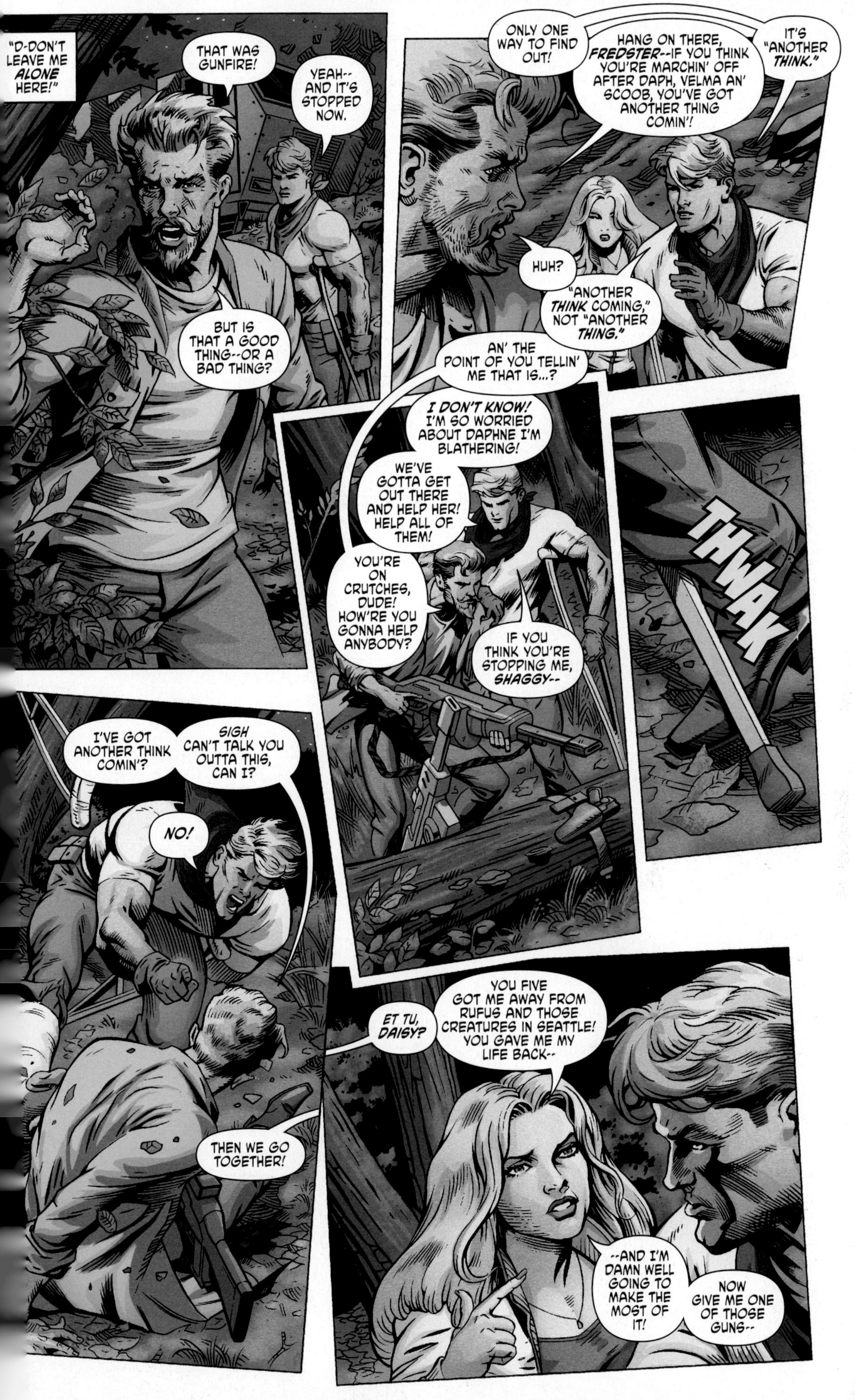
"D-DON'T LEAVE ME ALONE HERE!"
THAT WAS GUNFIRE!
YEAH--AND IT'S STOPPED NOW.
BUT IS THAT A GOOD THING--OR A BAD THING?
ONLY ONE WAY TO FIND OUT!
HANG ON THERE, FREDSTER--IF YOU THINK YOU'RE MARCHIN' OFF AFTER DAPH, VELMA AN' SCOOB, YOU'VE GOT ANOTHER THING COMIN'!
IT'S "ANOTHER THINK."
HUH?
"ANOTHER THINK COMING," NOT "ANOTHER THING."
AN' THE POINT OF YOU TELLIN' ME THAT IS...?
I DON'T KNOW! I'M SO WORRIED ABOUT DAPHNE I'M BLATHERING!
WE'VE GOTTA GET OUT THERE AND HELP HER! HELP ALL OF THEM!
YOU'RE ON CRUTCHES, DUDE! HOW'RE YOU GONNA HELP ANYBODY?
IF YOU THINK YOU'RE STOPPING ME, SHAGGY--
THWAK
I'VE GOT ANOTHER THINK COMIN'?
SIGH CAN'T TALK YOU OUTTA THIS, CAN I?
NO!
THEN WE GO TOGETHER!
ET TU, DAISY?
YOU FIVE GOT ME AWAY FROM RUFUS AND THOSE CREATURES IN SEATTLE! YOU GAVE ME MY LIFE BACK--
--AND I'M DAMN WELL GOING TO MAKE THE MOST OF IT!
NOW GIVE ME ONE OF THOSE GUNS--

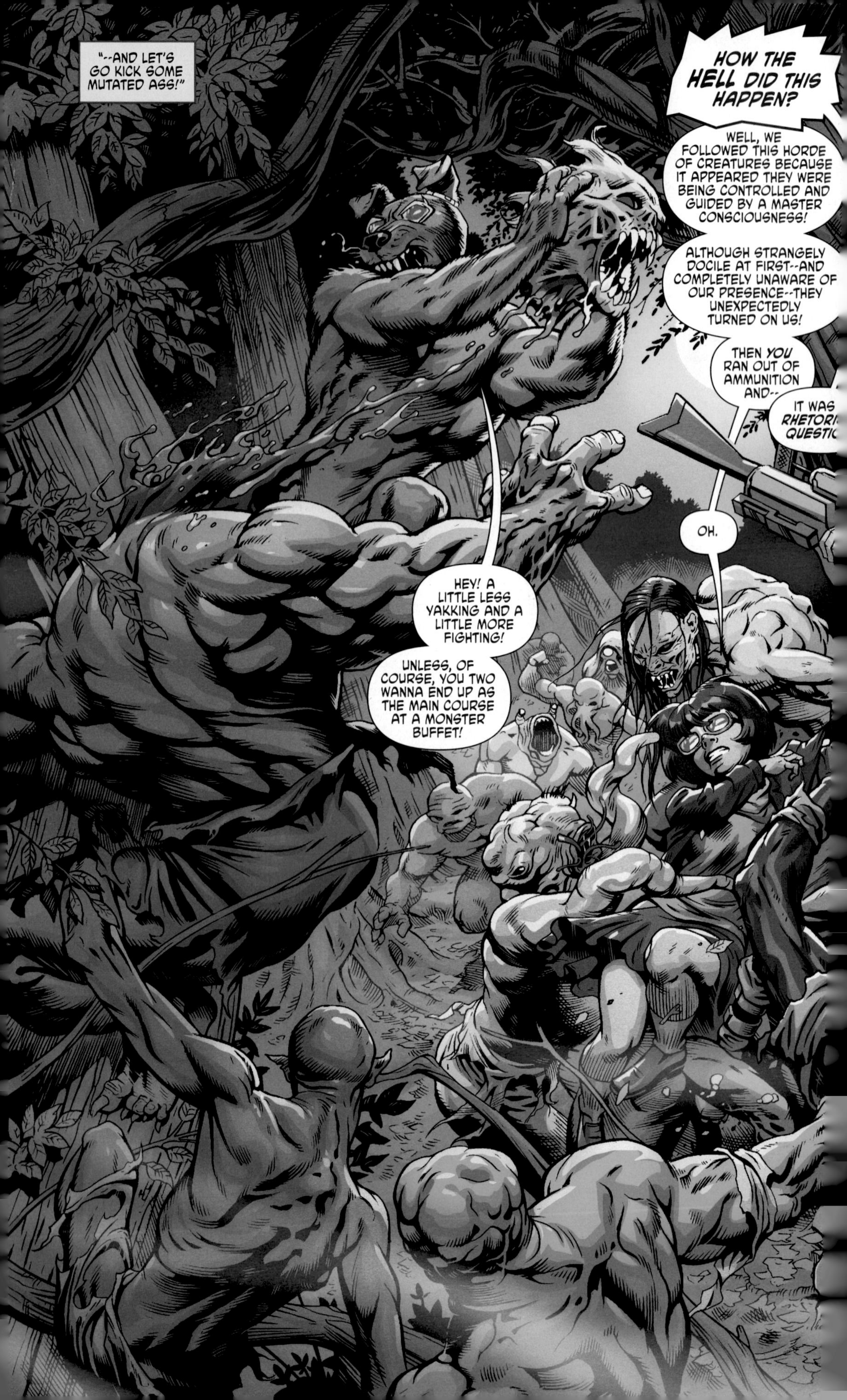
"--AND LET'S GO KICK SOME MUTATED ASS!"
HOW THE HELL DID THIS HAPPEN?
WELL, WE FOLLOWED THIS HORDE OF CREATURES BECAUSE IT APPEARED THEY WERE BEING CONTROLLED AND GUIDED BY A MASTER CONSCIOUSNESS!
ALTHOUGH STRANGELY DOCILE AT FIRST--AND COMPLETELY UNAWARE OF OUR PRESENCE--THEY UNEXPECTEDLY TURNED ON US!
THEN YOU RAN OUT OF AMMUNITION AND--
IT WAS RHETORI QUESTIC
OH.
HEY! A LITTLE LESS YAKKING AND A LITTLE MORE FIGHTING!
UNLESS, OF COURSE, YOU TWO WANNA END UP AS THE MAIN COURSE AT A MONSTER BUFFET!

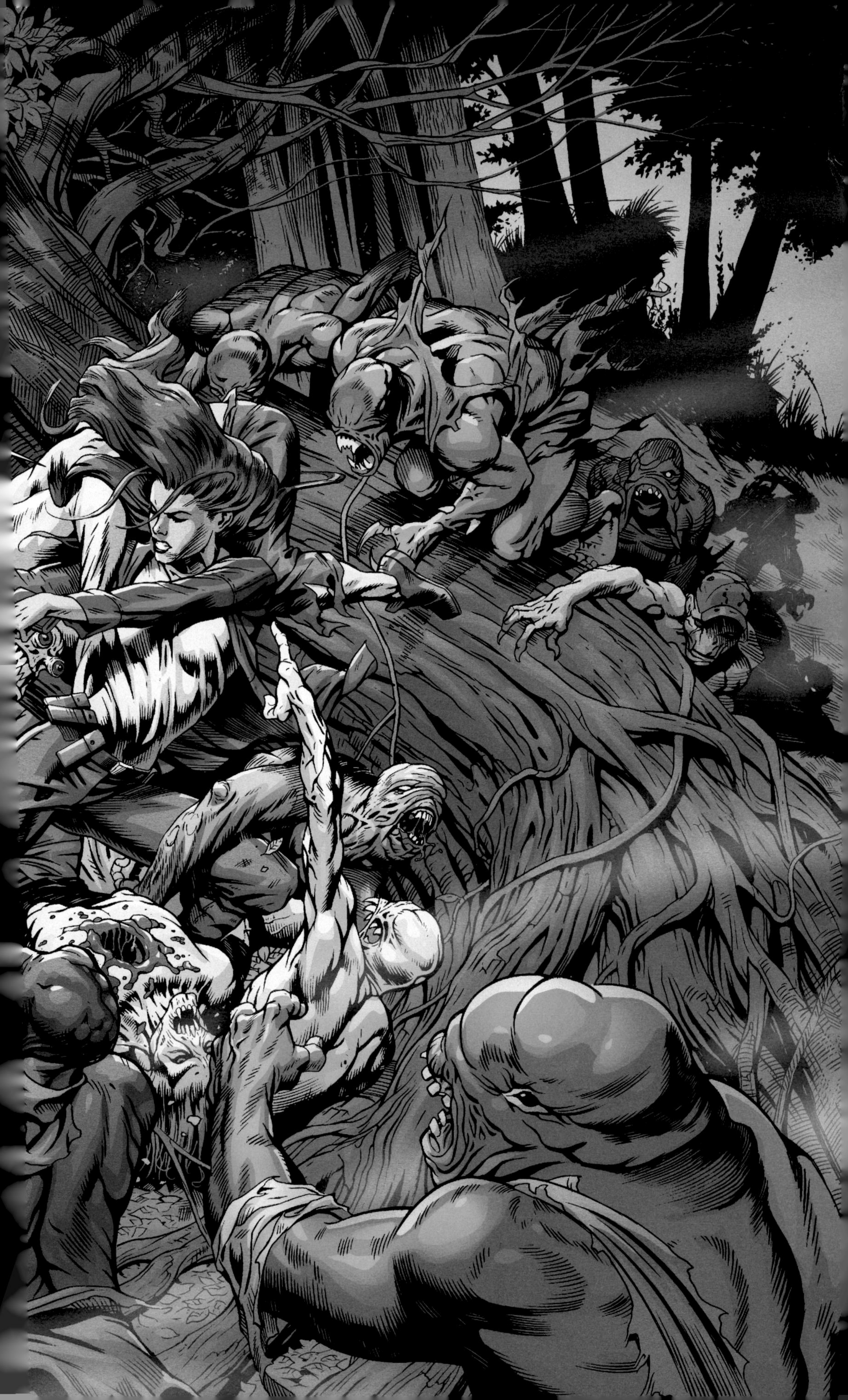

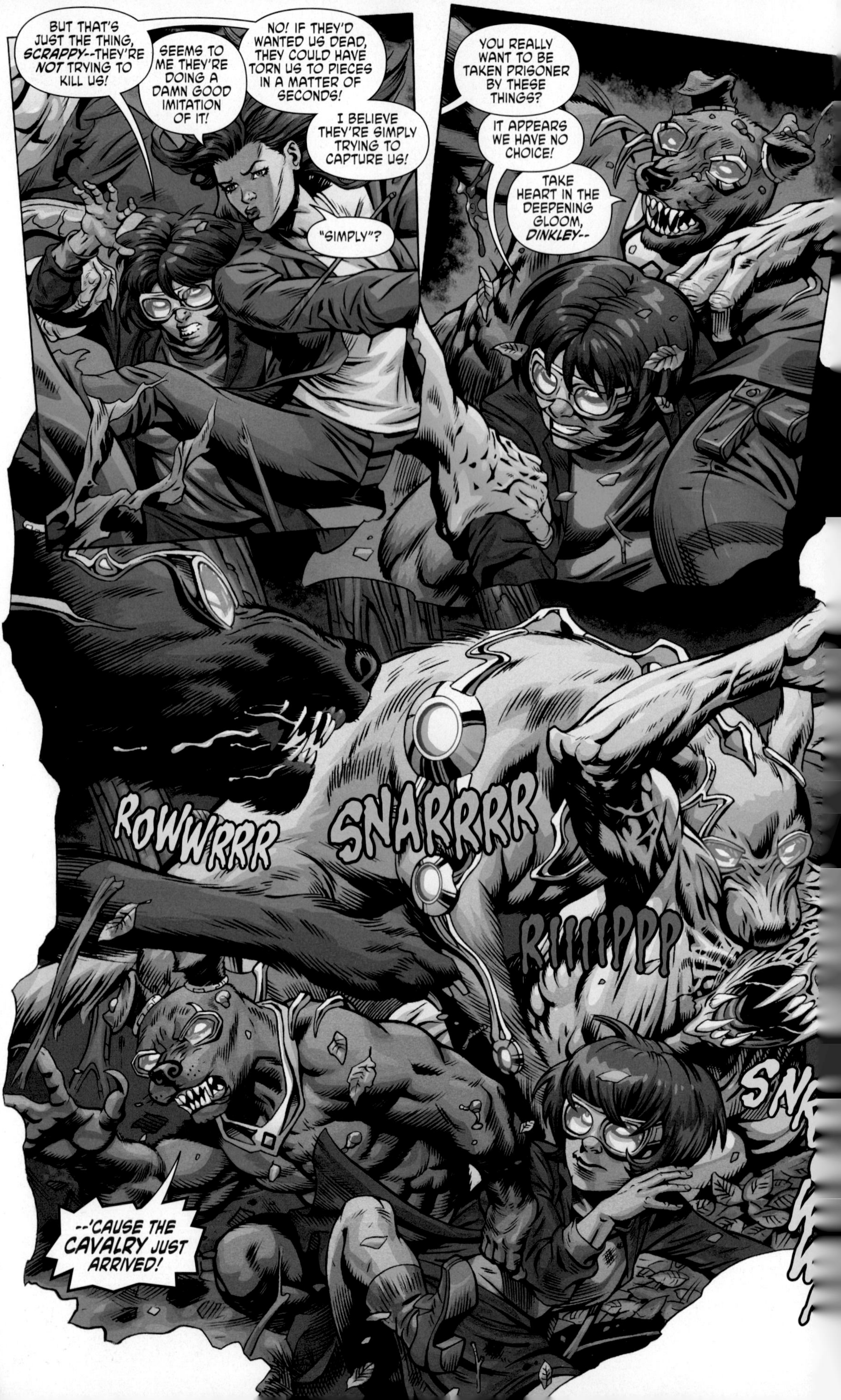
BUT THAT'S JUST THE THING, SCRAPPY--THEY'RE NOT TRYING TO KILL US!
SEEMS TO ME THEY'RE DOING A DAMN GOOD IMITATION OF IT!
NO! IF THEY'D WANTED US DEAD, THEY COULD HAVE TORN US TO PIECES IN A MATTER OF SECONDS!
I BELIEVE THEY'RE SIMPLY TRYING TO CAPTURE US!
"SIMPLY"?
YOU REALLY WANT TO BE TAKEN PRISONER BY THESE THINGS?
IT APPEARS WE HAVE NO CHOICE!
TAKE HEART IN THE DEEPENING GLOOM, DINKLEY--
ROWWRRR
SNARRRR
RIIIPPP
--'CAUSE THE CAVALRY JUST ARRIVED!

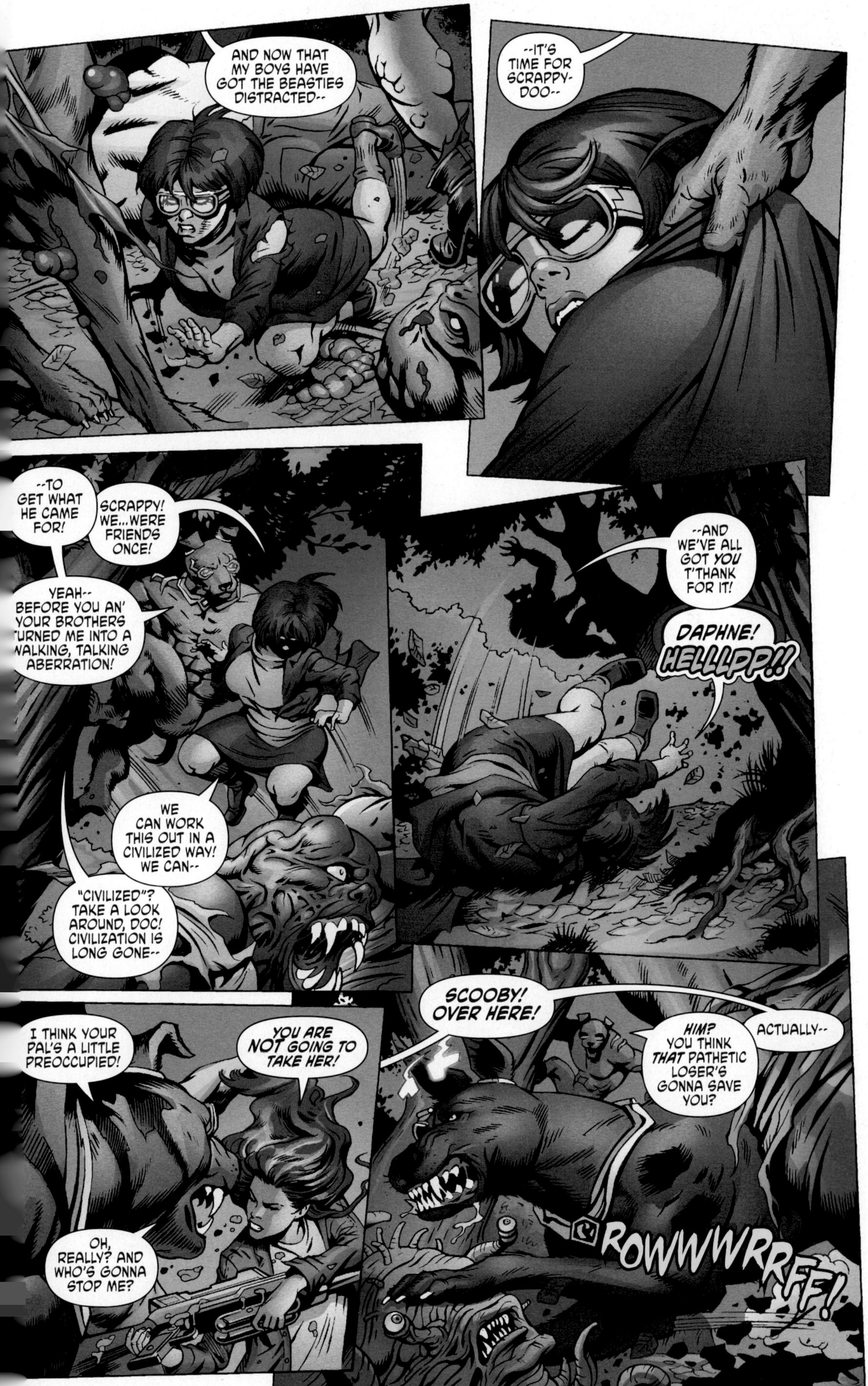
AND NOW THAT MY BOYS HAVE GOT THE BEASTIES DISTRACTED--
--IT'S TIME FOR SCRAPPY-DOO--
--TO GET WHAT HE CAME FOR!
SCRAPPY! WE...WERE FRIENDS ONCE!
YEAH-- BEFORE YOU AN' YOUR BROTHERS TURNED ME INTO A WALKING, TALKING ABERRATION!
WE CAN WORK THIS OUT IN A CIVILIZED WAY! WE CAN--
"CIVILIZED"? TAKE A LOOK AROUND, DOC! CIVILIZATION IS LONG GONE--
--AND WE'VE ALL GOT YOU T'THANK FOR IT!
DAPHNE! HELLLPP!!
I THINK YOUR PAL'S A LITTLE PREOCCUPIED!
YOU ARE NOT GOING TO TAKE HER!
OH, REALLY? AND WHO'S GONNA STOP ME?
SCOOBY! OVER HERE!
HIM? YOU THINK THAT PATHETIC LOSER'S GONNA SAVE YOU?
ACTUALLY--
ROWWWRRFF!

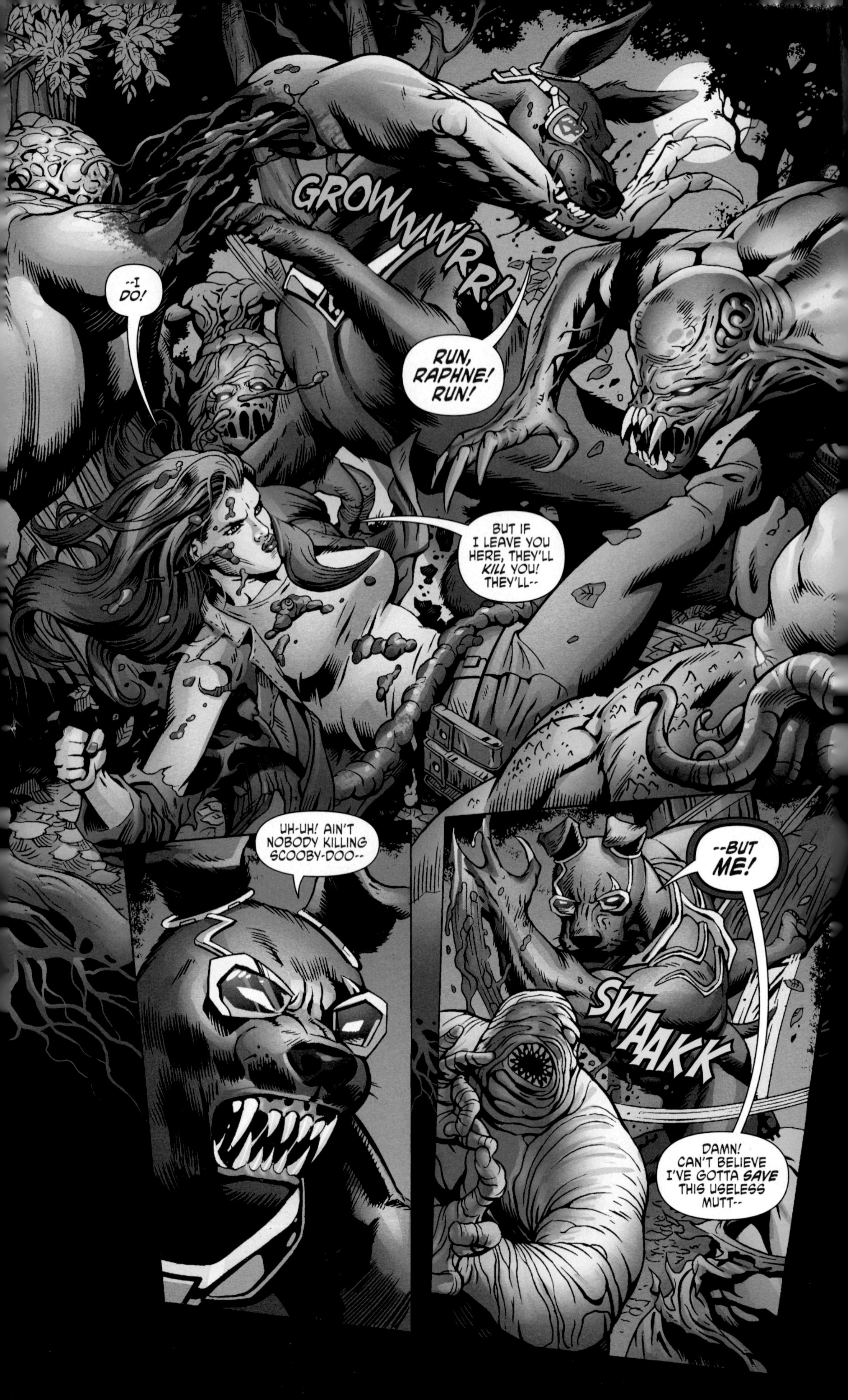
GROWWWRR!
RUN, RAPHNE! RUN!
--I DO!
BUT IF I LEAVE YOU HERE, THEY'LL KILL YOU! THEY'LL--
UH-UH! AIN'T NOBODY KILLING SCOOBY-DOO--
--BUT ME!
SWAAKK
DAMN! CAN'T BELIEVE I'VE GOTTA SAVE THIS USELESS MUTT--

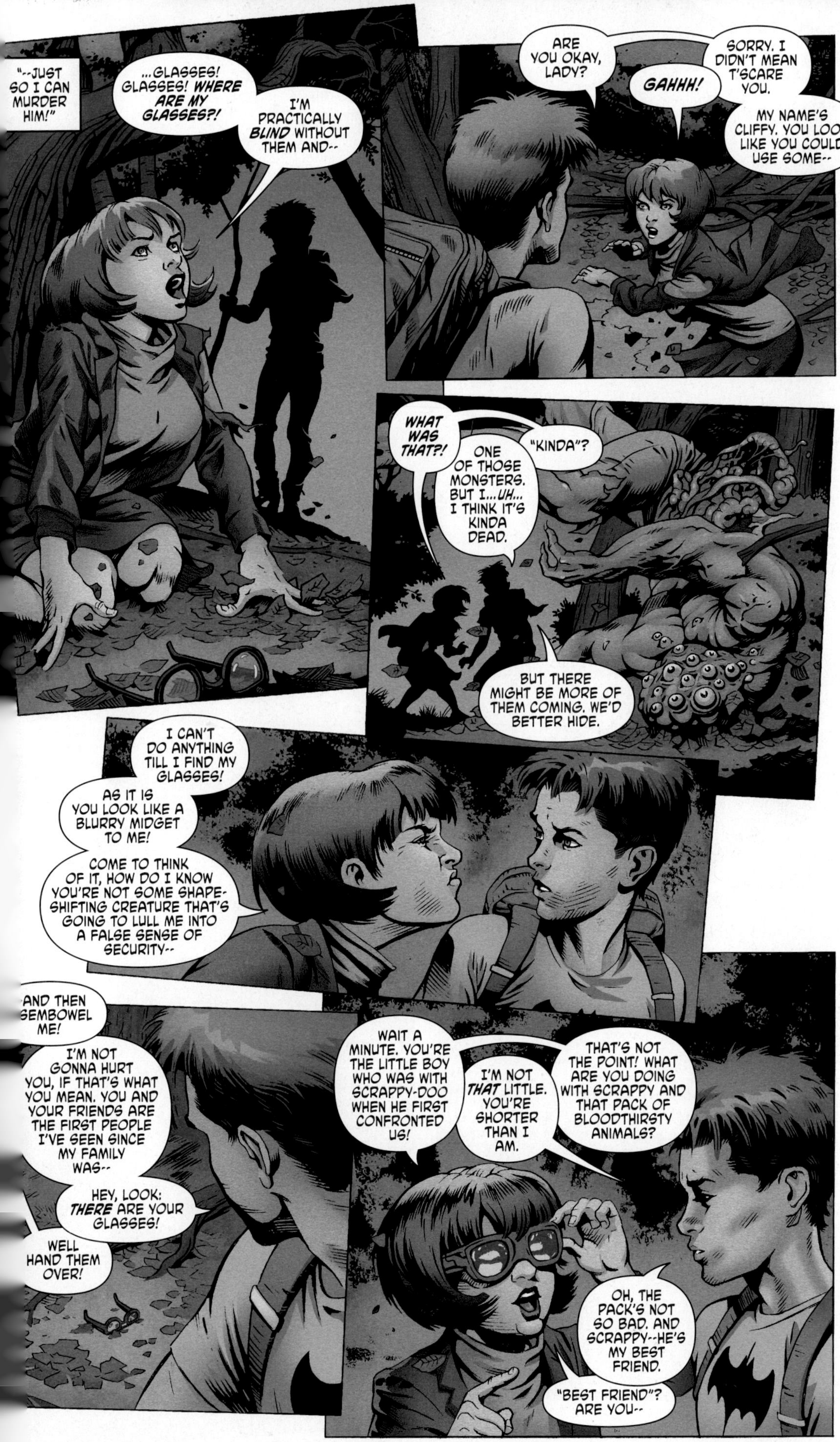
"--JUST SO I CAN MURDER HIM!"
...GLASSES! GLASSES! WHERE ARE MY GLASSES?!
I'M PRACTICALLY BLIND WITHOUT THEM AND--
ARE YOU OKAY, LADY?
GAHHH!
SORRY. I DIDN'T MEAN T'SCARE YOU.
MY NAME'S CLIFFY. YOU LOOK LIKE YOU COULD USE SOME--
WHAT WAS THAT?!
ONE OF THOSE MONSTERS. BUT I...UH... I THINK IT'S KINDA DEAD.
"KINDA"?
BUT THERE MIGHT BE MORE OF THEM COMING. WE'D BETTER HIDE.
I CAN'T DO ANYTHING TILL I FIND MY GLASSES!
AS IT IS YOU LOOK LIKE A BLURRY MIDGET TO ME!
COME TO THINK OF IT, HOW DO I KNOW YOU'RE NOT SOME SHAPE-SHIFTING CREATURE THAT'S GOING TO LULL ME INTO A FALSE SENSE OF SECURITY--
AND THEN EMBOWEL ME!
I'M NOT GONNA HURT YOU, IF THAT'S WHAT YOU MEAN. YOU AND YOUR FRIENDS ARE THE FIRST PEOPLE I'VE SEEN SINCE MY FAMILY WAS--
HEY, LOOK: THERE ARE YOUR GLASSES!
WELL HAND THEM OVER!
WAIT A MINUTE. YOU'RE THE LITTLE BOY WHO WAS WITH SCRAPPY-DOO WHEN HE FIRST CONFRONTED US!
I'M NOT THAT LITTLE. YOU'RE SHORTER THAN I AM.
THAT'S NOT THE POINT! WHAT ARE YOU DOING WITH SCRAPPY AND THAT PACK OF BLOODTHIRSTY ANIMALS?
OH, THE PACK'S NOT SO BAD. AND SCRAPPY--HE'S MY BEST FRIEND.
"BEST FRIEND"? ARE YOU--

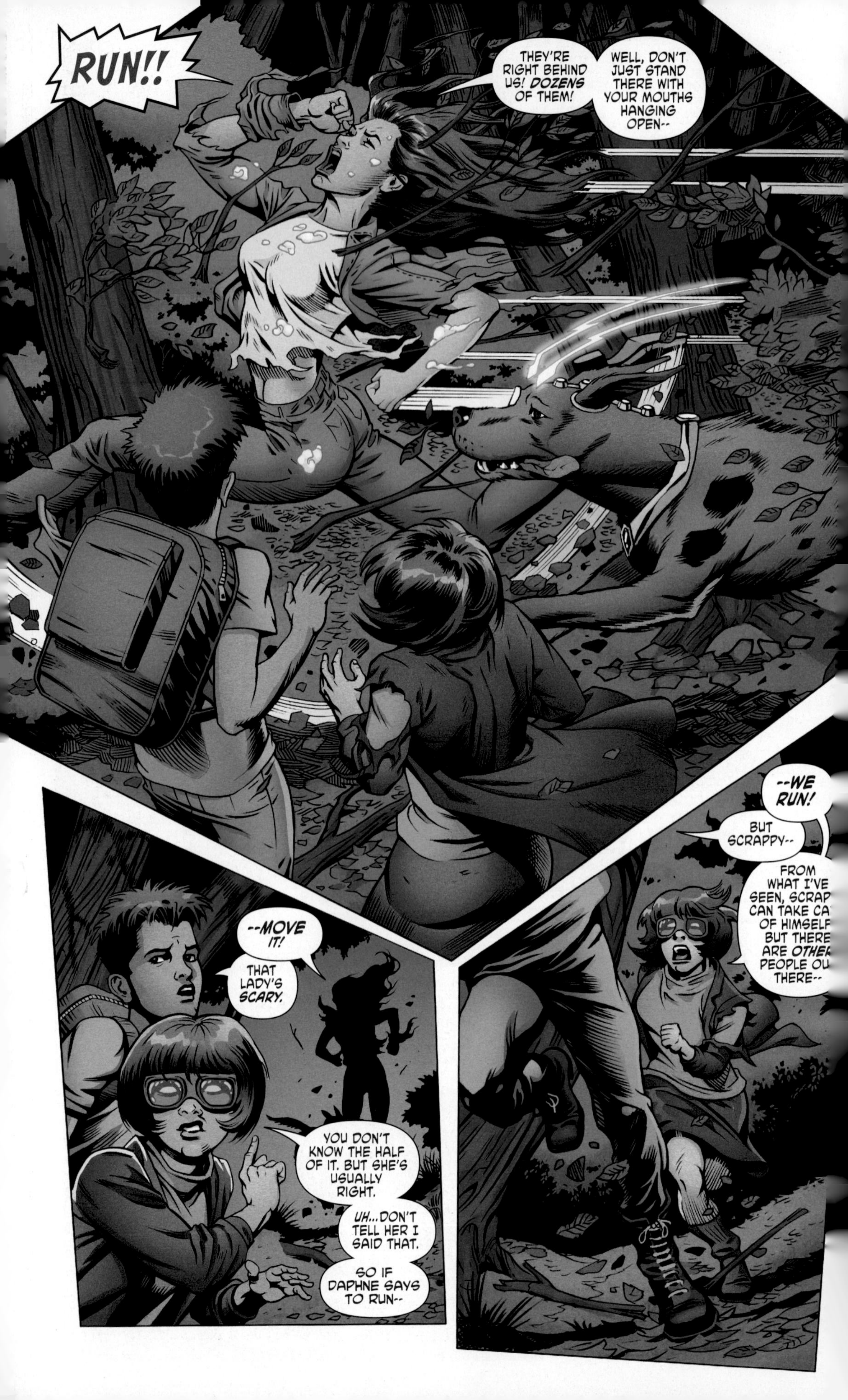
RUN!!
THEY'RE RIGHT BEHIND US! DOZENS OF THEM!
WELL, DON'T JUST STAND THERE WITH YOUR MOUTHS HANGING OPEN--
--MOVE IT!
THAT LADY'S SCARY.
YOU DON'T KNOW THE HALF OF IT. BUT SHE'S USUALLY RIGHT.
UH...DON'T TELL HER I SAID THAT.
SO IF DAPHNE SAYS TO RUN--
--WE RUN!
BUT SCRAPPY--
FROM WHAT I'VE SEEN, SCRAP CAN TAKE CA OF HIMSELF BUT THERE ARE OTHER PEOPLE OU THERE--

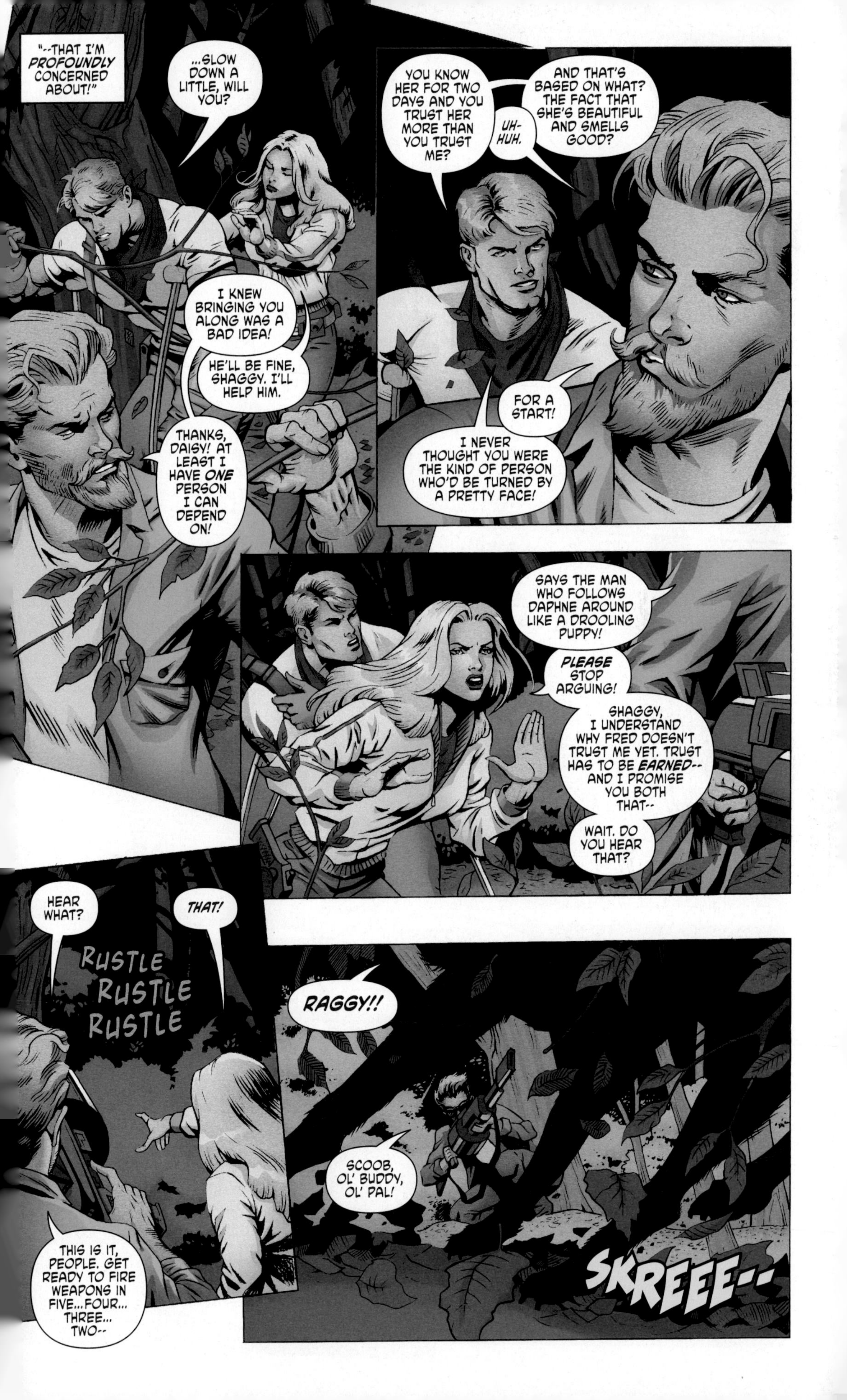
"--THAT I'M PROFOUNDLY CONCERNED ABOUT!"
...SLOW DOWN A LITTLE, WILL YOU?
I KNEW BRINGING YOU ALONG WAS A BAD IDEA!
HE'LL BE FINE, SHAGGY. I'LL HELP HIM.
THANKS, DAISY! AT LEAST I HAVE ONE PERSON I CAN DEPEND ON!
YOU KNOW HER FOR TWO DAYS AND YOU TRUST HER MORE THAN YOU TRUST ME?
UH-HUH.
AND THAT'S BASED ON WHAT? THE FACT THAT SHE'S BEAUTIFUL AND SMELLS GOOD?
FOR A START!
I NEVER THOUGHT YOU WERE THE KIND OF PERSON WHO'D BE TURNED BY A PRETTY FACE!
SAYS THE MAN WHO FOLLOWS DAPHNE AROUND LIKE A DROOLING PUPPY!
PLEASE STOP ARGUING!
SHAGGY, I UNDERSTAND WHY FRED DOESN'T TRUST ME YET. TRUST HAS TO BE EARNED-- AND I PROMISE YOU BOTH THAT--
WAIT. DO YOU HEAR THAT?
HEAR WHAT?
THAT!
RUSTLE RUSTLE RUSTLE
THIS IS IT, PEOPLE. GET READY TO FIRE WEAPONS IN FIVE...FOUR... THREE... TWO--
RAGGY!!
SCOOB, OL' BUDDY, OL' PAL!
SKREEE--

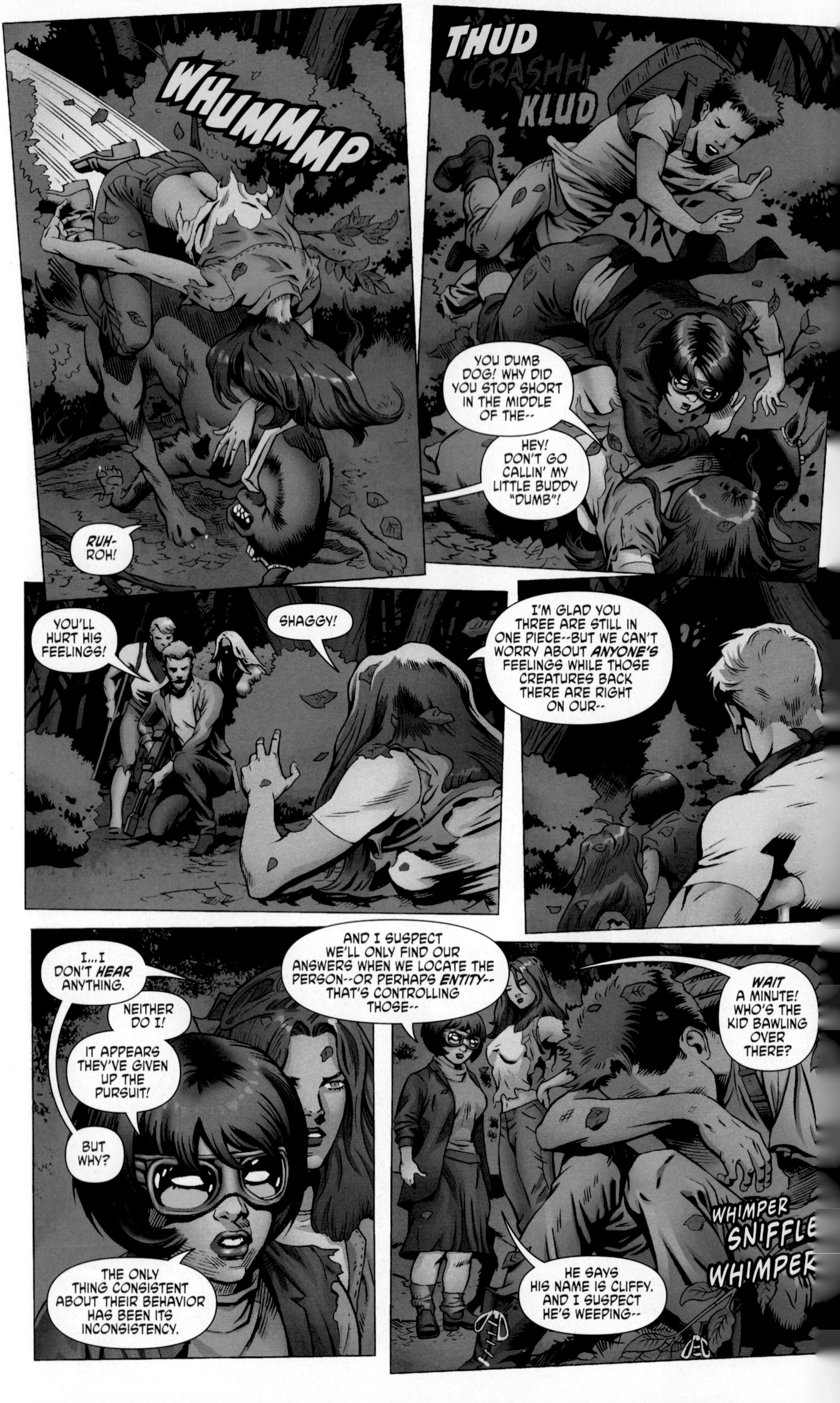
WHUMMMMP
RUH-ROH!
THUD
CRASHH
KLUD
YOU DUMB DOG! WHY DID YOU STOP SHORT IN THE MIDDLE OF THE--
HEY! DON'T GO CALLIN' MY LITTLE BUDDY "DUMB"!
YOU'LL HURT HIS FEELINGS!
SHAGGY!
I'M GLAD YOU THREE ARE STILL IN ONE PIECE--BUT WE CAN'T WORRY ABOUT ANYONE'S FEELINGS WHILE THOSE CREATURES BACK THERE ARE RIGHT ON OUR--
I...I DON'T HEAR ANYTHING.
NEITHER DO I!
IT APPEARS THEY'VE GIVEN UP THE PURSUIT!
BUT WHY?
THE ONLY THING CONSISTENT ABOUT THEIR BEHAVIOR HAS BEEN ITS INCONSISTENCY.
AND I SUSPECT WE'LL ONLY FIND OUR ANSWERS WHEN WE LOCATE THE PERSON--OR PERHAPS ENTITY--THAT'S CONTROLLING THOSE--
WAIT A MINUTE! WHO'S THE KID BAWLING OVER THERE?
WHIMPER
SNIFFLE
WHIMPER
HE SAYS HIS NAME IS CLIFFY. AND I SUSPECT HE'S WEEPING--

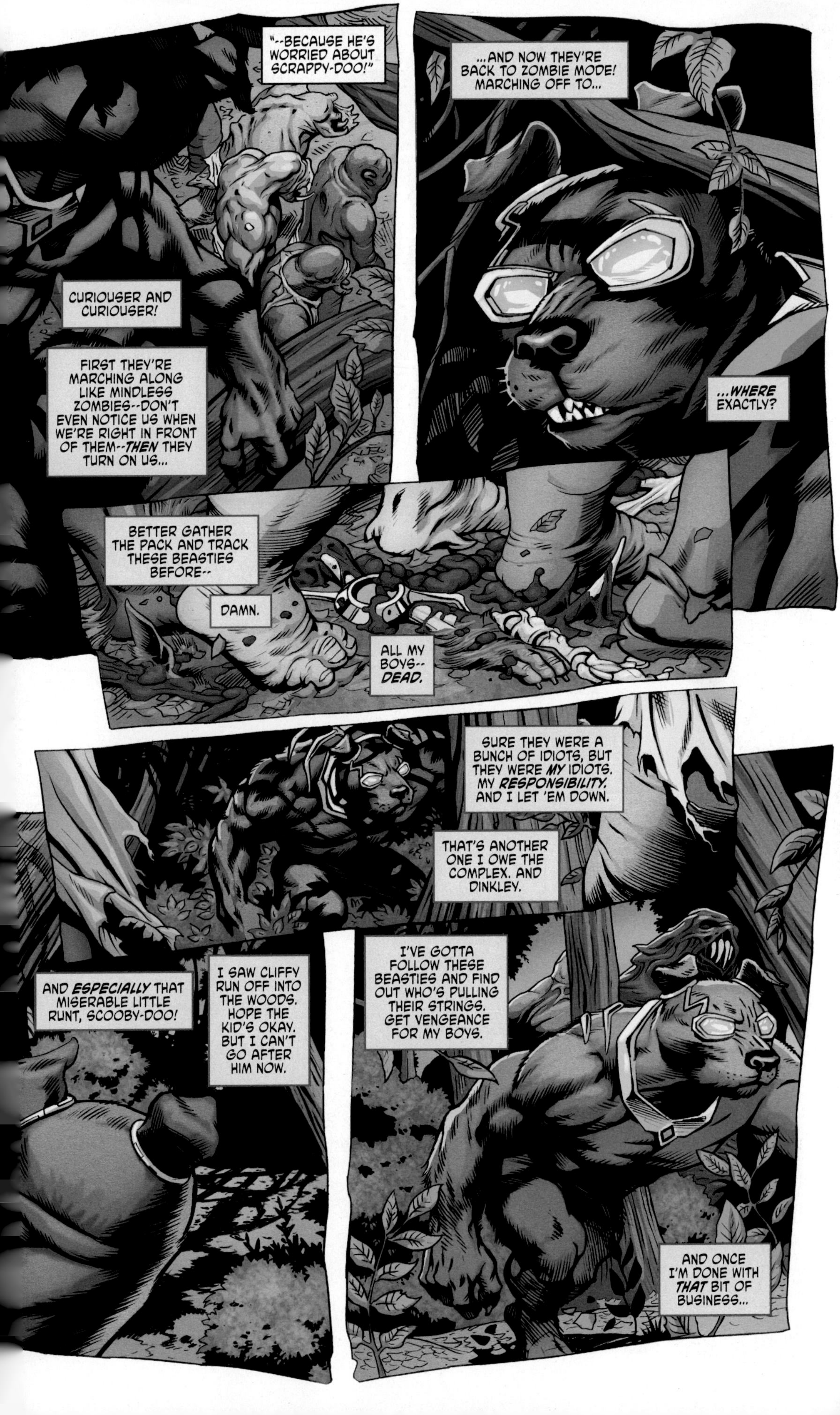
"--BECAUSE HE'S WORRIED ABOUT SCRAPPY-DOO!"
CURIOUSER AND CURIOUSER!
FIRST THEY'RE MARCHING ALONG LIKE MINDLESS ZOMBIES--DON'T EVEN NOTICE US WHEN WE'RE RIGHT IN FRONT OF THEM--*THEN* THEY TURN ON US...
...AND NOW THEY'RE BACK TO ZOMBIE MODE! MARCHING OFF TO...
...*WHERE* EXACTLY?
BETTER GATHER THE PACK AND TRACK THESE BEASTIES BEFORE--
DAMN.
ALL MY BOYS-- *DEAD.*
SURE THEY WERE A BUNCH OF IDIOTS, BUT THEY WERE *MY* IDIOTS. MY *RESPONSIBILITY.* AND I LET 'EM DOWN.
THAT'S ANOTHER ONE I OWE THE COMPLEX. AND DINKLEY.
AND *ESPECIALLY* THAT MISERABLE LITTLE RUNT, SCOOBY-DOO!
I SAW CLIFFY RUN OFF INTO THE WOODS. HOPE THE KID'S OKAY. BUT I CAN'T GO AFTER HIM NOW.
I'VE GOTTA FOLLOW THESE BEASTIES AND FIND OUT WHO'S PULLING THEIR STRINGS. GET VENGEANCE FOR MY BOYS.
AND ONCE I'M DONE WITH *THAT* BIT OF BUSINESS...

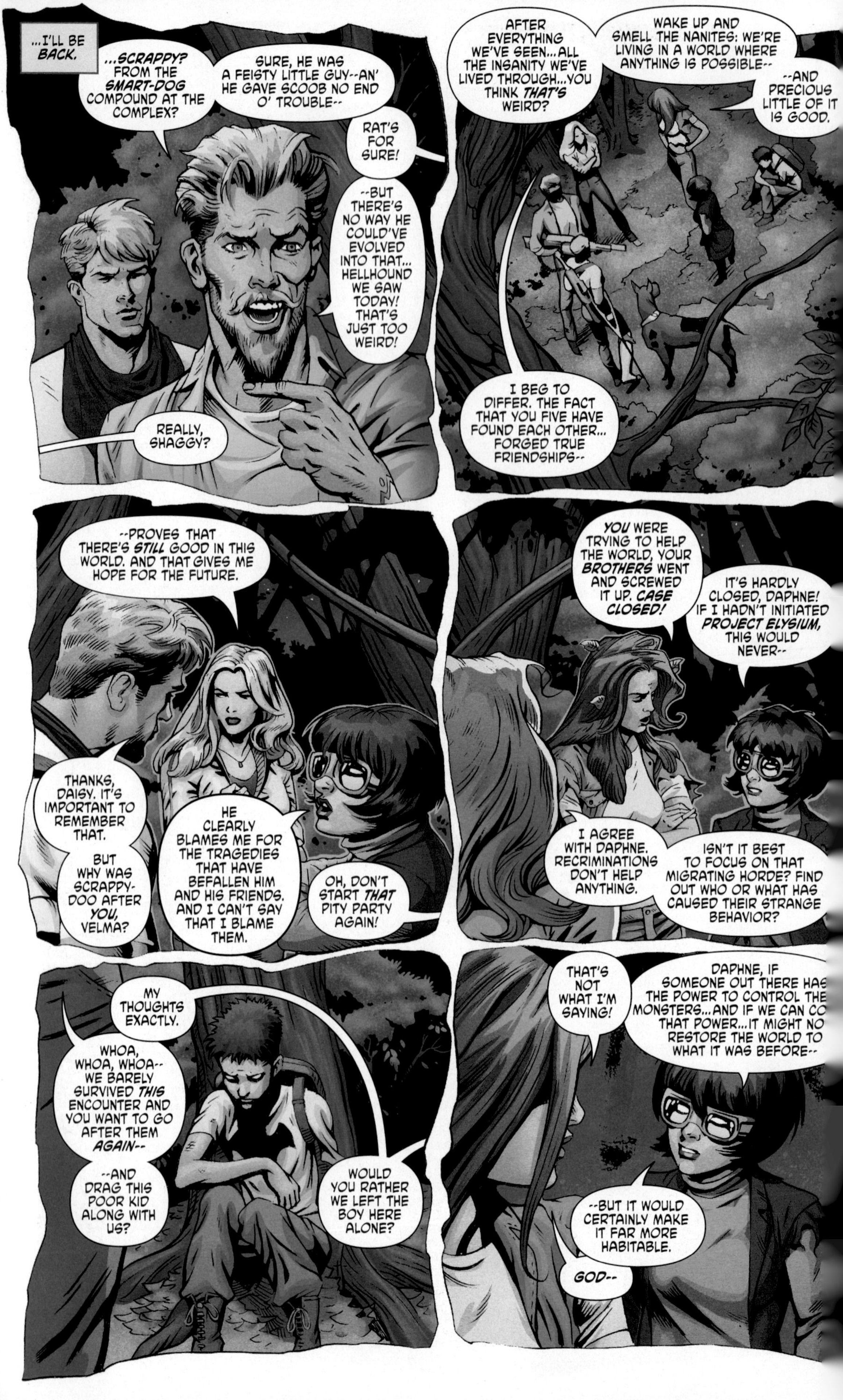

...I'LL BE BACK.
...SCRAPPY? FROM THE SMART-DOG COMPOUND AT THE COMPLEX?
SURE, HE WAS A FEISTY LITTLE GUY--AN' HE GAVE SCOOB NO END O' TROUBLE--
RAT'S FOR SURE!
--BUT THERE'S NO WAY HE COULD'VE EVOLVED INTO THAT... HELLHOUND WE SAW TODAY! THAT'S JUST TOO WEIRD!
REALLY, SHAGGY?
AFTER EVERYTHING WE'VE SEEN...ALL THE INSANITY WE'VE LIVED THROUGH...YOU THINK THAT'S WEIRD?
WAKE UP AND SMELL THE NANITES: WE'RE LIVING IN A WORLD WHERE ANYTHING IS POSSIBLE--
--AND PRECIOUS LITTLE OF IT IS GOOD.
I BEG TO DIFFER. THE FACT THAT YOU FIVE HAVE FOUND EACH OTHER... FORGED TRUE FRIENDSHIPS--
--PROVES THAT THERE'S STILL GOOD IN THIS WORLD. AND THAT GIVES ME HOPE FOR THE FUTURE.
THANKS, DAISY. IT'S IMPORTANT TO REMEMBER THAT.
BUT WHY WAS SCRAPPY-DOO AFTER YOU, VELMA?
HE CLEARLY BLAMES ME FOR THE TRAGEDIES THAT HAVE BEFALLEN HIM AND HIS FRIENDS. AND I CAN'T SAY THAT I BLAME THEM.
OH, DON'T START THAT PITY PARTY AGAIN!
YOU WERE TRYING TO HELP THE WORLD, YOUR BROTHERS WENT AND SCREWED IT UP. CASE CLOSED!
IT'S HARDLY CLOSED, DAPHNE! IF I HADN'T INITIATED PROJECT ELYSIUM, THIS WOULD NEVER--
I AGREE WITH DAPHNE. RECRIMINATIONS DON'T HELP ANYTHING.
ISN'T IT BEST TO FOCUS ON THAT MIGRATING HORDE? FIND OUT WHO OR WHAT HAS CAUSED THEIR STRANGE BEHAVIOR?
MY THOUGHTS EXACTLY.
WHOA, WHOA--WE BARELY SURVIVED THIS ENCOUNTER AND YOU WANT TO GO AFTER THEM AGAIN--
--AND DRAG THIS POOR KID ALONG WITH US?
WOULD YOU RATHER WE LEFT THE BOY HERE ALONE?
THAT'S NOT WHAT I'M SAYING!
DAPHNE, IF SOMEONE OUT THERE HAS THE POWER TO CONTROL THE MONSTERS...AND IF WE CAN CO THAT POWER...IT MIGHT NO RESTORE THE WORLD TO WHAT IT WAS BEFORE--
--BUT IT WOULD CERTAINLY MAKE IT FAR MORE HABITABLE.
GOD--

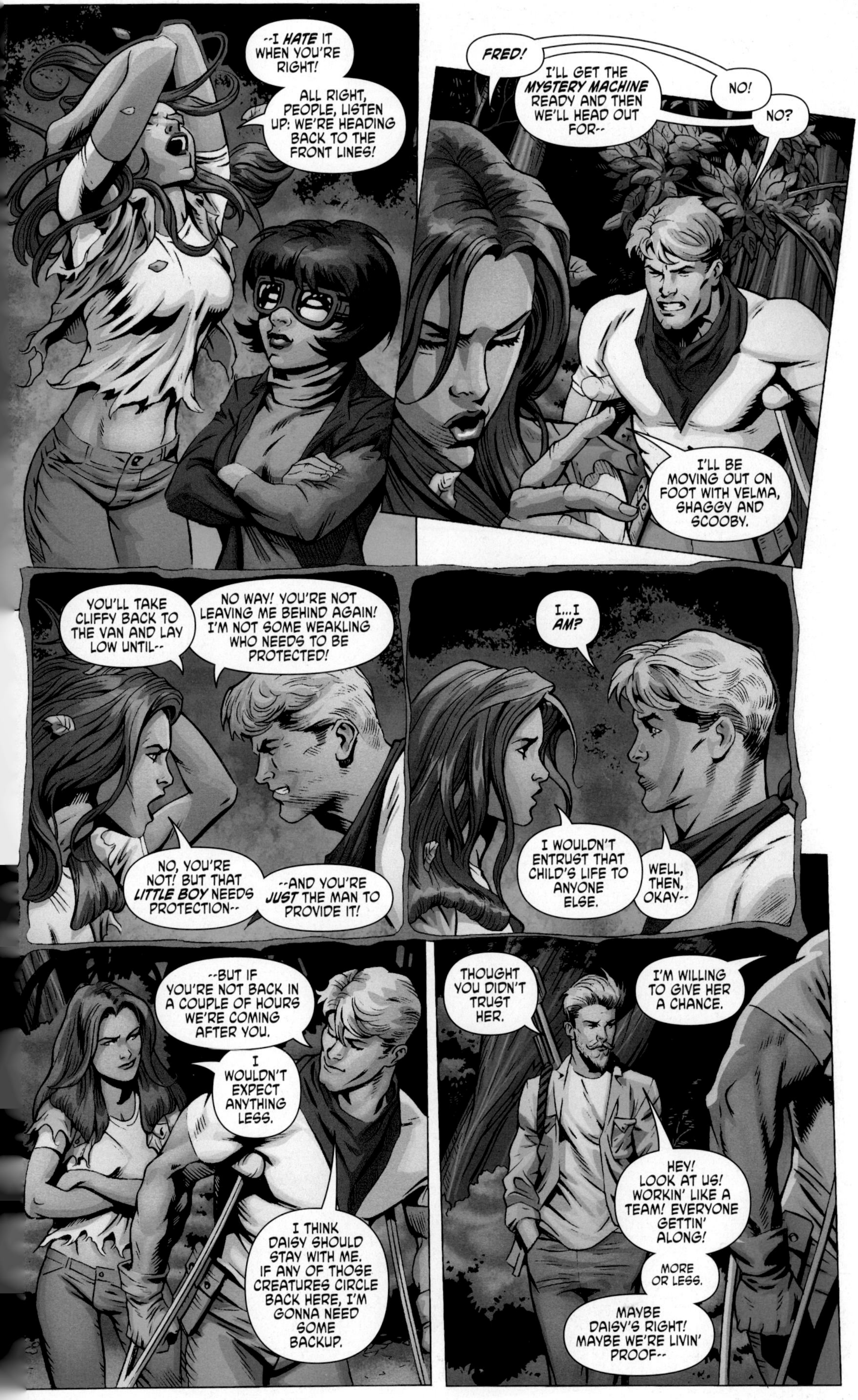

--I HATE IT WHEN YOU'RE RIGHT!
ALL RIGHT, PEOPLE, LISTEN UP: WE'RE HEADING BACK TO THE FRONT LINES!
FRED!
I'LL GET THE MYSTERY MACHINE READY AND THEN WE'LL HEAD OUT FOR--
NO!
NO?
I'LL BE MOVING OUT ON FOOT WITH VELMA, SHAGGY AND SCOOBY.
YOU'LL TAKE CLIFFY BACK TO THE VAN AND LAY LOW UNTIL--
NO WAY! YOU'RE NOT LEAVING ME BEHIND AGAIN! I'M NOT SOME WEAKLING WHO NEEDS TO BE PROTECTED!
NO, YOU'RE NOT! BUT THAT LITTLE BOY NEEDS PROTECTION--
--AND YOU'RE JUST THE MAN TO PROVIDE IT!
I...I AM?
I WOULDN'T ENTRUST THAT CHILD'S LIFE TO ANYONE ELSE.
WELL, THEN, OKAY--
--BUT IF YOU'RE NOT BACK IN A COUPLE OF HOURS WE'RE COMING AFTER YOU.
I WOULDN'T EXPECT ANYTHING LESS.
I THINK DAISY SHOULD STAY WITH ME. IF ANY OF THOSE CREATURES CIRCLE BACK HERE, I'M GONNA NEED SOME BACKUP.
THOUGHT YOU DIDN'T TRUST HER.
I'M WILLING TO GIVE HER A CHANCE.
HEY! LOOK AT US! WORKIN' LIKE A TEAM! EVERYONE GETTIN' ALONG!
MORE OR LESS.
MAYBE DAISY'S RIGHT! MAYBE WE'RE LIVIN' PROOF--

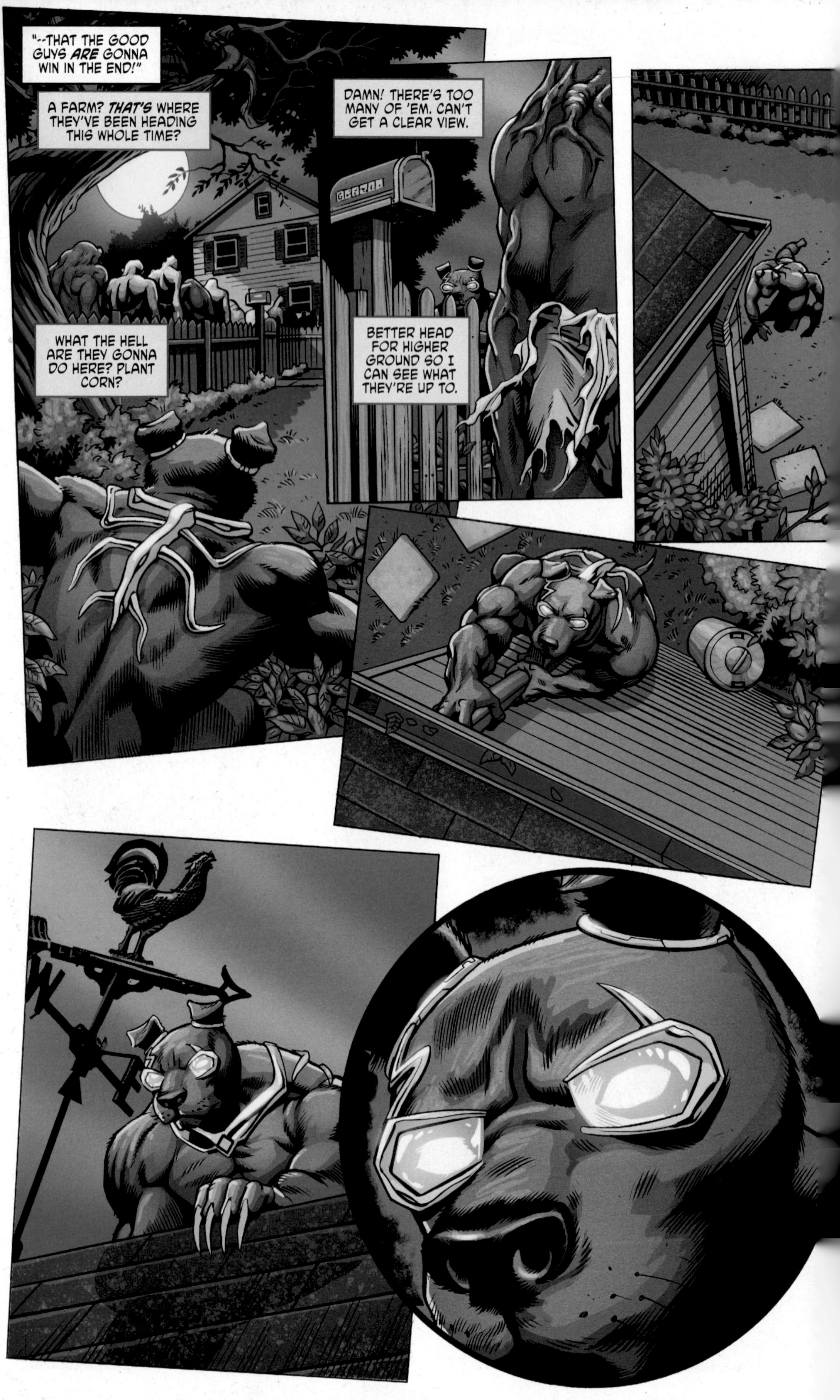
"--THAT THE GOOD GUYS ARE GONNA WIN IN THE END!"
A FARM? THAT'S WHERE THEY'VE BEEN HEADING THIS WHOLE TIME?
WHAT THE HELL ARE THEY GONNA DO HERE? PLANT CORN?
DAMN! THERE'S TOO MANY OF 'EM. CAN'T GET A CLEAR VIEW.
BETTER HEAD FOR HIGHER GROUND SO I CAN SEE WHAT THEY'RE UP TO.

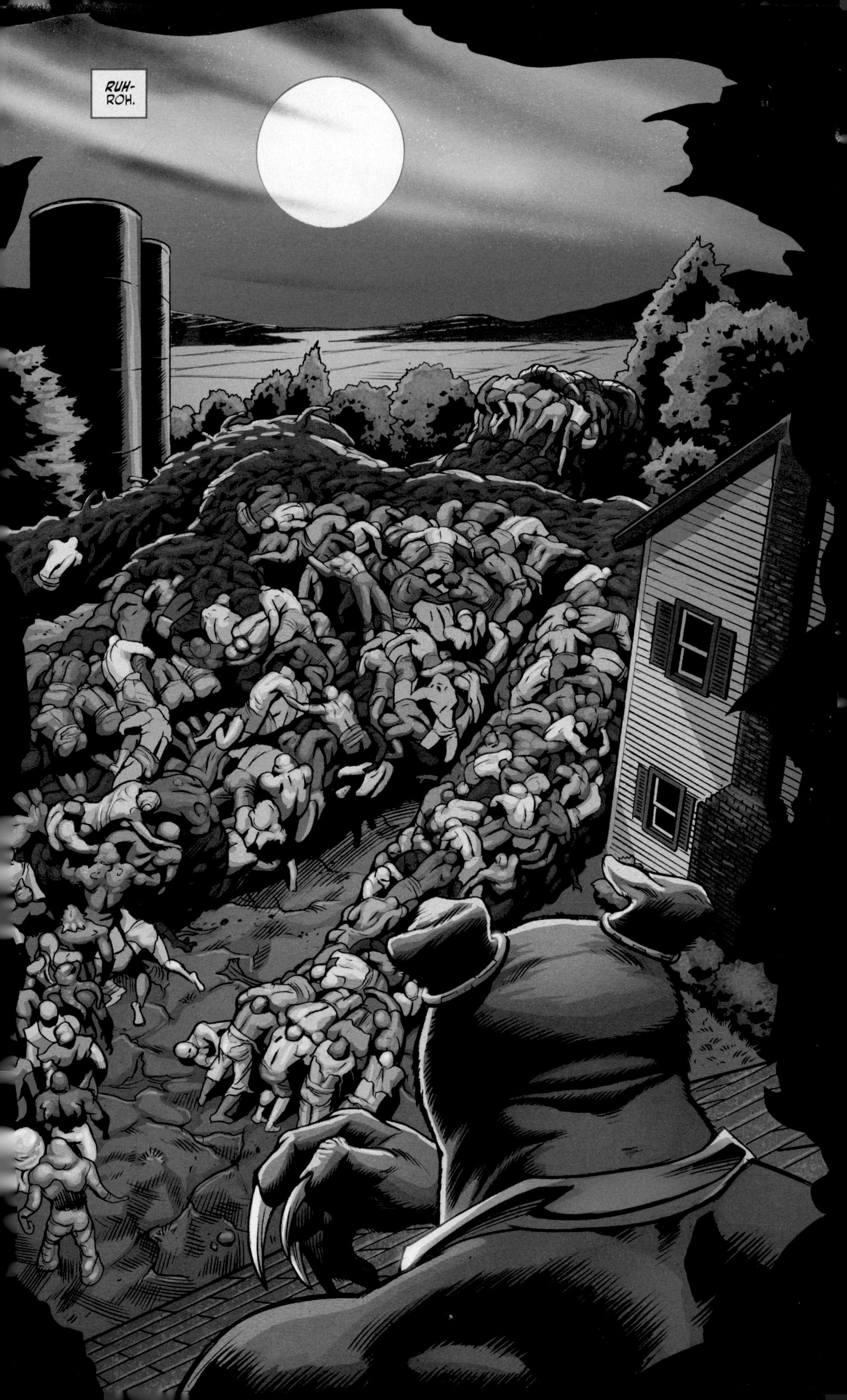
RUH-
ROH.

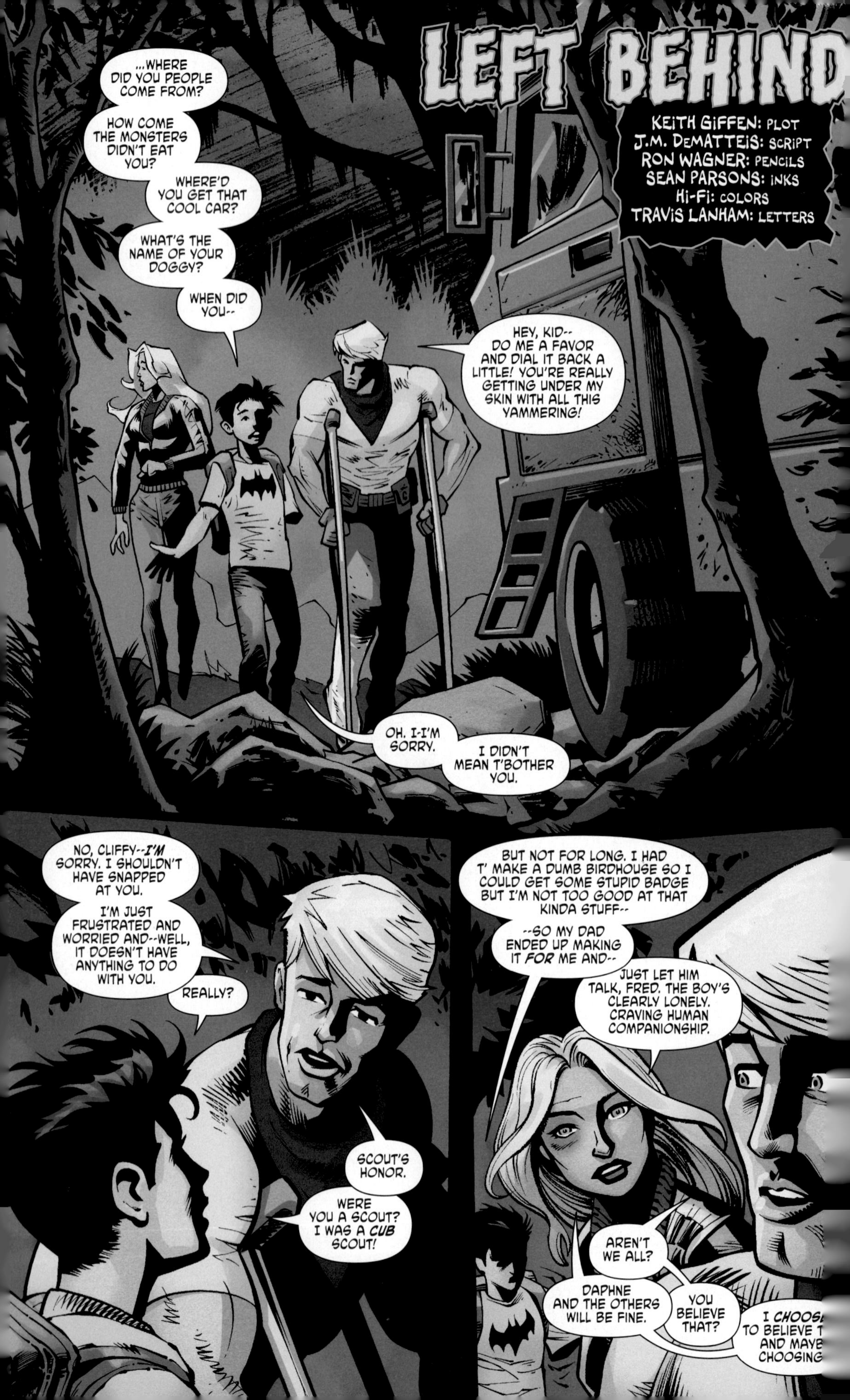
LEFT BEHIND
KEITH GIFFEN: PLOT
J.M. DeMATTEIS: SCRIPT
RON WAGNER: PENCILS
SEAN PARSONS: INKS
Hi-Fi: COLORS
TRAVIS LANHAM: LETTERS
...WHERE DID YOU PEOPLE COME FROM?
HOW COME THE MONSTERS DIDN'T EAT YOU?
WHERE'D YOU GET THAT COOL CAR?
WHAT'S THE NAME OF YOUR DOGGY?
WHEN DID YOU--
HEY, KID-- DO ME A FAVOR AND DIAL IT BACK A LITTLE! YOU'RE REALLY GETTING UNDER MY SKIN WITH ALL THIS YAMMERING!
OH. I-I'M SORRY.
I DIDN'T MEAN T'BOTHER YOU.
NO, CLIFFY--*I'M* SORRY. I SHOULDN'T HAVE SNAPPED AT YOU.
I'M JUST FRUSTRATED AND WORRIED AND--WELL, IT DOESN'T HAVE ANYTHING TO DO WITH YOU.
REALLY?
SCOUT'S HONOR.
WERE YOU A SCOUT? I WAS A *CUB* SCOUT!
BUT NOT FOR LONG. I HAD T' MAKE A DUMB BIRDHOUSE SO I COULD GET SOME STUPID BADGE BUT I'M NOT TOO GOOD AT THAT KINDA STUFF--
--SO MY DAD ENDED UP MAKING IT *FOR* ME AND--
JUST LET HIM TALK, FRED. THE BOY'S CLEARLY LONELY. CRAVING HUMAN COMPANIONSHIP.
AREN'T WE ALL?
DAPHNE AND THE OTHERS WILL BE FINE.
YOU BELIEVE THAT?
I *CHOOS*
TO BELIEVE T
AND MAYB
CHOOSING

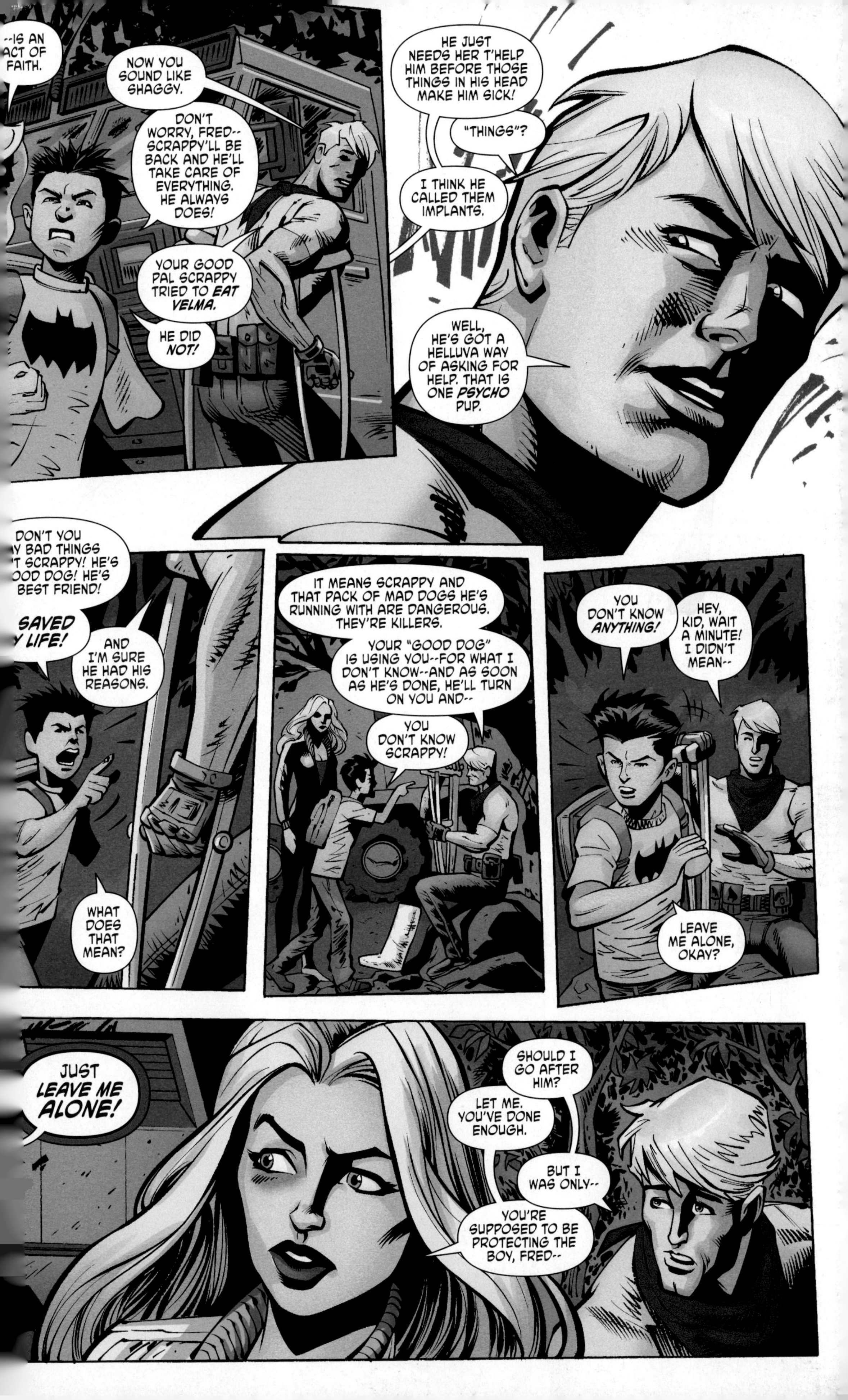
--IS AN ACT OF FAITH.
NOW YOU SOUND LIKE SHAGGY.
DON'T WORRY, FRED--SCRAPPY'LL BE BACK AND HE'LL TAKE CARE OF EVERYTHING. HE ALWAYS DOES!
YOUR GOOD PAL SCRAPPY TRIED TO EAT VELMA.
HE DID NOT!
HE JUST NEEDS HER T'HELP HIM BEFORE THOSE THINGS IN HIS HEAD MAKE HIM SICK!
"THINGS"?
I THINK HE CALLED THEM IMPLANTS.
WELL, HE'S GOT A HELLUVA WAY OF ASKING FOR HELP. THAT IS ONE PSYCHO PUP.
DON'T YOU
BAD THINGS
SCRAPPY! HE'S
OOD DOG! HE'S
BEST FRIEND!
SAVED
LIFE!
AND I'M SURE HE HAD HIS REASONS.
WHAT DOES THAT MEAN?
IT MEANS SCRAPPY AND THAT PACK OF MAD DOGS HE'S RUNNING WITH ARE DANGEROUS. THEY'RE KILLERS.
YOUR "GOOD DOG" IS USING YOU--FOR WHAT I DON'T KNOW--AND AS SOON AS HE'S DONE, HE'LL TURN ON YOU AND--
YOU DON'T KNOW SCRAPPY!
YOU DON'T KNOW ANYTHING!
HEY, KID, WAIT A MINUTE! I DIDN'T MEAN--
LEAVE ME ALONE, OKAY?
JUST LEAVE ME ALONE!
SHOULD I GO AFTER HIM?
LET ME. YOU'VE DONE ENOUGH.
BUT I WAS ONLY--
YOU'RE SUPPOSED TO BE PROTECTING THE BOY, FRED--

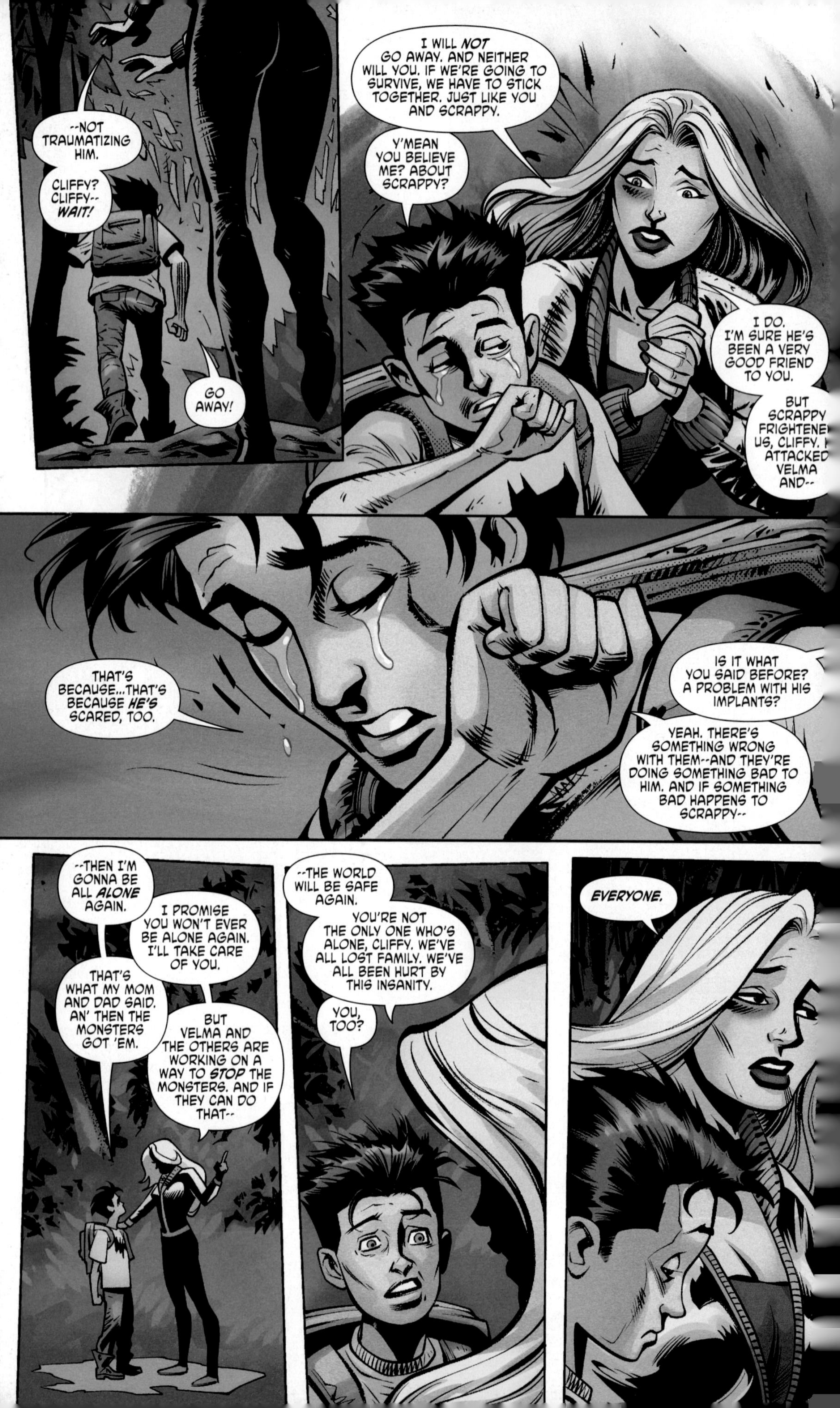
--NOT TRAUMATIZING HIM.
CLIFFY? CLIFFY-- *WAIT!*
GO AWAY!
I WILL *NOT* GO AWAY. AND NEITHER WILL YOU. IF WE'RE GOING TO SURVIVE, WE HAVE TO STICK TOGETHER. JUST LIKE YOU AND SCRAPPY.
Y'MEAN YOU BELIEVE ME? ABOUT SCRAPPY?
I DO. I'M SURE HE'S BEEN A VERY GOOD FRIEND TO YOU.
BUT SCRAPPY FRIGHTENE US, CLIFFY. ATTACKED VELMA AND--
THAT'S BECAUSE...THAT'S BECAUSE *HE'S* SCARED, TOO.
IS IT WHAT YOU SAID BEFORE? A PROBLEM WITH HIS IMPLANTS?
YEAH. THERE'S SOMETHING WRONG WITH THEM--AND THEY'RE DOING SOMETHING BAD TO HIM. AND IF SOMETHING BAD HAPPENS TO SCRAPPY--
--THEN I'M GONNA BE ALL *ALONE* AGAIN.
I PROMISE YOU WON'T EVER BE ALONE AGAIN. I'LL TAKE CARE OF YOU.
THAT'S WHAT MY MOM AND DAD SAID. AN' THEN THE MONSTERS GOT 'EM.
BUT VELMA AND THE OTHERS ARE WORKING ON A WAY TO *STOP* THE MONSTERS. AND IF THEY CAN DO THAT--
--THE WORLD WILL BE SAFE AGAIN.
YOU'RE NOT THE ONLY ONE WHO'S ALONE, CLIFFY. WE'VE ALL LOST FAMILY. WE'VE ALL BEEN HURT BY THIS INSANITY.
YOU, TOO?
EVERYONE.

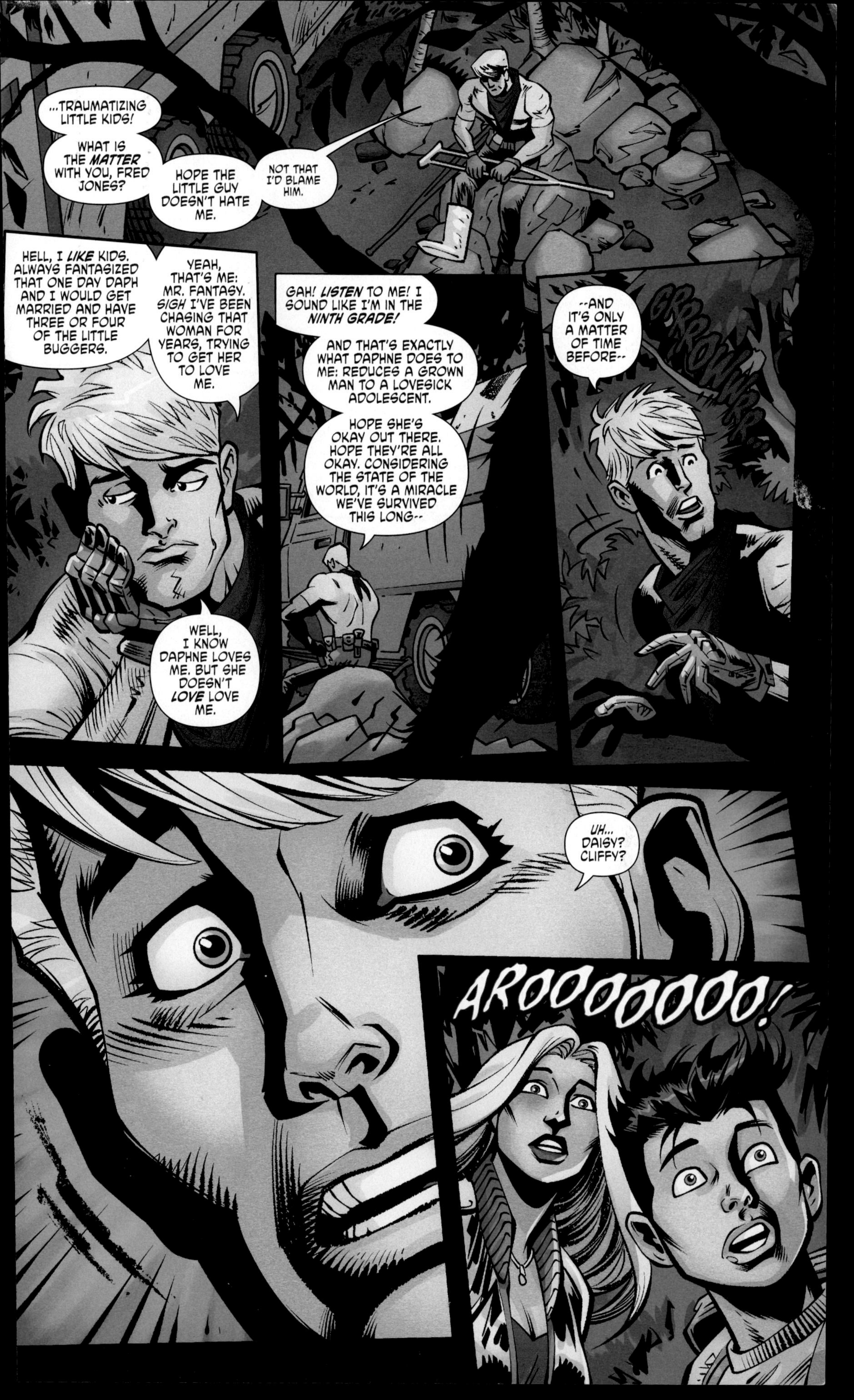
...TRAUMATIZING LITTLE KIDS!
WHAT IS THE MATTER WITH YOU, FRED JONES?
HOPE THE LITTLE GUY DOESN'T HATE ME.
NOT THAT I'D BLAME HIM.
HELL, I LIKE KIDS. ALWAYS FANTASIZED THAT ONE DAY DAPH AND I WOULD GET MARRIED AND HAVE THREE OR FOUR OF THE LITTLE BUGGERS.
YEAH, THAT'S ME: MR. FANTASY. SIGH I'VE BEEN CHASING THAT WOMAN FOR YEARS, TRYING TO GET HER TO LOVE ME.
WELL, I KNOW DAPHNE LOVES ME. BUT SHE DOESN'T LOVE LOVE ME.
GAH! LISTEN TO ME! I SOUND LIKE I'M IN THE NINTH GRADE!
AND THAT'S EXACTLY WHAT DAPHNE DOES TO ME: REDUCES A GROWN MAN TO A LOVESICK ADOLESCENT.
HOPE SHE'S OKAY OUT THERE. HOPE THEY'RE ALL OKAY. CONSIDERING THE STATE OF THE WORLD, IT'S A MIRACLE WE'VE SURVIVED THIS LONG--
--AND IT'S ONLY A MATTER OF TIME BEFORE--
GRROWWRR...
UH... DAISY? CLIFFY?
AROOOOOOOO!

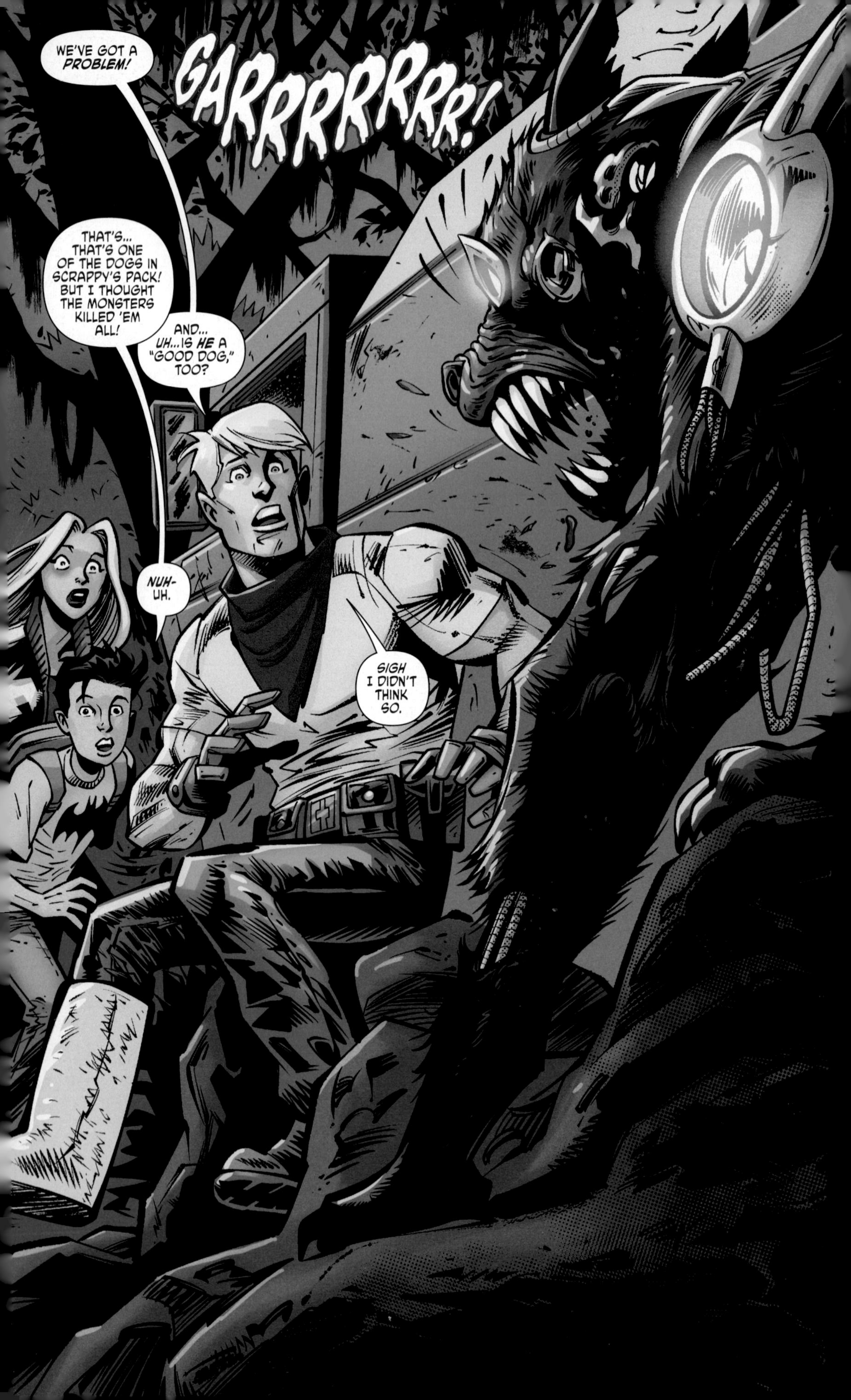
WE'VE GOT A PROBLEM!
GARRRRRRRR!
THAT'S... THAT'S ONE OF THE DOGS IN SCRAPPY'S PACK! BUT I THOUGHT THE MONSTERS KILLED 'EM ALL!
AND... UH...IS HE A "GOOD DOG," TOO?
NUH-UH.
SIGH I DIDN'T THINK SO.

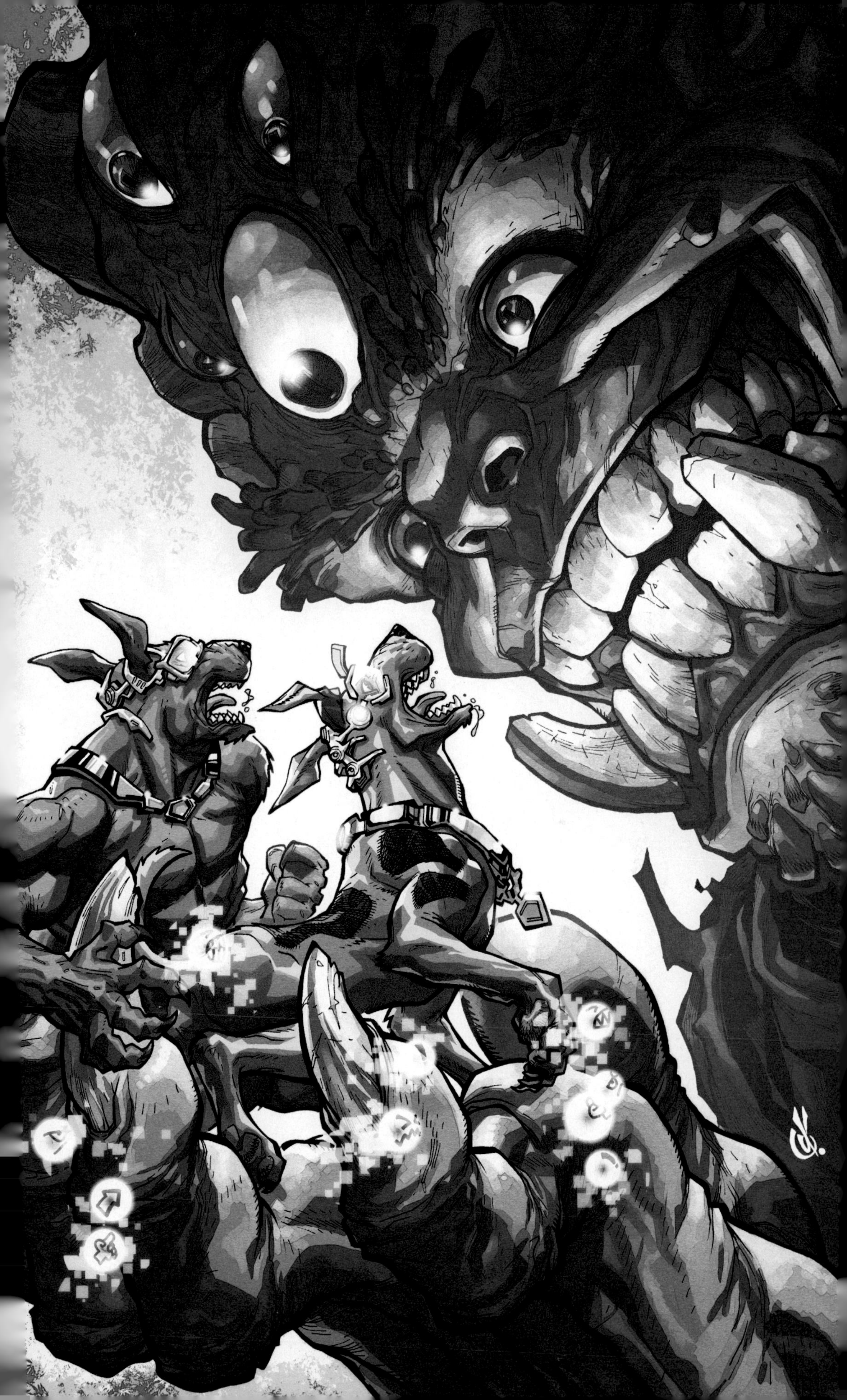

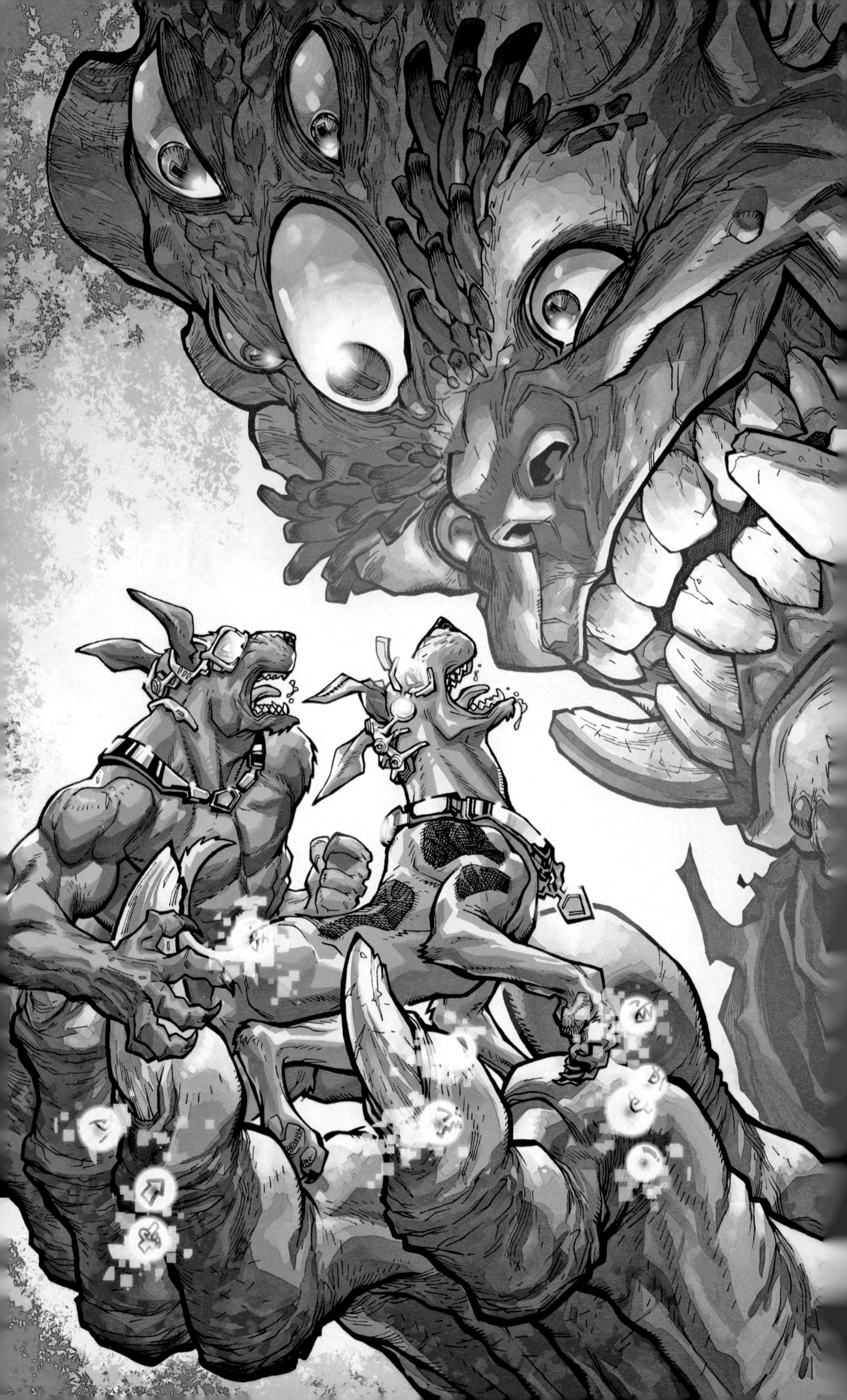

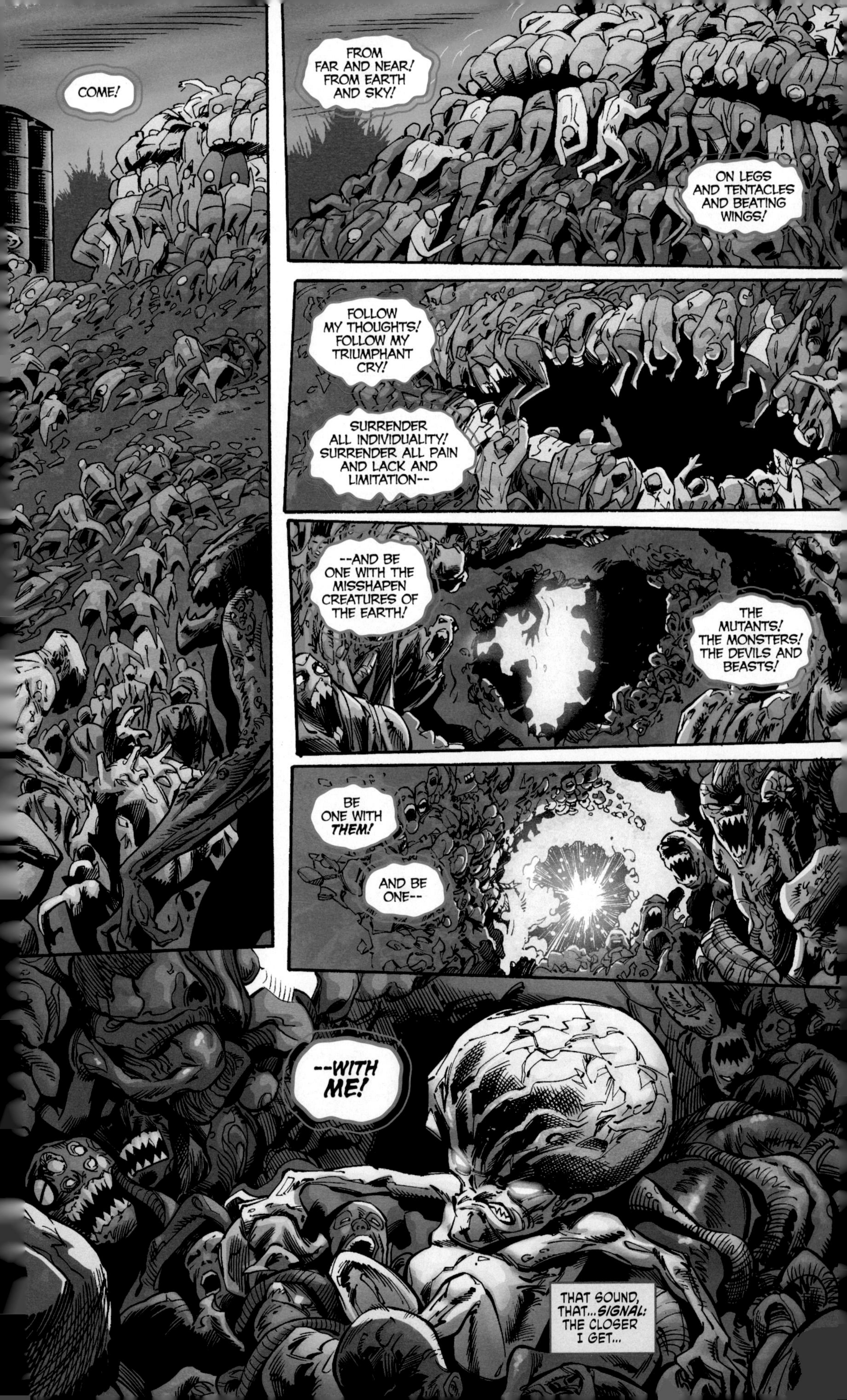
COME!
FROM FAR AND NEAR! FROM EARTH AND SKY!
ON LEGS AND TENTACLES AND BEATING WINGS!
FOLLOW MY THOUGHTS! FOLLOW MY TRIUMPHANT CRY!
SURRENDER ALL INDIVIDUALITY! SURRENDER ALL PAIN AND LACK AND LIMITATION--
--AND BE ONE WITH THE MISSHAPEN CREATURES OF THE EARTH!
THE MUTANTS! THE MONSTERS! THE DEVILS AND BEASTS!
BE ONE WITH *THEM!*
AND BE ONE--
--WITH ME!
THAT SOUND, THAT...*SIGNAL:* THE CLOSER I GET...

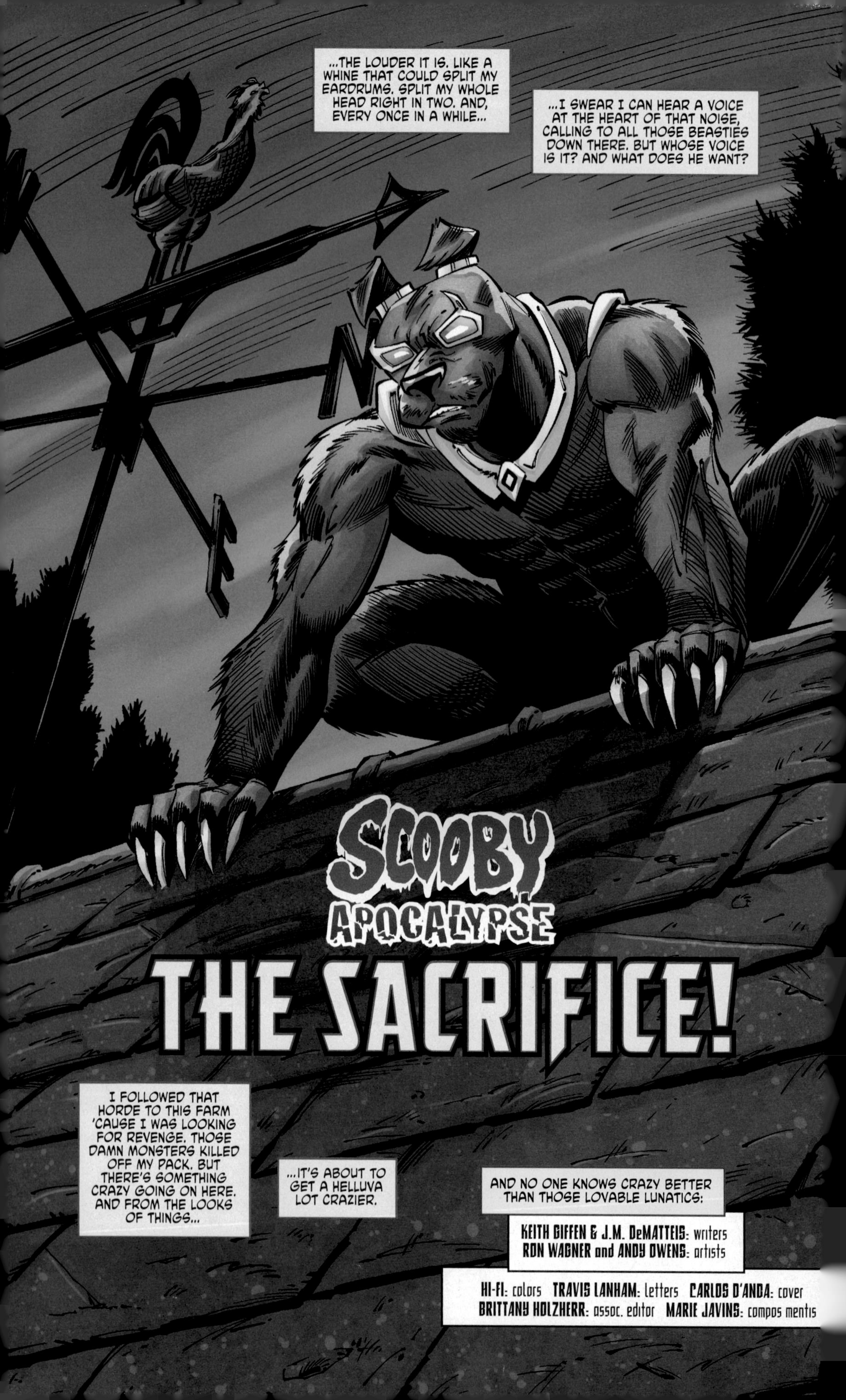
...THE LOUDER IT IS. LIKE A WHINE THAT COULD SPLIT MY EARDRUMS. SPLIT MY WHOLE HEAD RIGHT IN TWO. AND, EVERY ONCE IN A WHILE...
...I SWEAR I CAN HEAR A VOICE AT THE HEART OF THAT NOISE, CALLING TO ALL THOSE BEASTIES DOWN THERE. BUT WHOSE VOICE IS IT? AND WHAT DOES HE WANT?
SCOOBY APOCALYPSE
THE SACRIFICE!
I FOLLOWED THAT HORDE TO THIS FARM 'CAUSE I WAS LOOKING FOR REVENGE. THOSE DAMN MONSTERS KILLED OFF MY PACK. BUT THERE'S SOMETHING CRAZY GOING ON HERE. AND FROM THE LOOKS OF THINGS...
...IT'S ABOUT TO GET A HELLUVA LOT CRAZIER.
AND NO ONE KNOWS CRAZY BETTER THAN THOSE LOVABLE LUNATICS:
KEITH GIFFEN & J.M. DeMATTEIS: writers
RON WAGNER and ANDY OWENS: artists
HI-FI: colors TRAVIS LANHAM: letters CARLOS D'ANDA: cover
BRITTANY HOLZHERR: assoc. editor MARIE JAVINS: compos mentis

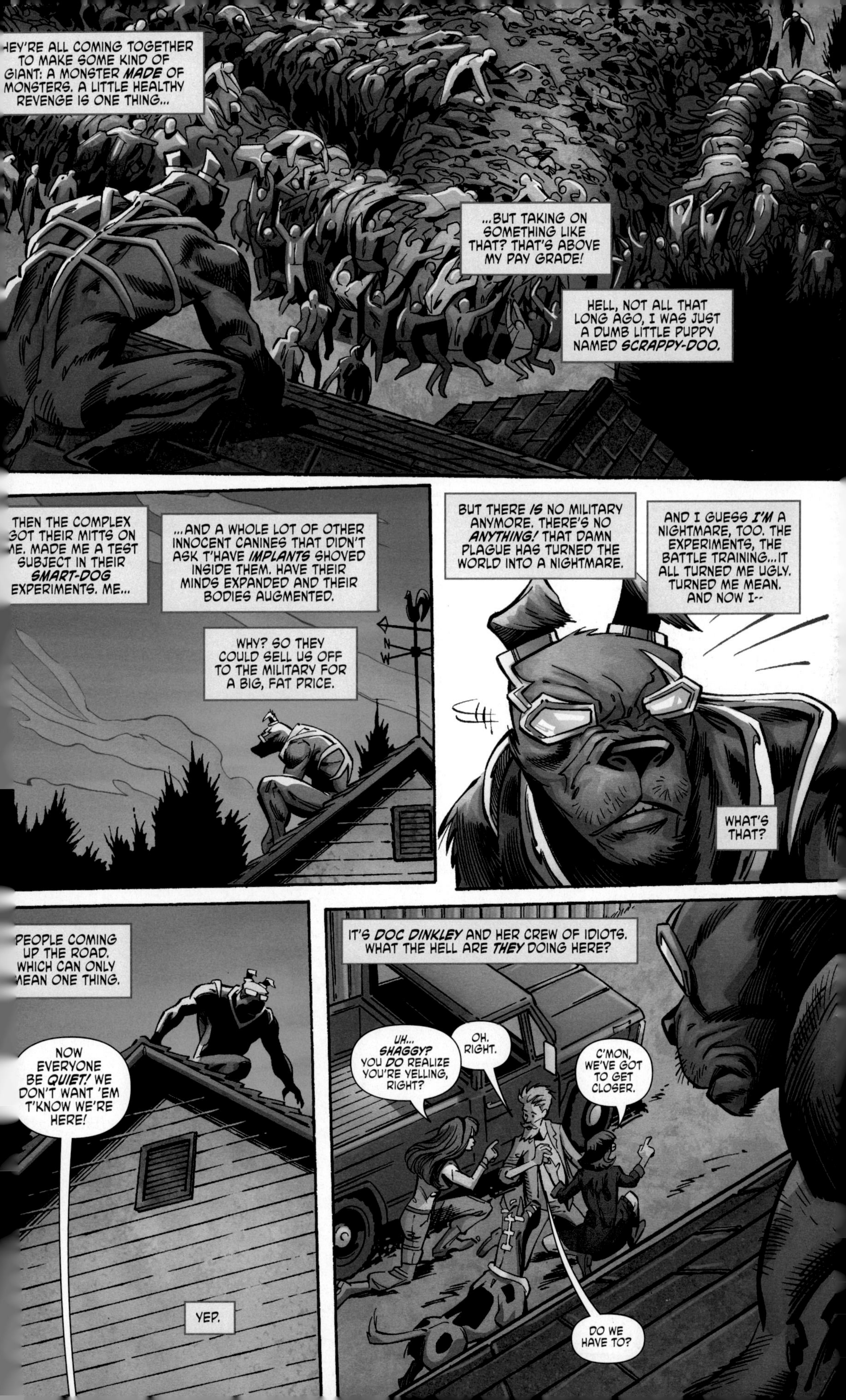
HEY'RE ALL COMING TOGETHER TO MAKE SOME KIND OF GIANT: A MONSTER MADE OF MONSTERS. A LITTLE HEALTHY REVENGE IS ONE THING...
...BUT TAKING ON SOMETHING LIKE THAT? THAT'S ABOVE MY PAY GRADE!
HELL, NOT ALL THAT LONG AGO, I WAS JUST A DUMB LITTLE PUPPY NAMED SCRAPPY-DOO.
THEN THE COMPLEX GOT THEIR MITTS ON ME. MADE ME A TEST SUBJECT IN THEIR SMART-DOG EXPERIMENTS. ME...
...AND A WHOLE LOT OF OTHER INNOCENT CANINES THAT DIDN'T ASK T'HAVE IMPLANTS SHOVED INSIDE THEM. HAVE THEIR MINDS EXPANDED AND THEIR BODIES AUGMENTED.
WHY? SO THEY COULD SELL US OFF TO THE MILITARY FOR A BIG, FAT PRICE.
N
W
BUT THERE IS NO MILITARY ANYMORE. THERE'S NO ANYTHING! THAT DAMN PLAGUE HAS TURNED THE WORLD INTO A NIGHTMARE.
AND I GUESS I'M A NIGHTMARE, TOO. THE EXPERIMENTS, THE BATTLE TRAINING...IT ALL TURNED ME UGLY. TURNED ME MEAN. AND NOW I--
WHAT'S THAT?
PEOPLE COMING UP THE ROAD. WHICH CAN ONLY MEAN ONE THING.
NOW EVERYONE BE QUIET! WE DON'T WANT 'EM T'KNOW WE'RE HERE!
YEP.
IT'S DOC DINKLEY AND HER CREW OF IDIOTS. WHAT THE HELL ARE THEY DOING HERE?
UH... SHAGGY? YOU DO REALIZE YOU'RE YELLING, RIGHT?
OH. RIGHT.
C'MON, WE'VE GOT TO GET CLOSER.
DO WE HAVE TO?

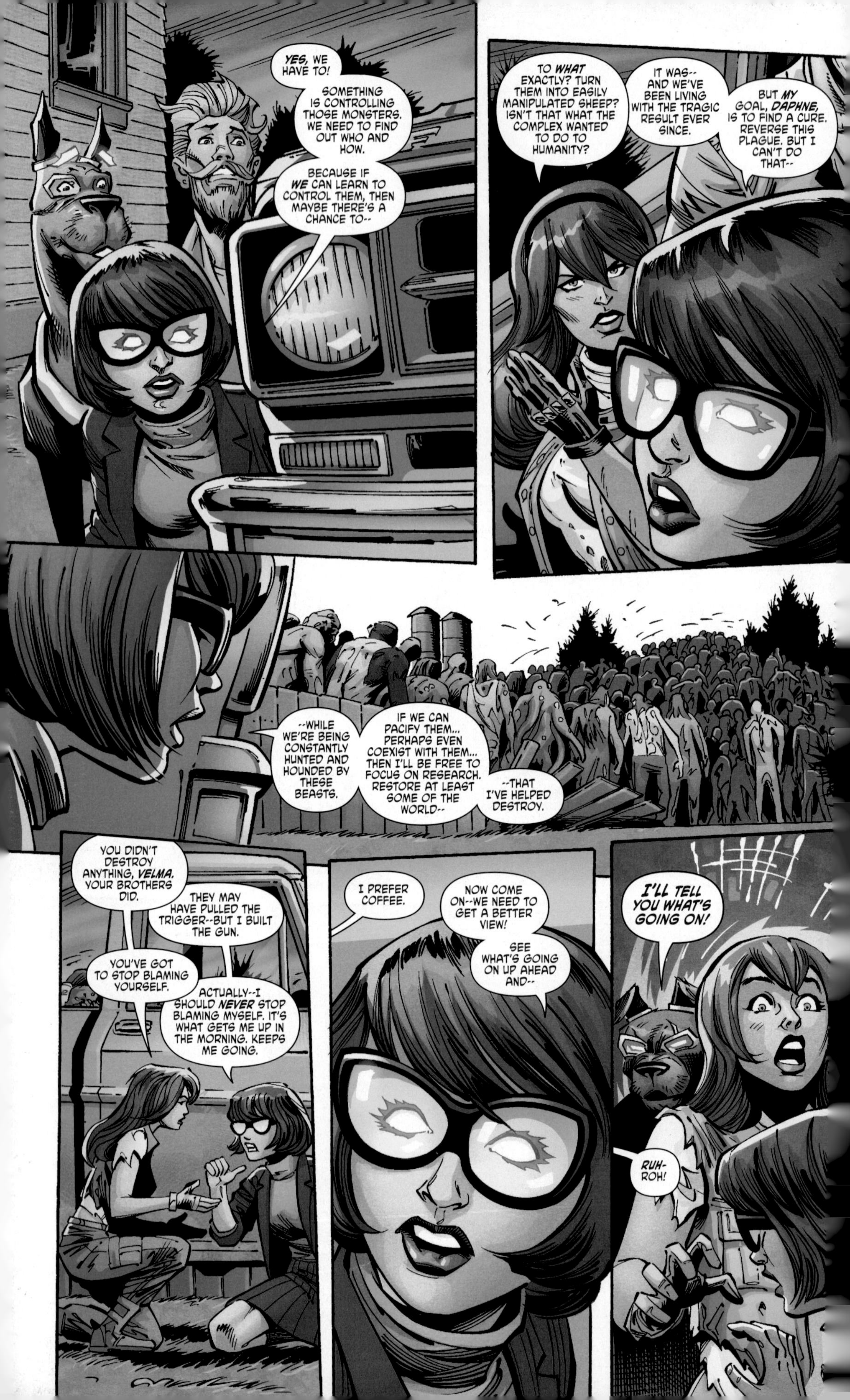
YES, WE HAVE TO!
SOMETHING IS CONTROLLING THOSE MONSTERS. WE NEED TO FIND OUT WHO AND HOW.
BECAUSE IF WE CAN LEARN TO CONTROL THEM, THEN MAYBE THERE'S A CHANCE TO--
TO WHAT EXACTLY? TURN THEM INTO EASILY MANIPULATED SHEEP? ISN'T THAT WHAT THE COMPLEX WANTED TO DO TO HUMANITY?
IT WAS-- AND WE'VE BEEN LIVING WITH THE TRAGIC RESULT EVER SINCE.
BUT MY GOAL, DAPHNE, IS TO FIND A CURE. REVERSE THIS PLAGUE. BUT I CAN'T DO THAT--
--WHILE WE'RE BEING CONSTANTLY HUNTED AND HOUNDED BY THESE BEASTS.
IF WE CAN PACIFY THEM... PERHAPS EVEN COEXIST WITH THEM... THEN I'LL BE FREE TO FOCUS ON RESEARCH. RESTORE AT LEAST SOME OF THE WORLD--
--THAT I'VE HELPED DESTROY.
YOU DIDN'T DESTROY ANYTHING, VELMA. YOUR BROTHERS DID.
THEY MAY HAVE PULLED THE TRIGGER--BUT I BUILT THE GUN.
YOU'VE GOT TO STOP BLAMING YOURSELF.
ACTUALLY--I SHOULD NEVER STOP BLAMING MYSELF. IT'S WHAT GETS ME UP IN THE MORNING. KEEPS ME GOING.
I PREFER COFFEE.
NOW COME ON--WE NEED TO GET A BETTER VIEW!
SEE WHAT'S GOING ON UP AHEAD AND--
I'LL TELL YOU WHAT'S GOING ON!
RUH-ROH!

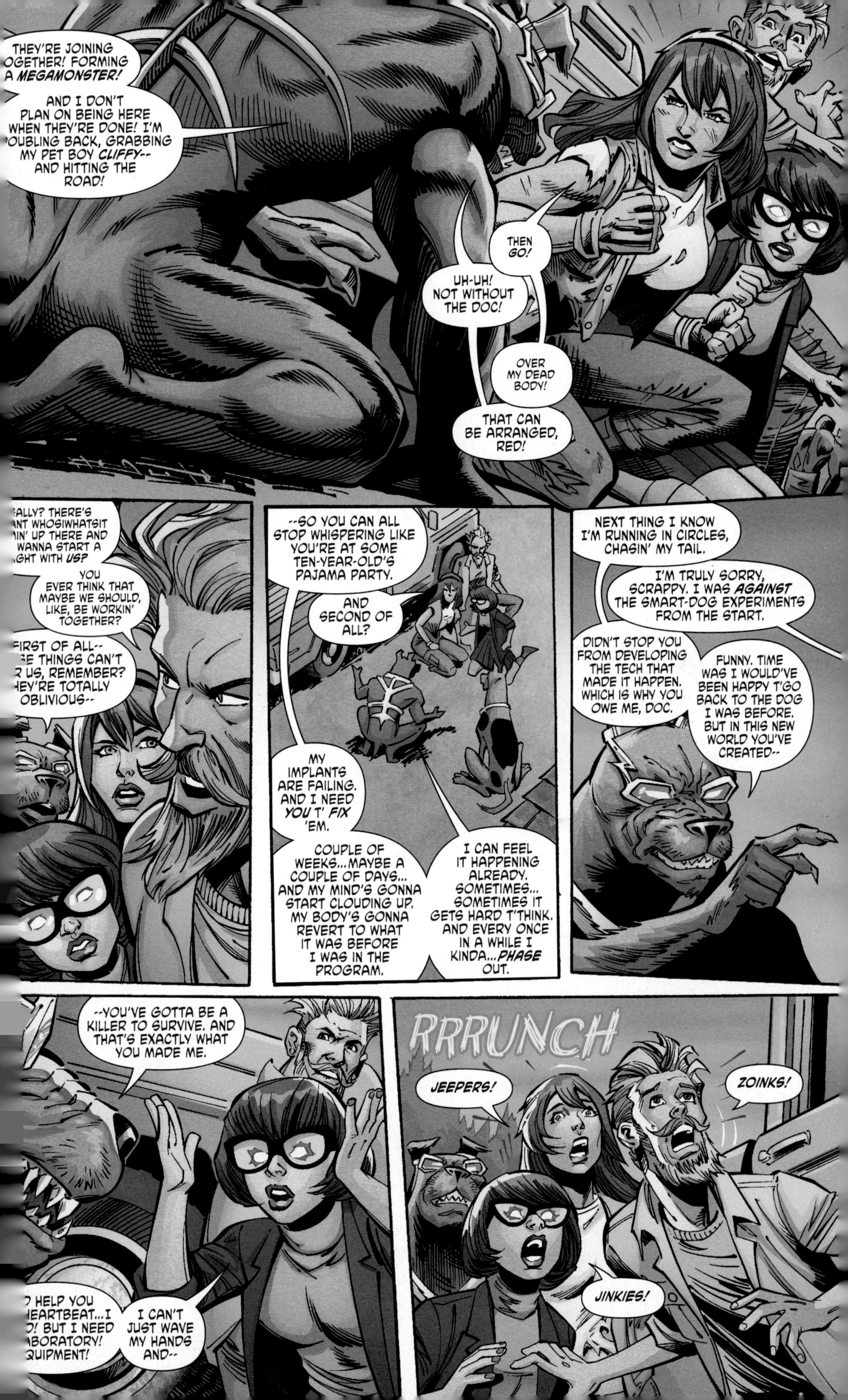
THEY'RE JOINING
OGETHER! FORMING A MEGAMONSTER!
AND I DON'T PLAN ON BEING HERE WHEN THEY'RE DONE! I'M OUBLING BACK, GRABBING MY PET BOY CLIFFY-- AND HITTING THE ROAD!
THEN GO!
UH-UH! NOT WITHOUT THE DOC!
OVER MY DEAD BODY!
THAT CAN BE ARRANGED, RED!
EALLY? THERE'S ANT WHOSIWHATSIT IN' UP THERE AND WANNA START A GHT WITH US?
YOU EVER THINK THAT MAYBE WE SHOULD, LIKE, BE WORKIN' TOGETHER?
FIRST OF ALL-- E THINGS CAN'T R US, REMEMBER? HEY'RE TOTALLY OBLIVIOUS--
--SO YOU CAN ALL STOP WHISPERING LIKE YOU'RE AT SOME TEN-YEAR-OLD'S PAJAMA PARTY.
AND SECOND OF ALL?
MY IMPLANTS ARE FAILING. AND I NEED YOU T' FIX 'EM.
COUPLE OF WEEKS...MAYBE A COUPLE OF DAYS... AND MY MIND'S GONNA START CLOUDING UP. MY BODY'S GONNA REVERT TO WHAT IT WAS BEFORE I WAS IN THE PROGRAM.
I CAN FEEL IT HAPPENING ALREADY. SOMETIMES... SOMETIMES IT GETS HARD T'THINK. AND EVERY ONCE IN A WHILE I KINDA...PHASE OUT.
NEXT THING I KNOW I'M RUNNING IN CIRCLES, CHASIN' MY TAIL.
I'M TRULY SORRY, SCRAPPY. I WAS AGAINST THE SMART-DOG EXPERIMENTS FROM THE START.
DIDN'T STOP YOU FROM DEVELOPING THE TECH THAT MADE IT HAPPEN. WHICH IS WHY YOU OWE ME, DOC.
FUNNY. TIME WAS I WOULD'VE BEEN HAPPY T'GO BACK TO THE DOG I WAS BEFORE. BUT IN THIS NEW WORLD YOU'VE CREATED--
--YOU'VE GOTTA BE A KILLER TO SURVIVE. AND THAT'S EXACTLY WHAT YOU MADE ME.
HELP YOU HEARTBEAT...I ! BUT I NEED BORATORY! QUIPMENT!
I CAN'T JUST WAVE MY HANDS AND--
RRRUNCH
JEEPERS!
ZOINKS!
JINKIES!

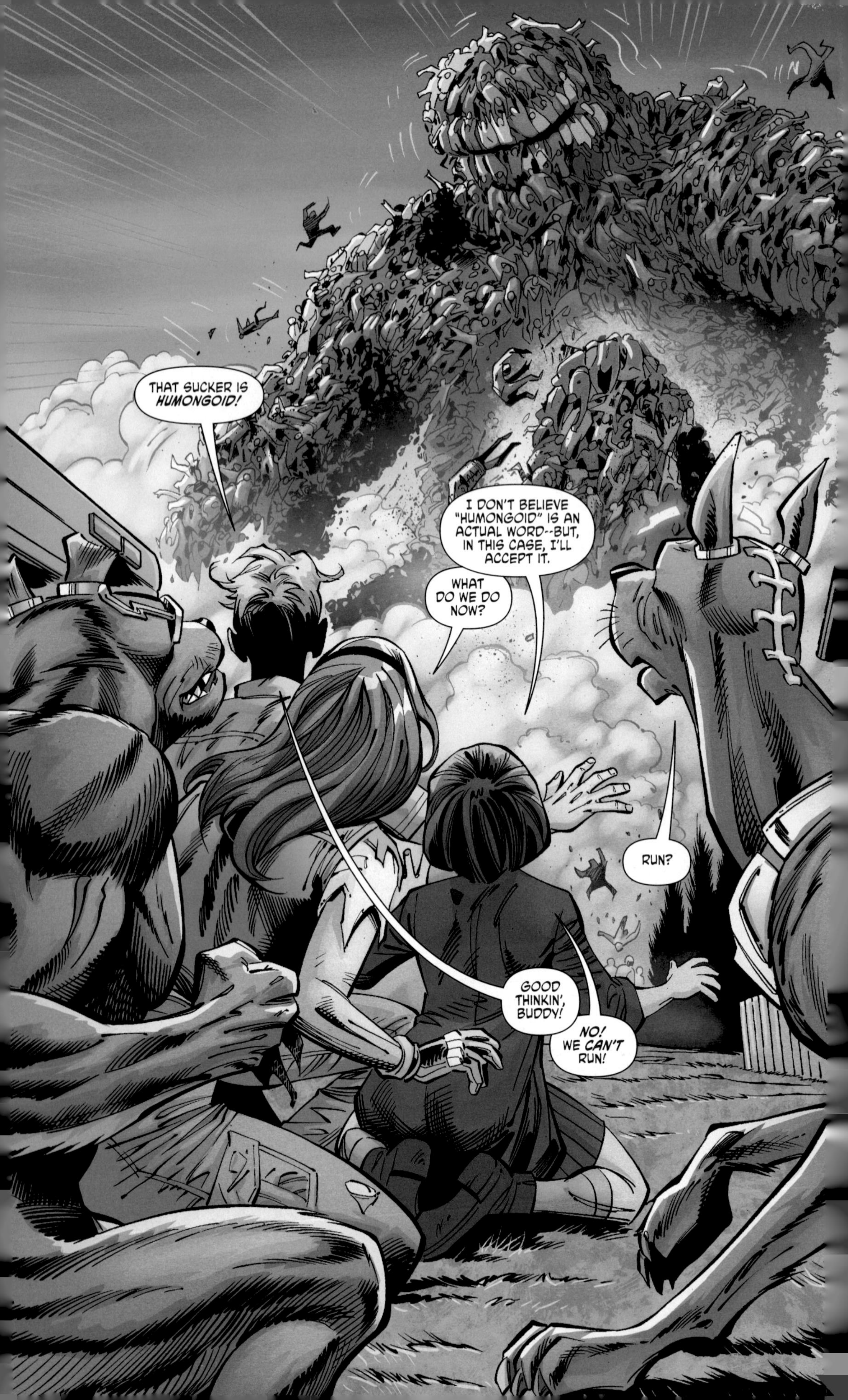
THAT SUCKER IS *HUMONGOID!*
I DON'T BELIEVE "HUMONGOID" IS AN ACTUAL WORD--BUT, IN THIS CASE, I'LL ACCEPT IT.
WHAT DO WE DO NOW?
RUN?
GOOD THINKIN', BUDDY!
NO! WE *CAN'T* RUN!

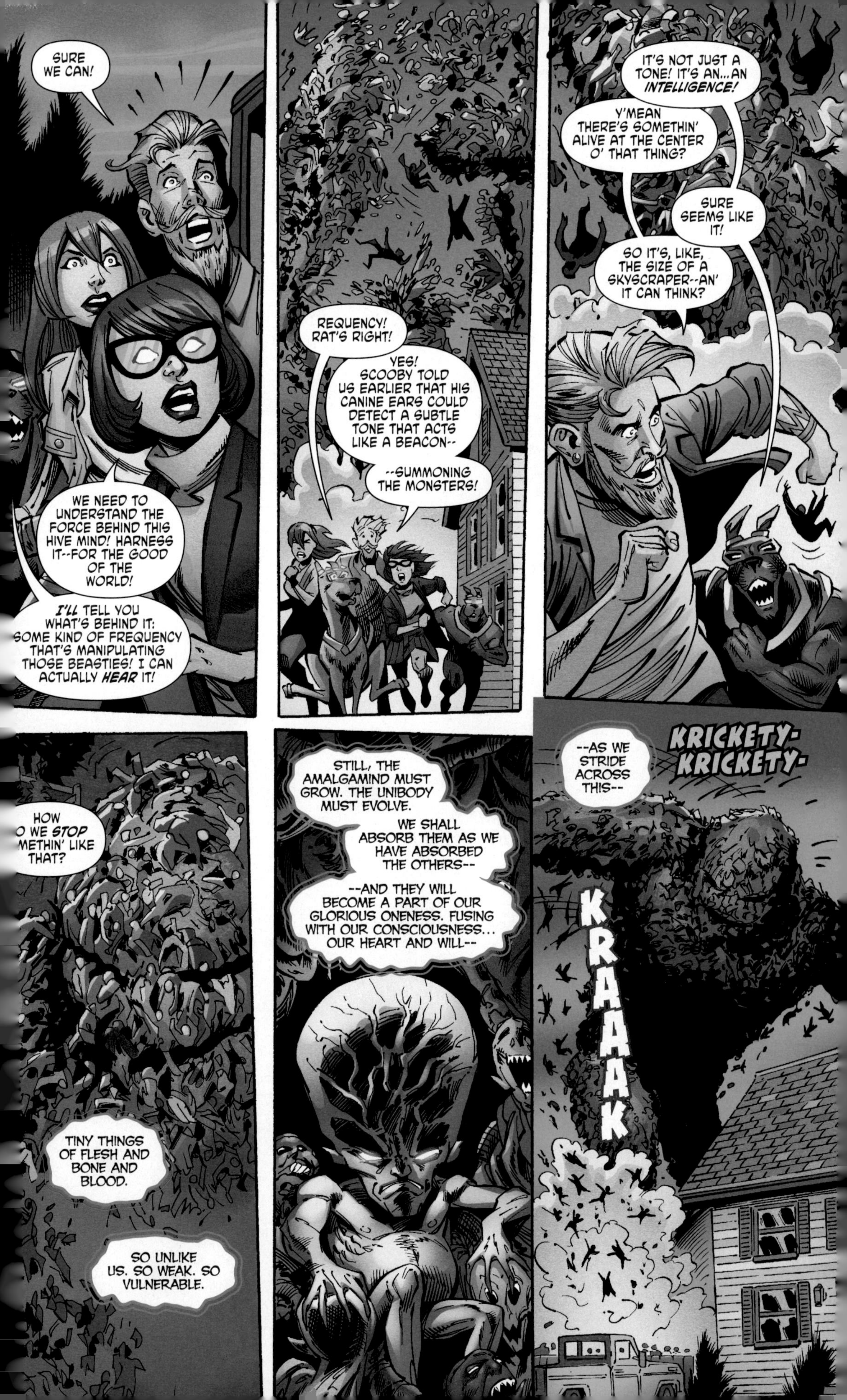
SURE WE CAN!
WE NEED TO UNDERSTAND THE FORCE BEHIND THIS HIVE MIND! HARNESS IT--FOR THE GOOD OF THE WORLD!
I'LL TELL YOU WHAT'S BEHIND IT: SOME KIND OF FREQUENCY THAT'S MANIPULATING THOSE BEASTIES! I CAN ACTUALLY HEAR IT!
REQUENCY! RAT'S RIGHT!
YES! SCOOBY TOLD US EARLIER THAT HIS CANINE EARS COULD DETECT A SUBTLE TONE THAT ACTS LIKE A BEACON--
--SUMMONING THE MONSTERS!
IT'S NOT JUST A TONE! IT'S AN...AN INTELLIGENCE!
Y'MEAN THERE'S SOMETHIN' ALIVE AT THE CENTER O' THAT THING?
SURE SEEMS LIKE IT!
SO IT'S, LIKE, THE SIZE OF A SKYSCRAPER--AN' IT CAN THINK?
HOW O WE STOP METHIN' LIKE THAT?
TINY THINGS OF FLESH AND BONE AND BLOOD.
SO UNLIKE US. SO WEAK. SO VULNERABLE.
STILL, THE AMALGAMIND MUST GROW. THE UNIBODY MUST EVOLVE.
WE SHALL ABSORB THEM AS WE HAVE ABSORBED THE OTHERS--
--AND THEY WILL BECOME A PART OF OUR GLORIOUS ONENESS. FUSING WITH OUR CONSCIOUSNESS... OUR HEART AND WILL--
--AS WE STRIDE ACROSS THIS--
KRICKETY-KRICKETY-
KRAAAK

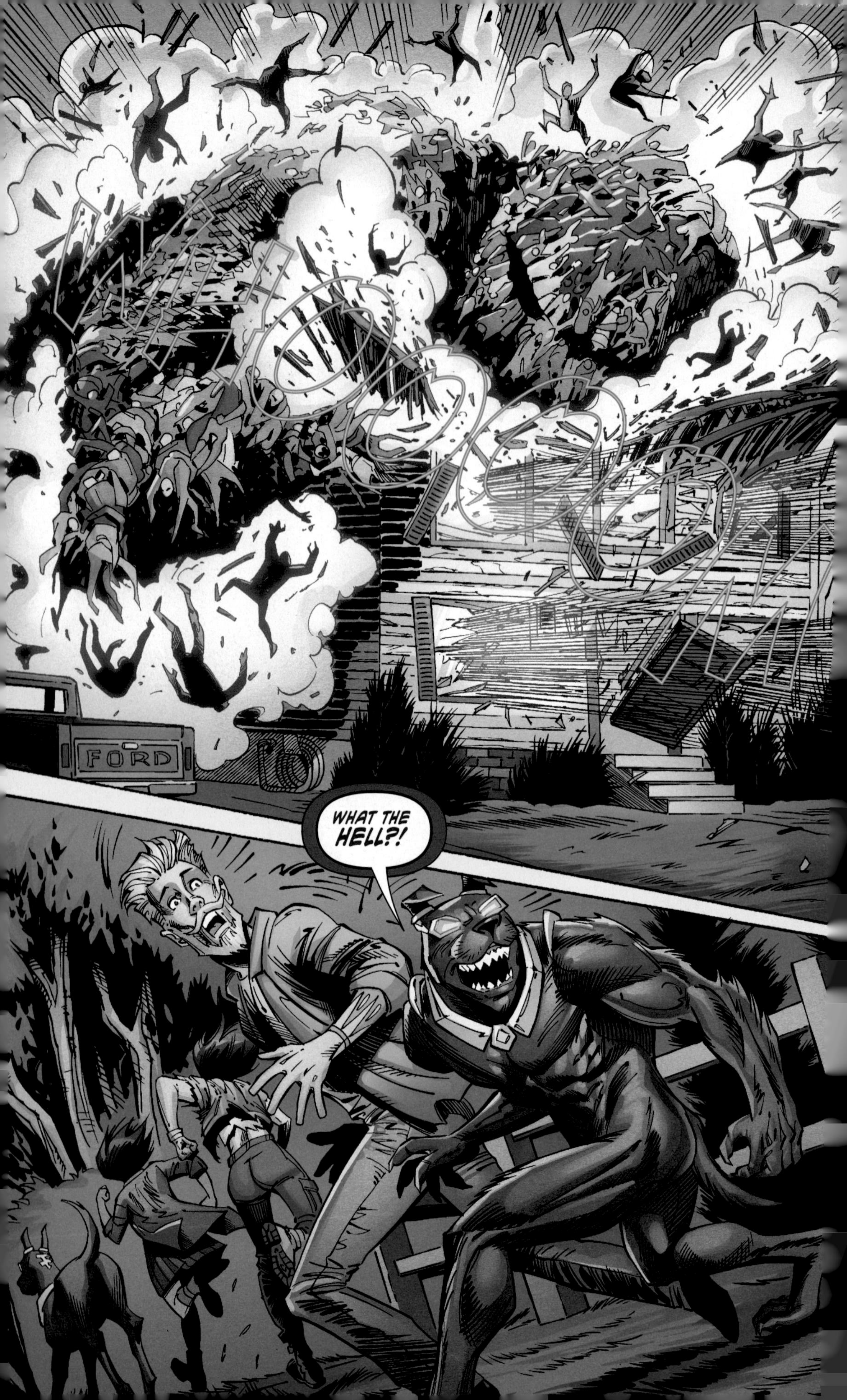
FORD
WHAT THE HELL?!

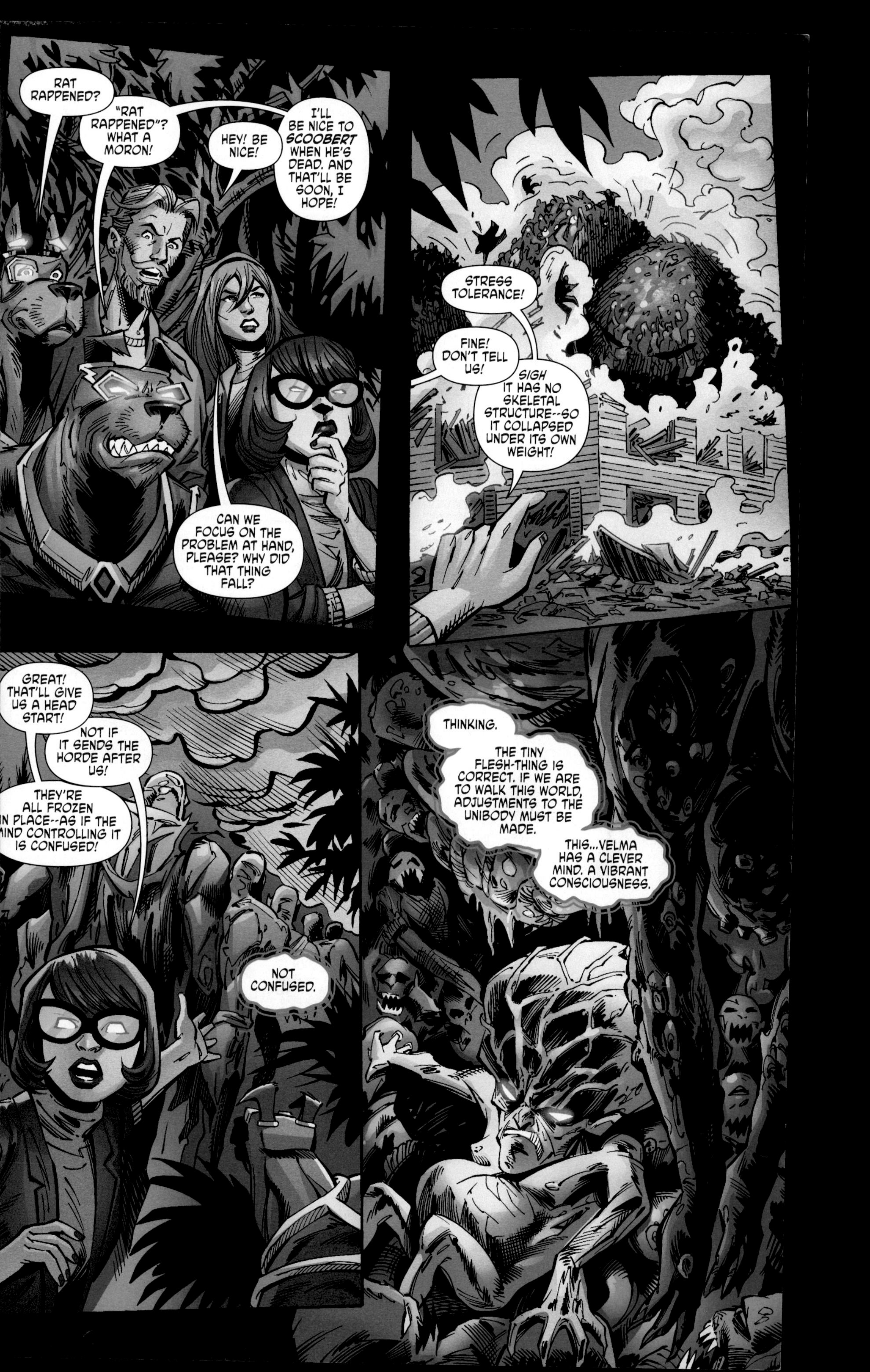
RAT RAPPENED?
"RAT RAPPENED"? WHAT A MORON!
HEY! BE NICE!
I'LL BE NICE TO SCOOBERT WHEN HE'S DEAD. AND THAT'LL BE SOON, I HOPE!
CAN WE FOCUS ON THE PROBLEM AT HAND, PLEASE? WHY DID THAT THING FALL?
STRESS TOLERANCE!
FINE! DON'T TELL US!
SIGH IT HAS NO SKELETAL STRUCTURE--SO IT COLLAPSED UNDER ITS OWN WEIGHT!
GREAT! THAT'LL GIVE US A HEAD START!
NOT IF IT SENDS THE HORDE AFTER US!
THEY'RE ALL FROZEN IN PLACE--AS IF THE MIND CONTROLLING IT IS CONFUSED!
NOT CONFUSED.
THINKING.
THE TINY FLESH-THING IS CORRECT. IF WE ARE TO WALK THIS WORLD, ADJUSTMENTS TO THE UNIBODY MUST BE MADE.
THIS...VELMA HAS A CLEVER MIND. A VIBRANT CONSCIOUSNESS.

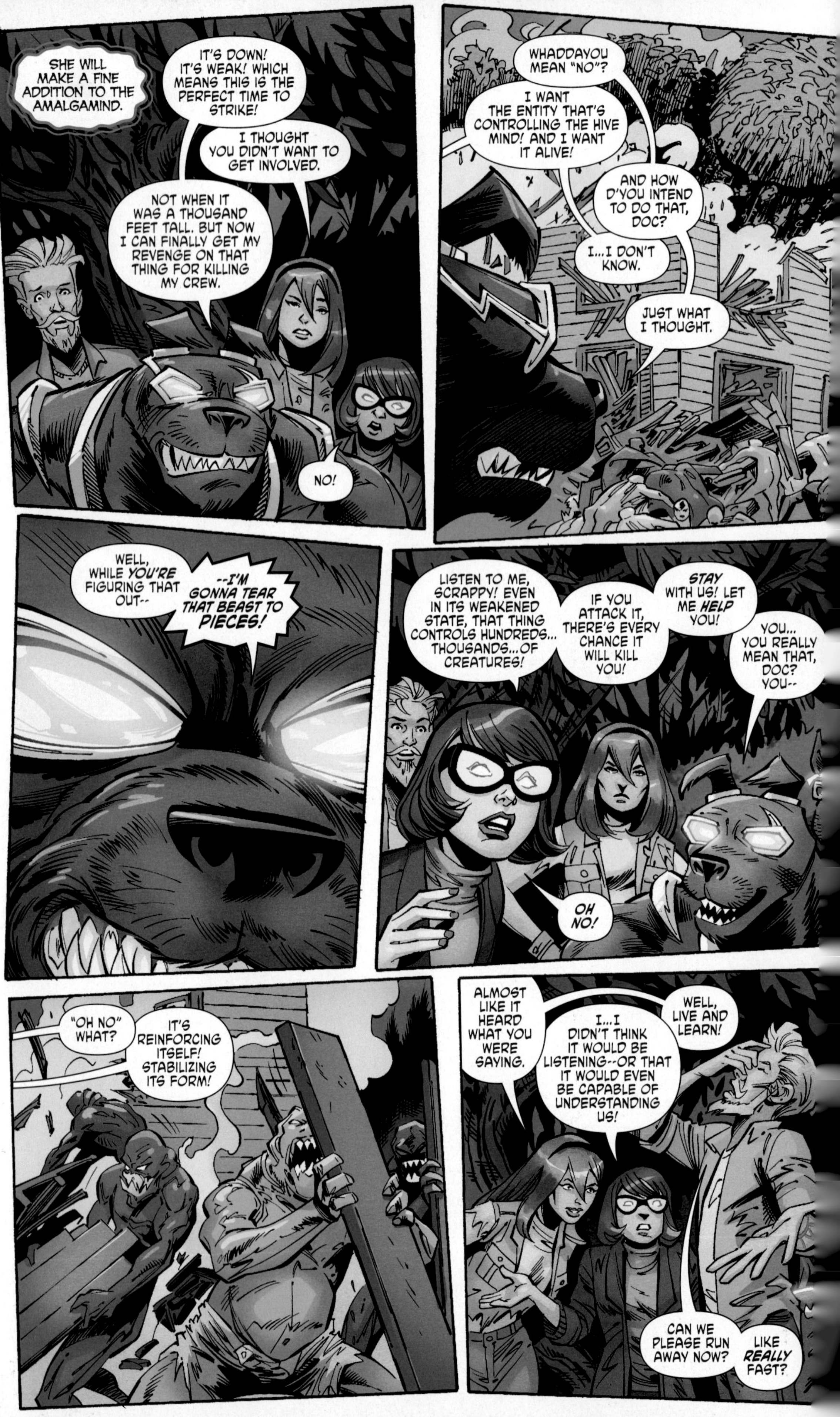

SHE WILL MAKE A FINE ADDITION TO THE AMALGAMIND.
IT'S DOWN! IT'S WEAK! WHICH MEANS THIS IS THE PERFECT TIME TO STRIKE!
I THOUGHT YOU DIDN'T WANT TO GET INVOLVED.
NOT WHEN IT WAS A THOUSAND FEET TALL. BUT NOW I CAN FINALLY GET MY REVENGE ON THAT THING FOR KILLING MY CREW.
NO!
WHADDAYOU MEAN "NO"?
I WANT THE ENTITY THAT'S CONTROLLING THE HIVE MIND! AND I WANT IT ALIVE!
AND HOW D'YOU INTEND TO DO THAT, DOC?
I...I DON'T KNOW.
JUST WHAT I THOUGHT.
WELL, WHILE *YOU'RE* FIGURING THAT OUT--
--I'M GONNA TEAR THAT BEAST TO PIECES!
LISTEN TO ME, SCRAPPY! EVEN IN ITS WEAKENED STATE, THAT THING CONTROLS HUNDREDS... THOUSANDS...OF CREATURES!
IF YOU ATTACK IT, THERE'S EVERY CHANCE IT WILL KILL YOU!
STAY WITH US! LET ME *HELP* YOU!
YOU... YOU REALLY MEAN THAT, DOC? YOU--
OH NO!
"OH NO" WHAT?
IT'S REINFORCING ITSELF! STABILIZING ITS FORM!
ALMOST LIKE IT HEARD WHAT YOU WERE SAYING.
I...I DIDN'T THINK IT WOULD BE LISTENING--OR THAT IT WOULD EVEN BE CAPABLE OF UNDERSTANDING US!
WELL, LIVE AND LEARN!
CAN WE PLEASE RUN AWAY NOW?
LIKE *REALLY* FAST?

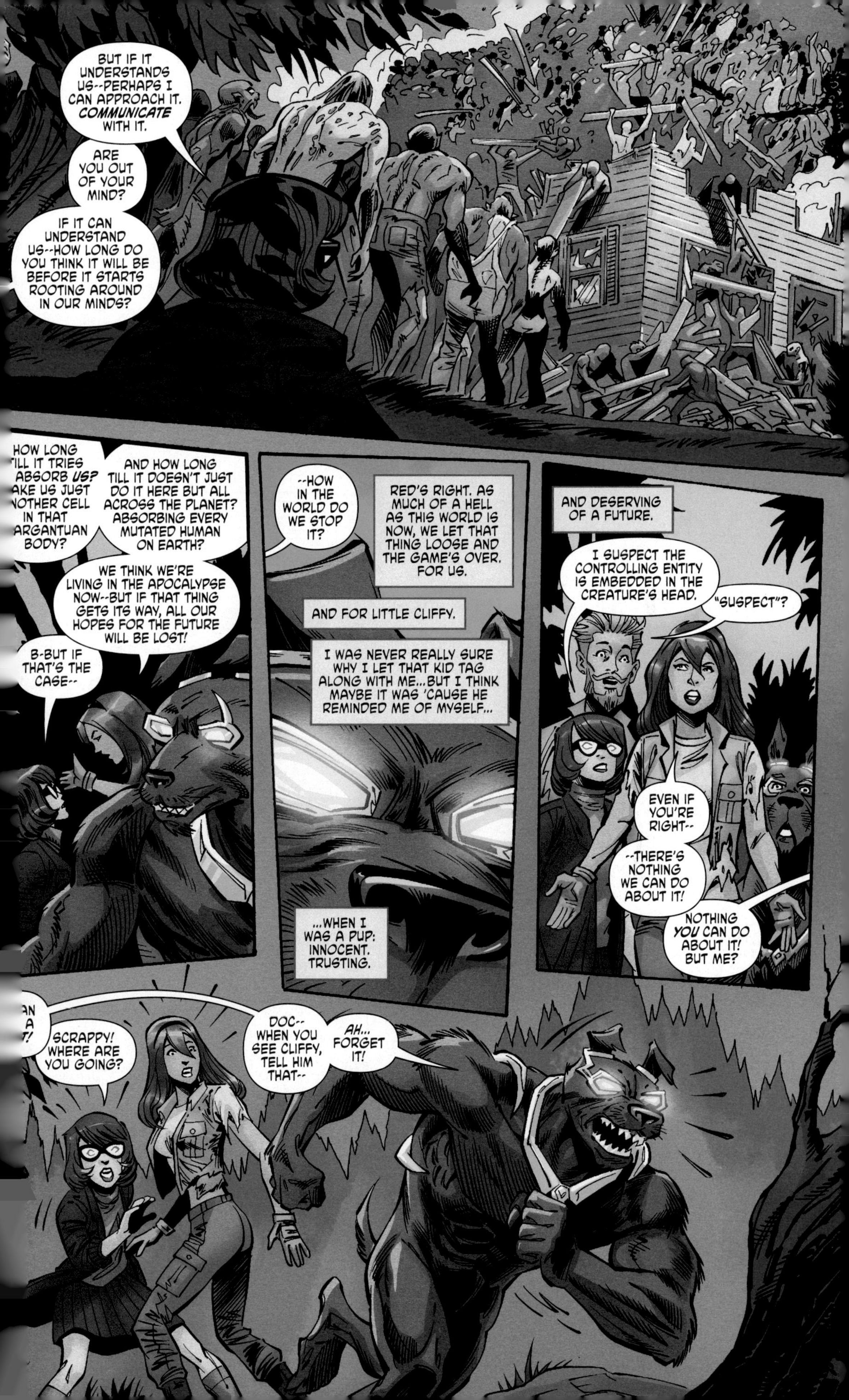

BUT IF IT UNDERSTANDS US--PERHAPS I CAN APPROACH IT. *COMMUNICATE* WITH IT.
ARE YOU OUT OF YOUR MIND?
IF IT CAN UNDERSTAND US--HOW LONG DO YOU THINK IT WILL BE BEFORE IT STARTS ROOTING AROUND IN OUR MINDS?
HOW LONG TILL IT TRIES ABSORB *US?* AKE US JUST NOTHER CELL IN THAT ARGANTUAN BODY?
AND HOW LONG TILL IT DOESN'T JUST DO IT HERE BUT ALL ACROSS THE PLANET? ABSORBING EVERY MUTATED HUMAN ON EARTH?
WE THINK WE'RE LIVING IN THE APOCALYPSE NOW--BUT IF THAT THING GETS ITS WAY, ALL OUR HOPES FOR THE FUTURE WILL BE LOST!
B-BUT IF THAT'S THE CASE--
--HOW IN THE WORLD DO WE STOP IT?
RED'S RIGHT. AS MUCH OF A HELL AS THIS WORLD IS NOW, WE LET THAT THING LOOSE AND THE GAME'S OVER. FOR US.
AND FOR LITTLE CLIFFY.
I WAS NEVER REALLY SURE WHY I LET THAT KID TAG ALONG WITH ME...BUT I THINK MAYBE IT WAS 'CAUSE HE REMINDED ME OF MYSELF...
...WHEN I WAS A PUP: INNOCENT. TRUSTING.
AND DESERVING OF A FUTURE.
I SUSPECT THE CONTROLLING ENTITY IS EMBEDDED IN THE CREATURE'S HEAD.
"SUSPECT"?
EVEN IF YOU'RE RIGHT--
--THERE'S NOTHING WE CAN DO ABOUT IT!
NOTHING *YOU* CAN DO ABOUT IT! BUT ME?
SCRAPPY! WHERE ARE YOU GOING?
DOC--WHEN YOU SEE CLIFFY, TELL HIM THAT--
AH... FORGET IT!

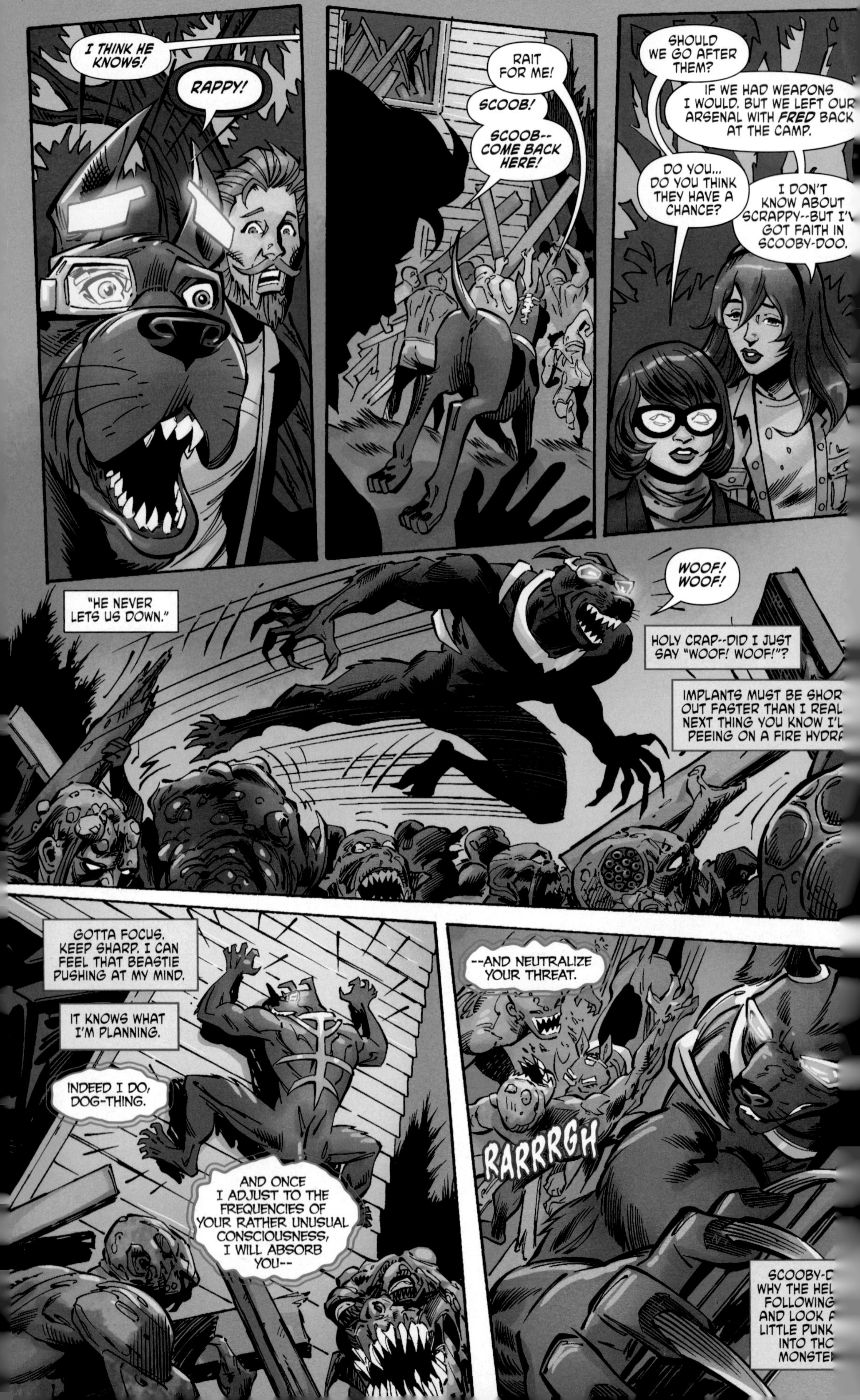
I THINK HE KNOWS!
RAPPY!
RAIT FOR ME!
SCOOB!
SCOOB-- COME BACK HERE!
SHOULD WE GO AFTER THEM?
IF WE HAD WEAPONS I WOULD. BUT WE LEFT OUR ARSENAL WITH FRED BACK AT THE CAMP.
DO YOU... DO YOU THINK THEY HAVE A CHANCE?
I DON'T KNOW ABOUT SCRAPPY--BUT I'V GOT FAITH IN SCOOBY-DOO.
"HE NEVER LETS US DOWN."
WOOF! WOOF!
HOLY CRAP--DID I JUST SAY "WOOF! WOOF!"?
IMPLANTS MUST BE SHOR OUT FASTER THAN I REAL NEXT THING YOU KNOW I'L PEEING ON A FIRE HYDRA
GOTTA FOCUS. KEEP SHARP. I CAN FEEL THAT BEASTIE PUSHING AT MY MIND.
IT KNOWS WHAT I'M PLANNING.
INDEED I DO, DOG-THING.
AND ONCE I ADJUST TO THE FREQUENCIES OF YOUR RATHER UNUSUAL CONSCIOUSNESS, I WILL ABSORB YOU--
--AND NEUTRALIZE YOUR THREAT.
RARRRGH
SCOOBY-D WHY THE HEL FOLLOWING AND LOOK A LITTLE PUNK INTO THO MONSTE

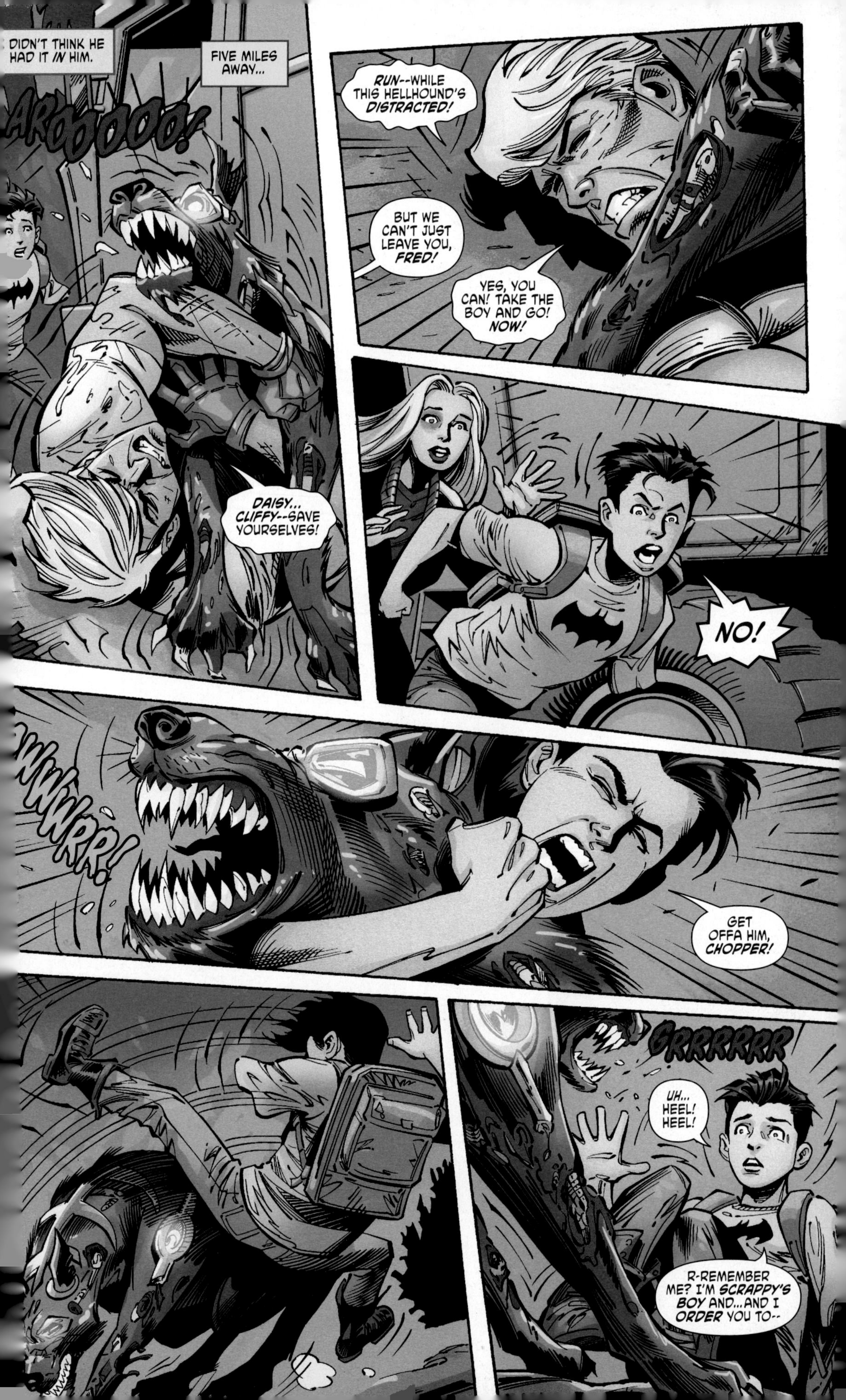

DIDN'T THINK HE HAD IT *IN* HIM.
FIVE MILES AWAY...
AROOOOO!
DAISY... CLIFFY--SAVE YOURSELVES!
RUN--WHILE THIS HELLHOUND'S *DISTRACTED!*
BUT WE CAN'T JUST LEAVE YOU, *FRED!*
YES, YOU CAN! TAKE THE BOY AND GO! *NOW!*
NO!
WWWRRR!
GET OFFA HIM, *CHOPPER!*
GRRRRRR
UH... HEEL! HEEL!
R-REMEMBER ME? I'M *SCRAPPY'S BOY* AND...AND I *ORDER* YOU TO--

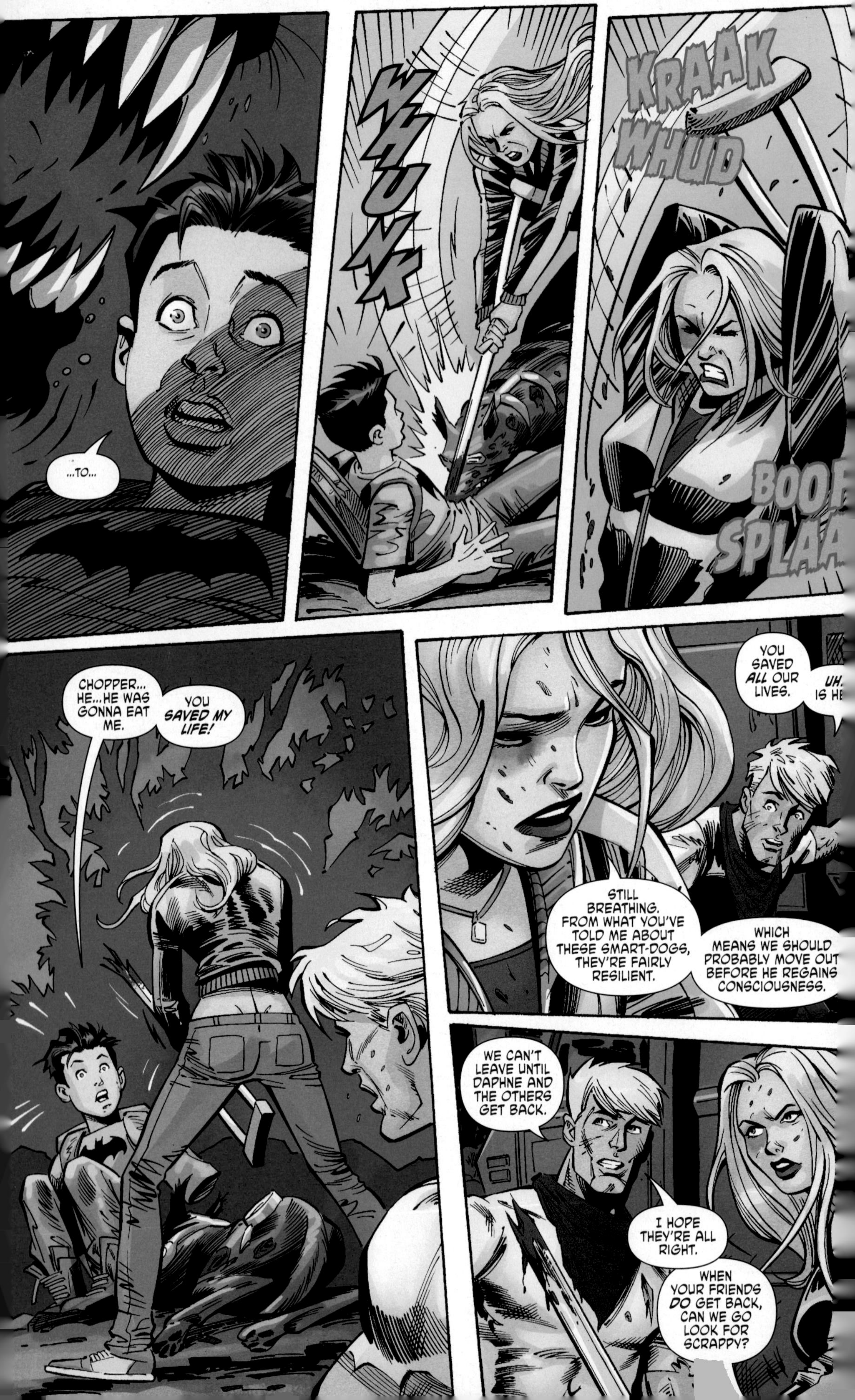

...TO...
WHUNK
KRAAK
WHUD
BOOF
SPLAA
CHOPPER... HE...HE WAS GONNA EAT ME.
YOU SAVED MY LIFE!
YOU SAVED ALL OUR LIVES.
UH. IS HE
STILL BREATHING. FROM WHAT YOU'VE TOLD ME ABOUT THESE SMART-DOGS, THEY'RE FAIRLY RESILIENT.
WHICH MEANS WE SHOULD PROBABLY MOVE OUT BEFORE HE REGAINS CONSCIOUSNESS.
WE CAN'T LEAVE UNTIL DAPHNE AND THE OTHERS GET BACK.
I HOPE THEY'RE ALL RIGHT.
WHEN YOUR FRIENDS DO GET BACK, CAN WE GO LOOK FOR SCRAPPY?

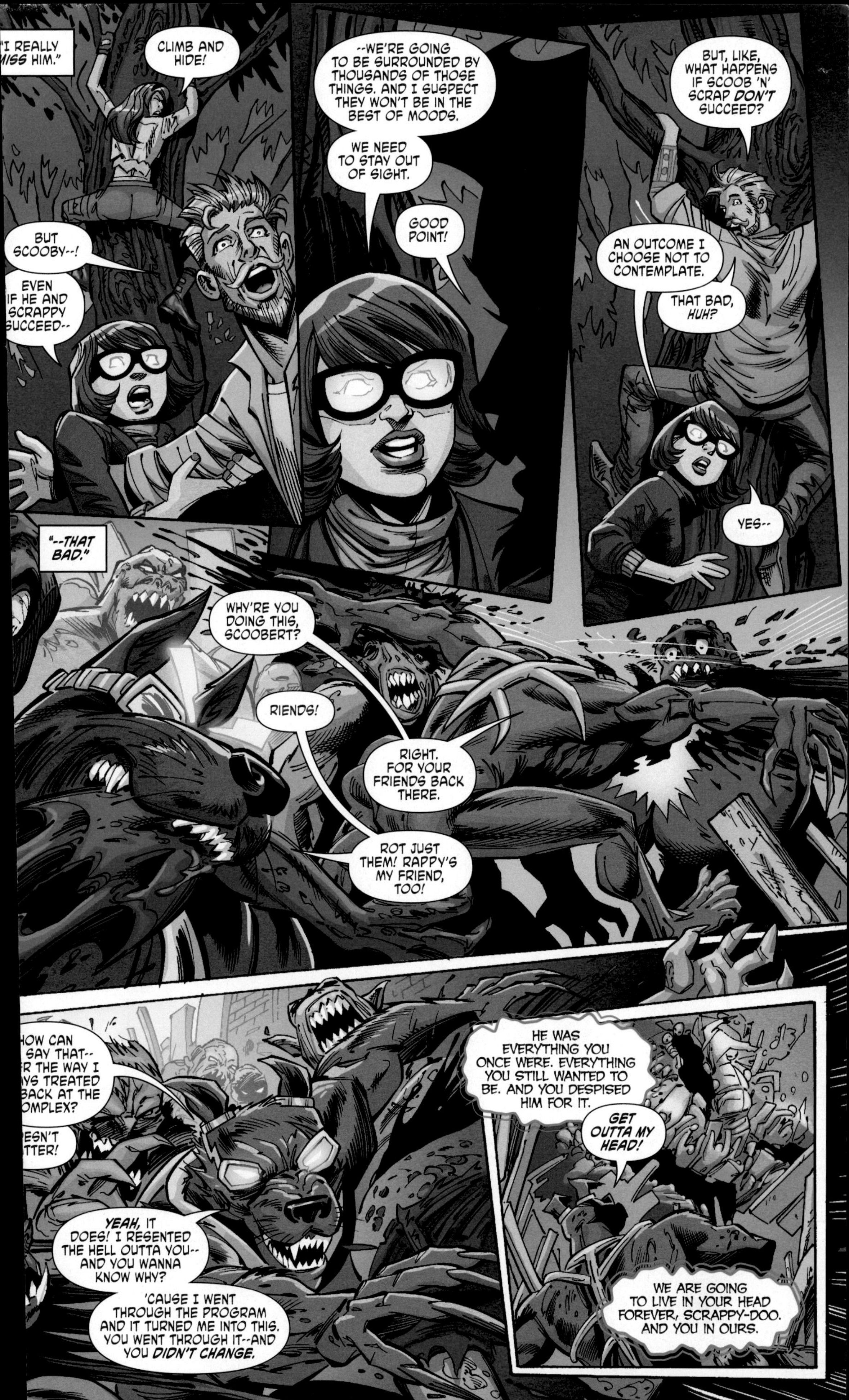
"I REALLY MISS HIM."
CLIMB AND HIDE!
BUT SCOOBY--!
EVEN IF HE AND SCRAPPY SUCCEED--
--WE'RE GOING TO BE SURROUNDED BY THOUSANDS OF THOSE THINGS. AND I SUSPECT THEY WON'T BE IN THE BEST OF MOODS.
WE NEED TO STAY OUT OF SIGHT.
GOOD POINT!
BUT, LIKE, WHAT HAPPENS IF SCOOB 'N' SCRAP DON'T SUCCEED?
AN OUTCOME I CHOOSE NOT TO CONTEMPLATE.
THAT BAD, HUH?
YES--
"--THAT BAD."
WHY'RE YOU DOING THIS, SCOOBERT?
RIENDS!
RIGHT. FOR YOUR FRIENDS BACK THERE.
ROT JUST THEM! RAPPY'S MY FRIEND, TOO!
HOW CAN SAY THAT-- ER THE WAY I AYS TREATED BACK AT THE OMPLEX?
ESN'T TTER!
YEAH, IT DOES! I RESENTED THE HELL OUTTA YOU-- AND YOU WANNA KNOW WHY?
'CAUSE I WENT THROUGH THE PROGRAM AND IT TURNED ME INTO THIS. YOU WENT THROUGH IT--AND YOU DIDN'T CHANGE.
HE WAS EVERYTHING YOU ONCE WERE. EVERYTHING YOU STILL WANTED TO BE. AND YOU DESPISED HIM FOR IT.
GET OUTTA MY HEAD!
WE ARE GOING TO LIVE IN YOUR HEAD FOREVER, SCRAPPY-DOO. AND YOU IN OURS.

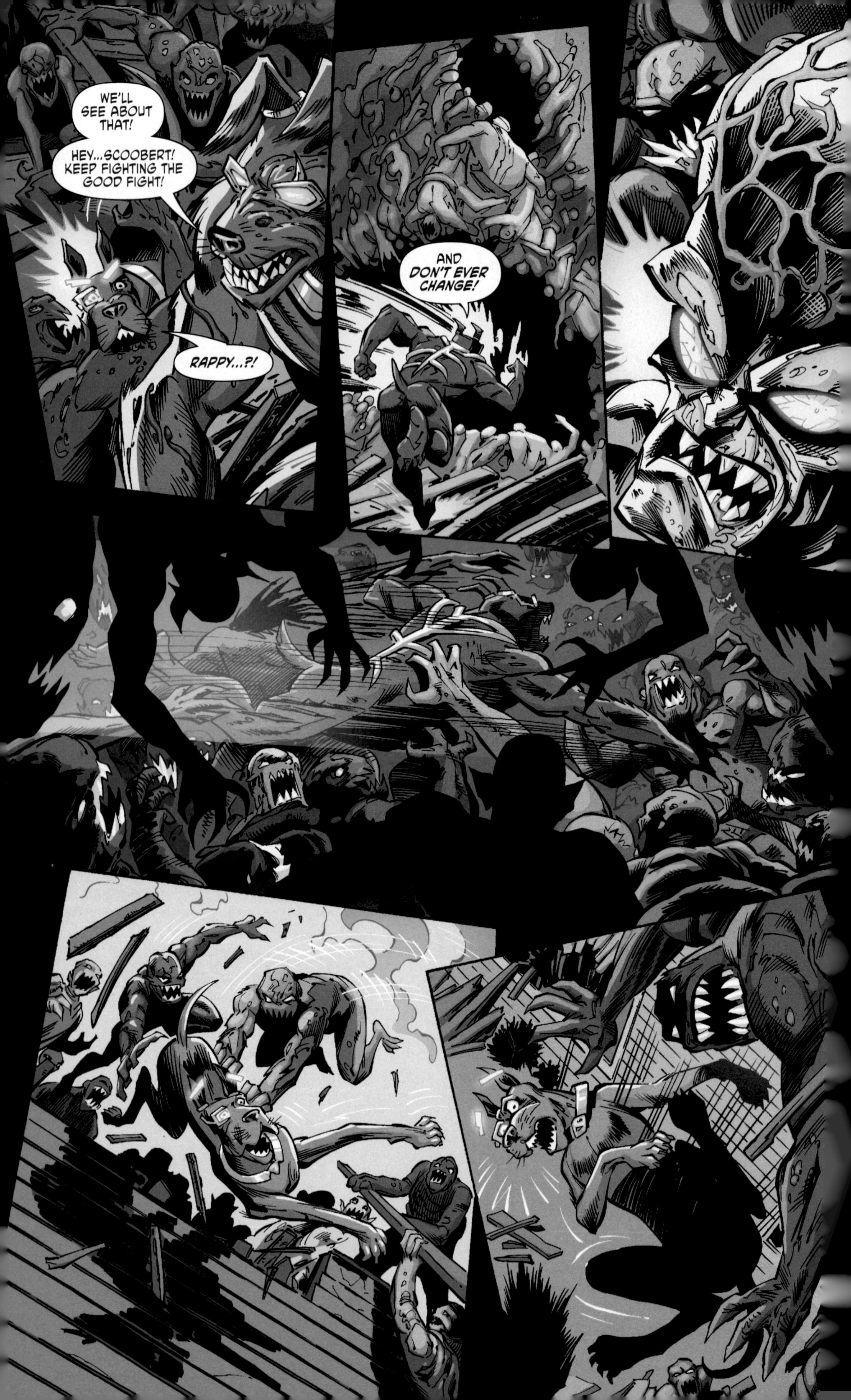
WE'LL SEE ABOUT THAT!
HEY...SCOOBERT! KEEP FIGHTING THE GOOD FIGHT!
RAPPY...?!
AND DON'T EVER CHANGE!

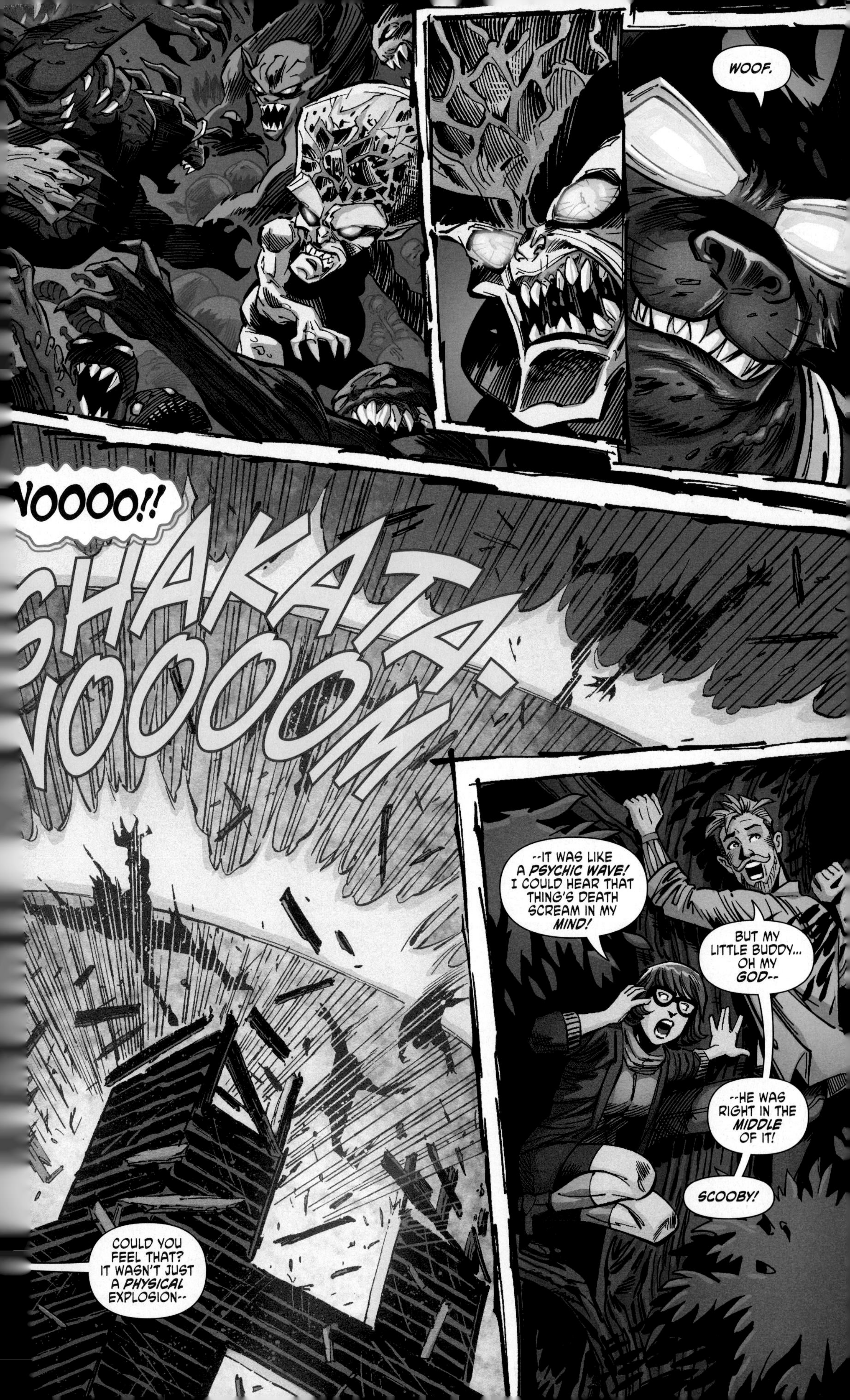
WOOF.
NOOOO!!
SHAKATA-VOOOOOM
COULD YOU FEEL THAT? IT WASN'T JUST A PHYSICAL EXPLOSION--
--IT WAS LIKE A PSYCHIC WAVE! I COULD HEAR THAT THING'S DEATH SCREAM IN MY MIND!
BUT MY LITTLE BUDDY... OH MY GOD--
--HE WAS RIGHT IN THE MIDDLE OF IT!
SCOOBY!

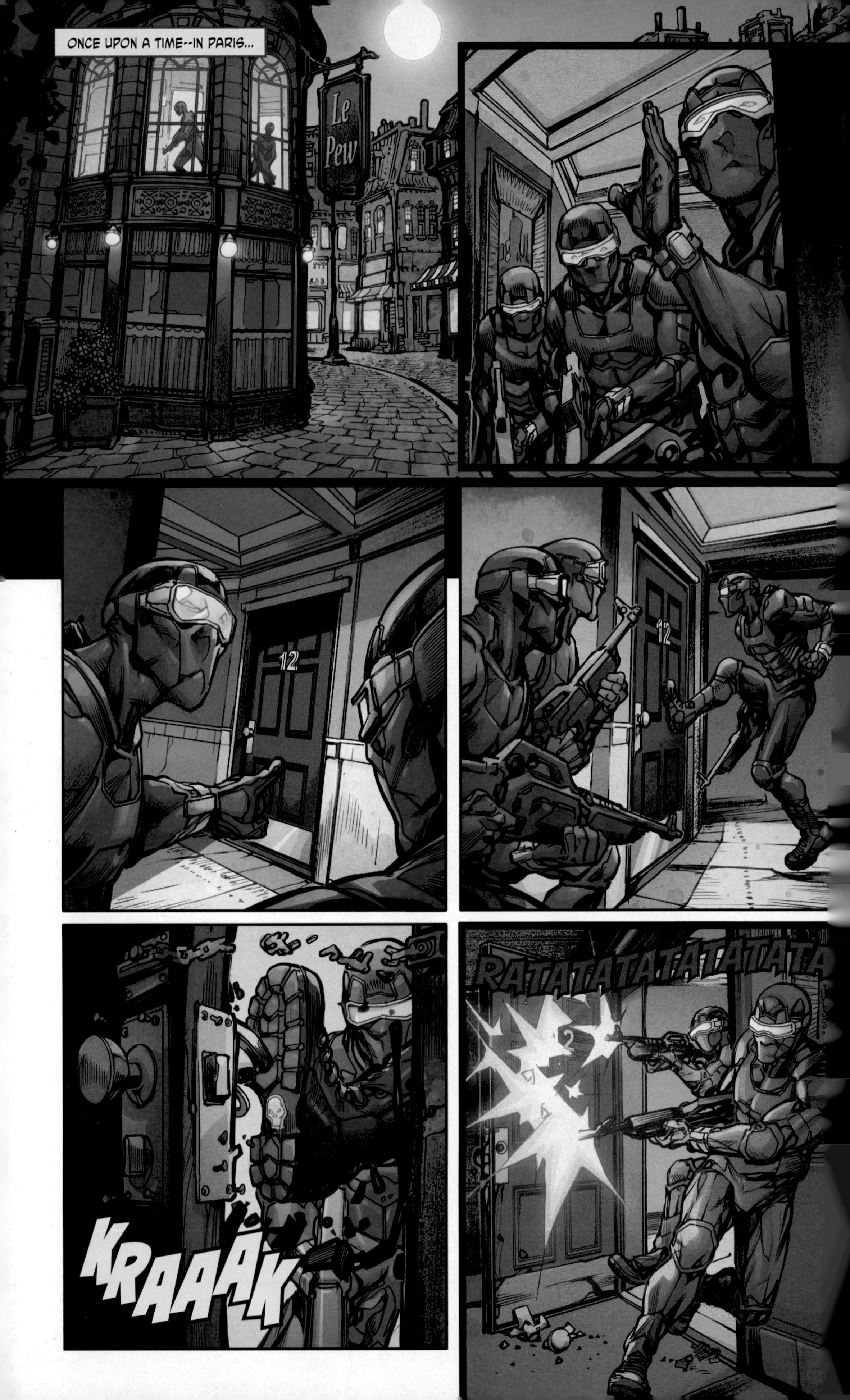
ONCE UPON A TIME--IN PARIS...
Le Pew
12
KRAAAK
RATATATATATATA

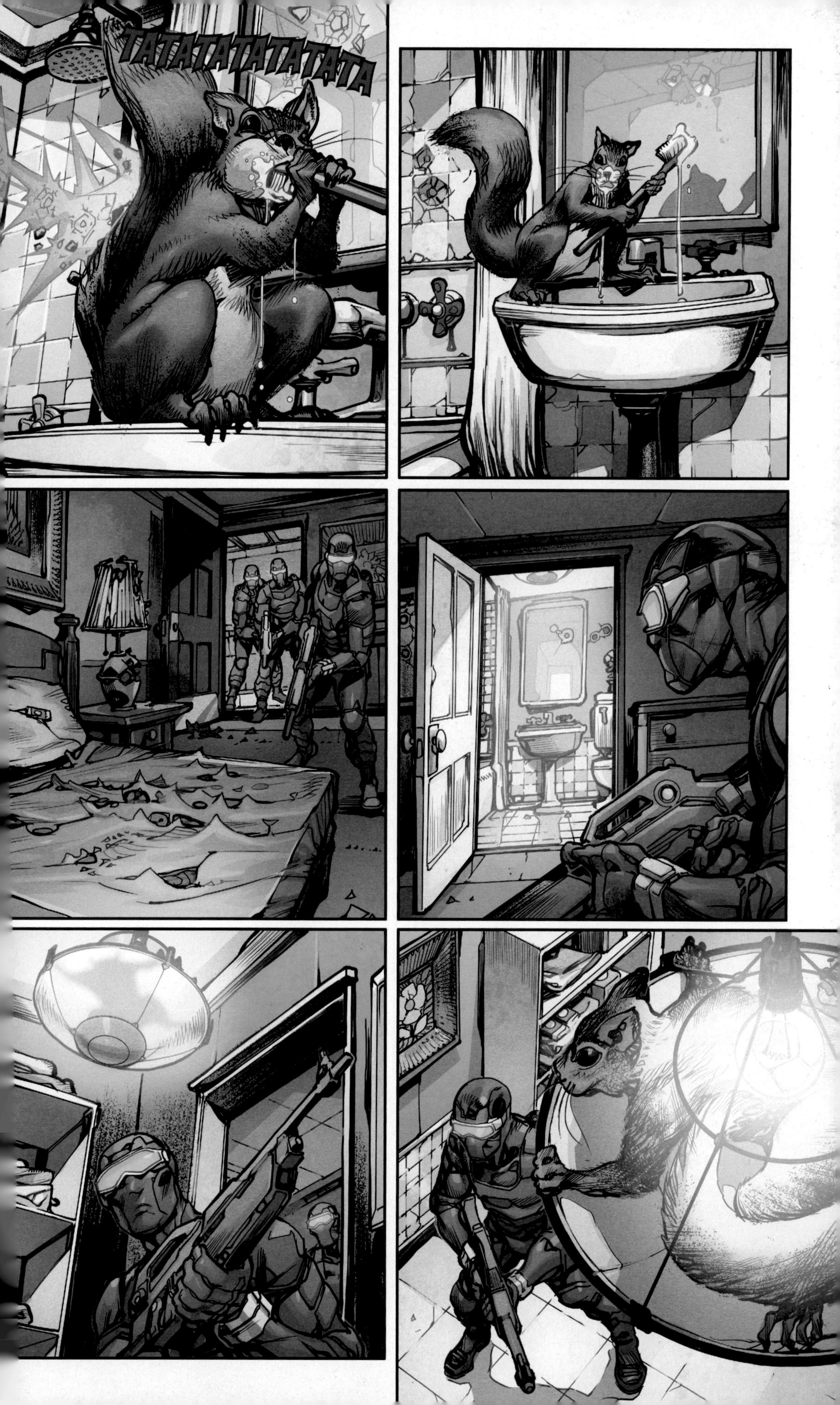
TATATATATATATA

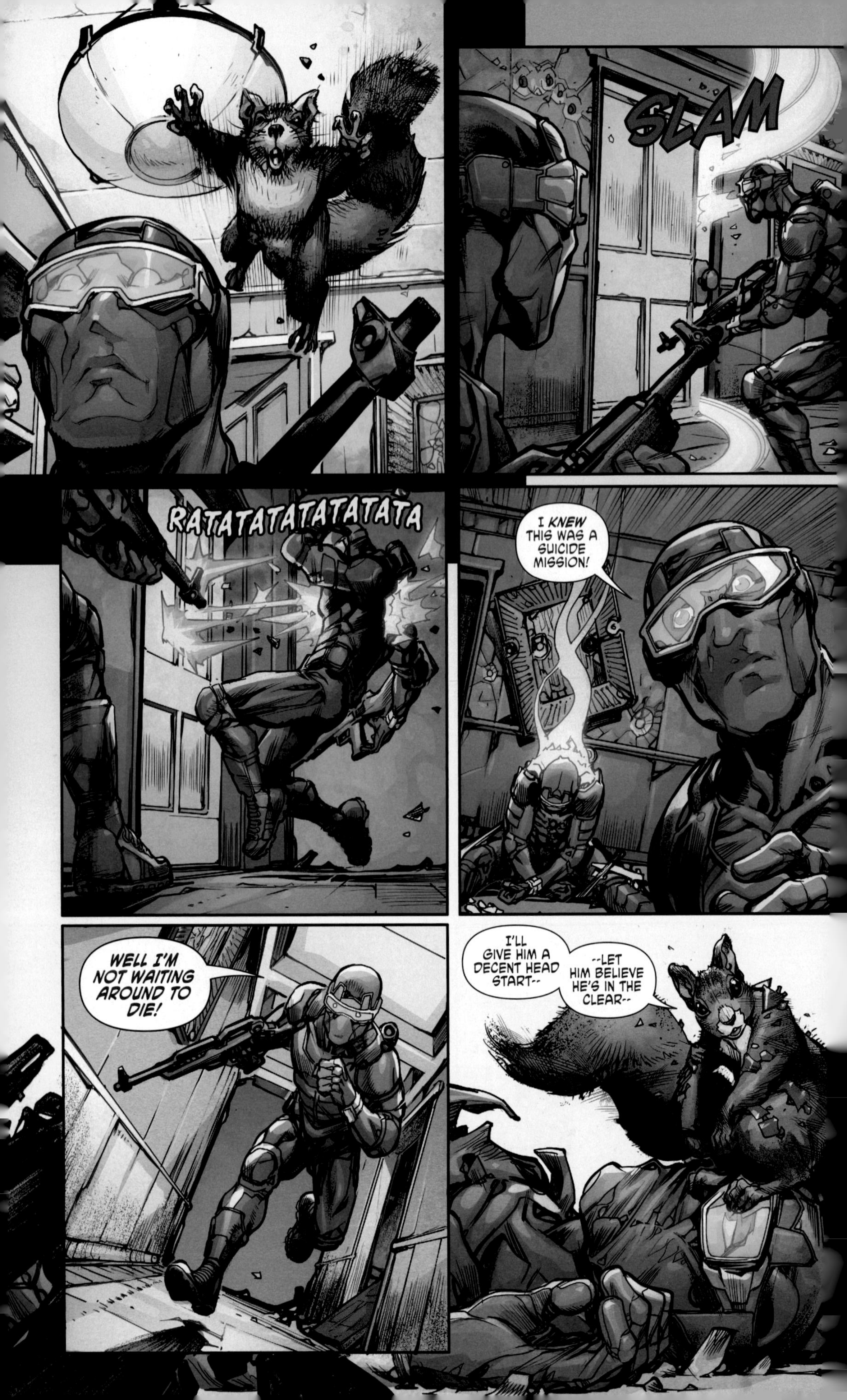
SLAM
RATATATATATATATA
I *KNEW* THIS WAS A SUICIDE MISSION!
WELL I'M NOT WAITING AROUND TO DIE!
I'LL GIVE HIM A DECENT HEAD START--
--LET HIM BELIEVE HE'S IN THE CLEAR--

"--AND *THEN* I'LL KILL HIM!"

'MORNING, *MELL.*

GOOD MORNING, *OOO.*

I.S.S.

U.S. HEADQUARTERS, LANGLEY, VIRGINIA...

IS THE CHIEF IN?

YES. AND HE'S IN A WRETCHED MOOD.

BOINK

BOINNNK

NATURALLY!

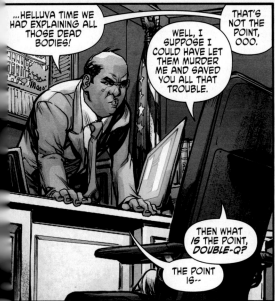

...HELLUVA TIME WE HAD EXPLAINING ALL THOSE DEAD BODIES!

THAT'S NOT THE POINT, *OOO.*

WELL, I SUPPOSE I COULD HAVE LET THEM MURDER ME AND SAVED YOU ALL THAT TROUBLE.

THEN WHAT *IS* THE POINT, *DOUBLE-Q?*

THE POINT IS--

--YOU WERE BETRAYED. BY A WOMAN. *AGAIN.*

OKAY, SO *PENNY* LEAKED MY IDENTITY TO *HY-SPY'S* GOONS. WE SUSPECTED SHE WAS A DOUBLE-AGENT GOING IN.

AND NOW WE HAVE PROOF.

AND THE ENCRYPTED FILES NAMING ALL THE POLITICIANS HY-SPY HAS COMPROMISED.

YOU SECURED THE FILES? HOW?

CHARM AND MENACE: MY TWO GREATEST QUALITIES.

WELL, LET'S HOPE THOSE QUALITIES HELP YOU WITH THIS MISSION.

SORRY, CHIEF-- I HAVE PLANS. A WEEKEND IN NORTHERN CALIFORNIA WITH TWIN SISTERS WHO CAN'T RESIST THE ALLURE OF A BUSHY TAIL.

CANCEL THEM--

--AND *READ THIS!*

DR. ROSA PINSK? NEVER HEARD OF HER.

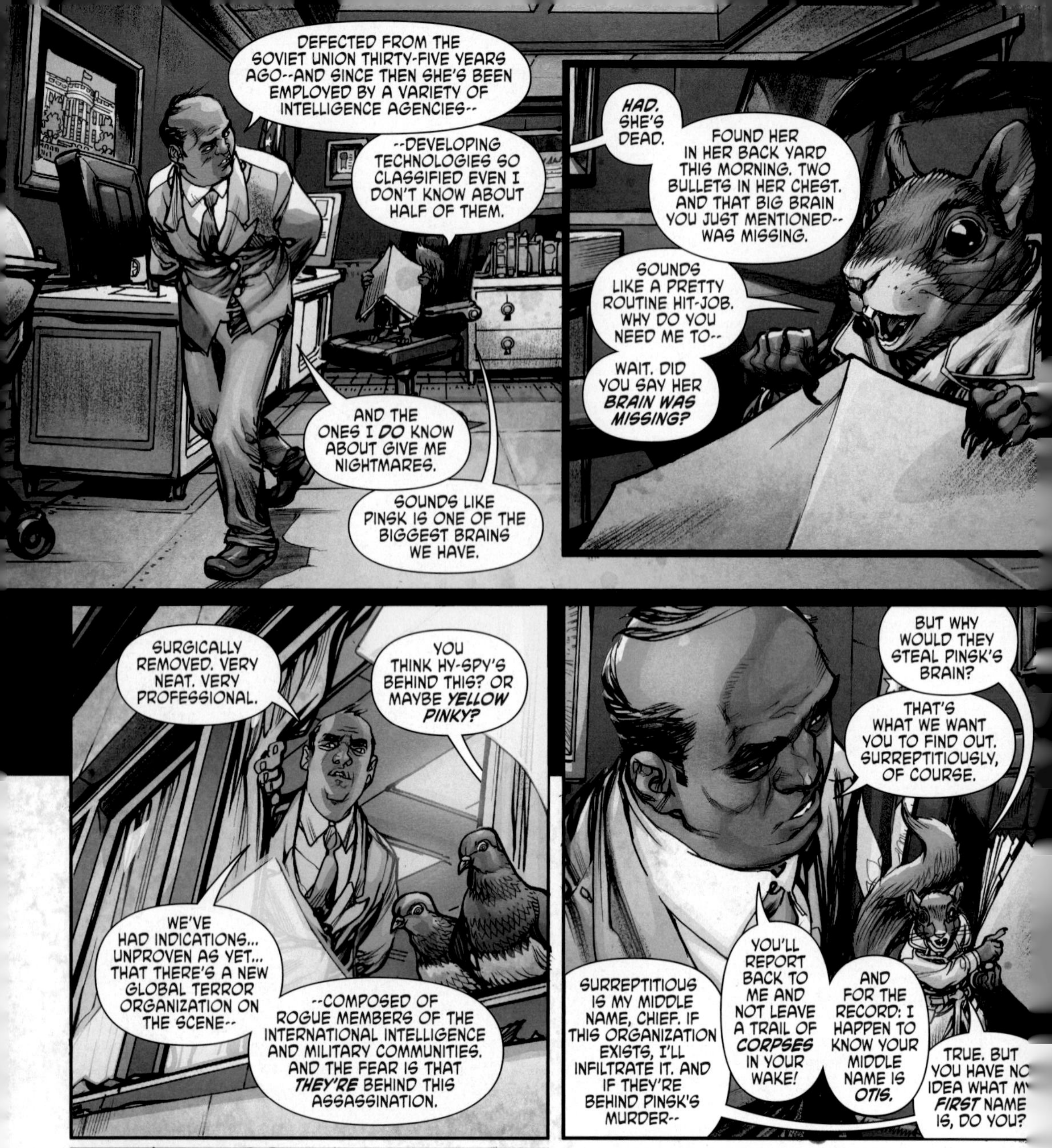
DEFECTED FROM THE SOVIET UNION THIRTY-FIVE YEARS AGO--AND SINCE THEN SHE'S BEEN EMPLOYED BY A VARIETY OF INTELLIGENCE AGENCIES--
--DEVELOPING TECHNOLOGIES SO CLASSIFIED EVEN I DON'T KNOW ABOUT HALF OF THEM.
AND THE ONES I *DO* KNOW ABOUT GIVE ME NIGHTMARES.
SOUNDS LIKE PINSK IS ONE OF THE BIGGEST BRAINS WE HAVE.
HAD. SHE'S DEAD.
FOUND HER IN HER BACK YARD THIS MORNING. TWO BULLETS IN HER CHEST. AND THAT BIG BRAIN YOU JUST MENTIONED--WAS MISSING.
SOUNDS LIKE A PRETTY ROUTINE HIT-JOB. WHY DO YOU NEED ME TO--
WAIT. DID YOU SAY HER *BRAIN WAS MISSING?*
SURGICALLY REMOVED. VERY NEAT. VERY PROFESSIONAL.
YOU THINK HY-SPY'S BEHIND THIS? OR MAYBE *YELLOW PINKY?*
WE'VE HAD INDICATIONS... UNPROVEN AS YET... THAT THERE'S A NEW GLOBAL TERROR ORGANIZATION ON THE SCENE--
--COMPOSED OF ROGUE MEMBERS OF THE INTERNATIONAL INTELLIGENCE AND MILITARY COMMUNITIES. AND THE FEAR IS THAT *THEY'RE* BEHIND THIS ASSASSINATION.
BUT WHY WOULD THEY STEAL PINSK'S BRAIN?
THAT'S WHAT WE WANT YOU TO FIND OUT. SURREPTITIOUSLY, OF COURSE.
SURREPTITIOUS IS MY MIDDLE NAME, CHIEF. IF THIS ORGANIZATION EXISTS, I'LL INFILTRATE IT. AND IF THEY'RE BEHIND PINSK'S MURDER--
YOU'LL REPORT BACK TO ME AND NOT LEAVE A TRAIL OF *CORPSES* IN YOUR WAKE!
AND FOR THE RECORD: I HAPPEN TO KNOW YOUR MIDDLE NAME IS *OTIS.*
TRUE. BUT YOU HAVE NO IDEA WHAT MY *FIRST* NAME IS, DO YOU?

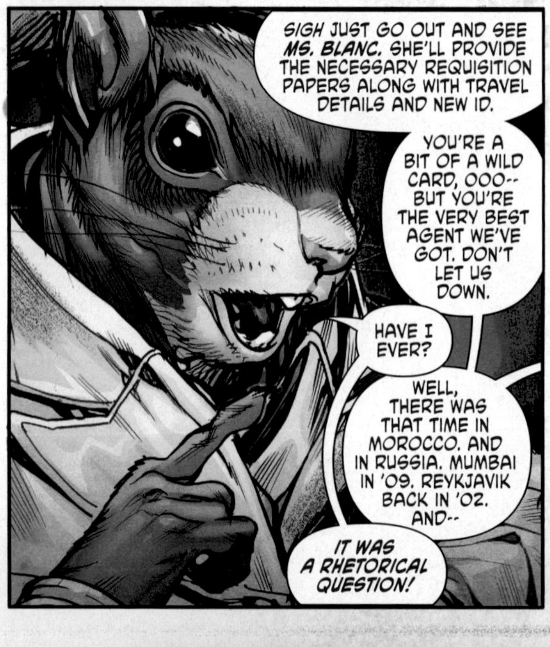
SIGH JUST GO OUT AND SEE *MS. BLANC.* SHE'LL PROVIDE THE NECESSARY REQUISITION PAPERS ALONG WITH TRAVEL DETAILS AND NEW ID.
YOU'RE A BIT OF A WILD CARD, OOO--BUT YOU'RE THE VERY BEST AGENT WE'VE GOT. DON'T LET US DOWN.
HAVE I EVER?
WELL, THERE WAS THAT TIME IN MOROCCO. AND IN RUSSIA. MUMBAI IN '09. REYKJAVIK BACK IN '02. AND--
IT WAS A RHETORICAL QUESTION!

SECRET SQUIRREL!

A Giffen-DeMatteis-Porter production

Hi-Fi
Colors

Travis Lanham
Letters

Brittany Holzherr
Assoc. Editor

Marie Javins
Under Surveillance

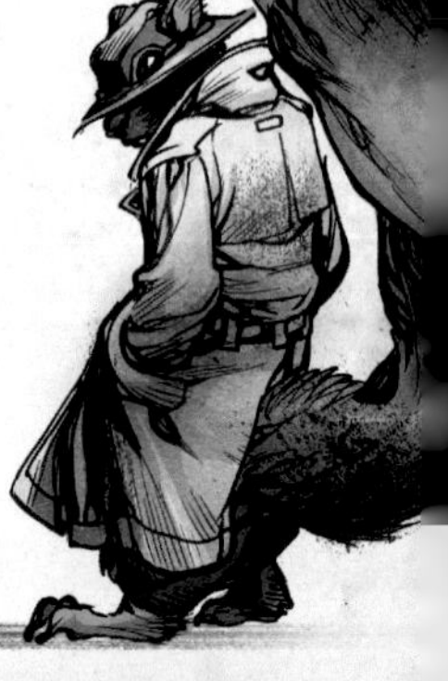

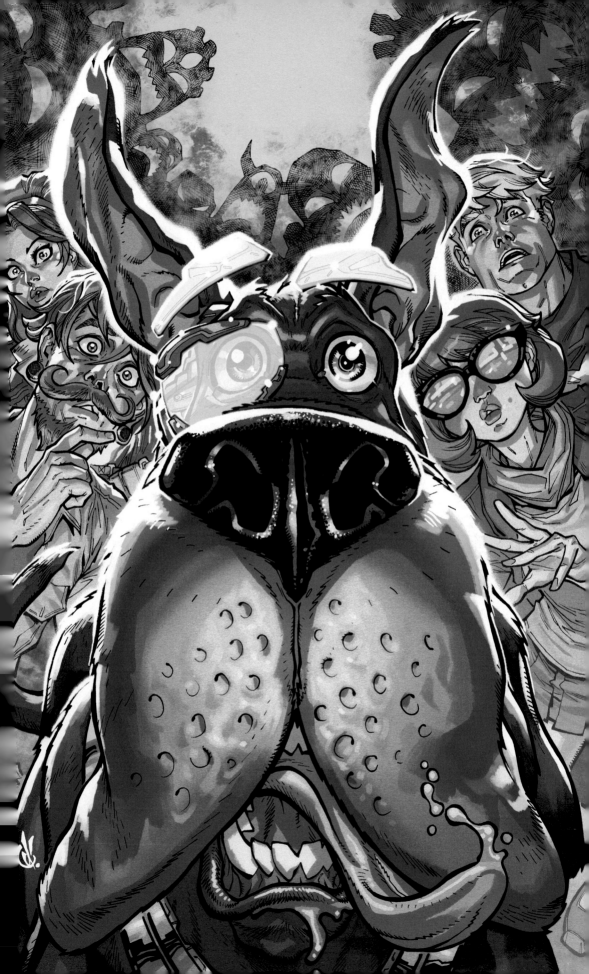

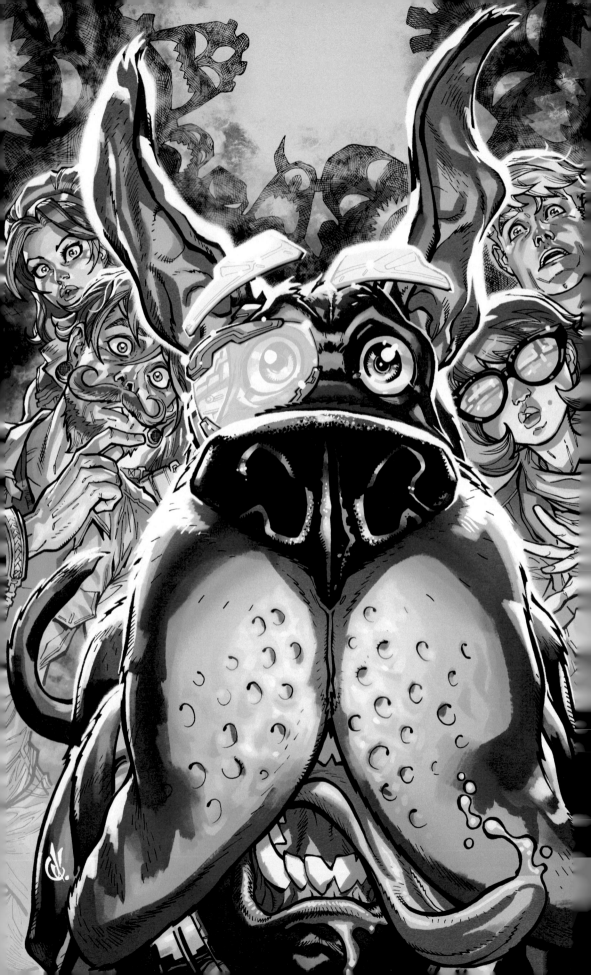

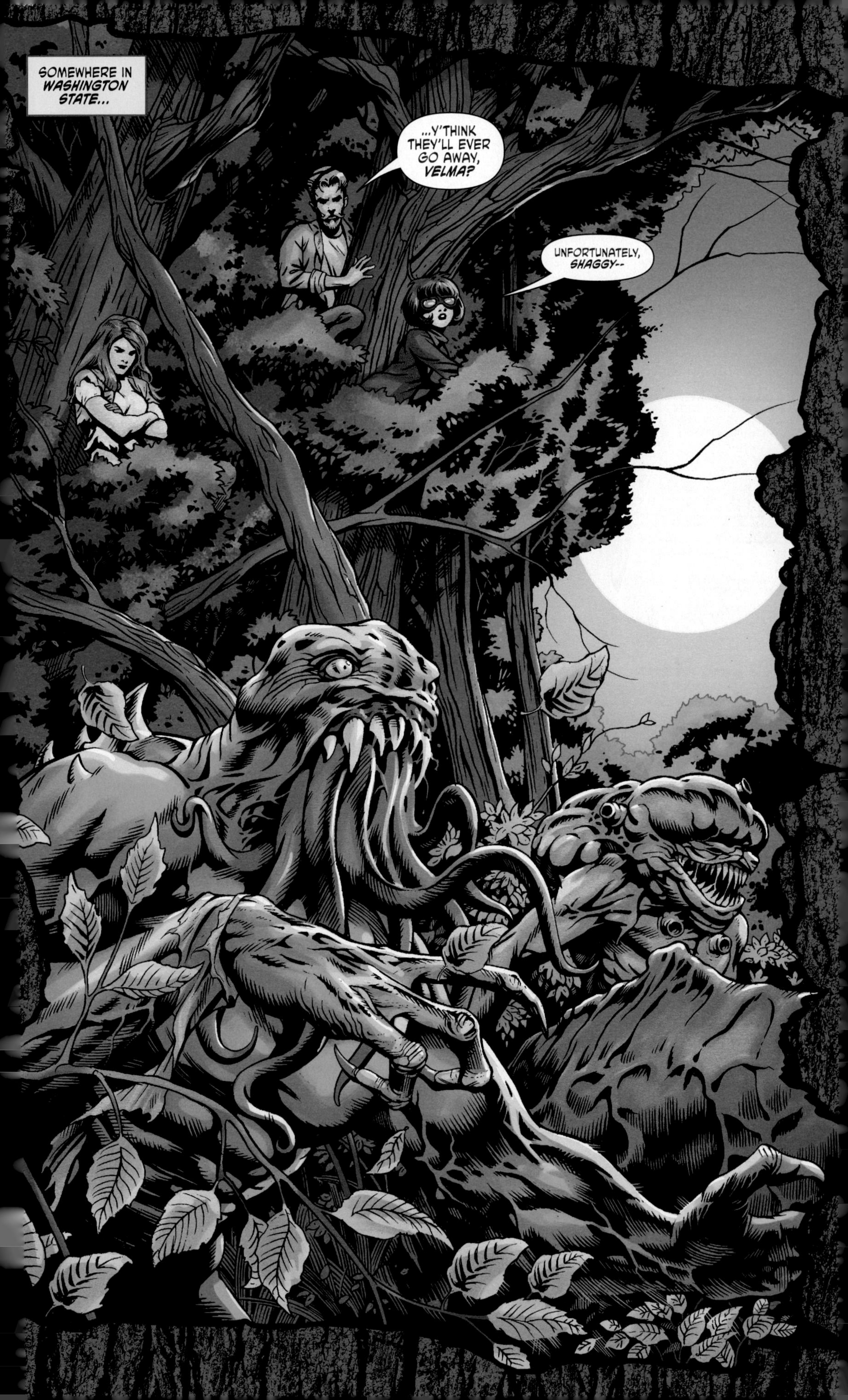
SOMEWHERE IN WASHINGTON STATE...
...Y'THINK THEY'LL EVER GO AWAY, VELMA?
UNFORTUNATELY, SHAGGY--

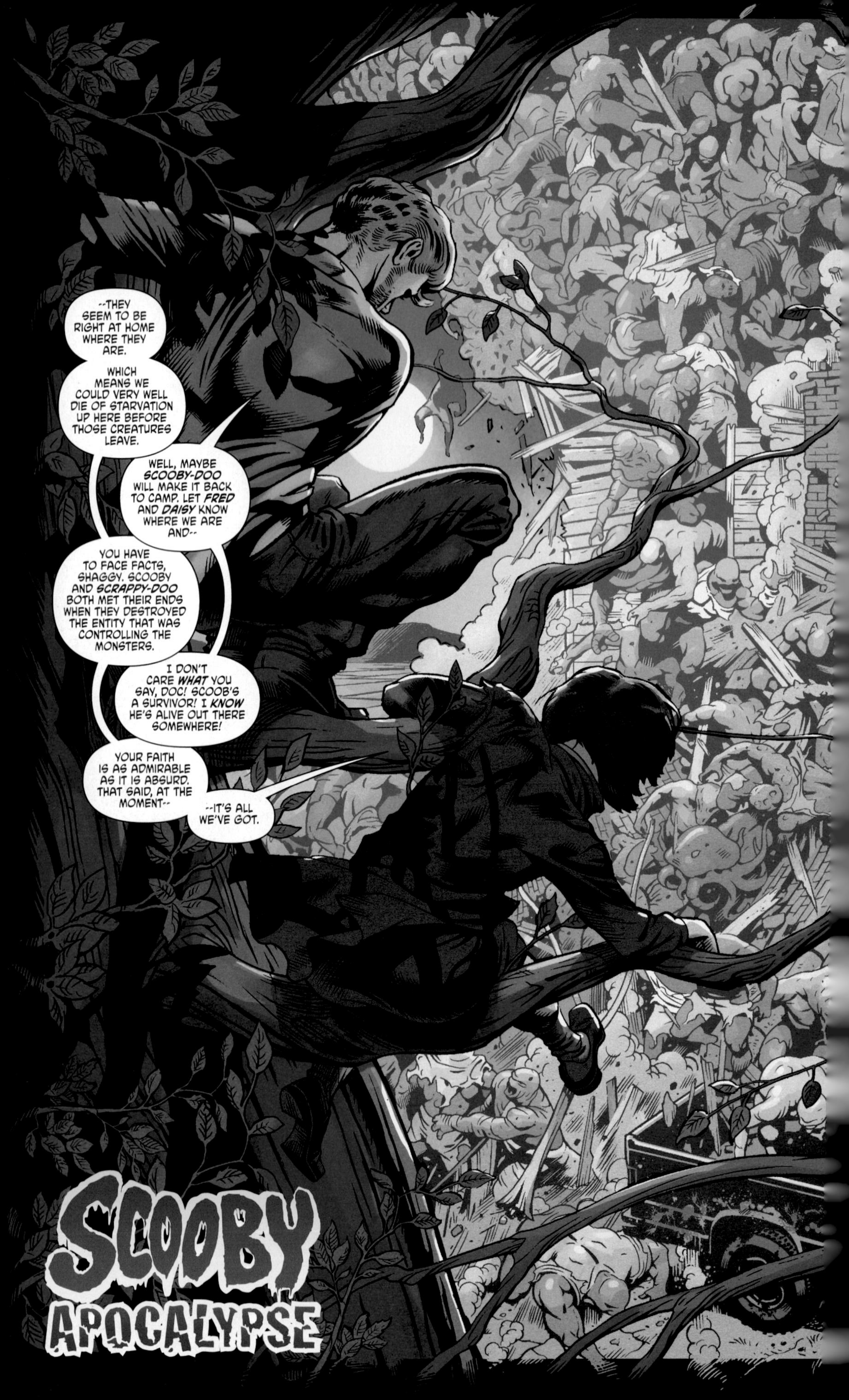
--THEY SEEM TO BE RIGHT AT HOME WHERE THEY ARE.
WHICH MEANS WE COULD VERY WELL DIE OF STARVATION UP HERE BEFORE THOSE CREATURES LEAVE.
WELL, MAYBE SCOOBY-DOO WILL MAKE IT BACK TO CAMP. LET FRED AND DAISY KNOW WHERE WE ARE AND--
YOU HAVE TO FACE FACTS, SHAGGY. SCOOBY AND SCRAPPY-DOO BOTH MET THEIR ENDS WHEN THEY DESTROYED THE ENTITY THAT WAS CONTROLLING THE MONSTERS.
I DON'T CARE WHAT YOU SAY, DOC! SCOOB'S A SURVIVOR! I KNOW HE'S ALIVE OUT THERE SOMEWHERE!
YOUR FAITH IS AS ADMIRABLE AS IT IS ABSURD. THAT SAID, AT THE MOMENT--
--IT'S ALL WE'VE GOT.
SCOOBY
APOCALYPSE

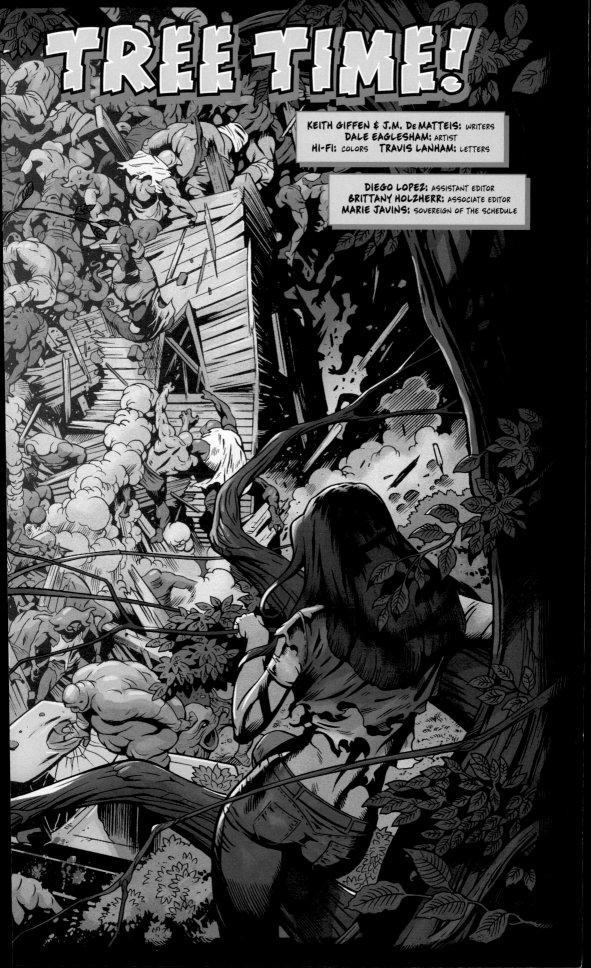

TREE TIME!

KEITH GIFFEN & J.M. DeMATTEIS: WRITERS
DALE EAGLESHAM: ARTIST
HI-FI: COLORS   TRAVIS LANHAM: LETTERS

DIEGO LOPEZ: ASSISTANT EDITOR
BRITTANY HOLZHERR: ASSOCIATE EDITOR
MARIE JAVINS: SOVEREIGN OF THE SCHEDULE

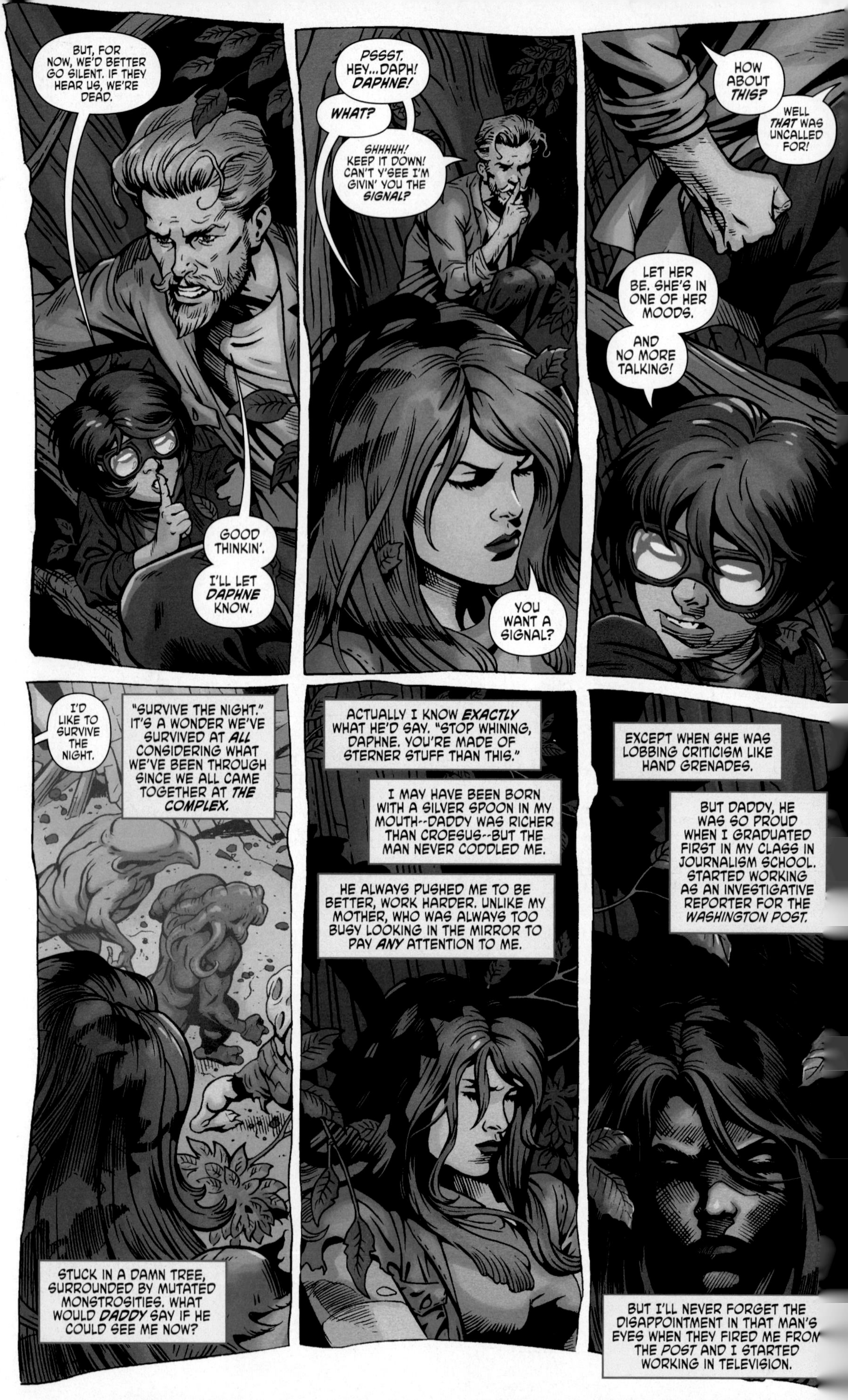
BUT, FOR NOW, WE'D BETTER GO SILENT. IF THEY HEAR US, WE'RE DEAD.
GOOD THINKIN'.
I'LL LET DAPHNE KNOW.
PSSST. HEY...DAPH! DAPHNE!
WHAT?
SHHHHH! KEEP IT DOWN! CAN'T Y'SEE I'M GIVIN' YOU THE SIGNAL?
YOU WANT A SIGNAL?
HOW ABOUT THIS?
WELL THAT WAS UNCALLED FOR!
LET HER BE. SHE'S IN ONE OF HER MOODS.
AND NO MORE TALKING!
I'D LIKE TO SURVIVE THE NIGHT.
"SURVIVE THE NIGHT." IT'S A WONDER WE'VE SURVIVED AT ALL CONSIDERING WHAT WE'VE BEEN THROUGH SINCE WE ALL CAME TOGETHER AT THE COMPLEX.
STUCK IN A DAMN TREE, SURROUNDED BY MUTATED MONSTROSITIES. WHAT WOULD DADDY SAY IF HE COULD SEE ME NOW?
ACTUALLY I KNOW EXACTLY WHAT HE'D SAY. "STOP WHINING, DAPHNE. YOU'RE MADE OF STERNER STUFF THAN THIS."
I MAY HAVE BEEN BORN WITH A SILVER SPOON IN MY MOUTH--DADDY WAS RICHER THAN CROESUS--BUT THE MAN NEVER CODDLED ME.
HE ALWAYS PUSHED ME TO BE BETTER, WORK HARDER. UNLIKE MY MOTHER, WHO WAS ALWAYS TOO BUSY LOOKING IN THE MIRROR TO PAY ANY ATTENTION TO ME.
EXCEPT WHEN SHE WAS LOBBING CRITICISM LIKE HAND GRENADES.
BUT DADDY, HE WAS SO PROUD WHEN I GRADUATED FIRST IN MY CLASS IN JOURNALISM SCHOOL. STARTED WORKING AS AN INVESTIGATIVE REPORTER FOR THE WASHINGTON POST.
BUT I'LL NEVER FORGET THE DISAPPOINTMENT IN THAT MAN'S EYES WHEN THEY FIRED ME FROM THE POST AND I STARTED WORKING IN TELEVISION.

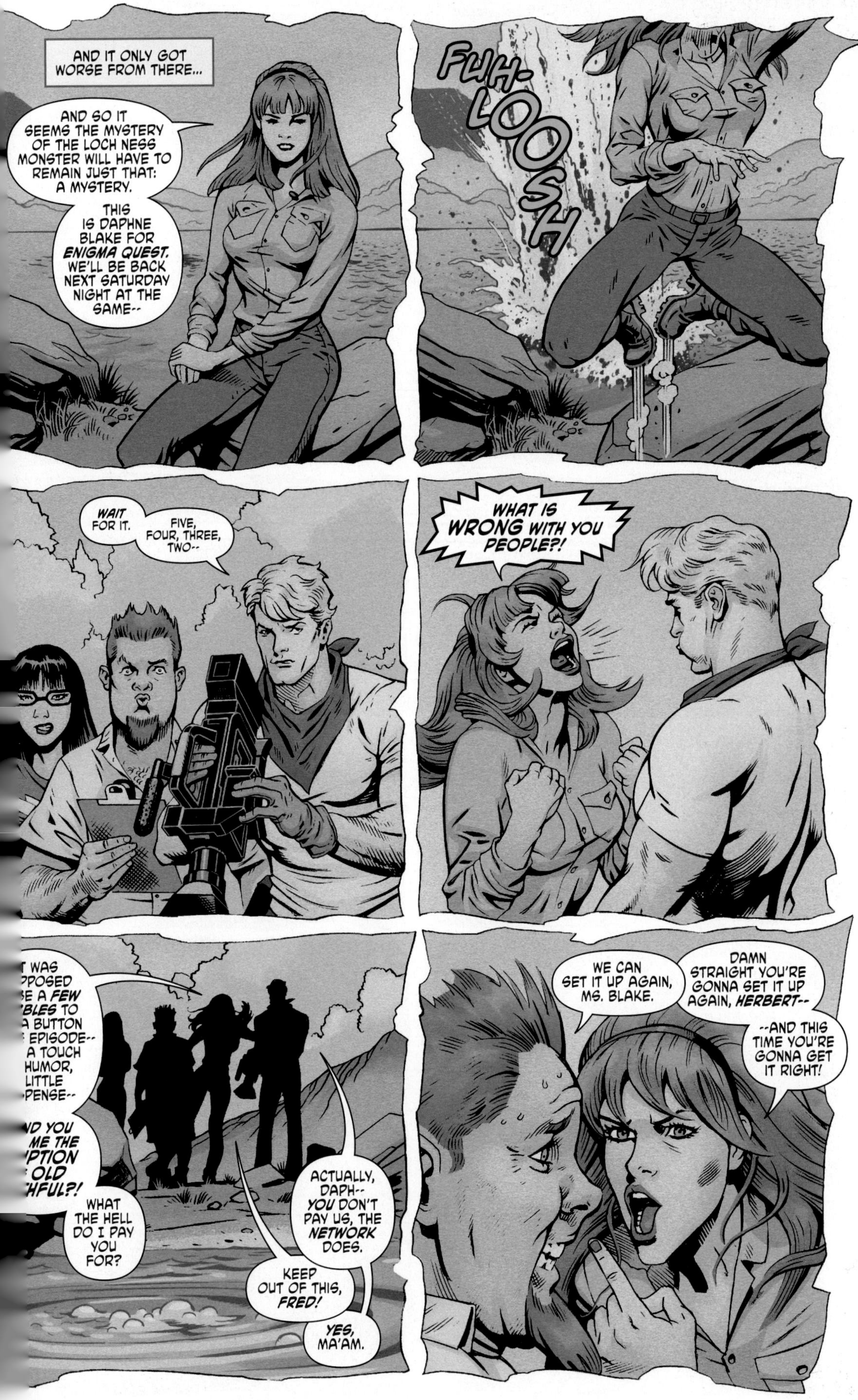
AND IT ONLY GOT WORSE FROM THERE...
AND SO IT SEEMS THE MYSTERY OF THE LOCH NESS MONSTER WILL HAVE TO REMAIN JUST THAT: A MYSTERY.
THIS IS DAPHNE BLAKE FOR *ENIGMA QUEST.* WE'LL BE BACK NEXT SATURDAY NIGHT AT THE SAME--
FUH-LOOSH
WAIT FOR IT.
FIVE, FOUR, THREE, TWO--
WHAT IS *WRONG* WITH YOU PEOPLE?!
T WAS PPOSED E A *FEW BLES* TO A BUTTON EPISODE-- A TOUCH HUMOR, LITTLE PENSE--
ND YOU ME THE PTION OLD HFUL?!
WHAT THE HELL DO I PAY YOU FOR?
ACTUALLY, DAPH-- *YOU* DON'T PAY US, THE *NETWORK* DOES.
KEEP OUT OF THIS, *FRED!*
YES, MA'AM.
WE CAN SET IT UP AGAIN, MS. BLAKE.
DAMN STRAIGHT YOU'RE GONNA SET IT UP AGAIN, *HERBERT--*
--AND THIS TIME YOU'RE GONNA GET IT RIGHT!

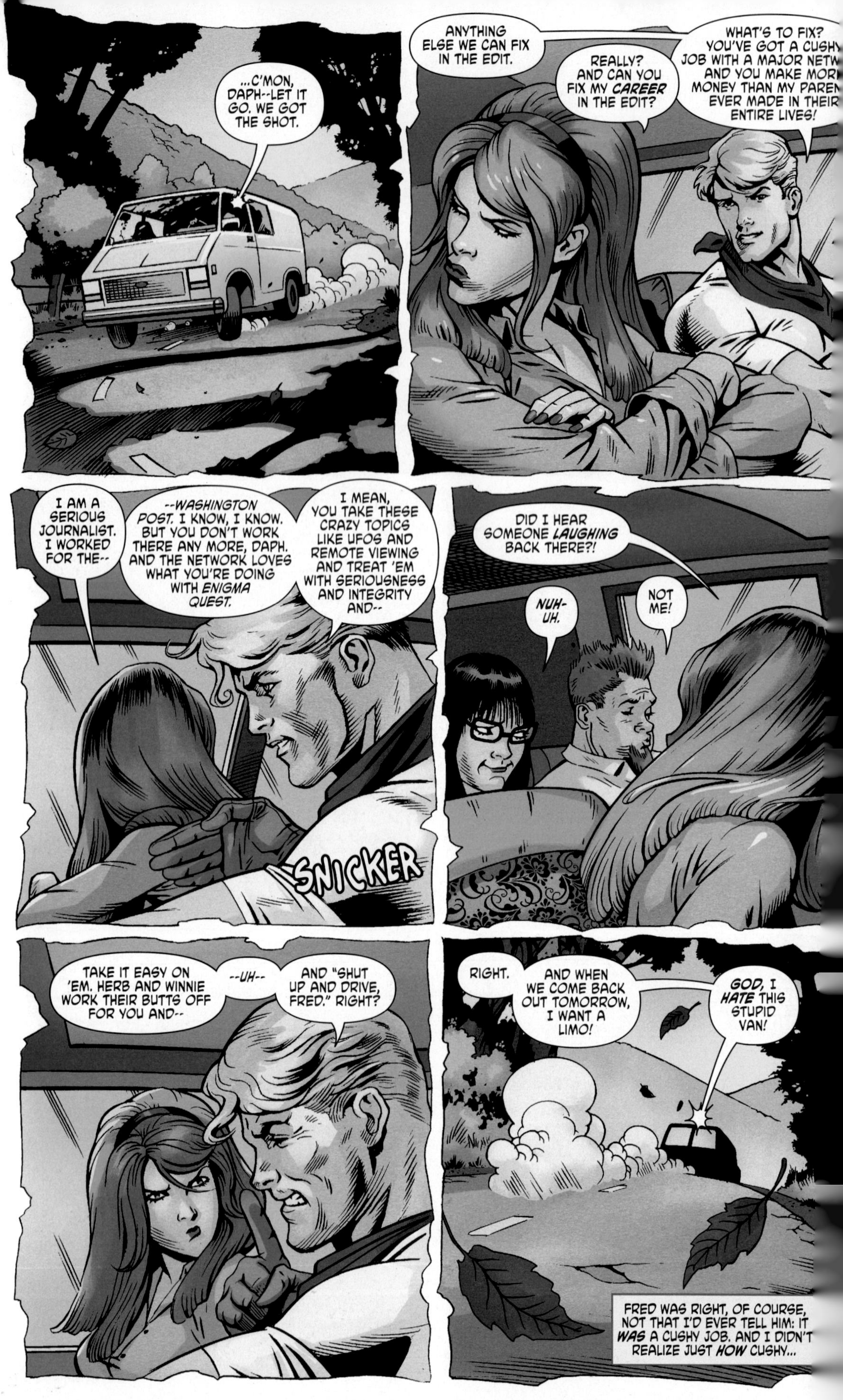
...C'MON, DAPH--LET IT GO. WE GOT THE SHOT.
ANYTHING ELSE WE CAN FIX IN THE EDIT.
REALLY? AND CAN YOU FIX MY CAREER IN THE EDIT?
WHAT'S TO FIX? YOU'VE GOT A CUSHY JOB WITH A MAJOR NETW AND YOU MAKE MOR MONEY THAN MY PAREN EVER MADE IN THEIR ENTIRE LIVES!
I AM A SERIOUS JOURNALIST. I WORKED FOR THE--
--WASHINGTON POST. I KNOW, I KNOW. BUT YOU DON'T WORK THERE ANY MORE, DAPH. AND THE NETWORK LOVES WHAT YOU'RE DOING WITH ENIGMA QUEST.
I MEAN, YOU TAKE THESE CRAZY TOPICS LIKE UFOS AND REMOTE VIEWING AND TREAT 'EM WITH SERIOUSNESS AND INTEGRITY AND--
SNICKER
DID I HEAR SOMEONE LAUGHING BACK THERE?!
NUH-UH.
NOT ME!
TAKE IT EASY ON 'EM. HERB AND WINNIE WORK THEIR BUTTS OFF FOR YOU AND--
--UH--
AND "SHUT UP AND DRIVE, FRED." RIGHT?
RIGHT.
AND WHEN WE COME BACK OUT TOMORROW, I WANT A LIMO!
GOD, I HATE THIS STUPID VAN!
FRED WAS RIGHT, OF COURSE, NOT THAT I'D EVER TELL HIM: IT WAS A CUSHY JOB. AND I DIDN'T REALIZE JUST HOW CUSHY...

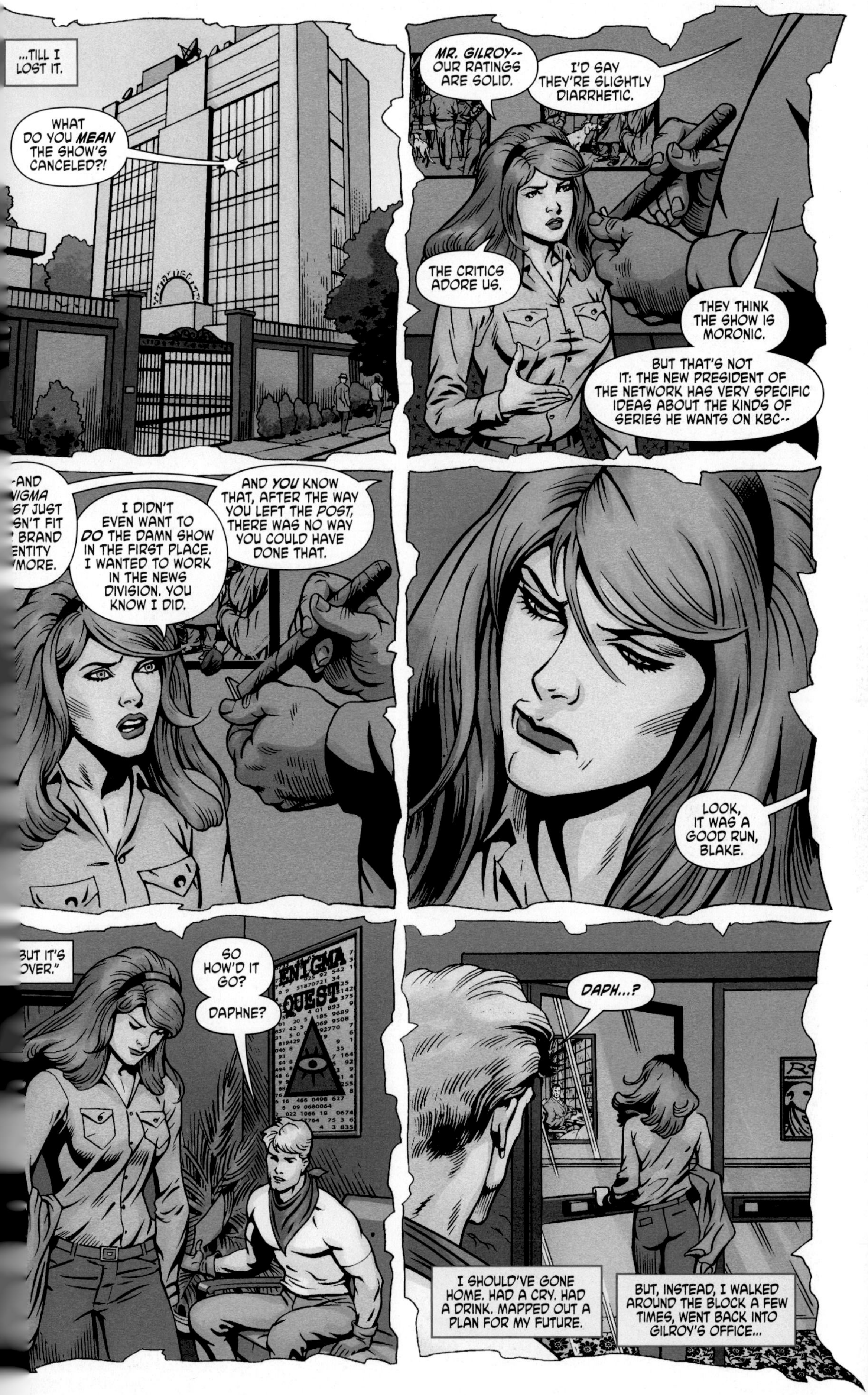
...TILL I LOST IT.
WHAT DO YOU MEAN THE SHOW'S CANCELED?!
MR. GILROY-- OUR RATINGS ARE SOLID.
I'D SAY THEY'RE SLIGHTLY DIARRHETIC.
THE CRITICS ADORE US.
THEY THINK THE SHOW IS MORONIC.
BUT THAT'S NOT IT: THE NEW PRESIDENT OF THE NETWORK HAS VERY SPECIFIC IDEAS ABOUT THE KINDS OF SERIES HE WANTS ON KBC--
-AND NIGMA ST JUST SN'T FIT BRAND ENTITY YMORE.
I DIDN'T EVEN WANT TO DO THE DAMN SHOW IN THE FIRST PLACE. I WANTED TO WORK IN THE NEWS DIVISION. YOU KNOW I DID.
AND YOU KNOW THAT, AFTER THE WAY YOU LEFT THE POST, THERE WAS NO WAY YOU COULD HAVE DONE THAT.
LOOK, IT WAS A GOOD RUN, BLAKE.
BUT IT'S OVER."
SO HOW'D IT GO?
DAPHNE?
ENIGMA QUEST
DAPH...?
I SHOULD'VE GONE HOME. HAD A CRY. HAD A DRINK. MAPPED OUT A PLAN FOR MY FUTURE.
BUT, INSTEAD, I WALKED AROUND THE BLOCK A FEW TIMES, WENT BACK INTO GILROY'S OFFICE...

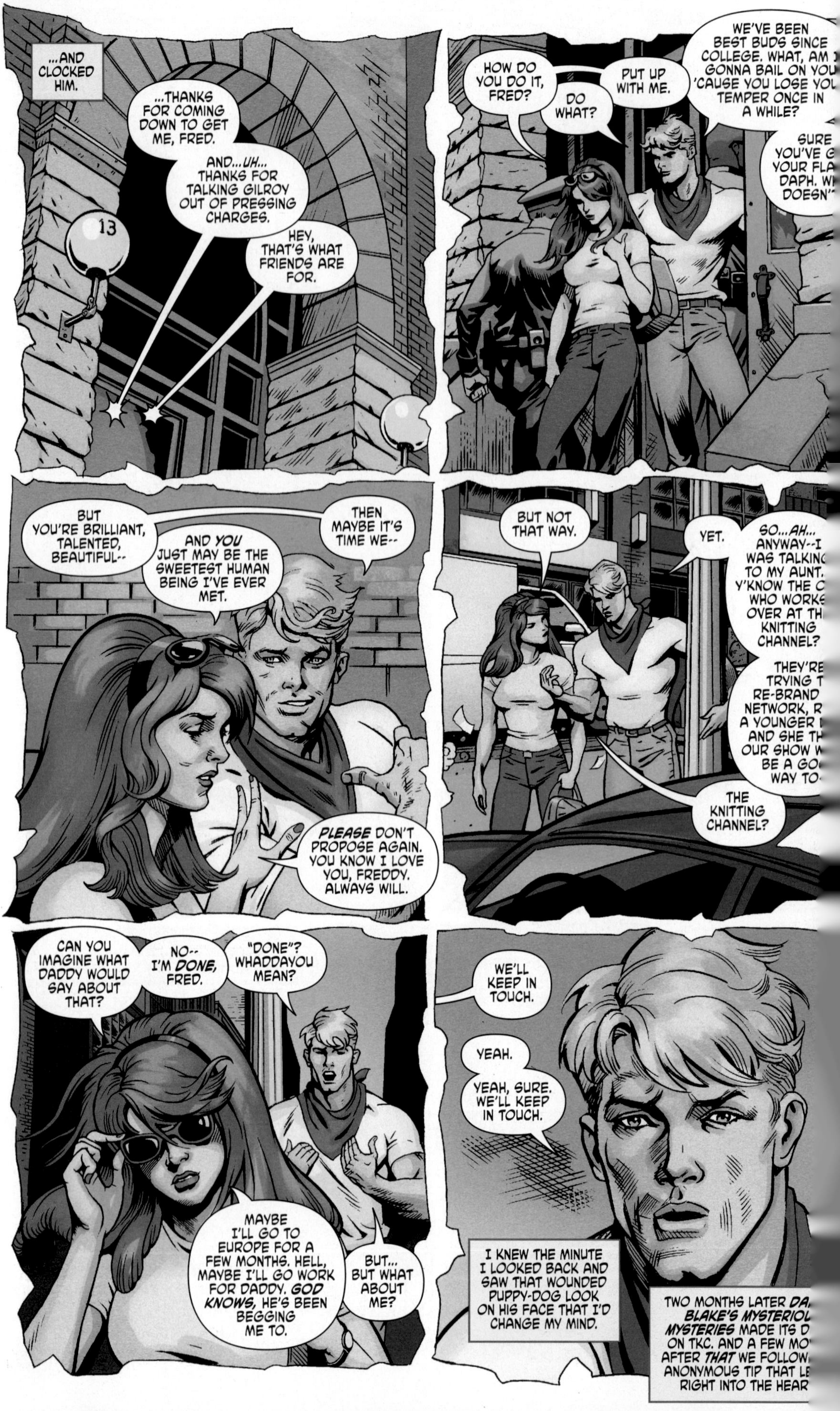

...AND CLOCKED HIM.
...THANKS FOR COMING DOWN TO GET ME, FRED.
AND...UH... THANKS FOR TALKING GILROY OUT OF PRESSING CHARGES.
HEY, THAT'S WHAT FRIENDS ARE FOR.
13
HOW DO YOU DO IT, FRED?
DO WHAT?
PUT UP WITH ME.
WE'VE BEEN BEST BUDS SINCE COLLEGE. WHAT, AM I GONNA BAIL ON YOU 'CAUSE YOU LOSE YOUR TEMPER ONCE IN A WHILE?
BUT YOU'RE BRILLIANT, TALENTED, BEAUTIFUL--
THEN MAYBE IT'S TIME WE--
AND YOU JUST MAY BE THE SWEETEST HUMAN BEING I'VE EVER MET.
PLEASE DON'T PROPOSE AGAIN. YOU KNOW I LOVE YOU, FREDDY. ALWAYS WILL.
BUT NOT THAT WAY.
YET.
THE KNITTING CHANNEL?
CAN YOU IMAGINE WHAT DADDY WOULD SAY ABOUT THAT?
NO-- I'M DONE, FRED.
"DONE"? WHADDAYOU MEAN?
MAYBE I'LL GO TO EUROPE FOR A FEW MONTHS. HELL, MAYBE I'LL GO WORK FOR DADDY. GOD KNOWS, HE'S BEEN BEGGING ME TO.
BUT... BUT WHAT ABOUT ME?
WE'LL KEEP IN TOUCH.
YEAH.
YEAH, SURE. WE'LL KEEP IN TOUCH.
I KNEW THE MINUTE I LOOKED BACK AND SAW THAT WOUNDED PUPPY-DOG LOOK ON HIS FACE THAT I'D CHANGE MY MIND.

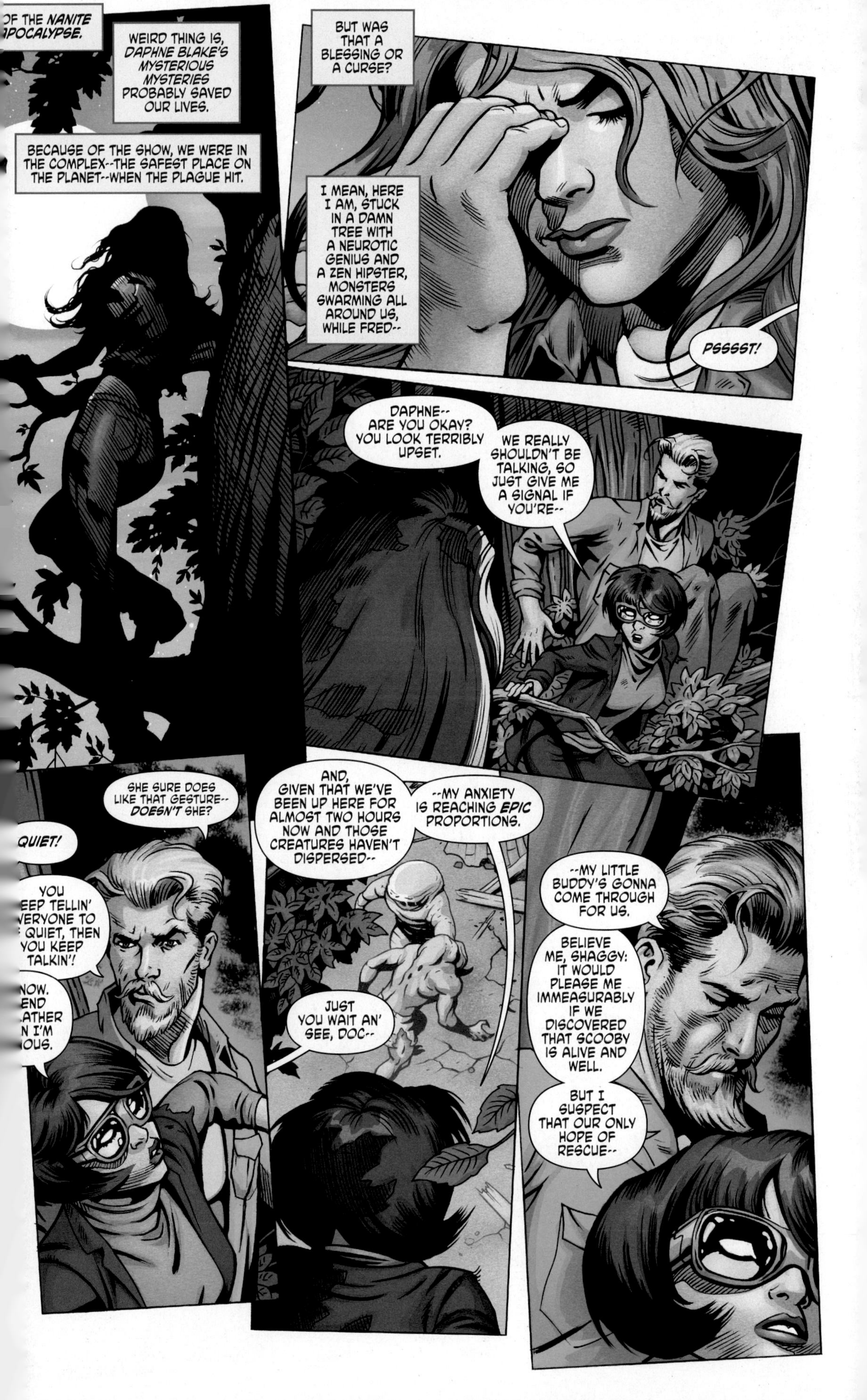
OF THE *NANITE* APOCALYPSE.
WEIRD THING IS, *DAPHNE BLAKE'S MYSTERIOUS MYSTERIES* PROBABLY SAVED OUR LIVES.
BECAUSE OF THE SHOW, WE WERE IN THE COMPLEX--THE SAFEST PLACE ON THE PLANET--WHEN THE PLAGUE HIT.
BUT WAS THAT A BLESSING OR A CURSE?
I MEAN, HERE I AM, STUCK IN A DAMN TREE WITH A NEUROTIC GENIUS AND A ZEN HIPSTER, MONSTERS SWARMING ALL AROUND US, WHILE FRED--
PSSSST!
DAPHNE-- ARE YOU OKAY? YOU LOOK TERRIBLY UPSET.
WE REALLY SHOULDN'T BE TALKING, SO JUST GIVE ME A SIGNAL IF YOU'RE--
SHE SURE DOES LIKE THAT GESTURE-- *DOESN'T* SHE?
QUIET!
YOU EEP TELLIN' VERYONE TO QUIET, THEN YOU KEEP TALKIN'!
NOW. END LATHER N I'M OUS.
AND, GIVEN THAT WE'VE BEEN UP HERE FOR ALMOST TWO HOURS NOW AND THOSE CREATURES HAVEN'T DISPERSED--
--MY ANXIETY IS REACHING *EPIC* PROPORTIONS.
JUST YOU WAIT AN' SEE, DOC--
--MY LITTLE BUDDY'S GONNA COME THROUGH FOR US.
BELIEVE ME, SHAGGY: IT WOULD PLEASE ME IMMEASURABLY IF WE DISCOVERED THAT SCOOBY IS ALIVE AND WELL.
BUT I SUSPECT THAT OUR ONLY HOPE OF RESCUE--

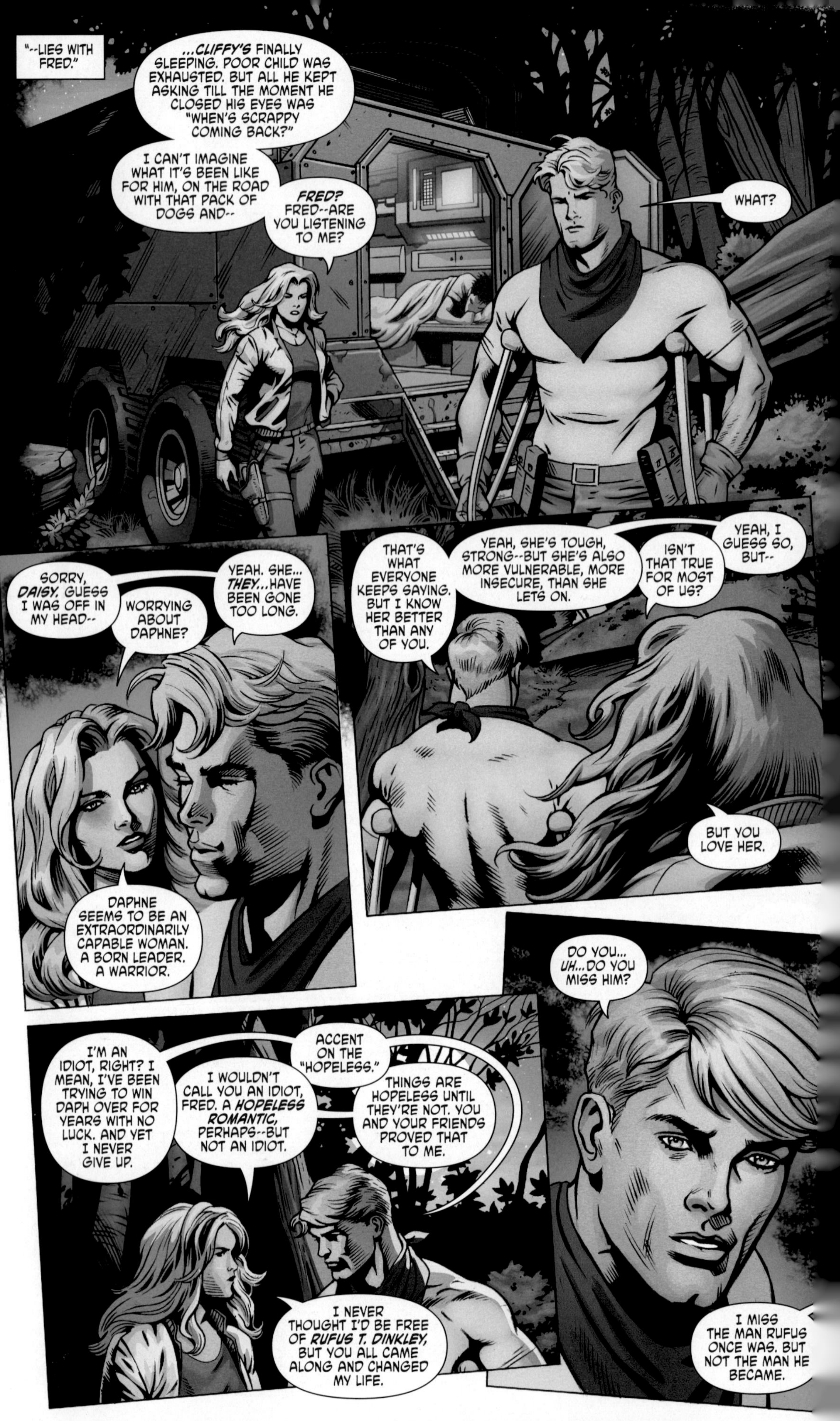
"--LIES WITH FRED."
...CLIFFY'S FINALLY SLEEPING. POOR CHILD WAS EXHAUSTED. BUT ALL HE KEPT ASKING TILL THE MOMENT HE CLOSED HIS EYES WAS "WHEN'S SCRAPPY COMING BACK?"
I CAN'T IMAGINE WHAT IT'S BEEN LIKE FOR HIM, ON THE ROAD WITH THAT PACK OF DOGS AND--
FRED? FRED--ARE YOU LISTENING TO ME?
WHAT?
SORRY, DAISY. GUESS I WAS OFF IN MY HEAD--
WORRYING ABOUT DAPHNE?
YEAH. SHE... THEY...HAVE BEEN GONE TOO LONG.
DAPHNE SEEMS TO BE AN EXTRAORDINARILY CAPABLE WOMAN. A BORN LEADER. A WARRIOR.
THAT'S WHAT EVERYONE KEEPS SAYING. BUT I KNOW HER BETTER THAN ANY OF YOU.
YEAH, SHE'S TOUGH, STRONG--BUT SHE'S ALSO MORE VULNERABLE, MORE INSECURE, THAN SHE LETS ON.
ISN'T THAT TRUE FOR MOST OF US?
YEAH, I GUESS SO, BUT--
BUT YOU LOVE HER.
I'M AN IDIOT, RIGHT? I MEAN, I'VE BEEN TRYING TO WIN DAPH OVER FOR YEARS WITH NO LUCK. AND YET I NEVER GIVE UP.
I WOULDN'T CALL YOU AN IDIOT, FRED. A HOPELESS ROMANTIC, PERHAPS--BUT NOT AN IDIOT.
ACCENT ON THE "HOPELESS."
THINGS ARE HOPELESS UNTIL THEY'RE NOT. YOU AND YOUR FRIENDS PROVED THAT TO ME.
I NEVER THOUGHT I'D BE FREE OF RUFUS T. DINKLEY, BUT YOU ALL CAME ALONG AND CHANGED MY LIFE.
DO YOU... UH...DO YOU MISS HIM?
I MISS THE MAN RUFUS ONCE WAS. BUT NOT THE MAN HE BECAME.

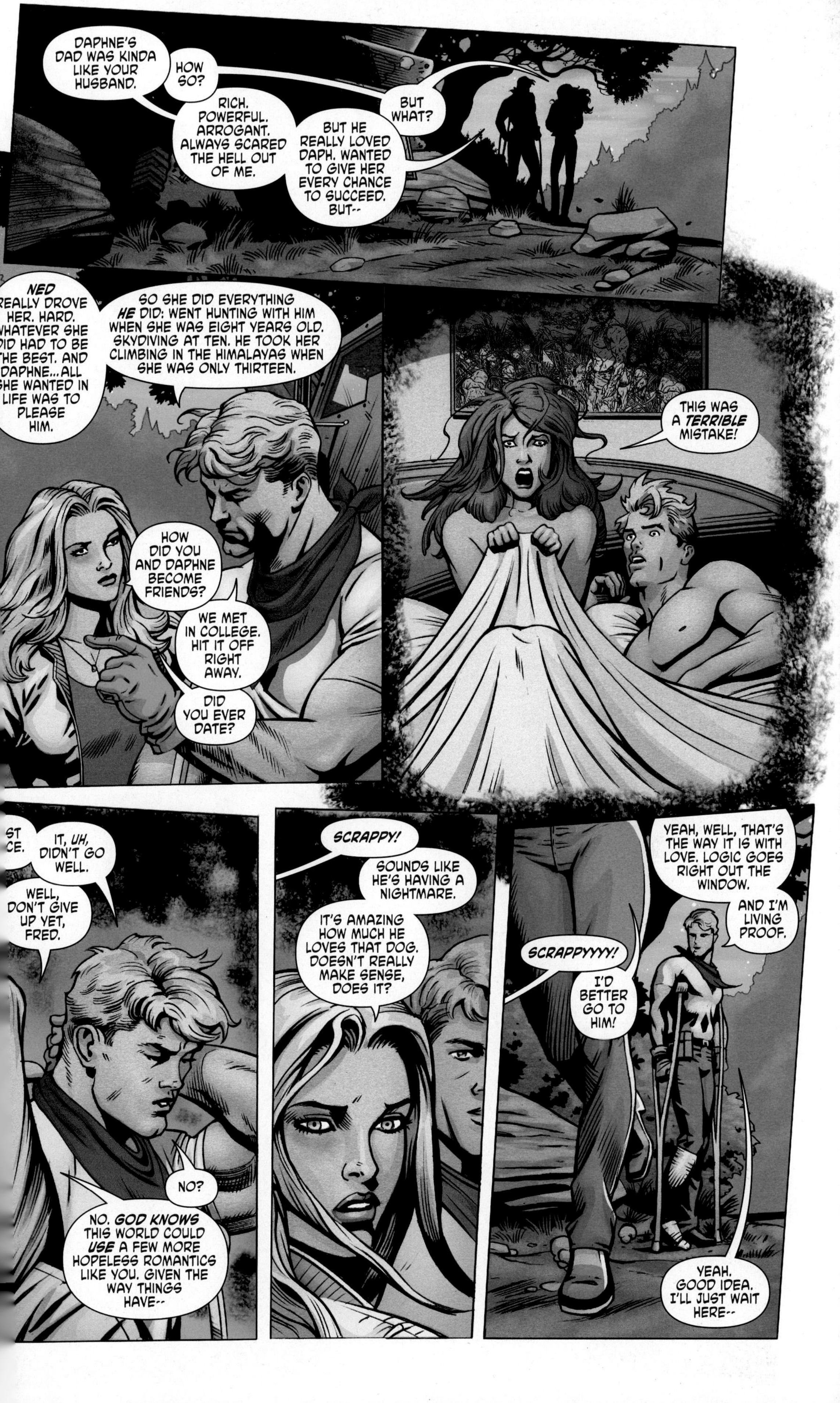
DAPHNE'S DAD WAS KINDA LIKE YOUR HUSBAND.
HOW SO?
RICH. POWERFUL. ARROGANT. ALWAYS SCARED THE HELL OUT OF ME.
BUT HE REALLY LOVED DAPH. WANTED TO GIVE HER EVERY CHANCE TO SUCCEED. BUT--
BUT WHAT?
NED REALLY DROVE HER. HARD. WHATEVER SHE DID HAD TO BE THE BEST. AND DAPHNE...ALL SHE WANTED IN LIFE WAS TO PLEASE HIM.
SO SHE DID EVERYTHING HE DID: WENT HUNTING WITH HIM WHEN SHE WAS EIGHT YEARS OLD. SKYDIVING AT TEN. HE TOOK HER CLIMBING IN THE HIMALAYAS WHEN SHE WAS ONLY THIRTEEN.
HOW DID YOU AND DAPHNE BECOME FRIENDS?
WE MET IN COLLEGE. HIT IT OFF RIGHT AWAY.
DID YOU EVER DATE?
THIS WAS A TERRIBLE MISTAKE!
IT, UH, DIDN'T GO WELL.
WELL, DON'T GIVE UP YET, FRED.
NO?
NO. GOD KNOWS THIS WORLD COULD USE A FEW MORE HOPELESS ROMANTICS LIKE YOU. GIVEN THE WAY THINGS HAVE--
SCRAPPY!
SOUNDS LIKE HE'S HAVING A NIGHTMARE.
IT'S AMAZING HOW MUCH HE LOVES THAT DOG. DOESN'T REALLY MAKE SENSE, DOES IT?
YEAH, WELL, THAT'S THE WAY IT IS WITH LOVE. LOGIC GOES RIGHT OUT THE WINDOW.
AND I'M LIVING PROOF.
SCRAPPYYYY!
I'D BETTER GO TO HIM!
YEAH. GOOD IDEA. I'LL JUST WAIT HERE--

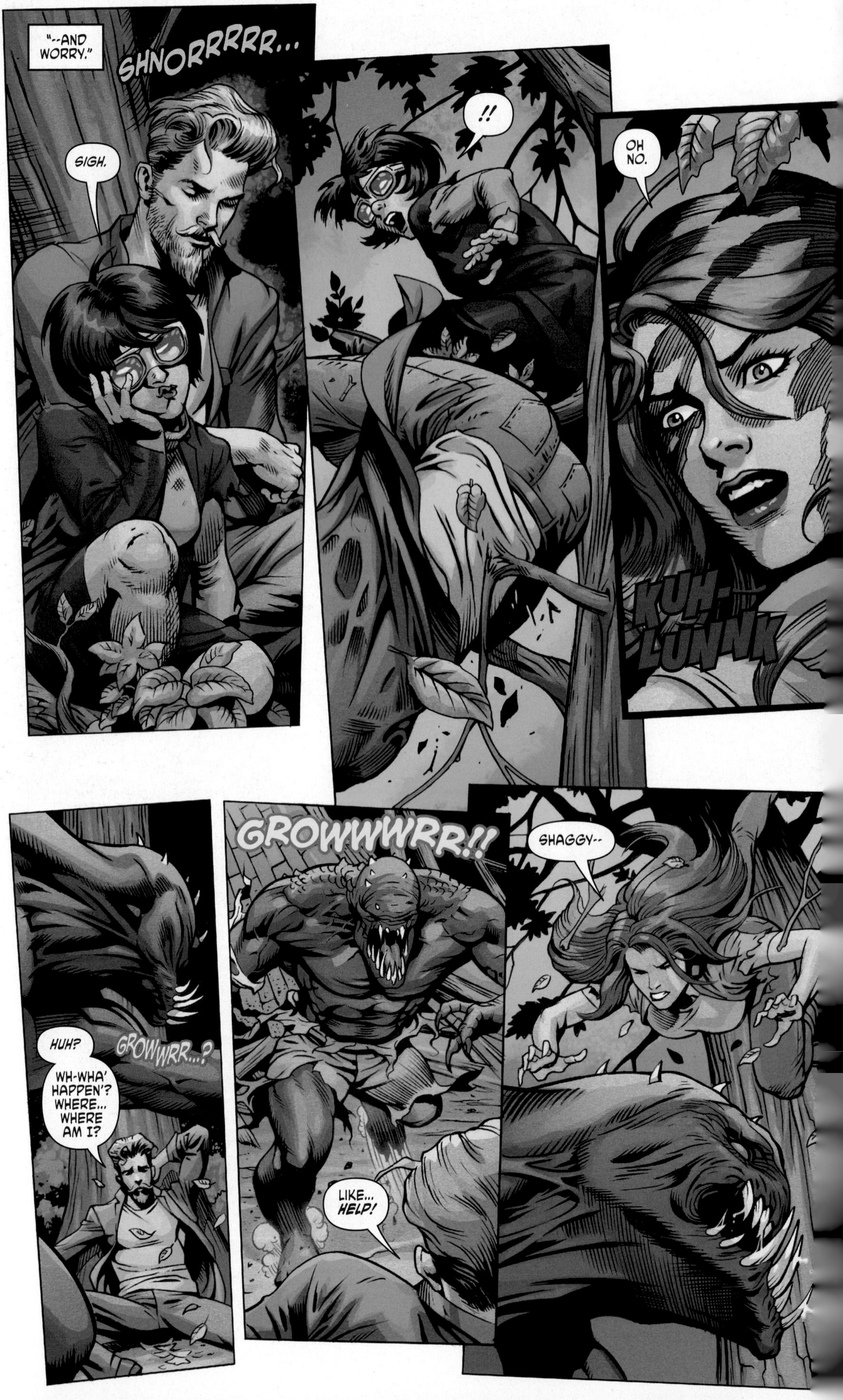
"--AND WORRY."
SHNORRRRR...
SIGH.
!!
OH NO.
KUH-LUNNK
HUH?
WH-WHA' HAPPEN'? WHERE... WHERE AM I?
GROWWRR...?
GROWWWRR!!
LIKE... HELP!
SHAGGY--

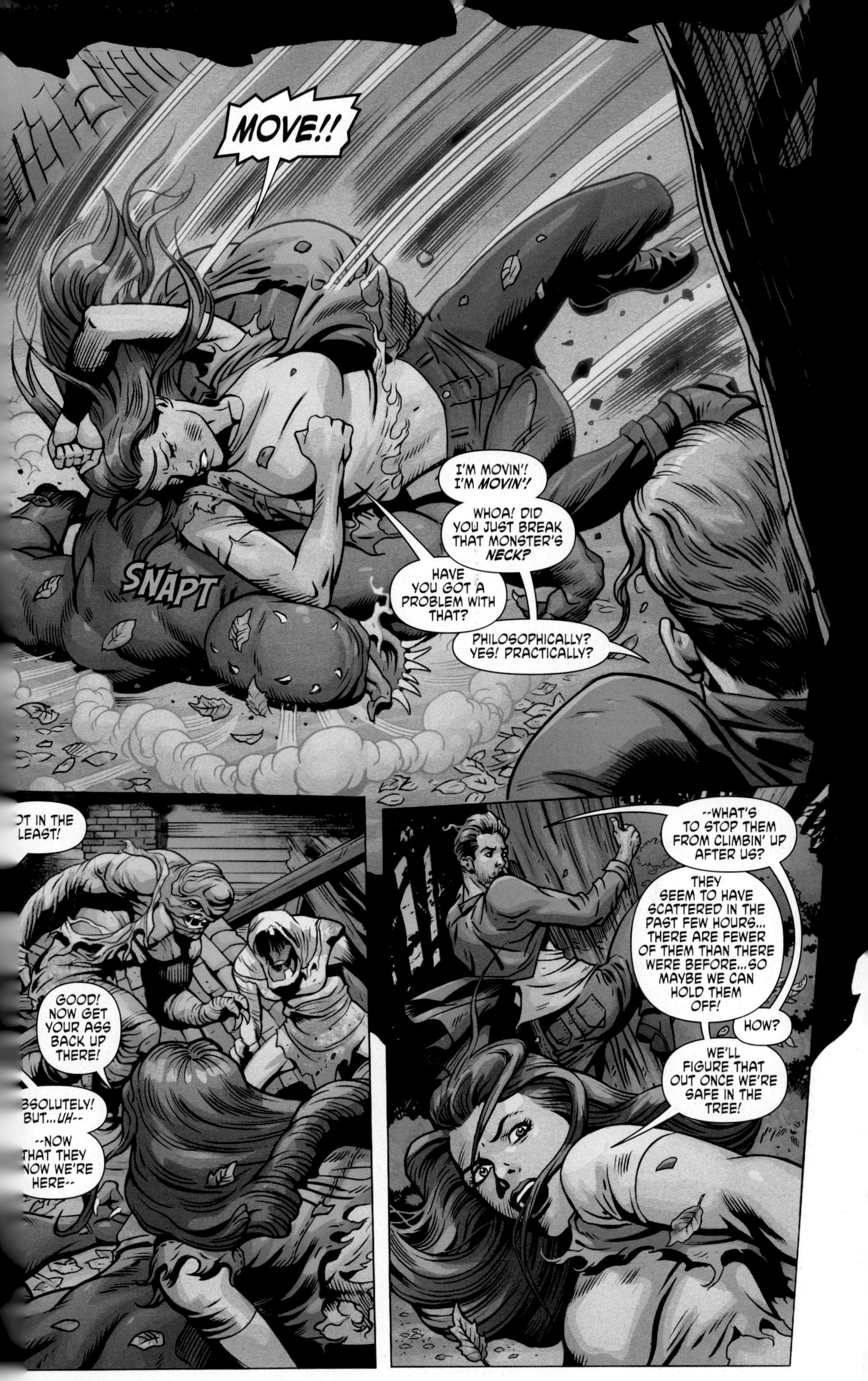
MOVE!!
I'M MOVIN'! I'M *MOVIN'!*
WHOA! DID YOU JUST BREAK THAT MONSTER'S *NECK?*
SNAPT
HAVE YOU GOT A PROBLEM WITH THAT?
PHILOSOPHICALLY? YES! PRACTICALLY?
OT IN THE LEAST!
GOOD! NOW GET YOUR ASS BACK UP THERE!
BSOLUTELY! BUT...*UH--*
--NOW THAT THEY NOW WE'RE HERE--
--WHAT'S TO STOP THEM FROM CLIMBIN' UP AFTER US?
THEY SEEM TO HAVE SCATTERED IN THE PAST FEW HOURS... THERE ARE FEWER OF THEM THAN THERE WERE BEFORE...SO MAYBE WE CAN HOLD THEM OFF!
HOW?
WE'LL FIGURE THAT OUT ONCE WE'RE SAFE IN THE TREE!

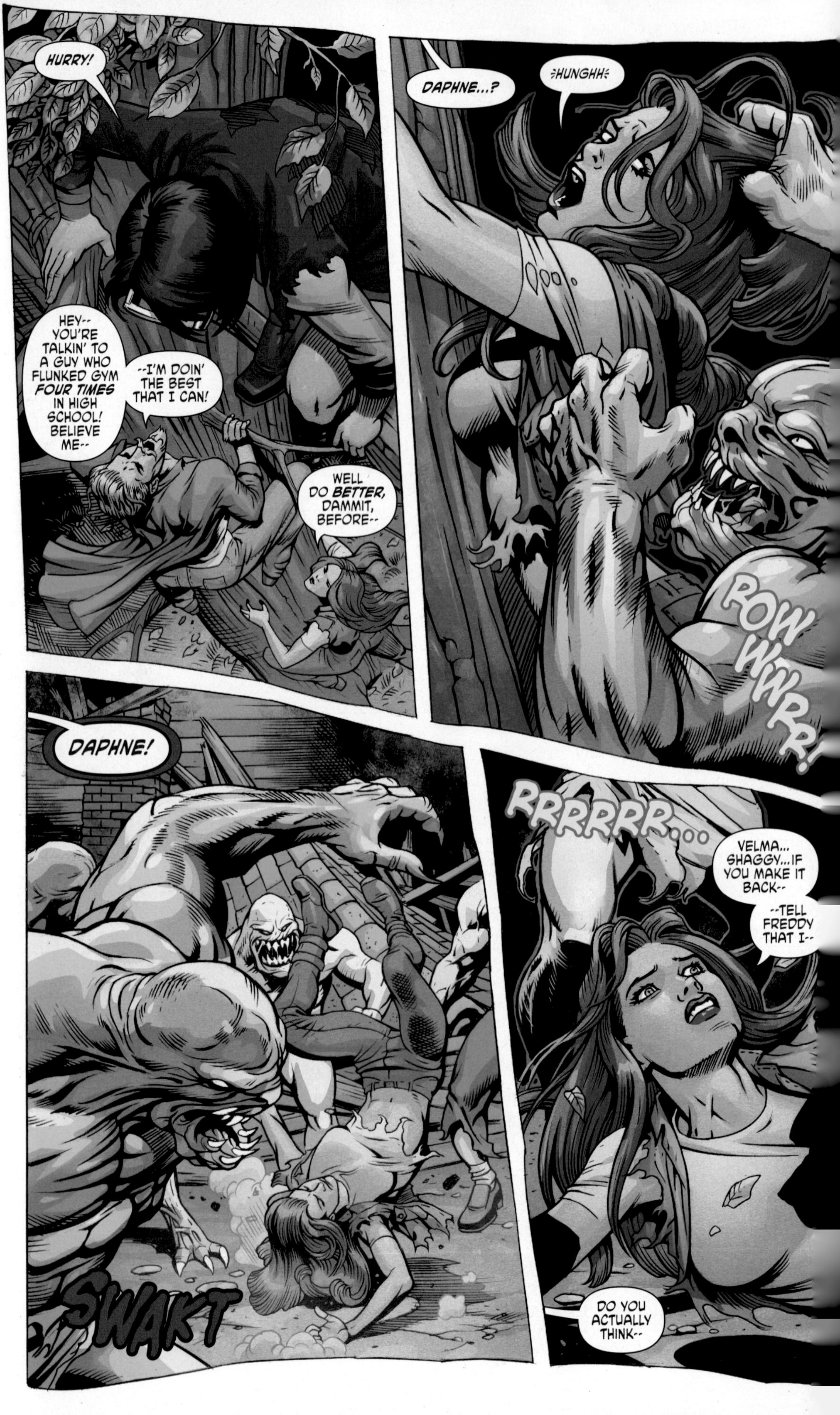
HURRY!
HEY-- YOU'RE TALKIN' TO A GUY WHO FLUNKED GYM FOUR TIMES IN HIGH SCHOOL! BELIEVE ME--
--I'M DOIN' THE BEST THAT I CAN!
WELL DO BETTER, DAMMIT, BEFORE--
DAPHNE...?
HUNGHH
ROWWWRR!
DAPHNE!
SWAKT
RRRRRR...
VELMA... SHAGGY...IF YOU MAKE IT BACK--
--TELL FREDDY THAT I--
DO YOU ACTUALLY THINK--

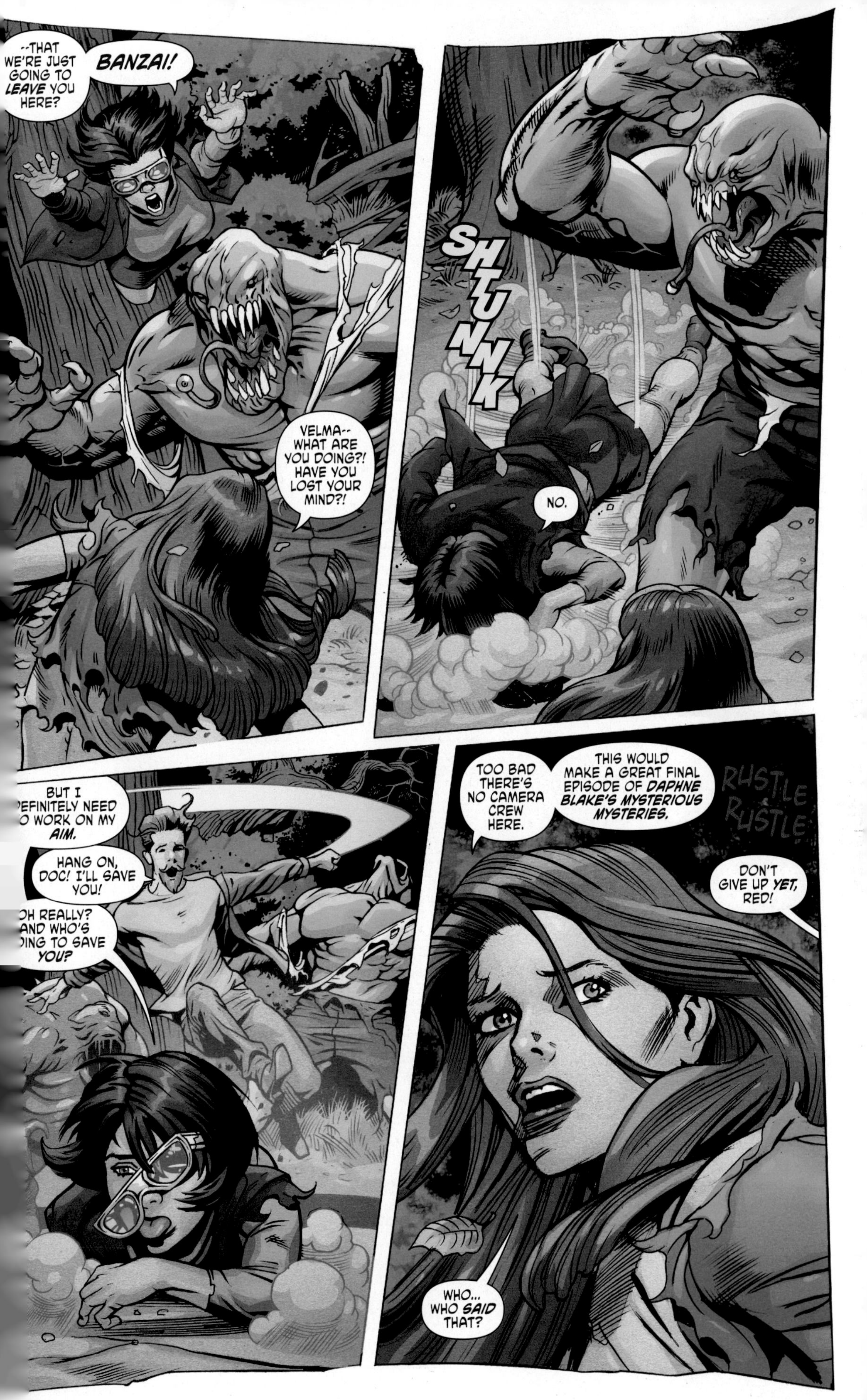
--THAT WE'RE JUST GOING TO LEAVE YOU HERE?
BANZAI!
VELMA-- WHAT ARE YOU DOING?! HAVE YOU LOST YOUR MIND?!
SHTUNNK
NO.
BUT I EFINITELY NEED O WORK ON MY AIM.
HANG ON, DOC! I'LL SAVE YOU!
OH REALLY? AND WHO'S OING TO SAVE YOU?
TOO BAD THERE'S NO CAMERA CREW HERE.
THIS WOULD MAKE A GREAT FINAL EPISODE OF DAPHNE BLAKE'S MYSTERIOUS MYSTERIES.
RUSTLE RUSTLE
DON'T GIVE UP YET, RED!
WHO... WHO SAID THAT?

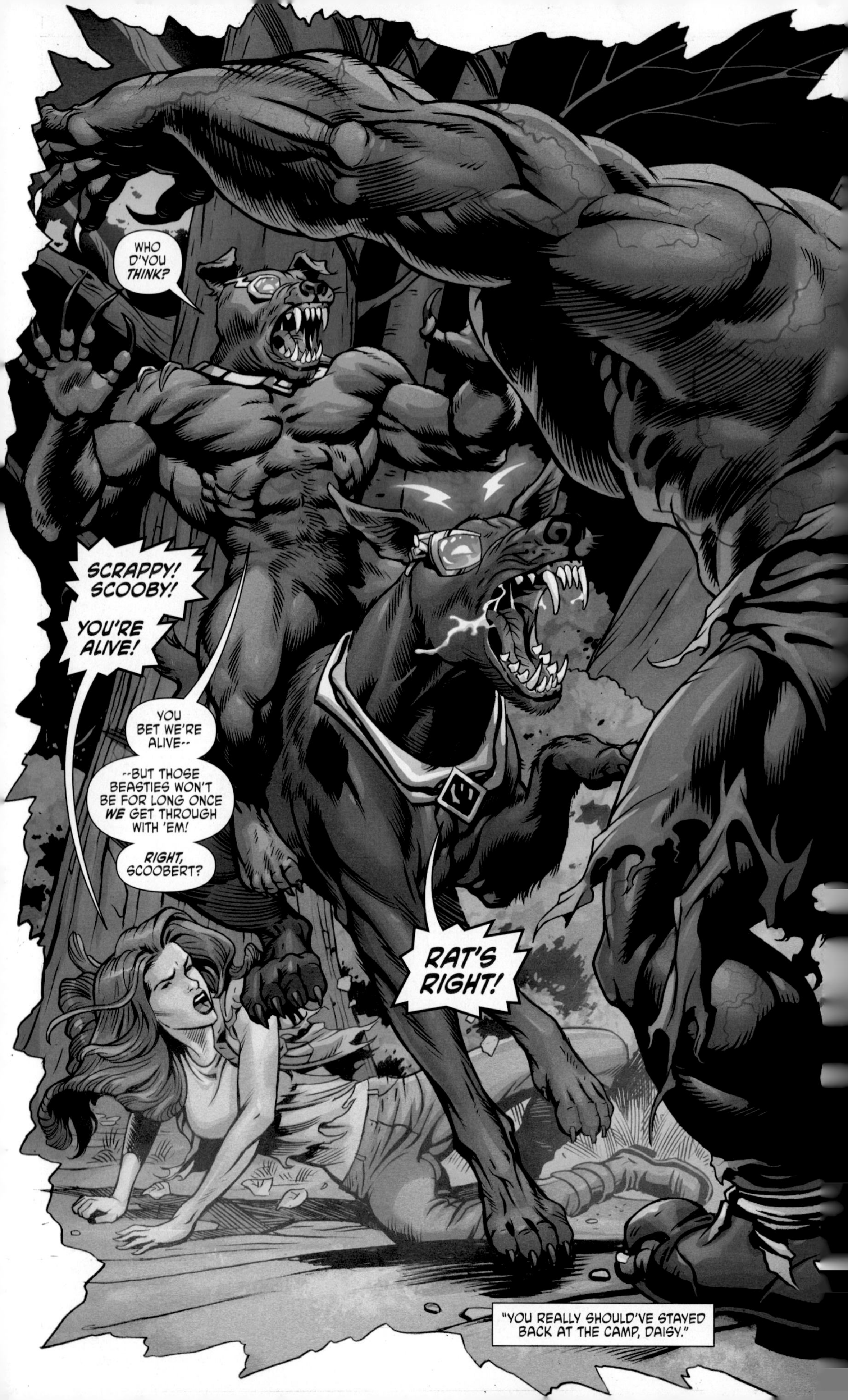
WHO D'YOU *THINK?*
SCRAPPY! SCOOBY!
YOU'RE ALIVE!
YOU BET WE'RE ALIVE--
--BUT THOSE BEASTIES WON'T BE FOR LONG ONCE *WE* GET THROUGH WITH 'EM!
RIGHT, SCOOBERT?
RAT'S RIGHT!
"YOU REALLY SHOULD'VE STAYED BACK AT THE CAMP, DAISY."

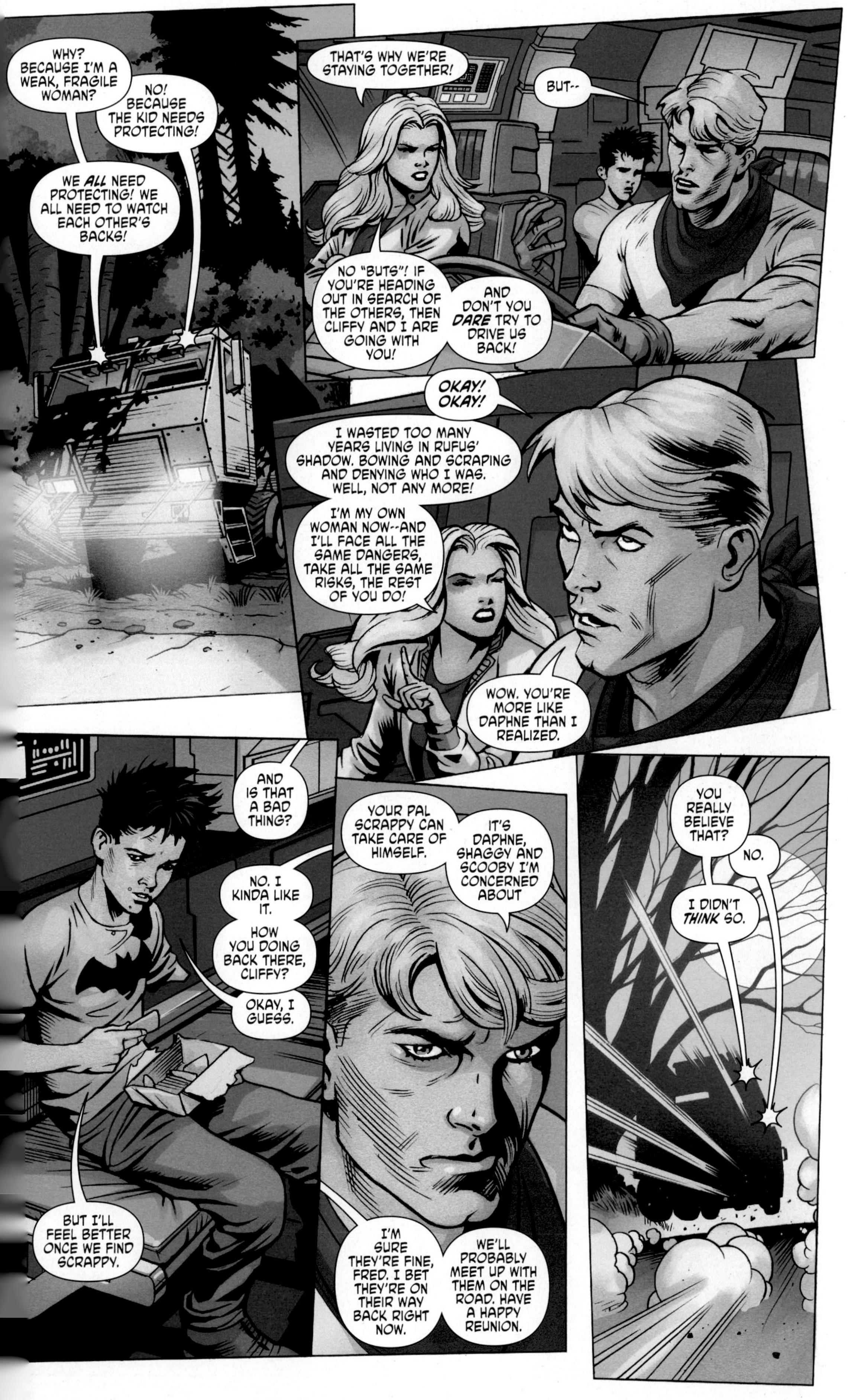

WHY? BECAUSE I'M A WEAK, FRAGILE WOMAN?
NO! BECAUSE THE KID NEEDS PROTECTING!
WE ALL NEED PROTECTING! WE ALL NEED TO WATCH EACH OTHER'S BACKS!
THAT'S WHY WE'RE STAYING TOGETHER!
BUT--
NO "BUTS"! IF YOU'RE HEADING OUT IN SEARCH OF THE OTHERS, THEN CLIFFY AND I ARE GOING WITH YOU!
AND DON'T YOU DARE TRY TO DRIVE US BACK!
OKAY! OKAY!
I WASTED TOO MANY YEARS LIVING IN RUFUS' SHADOW. BOWING AND SCRAPING AND DENYING WHO I WAS. WELL, NOT ANY MORE!
I'M MY OWN WOMAN NOW--AND I'LL FACE ALL THE SAME DANGERS, TAKE ALL THE SAME RISKS, THE REST OF YOU DO!
WOW. YOU'RE MORE LIKE DAPHNE THAN I REALIZED.
AND IS THAT A BAD THING?
NO. I KINDA LIKE IT.
HOW YOU DOING BACK THERE, CLIFFY?
OKAY, I GUESS.
BUT I'LL FEEL BETTER ONCE WE FIND SCRAPPY.
YOUR PAL SCRAPPY CAN TAKE CARE OF HIMSELF.
IT'S DAPHNE, SHAGGY AND SCOOBY I'M CONCERNED ABOUT
I'M SURE THEY'RE FINE, FRED. I BET THEY'RE ON THEIR WAY BACK RIGHT NOW.
WE'LL PROBABLY MEET UP WITH THEM ON THE ROAD. HAVE A HAPPY REUNION.
YOU REALLY BELIEVE THAT?
NO.
I DIDN'T THINK SO.

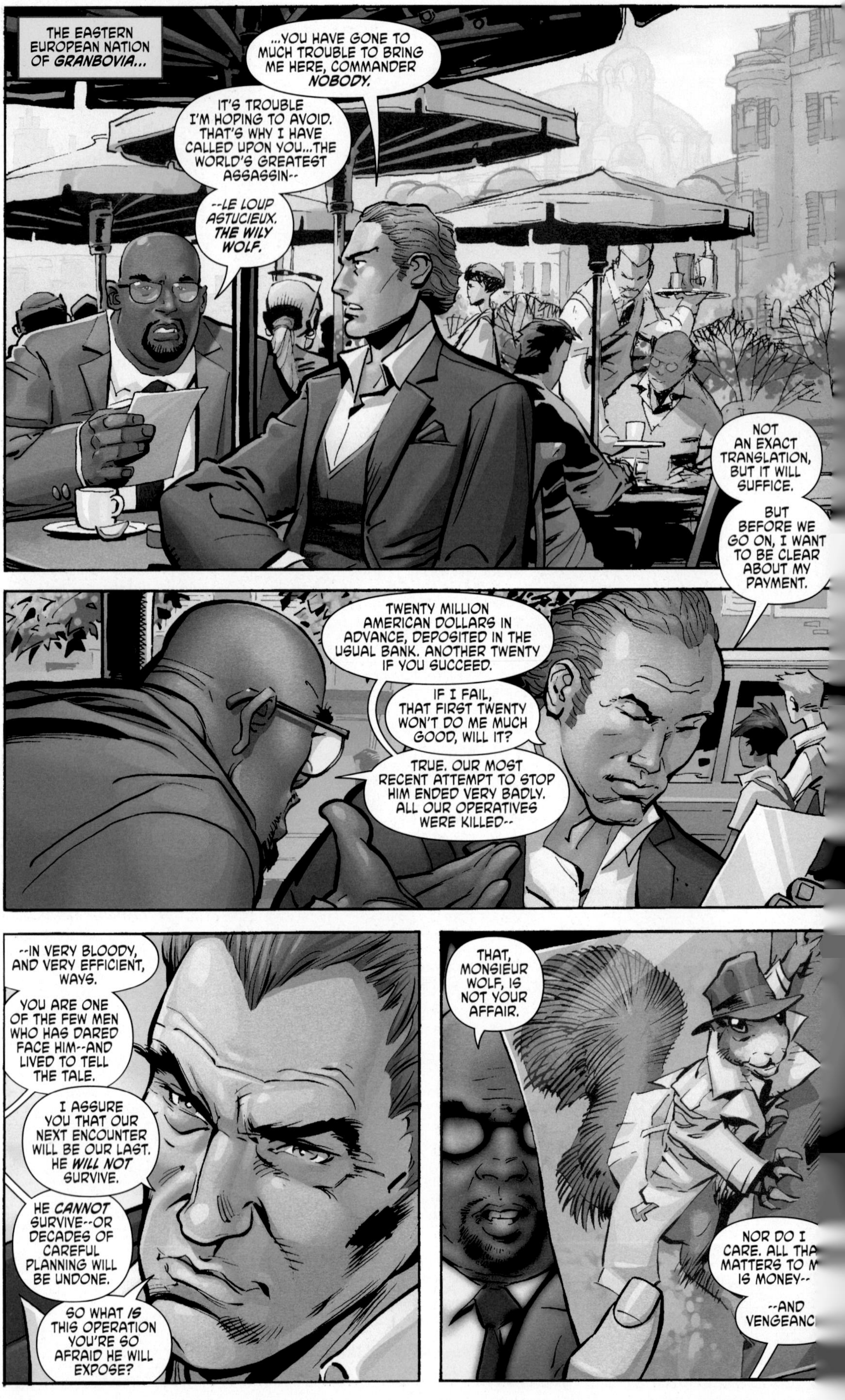
THE EASTERN EUROPEAN NATION OF GRANBOVIA...
...YOU HAVE GONE TO MUCH TROUBLE TO BRING ME HERE, COMMANDER NOBODY.
IT'S TROUBLE I'M HOPING TO AVOID. THAT'S WHY I HAVE CALLED UPON YOU...THE WORLD'S GREATEST ASSASSIN--
--LE LOUP ASTUCIEUX. THE WILY WOLF.
NOT AN EXACT TRANSLATION, BUT IT WILL SUFFICE.
BUT BEFORE WE GO ON, I WANT TO BE CLEAR ABOUT MY PAYMENT.
TWENTY MILLION AMERICAN DOLLARS IN ADVANCE, DEPOSITED IN THE USUAL BANK. ANOTHER TWENTY IF YOU SUCCEED.
IF I FAIL, THAT FIRST TWENTY WON'T DO ME MUCH GOOD, WILL IT?
TRUE. OUR MOST RECENT ATTEMPT TO STOP HIM ENDED VERY BADLY. ALL OUR OPERATIVES WERE KILLED--
--IN VERY BLOODY, AND VERY EFFICIENT, WAYS.
YOU ARE ONE OF THE FEW MEN WHO HAS DARED FACE HIM--AND LIVED TO TELL THE TALE.
I ASSURE YOU THAT OUR NEXT ENCOUNTER WILL BE OUR LAST. HE WILL NOT SURVIVE.
HE CANNOT SURVIVE--OR DECADES OF CAREFUL PLANNING WILL BE UNDONE.
SO WHAT IS THIS OPERATION YOU'RE SO AFRAID HE WILL EXPOSE?
THAT, MONSIEUR WOLF, IS NOT YOUR AFFAIR.
NOR DO I CARE. ALL THA MATTERS TO M IS MONEY--
--AND VENGEANC

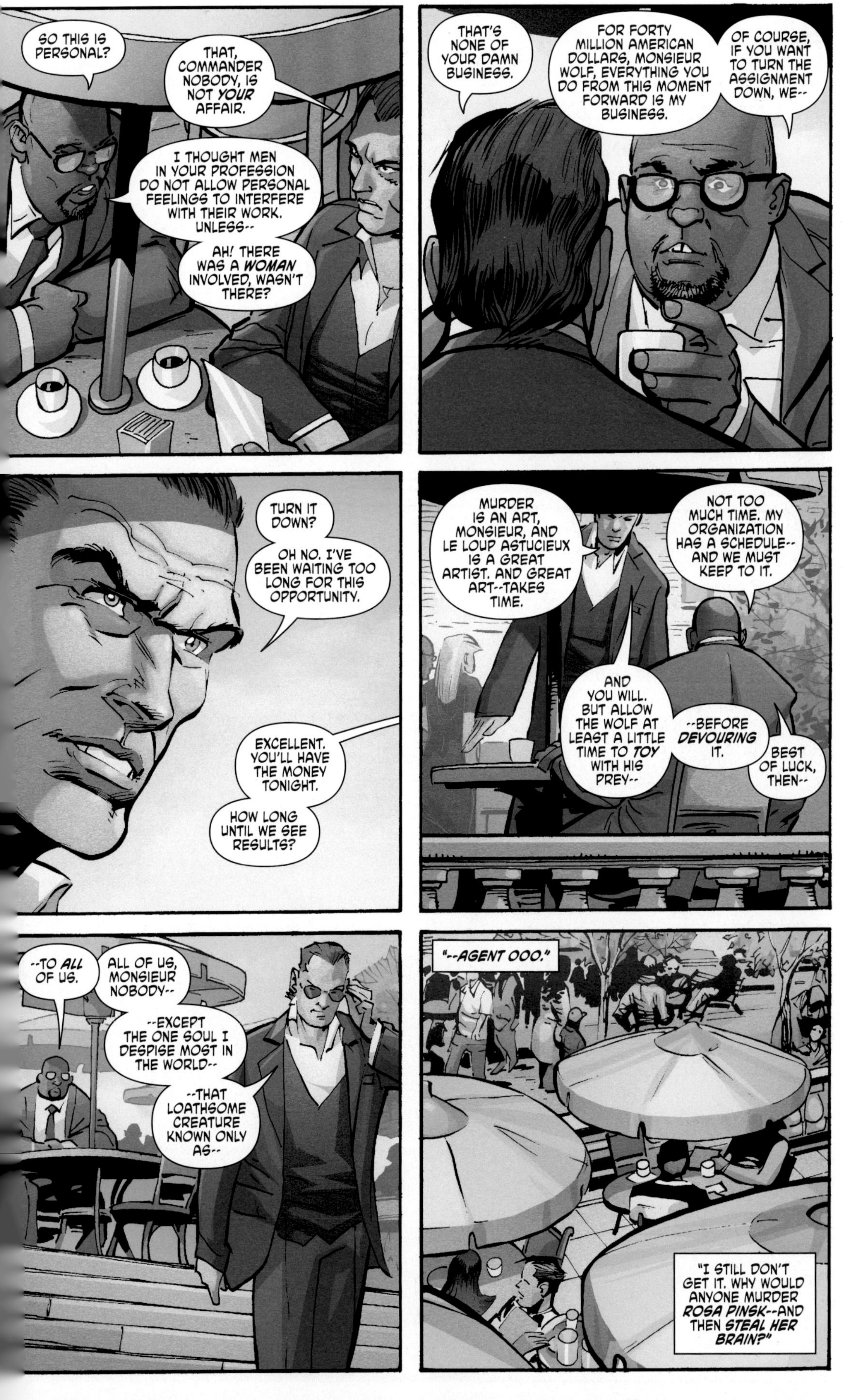
SO THIS IS PERSONAL?
THAT, COMMANDER NOBODY, IS NOT *YOUR* AFFAIR.
I THOUGHT MEN IN YOUR PROFESSION DO NOT ALLOW PERSONAL FEELINGS TO INTERFERE WITH THEIR WORK. UNLESS--
AH! THERE WAS A *WOMAN* INVOLVED, WASN'T THERE?
THAT'S NONE OF YOUR DAMN BUSINESS.
FOR FORTY MILLION AMERICAN DOLLARS, MONSIEUR WOLF, EVERYTHING YOU DO FROM THIS MOMENT FORWARD IS MY BUSINESS.
OF COURSE, IF YOU WANT TO TURN THE ASSIGNMENT DOWN, WE--
TURN IT DOWN?
OH NO. I'VE BEEN WAITING TOO LONG FOR THIS OPPORTUNITY.
EXCELLENT. YOU'LL HAVE THE MONEY TONIGHT.
HOW LONG UNTIL WE SEE RESULTS?
MURDER IS AN ART, MONSIEUR, AND LE LOUP ASTUCIEUX IS A GREAT ARTIST. AND GREAT ART--TAKES TIME.
NOT TOO MUCH TIME. MY ORGANIZATION HAS A SCHEDULE--AND WE MUST KEEP TO IT.
AND YOU WILL. BUT ALLOW THE WOLF AT LEAST A LITTLE TIME TO *TOY* WITH HIS PREY--
--BEFORE *DEVOURING* IT.
BEST OF LUCK, THEN--
--TO *ALL* OF US.
ALL OF US, MONSIEUR NOBODY--
--EXCEPT THE ONE SOUL I DESPISE MOST IN THE WORLD--
--THAT LOATHSOME CREATURE KNOWN ONLY AS--
"--AGENT OOO."
"I STILL DON'T GET IT. WHY WOULD ANYONE MURDER *ROSA PINSK*--AND THEN *STEAL HER BRAIN?*"

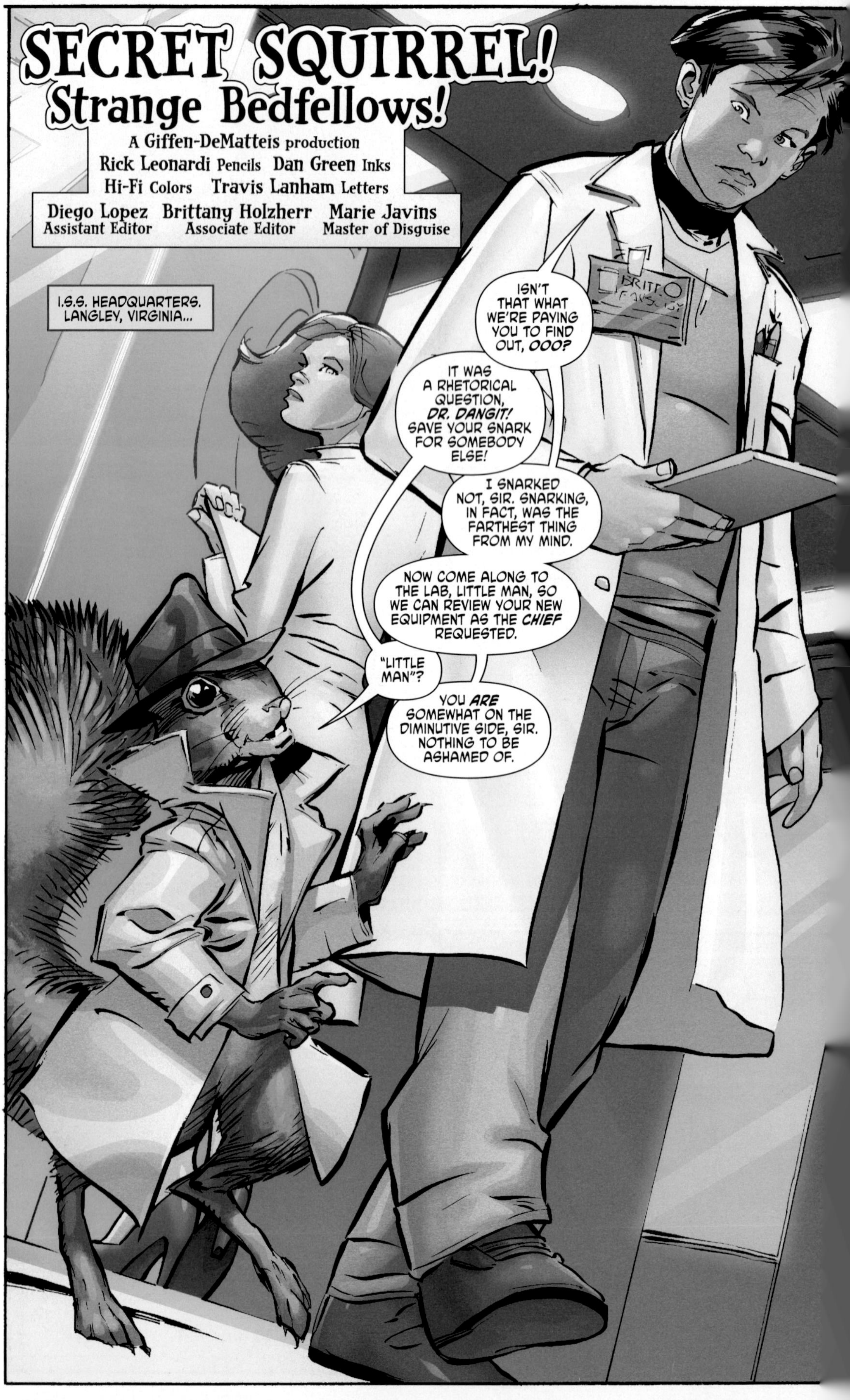
SECRET SQUIRREL!
Strange Bedfellows!
A Giffen-DeMatteis production
Rick Leonardi Pencils Dan Green Inks
Hi-Fi Colors Travis Lanham Letters
Diego Lopez Assistant Editor
Brittany Holzherr Associate Editor
Marie Javins Master of Disguise
I.S.S. HEADQUARTERS. LANGLEY, VIRGINIA...
ISN'T THAT WHAT WE'RE PAYING YOU TO FIND OUT, OOO?
IT WAS A RHETORICAL QUESTION, DR. DANGIT! SAVE YOUR SNARK FOR SOMEBODY ELSE!
I SNARKED NOT, SIR. SNARKING, IN FACT, WAS THE FARTHEST THING FROM MY MIND.
NOW COME ALONG TO THE LAB, LITTLE MAN, SO WE CAN REVIEW YOUR NEW EQUIPMENT AS THE CHIEF REQUESTED.
"LITTLE MAN"?
YOU ARE SOMEWHAT ON THE DIMINUTIVE SIDE, SIR. NOTHING TO BE ASHAMED OF.

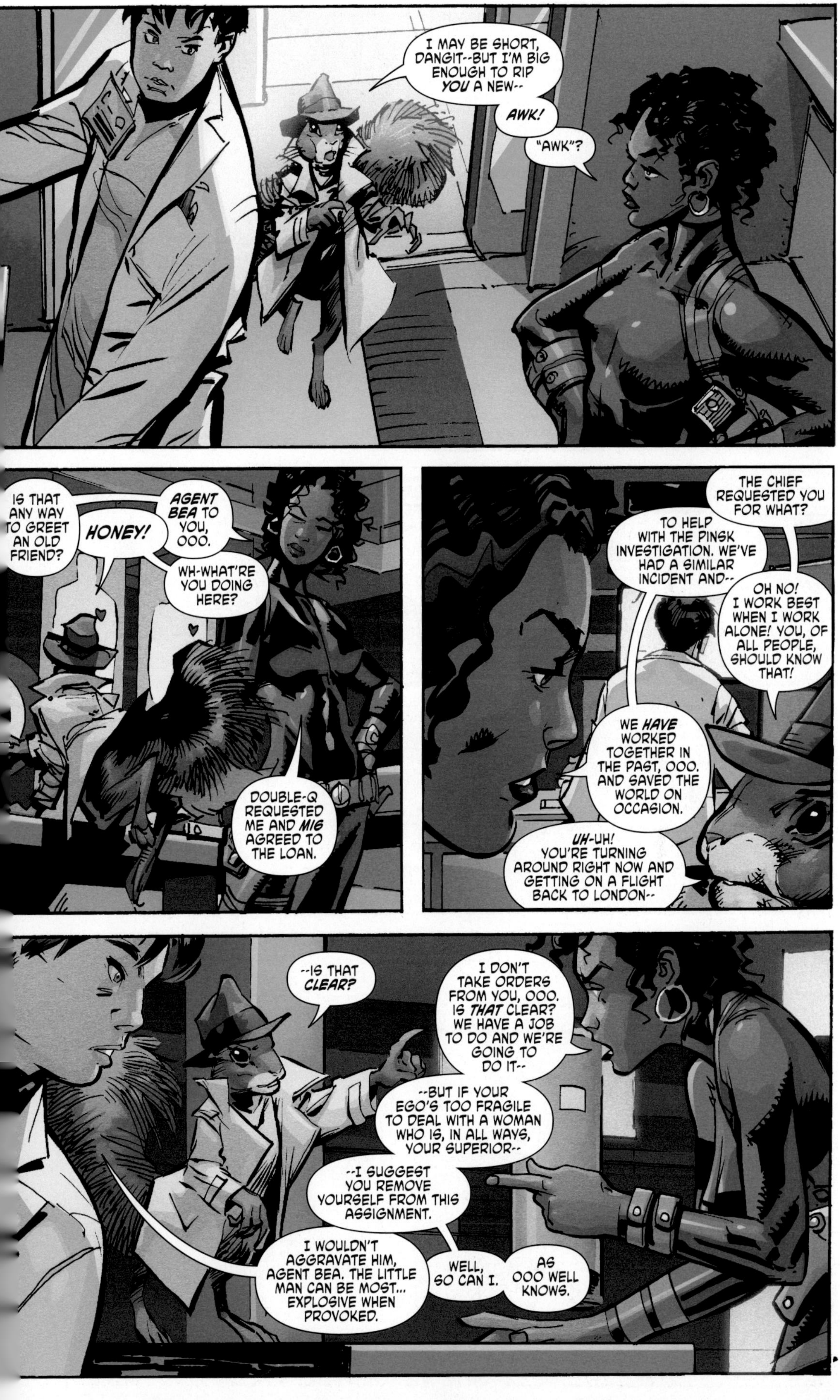
I MAY BE SHORT, DANGIT--BUT I'M BIG ENOUGH TO RIP *YOU* A NEW--
AWK!
"AWK"?
IS THAT ANY WAY TO GREET AN OLD FRIEND?
HONEY!
AGENT BEA TO YOU, OOO.
WH-WHAT'RE YOU DOING HERE?
DOUBLE-Q REQUESTED ME AND *MI6* AGREED TO THE LOAN.
THE CHIEF REQUESTED YOU FOR WHAT?
TO HELP WITH THE PINSK INVESTIGATION. WE'VE HAD A SIMILAR INCIDENT AND--
OH NO! I WORK BEST WHEN I WORK ALONE! YOU, OF ALL PEOPLE, SHOULD KNOW THAT!
WE *HAVE* WORKED TOGETHER IN THE PAST, OOO. AND SAVED THE WORLD ON OCCASION.
UH-UH! YOU'RE TURNING AROUND RIGHT NOW AND GETTING ON A FLIGHT BACK TO LONDON--
--IS THAT *CLEAR?*
I DON'T TAKE ORDERS FROM YOU, OOO. IS *THAT* CLEAR? WE HAVE A JOB TO DO AND WE'RE GOING TO DO IT--
--BUT IF YOUR EGO'S TOO FRAGILE TO DEAL WITH A WOMAN WHO IS, IN ALL WAYS, YOUR SUPERIOR--
--I SUGGEST YOU REMOVE YOURSELF FROM THIS ASSIGNMENT.
I WOULDN'T AGGRAVATE HIM, AGENT BEA. THE LITTLE MAN CAN BE MOST... EXPLOSIVE WHEN PROVOKED.
WELL, SO CAN I.
AS OOO WELL KNOWS.

OKAY, OKAY, *OKAY*--YOU CAN COME ALONG FOR THE RIDE. BUT I CALL THE SHOTS, UNDERSTAND?

AND, *UH,* JUST TO PROVE THAT WE CAN PUT THE PAST BEHIND US--I WANT TO APOLOGIZE FOR WHAT HAPPENED IN HONG KONG.

YOU MEAN WHEN YOU ALMOST GOT US INCINERATED BY *HY-SPY'S* INVISIBLE ROBOTS?

THAT? *PSSH!* THAT WAS *NOTHING!*

I'M TALKING ABOUT THE WAY I LEFT. I KNOW I BROKE YOUR HEART, BABE...I HAVE A NASTY HABIT OF DOING THAT TO WOMEN...AND I JUST WANT TO SAY THAT--

YOU BROKE MY HEART?

HARD T'TALK ABOUT, SURE, BUT I THINK THAT, ONCE WE GET IT ALL OUT IN THE OPEN--

KRAAK

--WE CAN MOVE ON LIKE TWO PROFESSIONALS AND NOT LET--

YOU BROKE *MY* HEART?!

YOU ARROGANT, EGOTISTICAL, NARCISSISTIC, INSUFFERABLE--!

I LEFT YOU IN THAT HOTEL ROOM WEEPING IN YOUR RUM BECAUSE I WOULDN'T *MARRY* YOU!

YOU WERE CLINGING TO MY ANKLES ALL THE WAY DOWN TO THE LOBBY, *BEGGING* ME NOT TO LEAVE YOU!

AND YOU HAVE THE TEMERITY TO SAY THAT YOU *BROKE MY HEART?!*

WHUMP

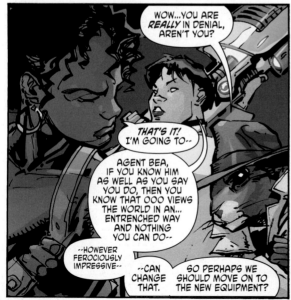

WOW...YOU ARE *REALLY* IN DENIAL, AREN'T YOU?

THAT'S IT! I'M GOING TO--

AGENT BEA, IF YOU KNOW HIM AS WELL AS YOU SAY YOU DO, THEN YOU KNOW THAT OOO VIEWS THE WORLD IN AN... ENTRENCHED WAY AND NOTHING YOU CAN DO--

--HOWEVER FEROCIOUSLY IMPRESSIVE--

--CAN CHANGE THAT.

SO PERHAPS WE SHOULD MOVE ON TO THE NEW EQUIPMENT?

SIGH YOU'RE A WISE MAN, DANGIT.

I TRY, AGENT BEA. I TRY.

NOW THIS IS A *SUPER- FUSION, TWELVE-SHOT QUANTUM GRENADE LAUNCHER* AND--

HEY! THAT'S *MINE!*

OH, *SHUT UP!*

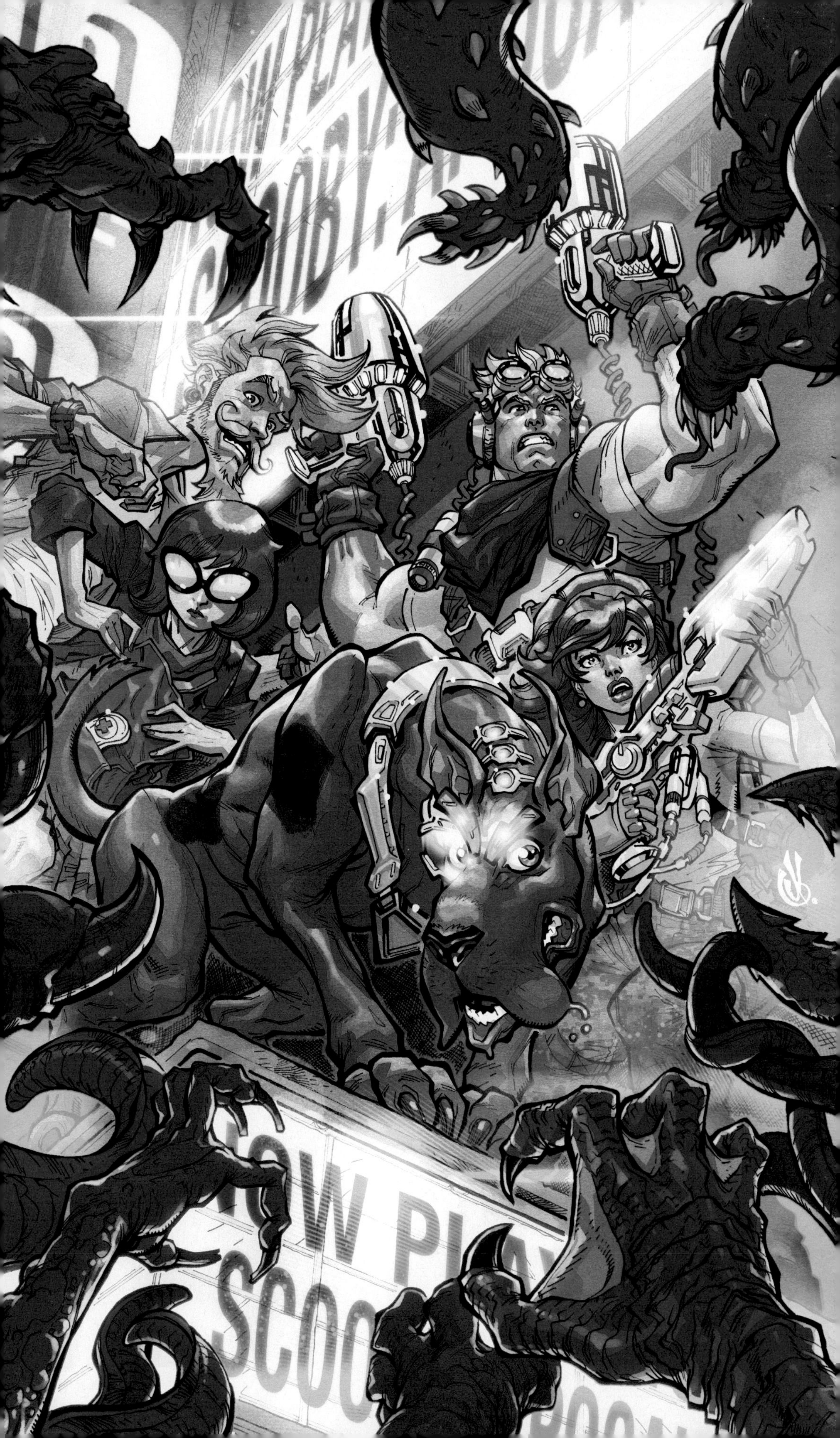

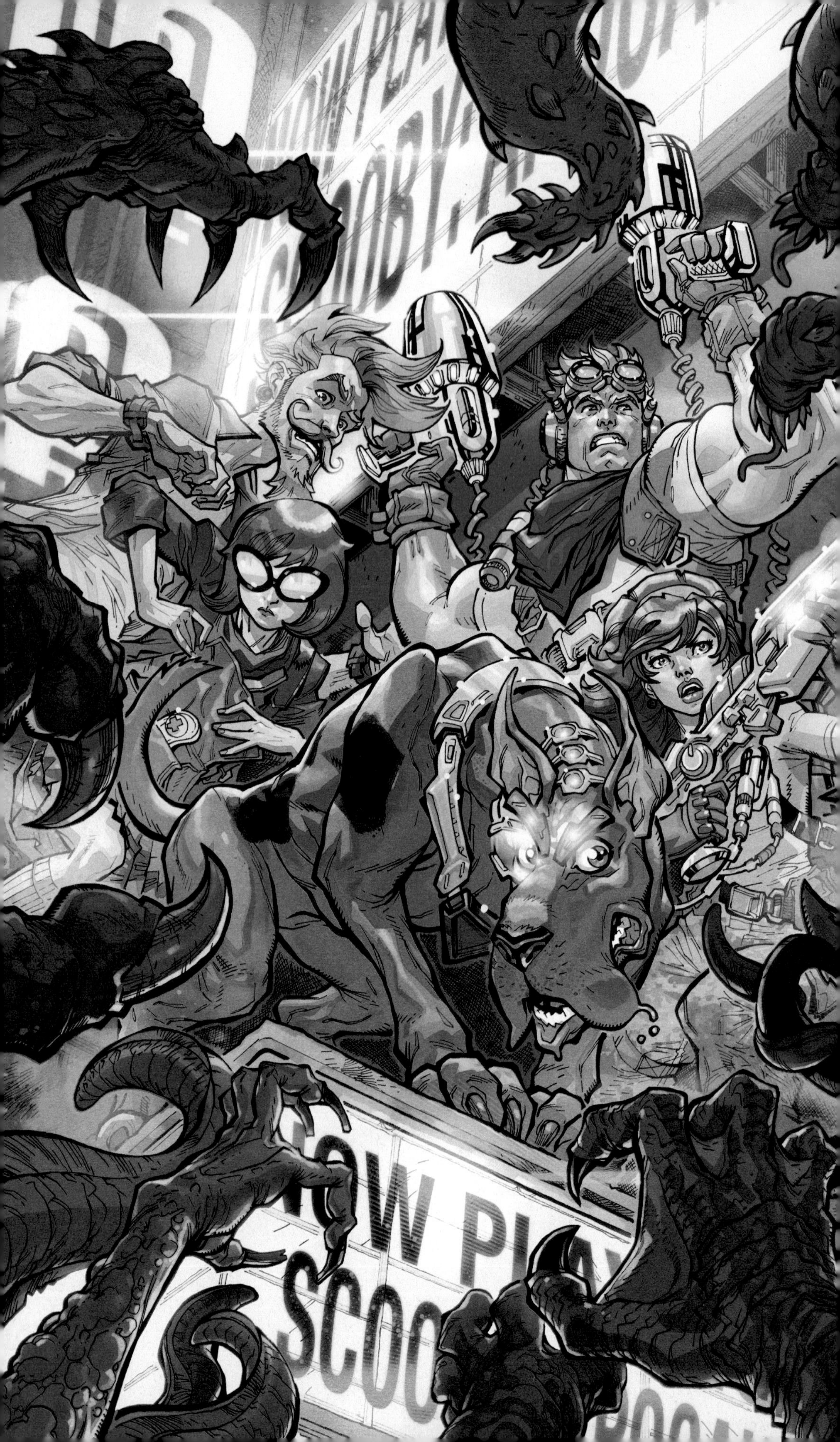

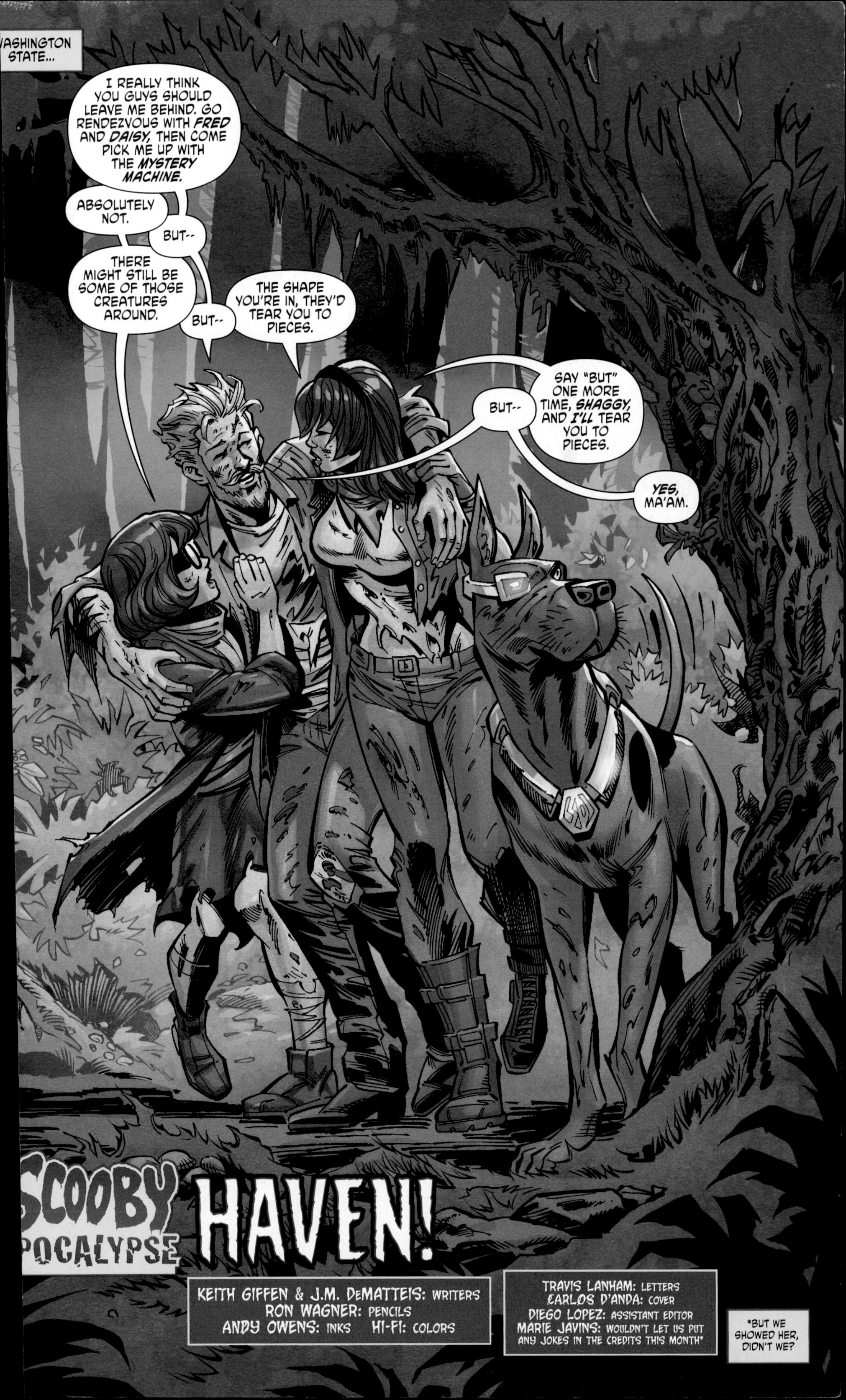
WASHINGTON STATE...
I REALLY THINK YOU GUYS SHOULD LEAVE ME BEHIND. GO RENDEZVOUS WITH FRED AND DAISY, THEN COME PICK ME UP WITH THE MYSTERY MACHINE.
ABSOLUTELY NOT.
BUT--
THERE MIGHT STILL BE SOME OF THOSE CREATURES AROUND.
BUT--
THE SHAPE YOU'RE IN, THEY'D TEAR YOU TO PIECES.
BUT--
SAY "BUT" ONE MORE TIME, SHAGGY, AND I'LL TEAR YOU TO PIECES.
YES, MA'AM.
SCOOBY APOCALYPSE
HAVEN!
KEITH GIFFEN & J.M. DeMATTEIS: WRITERS
RON WAGNER: PENCILS
ANDY OWENS: INKS HI-FI: COLORS
TRAVIS LANHAM: LETTERS
CARLOS D'ANDA: COVER
DIEGO LOPEZ: ASSISTANT EDITOR
MARIE JAVINS: WOULDN'T LET US PUT ANY JOKES IN THE CREDITS THIS MONTH*
*BUT WE SHOWED HER, DIDN'T WE?

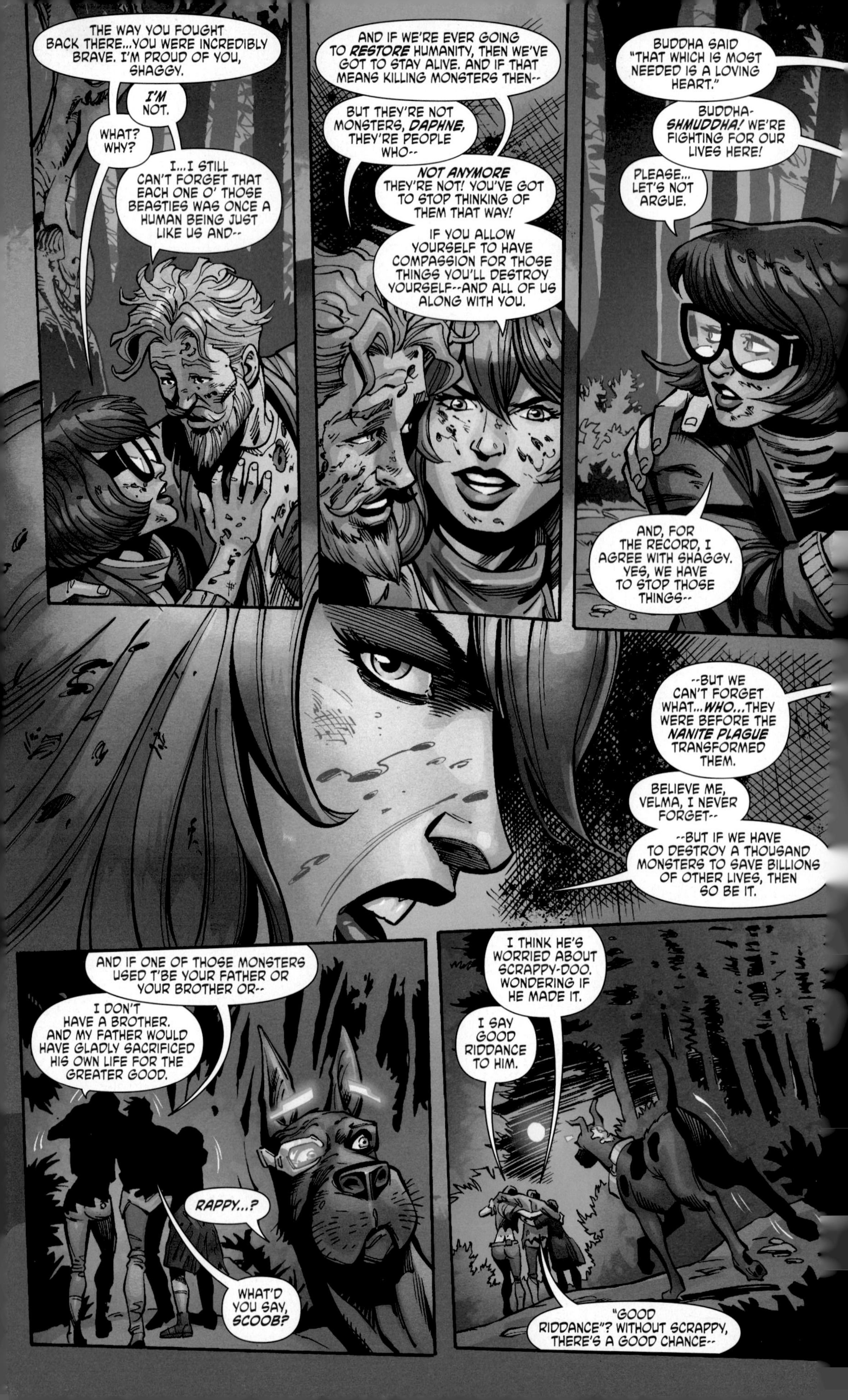
THE WAY YOU FOUGHT BACK THERE...YOU WERE INCREDIBLY BRAVE. I'M PROUD OF YOU, SHAGGY.
I'M NOT.
WHAT? WHY?
I...I STILL CAN'T FORGET THAT EACH ONE O' THOSE BEASTIES WAS ONCE A HUMAN BEING JUST LIKE US AND--
AND IF WE'RE EVER GOING TO ***RESTORE*** HUMANITY, THEN WE'VE GOT TO STAY ALIVE. AND IF THAT MEANS KILLING MONSTERS THEN--
BUT THEY'RE NOT MONSTERS, ***DAPHNE,*** THEY'RE PEOPLE WHO--
NOT ANYMORE THEY'RE NOT! YOU'VE GOT TO STOP THINKING OF THEM THAT WAY!
IF YOU ALLOW YOURSELF TO HAVE COMPASSION FOR THOSE THINGS YOU'LL DESTROY YOURSELF--AND ALL OF US ALONG WITH YOU.
BUDDHA SAID "THAT WHICH IS MOST NEEDED IS A LOVING HEART."
BUDDHA-***SHMUDDHA!*** WE'RE FIGHTING FOR OUR LIVES HERE!
PLEASE... LET'S NOT ARGUE.
AND, FOR THE RECORD, I AGREE WITH SHAGGY. YES, WE HAVE TO STOP THOSE THINGS--
--BUT WE CAN'T FORGET WHAT...***WHO...***THEY WERE BEFORE THE ***NANITE PLAGUE*** TRANSFORMED THEM.
BELIEVE ME, VELMA, I NEVER FORGET--
--BUT IF WE HAVE TO DESTROY A THOUSAND MONSTERS TO SAVE BILLIONS OF OTHER LIVES, THEN SO BE IT.
AND IF ONE OF THOSE MONSTERS USED T'BE YOUR FATHER OR YOUR BROTHER OR--
I DON'T HAVE A BROTHER. AND MY FATHER WOULD HAVE GLADLY SACRIFICED HIS OWN LIFE FOR THE GREATER GOOD.
RAPPY...?
WHAT'D YOU SAY, ***SCOOB?***
I THINK HE'S WORRIED ABOUT SCRAPPY-DOO. WONDERING IF HE MADE IT.
I SAY GOOD RIDDANCE TO HIM.
"GOOD RIDDANCE"? WITHOUT SCRAPPY, THERE'S A GOOD CHANCE--

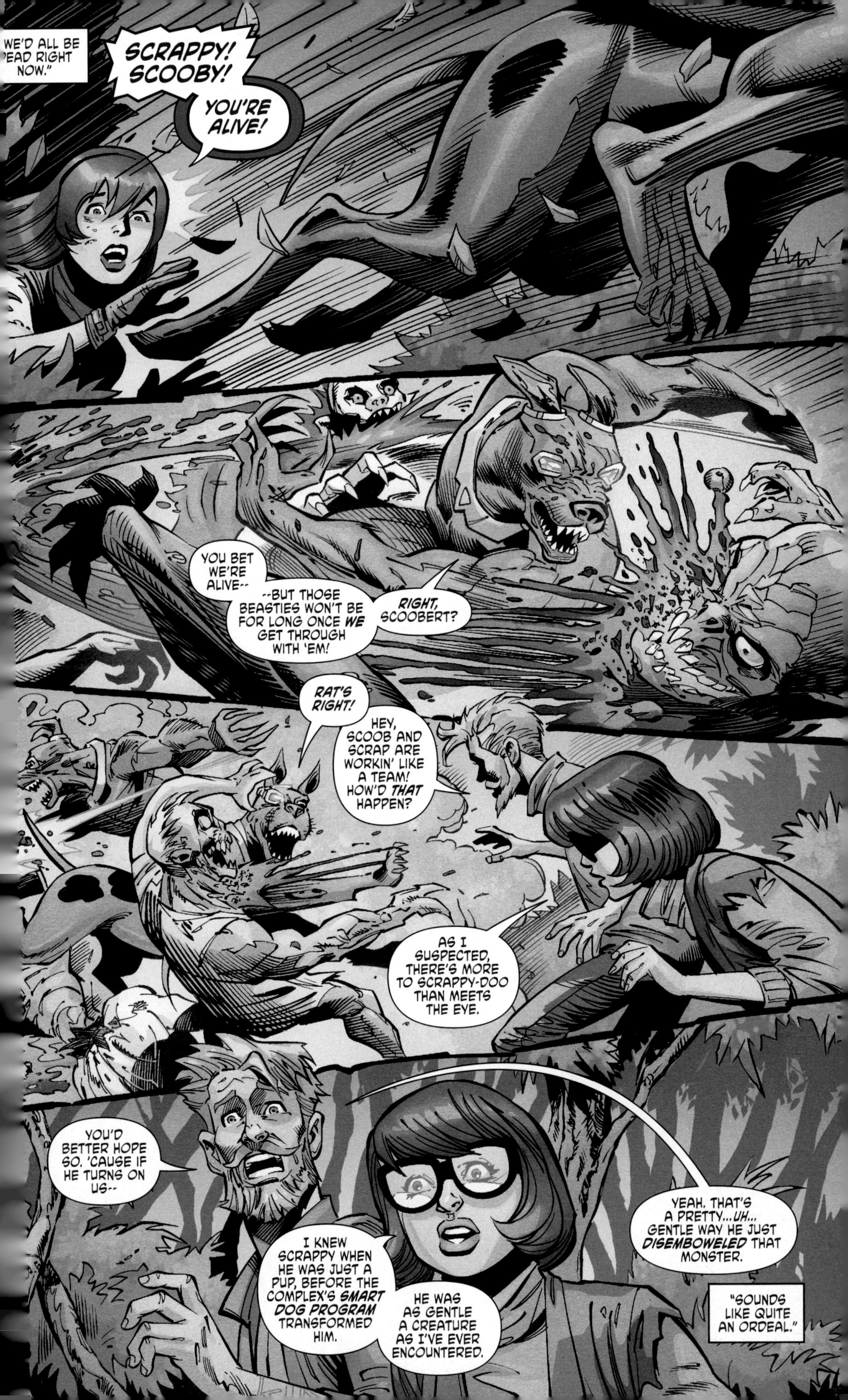

WE'D ALL BE DEAD RIGHT NOW."
SCRAPPY! SCOOBY!
YOU'RE ALIVE!
YOU BET WE'RE ALIVE--
--BUT THOSE BEASTIES WON'T BE FOR LONG ONCE WE GET THROUGH WITH 'EM!
RIGHT, SCOOBERT?
RAT'S RIGHT!
HEY, SCOOB AND SCRAP ARE WORKIN' LIKE A TEAM! HOW'D THAT HAPPEN?
AS I SUSPECTED, THERE'S MORE TO SCRAPPY-DOO THAN MEETS THE EYE.
YOU'D BETTER HOPE SO. 'CAUSE IF HE TURNS ON US--
YEAH. THAT'S A PRETTY...UH... GENTLE WAY HE JUST DISEMBOWELED THAT MONSTER.
I KNEW SCRAPPY WHEN HE WAS JUST A PUP, BEFORE THE COMPLEX'S SMART DOG PROGRAM TRANSFORMED HIM.
HE WAS AS GENTLE A CREATURE AS I'VE EVER ENCOUNTERED.
"SOUNDS LIKE QUITE AN ORDEAL."

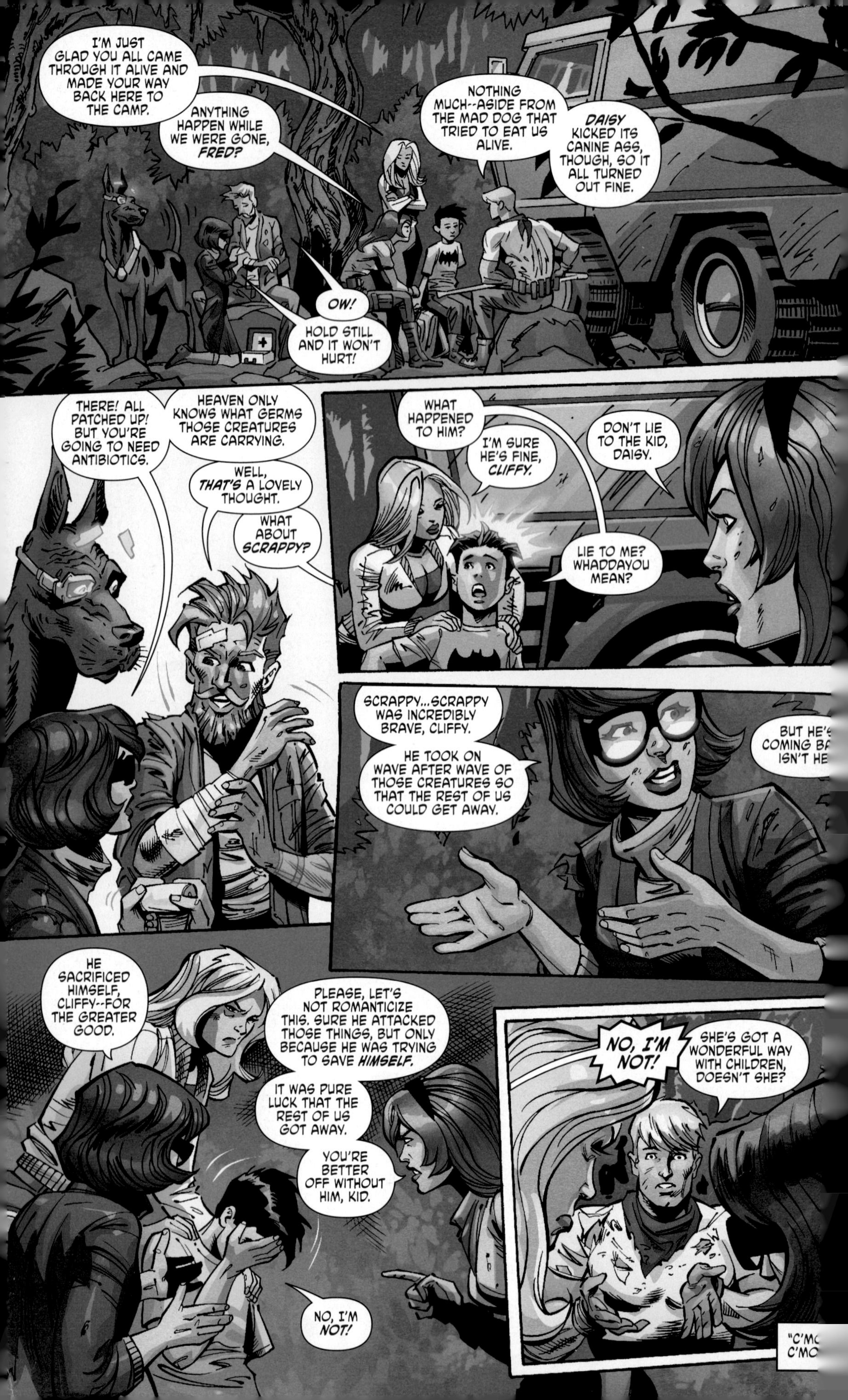
I'M JUST GLAD YOU ALL CAME THROUGH IT ALIVE AND MADE YOUR WAY BACK HERE TO THE CAMP.
ANYTHING HAPPEN WHILE WE WERE GONE, FRED?
NOTHING MUCH--ASIDE FROM THE MAD DOG THAT TRIED TO EAT US ALIVE.
DAISY KICKED ITS CANINE ASS, THOUGH, SO IT ALL TURNED OUT FINE.
OW!
HOLD STILL AND IT WON'T HURT!
THERE! ALL PATCHED UP! BUT YOU'RE GOING TO NEED ANTIBIOTICS.
HEAVEN ONLY KNOWS WHAT GERMS THOSE CREATURES ARE CARRYING.
WELL, THAT'S A LOVELY THOUGHT.
WHAT ABOUT SCRAPPY?
WHAT HAPPENED TO HIM?
I'M SURE HE'S FINE, CLIFFY.
DON'T LIE TO THE KID, DAISY.
LIE TO ME? WHADDAYOU MEAN?
SCRAPPY...SCRAPPY WAS INCREDIBLY BRAVE, CLIFFY.
HE TOOK ON WAVE AFTER WAVE OF THOSE CREATURES SO THAT THE REST OF US COULD GET AWAY.
HE SACRIFICED HIMSELF, CLIFFY--FOR THE GREATER GOOD.
PLEASE, LET'S NOT ROMANTICIZE THIS. SURE HE ATTACKED THOSE THINGS, BUT ONLY BECAUSE HE WAS TRYING TO SAVE HIMSELF.
IT WAS PURE LUCK THAT THE REST OF US GOT AWAY.
YOU'RE BETTER OFF WITHOUT HIM, KID.
NO, I'M NOT!
NO, I'M NOT!
SHE'S GOT A WONDERFUL WAY WITH CHILDREN, DOESN'T SHE?

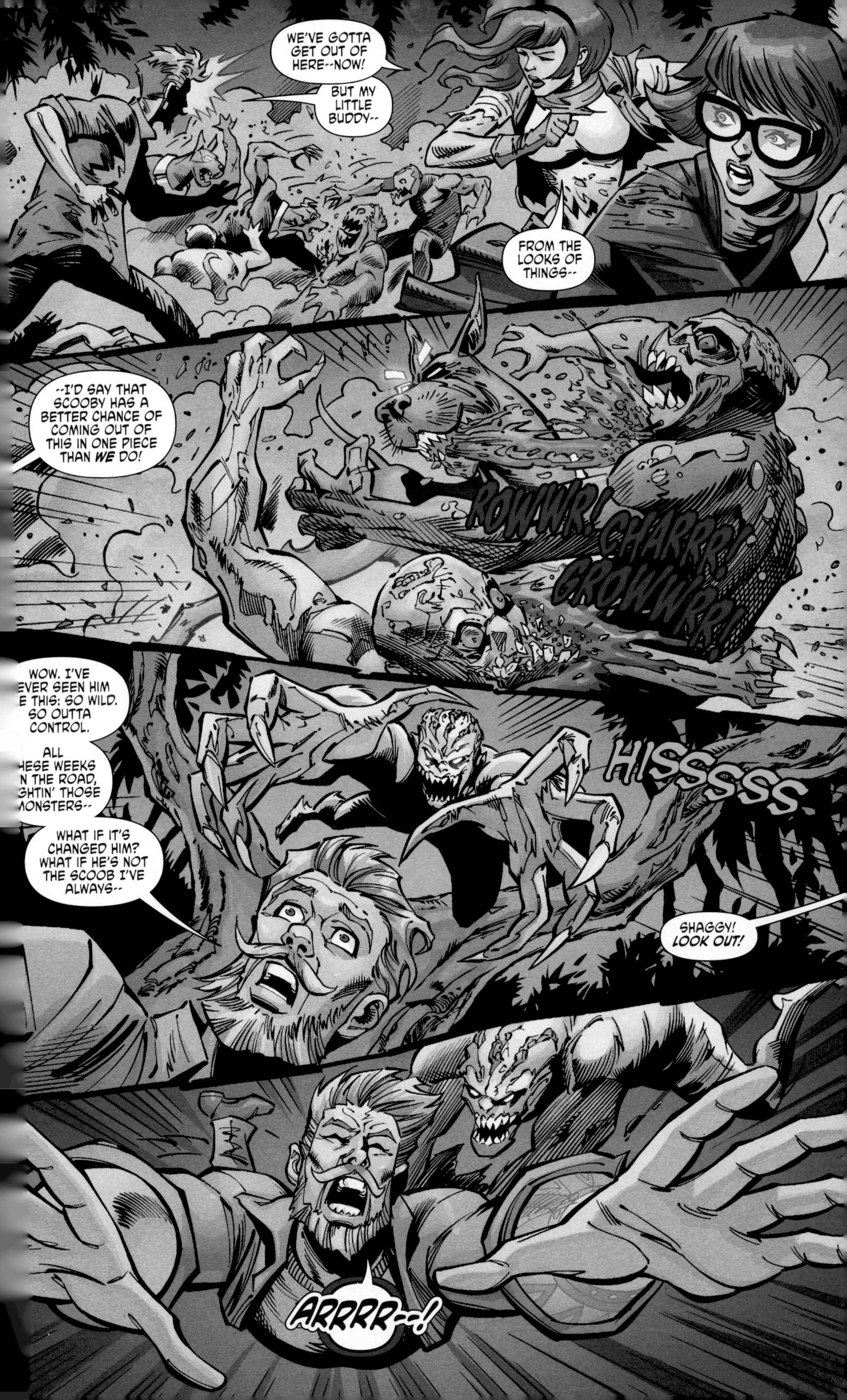
WE'VE GOTTA GET OUT OF HERE--NOW!
BUT MY LITTLE BUDDY--
FROM THE LOOKS OF THINGS--
--I'D SAY THAT SCOOBY HAS A BETTER CHANCE OF COMING OUT OF THIS IN ONE PIECE THAN WE DO!
ROWWR! CHARRR! GROWWRR!
WOW. I'VE EVER SEEN HIM E THIS: SO WILD. SO OUTTA CONTROL.
ALL HESE WEEKS N THE ROAD, GHTIN' THOSE MONSTERS--
WHAT IF IT'S CHANGED HIM? WHAT IF HE'S NOT THE SCOOB I'VE ALWAYS--
HISSSSS
SHAGGY! LOOK OUT!
ARRRR--!

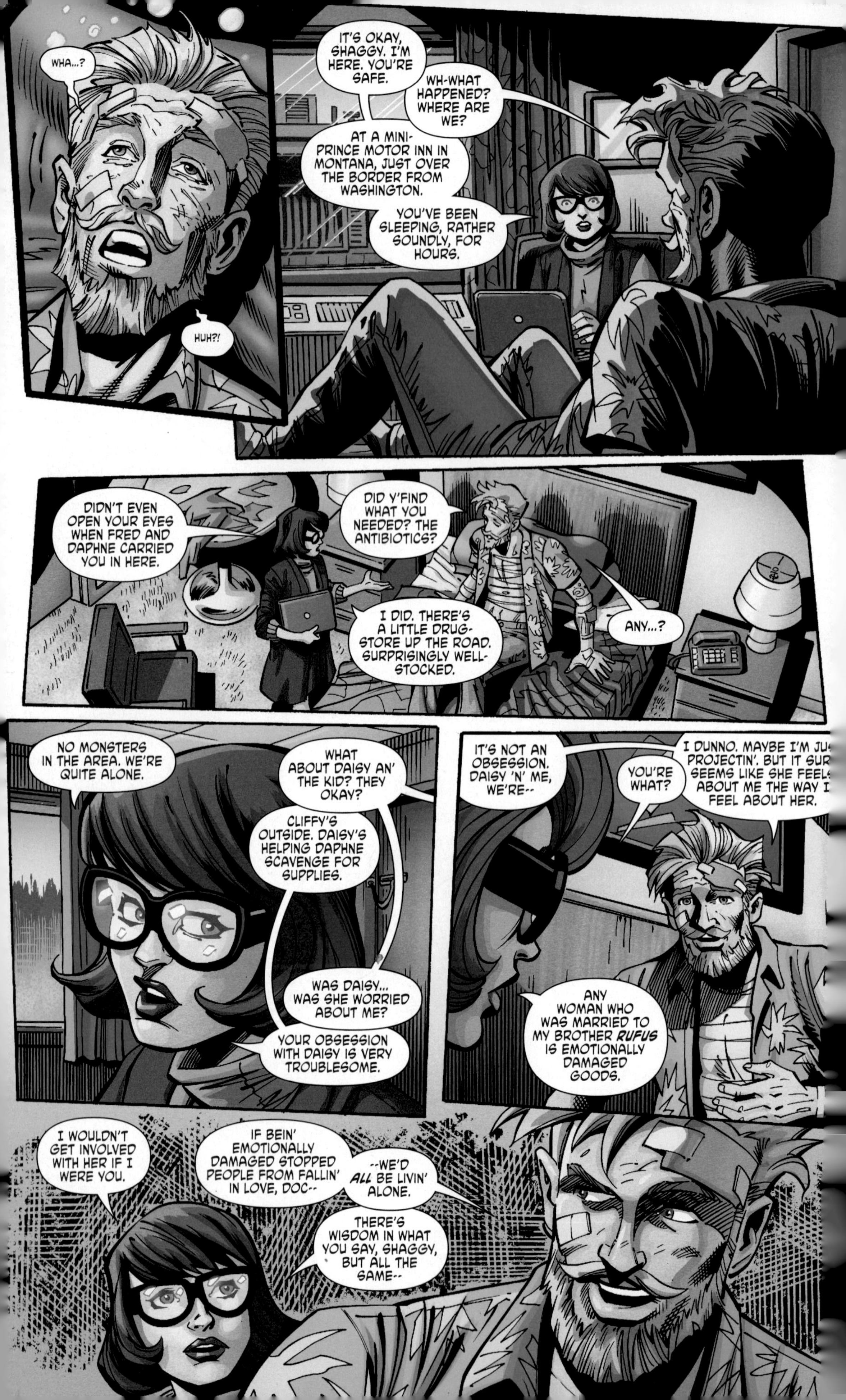
WHA...?
IT'S OKAY, SHAGGY. I'M HERE. YOU'RE SAFE.
WH-WHAT HAPPENED? WHERE ARE WE?
AT A MINI-PRINCE MOTOR INN IN MONTANA, JUST OVER THE BORDER FROM WASHINGTON.
YOU'VE BEEN SLEEPING, RATHER SOUNDLY, FOR HOURS.
HUH?!
DIDN'T EVEN OPEN YOUR EYES WHEN FRED AND DAPHNE CARRIED YOU IN HERE.
DID Y'FIND WHAT YOU NEEDED? THE ANTIBIOTICS?
I DID. THERE'S A LITTLE DRUG-STORE UP THE ROAD. SURPRISINGLY WELL-STOCKED.
ANY...?
NO MONSTERS IN THE AREA. WE'RE QUITE ALONE.
WHAT ABOUT DAISY AN' THE KID? THEY OKAY?
CLIFFY'S OUTSIDE. DAISY'S HELPING DAPHNE SCAVENGE FOR SUPPLIES.
WAS DAISY... WAS SHE WORRIED ABOUT ME?
YOUR OBSESSION WITH DAISY IS VERY TROUBLESOME.
IT'S NOT AN OBSESSION. DAISY 'N' ME, WE'RE--
YOU'RE WHAT?
I DUNNO. MAYBE I'M JUS PROJECTIN'. BUT IT SUR SEEMS LIKE SHE FEEL ABOUT ME THE WAY I FEEL ABOUT HER.
ANY WOMAN WHO WAS MARRIED TO MY BROTHER *RUFUS* IS EMOTIONALLY DAMAGED GOODS.
I WOULDN'T GET INVOLVED WITH HER IF I WERE YOU.
IF BEIN' EMOTIONALLY DAMAGED STOPPED PEOPLE FROM FALLIN' IN LOVE, DOC--
--WE'D *ALL* BE LIVIN' ALONE.
THERE'S WISDOM IN WHAT YOU SAY, SHAGGY, BUT ALL THE SAME--

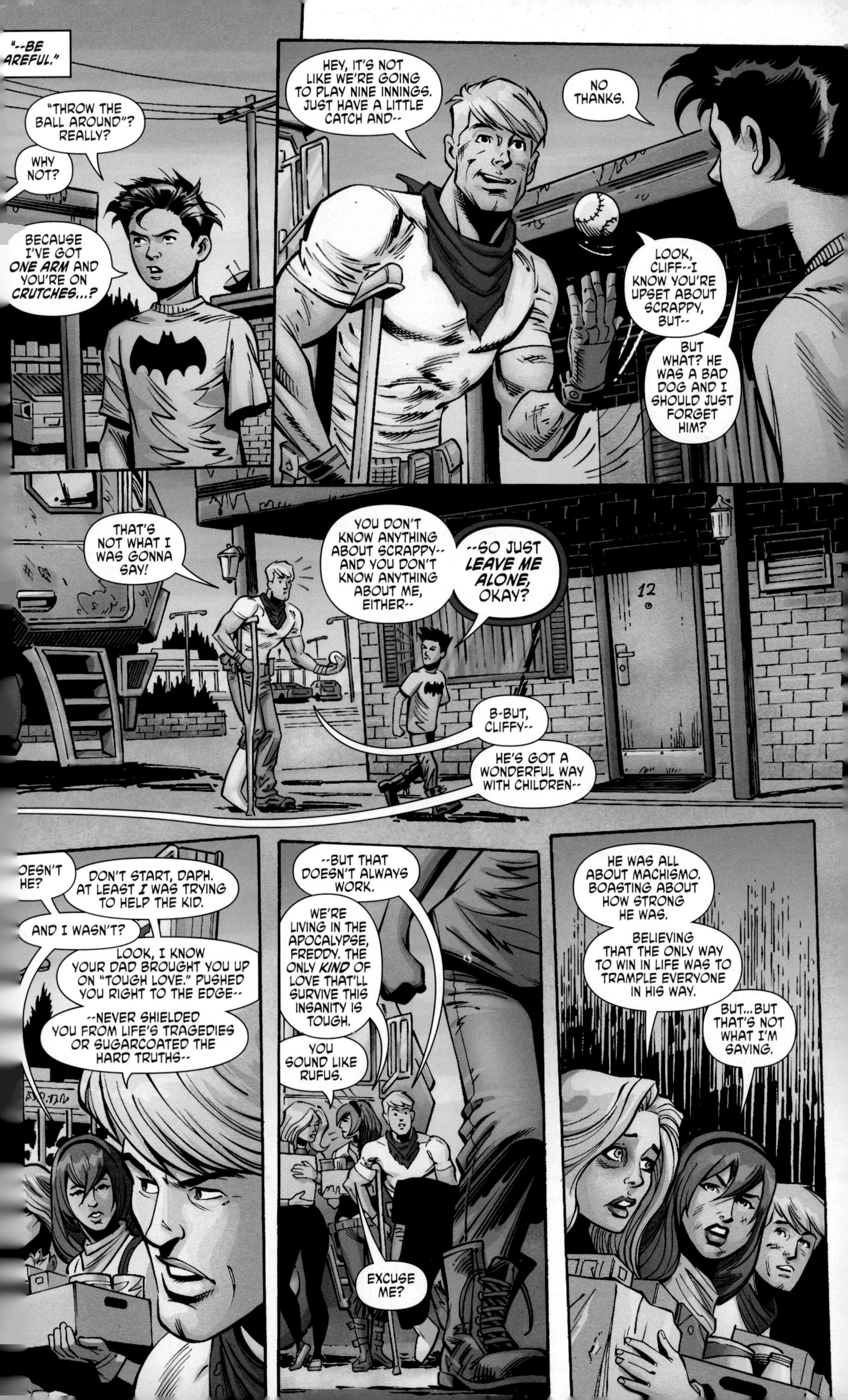
"--BE
AREFUL."
"THROW THE BALL AROUND"? REALLY?
WHY NOT?
BECAUSE I'VE GOT ONE ARM AND YOU'RE ON CRUTCHES...?
HEY, IT'S NOT LIKE WE'RE GOING TO PLAY NINE INNINGS. JUST HAVE A LITTLE CATCH AND--
NO THANKS.
LOOK, CLIFF--I KNOW YOU'RE UPSET ABOUT SCRAPPY, BUT--
BUT WHAT? HE WAS A BAD DOG AND I SHOULD JUST FORGET HIM?
THAT'S NOT WHAT I WAS GONNA SAY!
YOU DON'T KNOW ANYTHING ABOUT SCRAPPY-- AND YOU DON'T KNOW ANYTHING ABOUT ME, EITHER--
--SO JUST LEAVE ME ALONE, OKAY?
12
B-BUT, CLIFFY--
HE'S GOT A WONDERFUL WAY WITH CHILDREN--
OESN'T HE?
DON'T START, DAPH. AT LEAST I WAS TRYING TO HELP THE KID.
AND I WASN'T?
LOOK, I KNOW YOUR DAD BROUGHT YOU UP ON "TOUGH LOVE." PUSHED YOU RIGHT TO THE EDGE--
--NEVER SHIELDED YOU FROM LIFE'S TRAGEDIES OR SUGARCOATED THE HARD TRUTHS--
--BUT THAT DOESN'T ALWAYS WORK.
WE'RE LIVING IN THE APOCALYPSE, FREDDY. THE ONLY KIND OF LOVE THAT'LL SURVIVE THIS INSANITY IS TOUGH.
YOU SOUND LIKE RUFUS.
EXCUSE ME?
HE WAS ALL ABOUT MACHISMO. BOASTING ABOUT HOW STRONG HE WAS.
BELIEVING THAT THE ONLY WAY TO WIN IN LIFE WAS TO TRAMPLE EVERYONE IN HIS WAY.
BUT...BUT THAT'S NOT WHAT I'M SAYING.

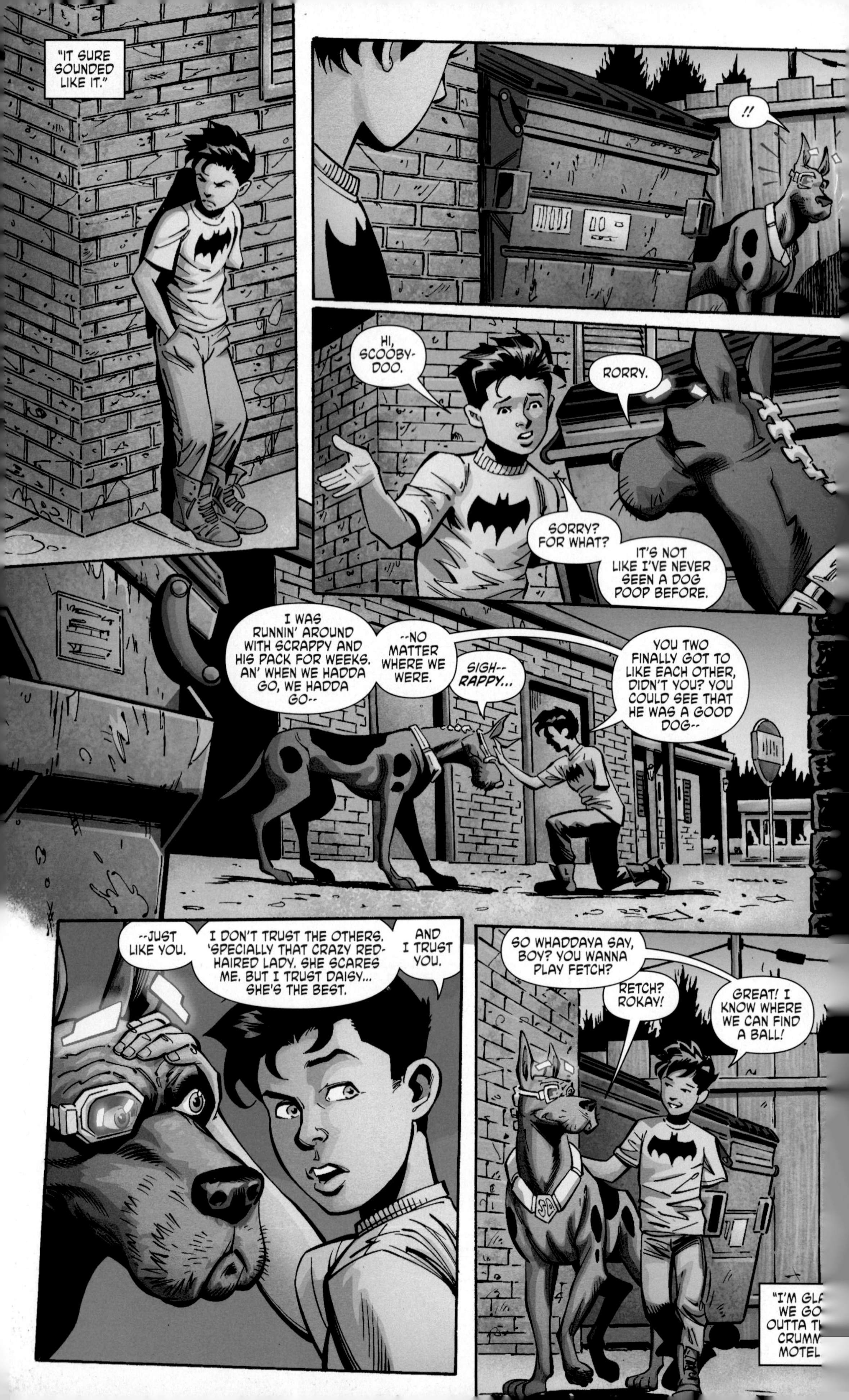
"IT SURE SOUNDED LIKE IT."
!!
HI, SCOOBY-DOO.
RORRY.
SORRY? FOR WHAT?
IT'S NOT LIKE I'VE NEVER SEEN A DOG POOP BEFORE.
I WAS RUNNIN' AROUND WITH SCRAPPY AND HIS PACK FOR WEEKS. AN' WHEN WE HADDA GO, WE HADDA GO--
--NO MATTER WHERE WE WERE.
SIGH-- RAPPY...
YOU TWO FINALLY GOT TO LIKE EACH OTHER, DIDN'T YOU? YOU COULD SEE THAT HE WAS A GOOD DOG--
--JUST LIKE YOU.
I DON'T TRUST THE OTHERS. 'SPECIALLY THAT CRAZY RED-HAIRED LADY. SHE SCARES ME. BUT I TRUST DAISY... SHE'S THE BEST.
AND I TRUST YOU.
SO WHADDAYA SAY, BOY? YOU WANNA PLAY FETCH?
RETCH? ROKAY!
GREAT! I KNOW WHERE WE CAN FIND A BALL!

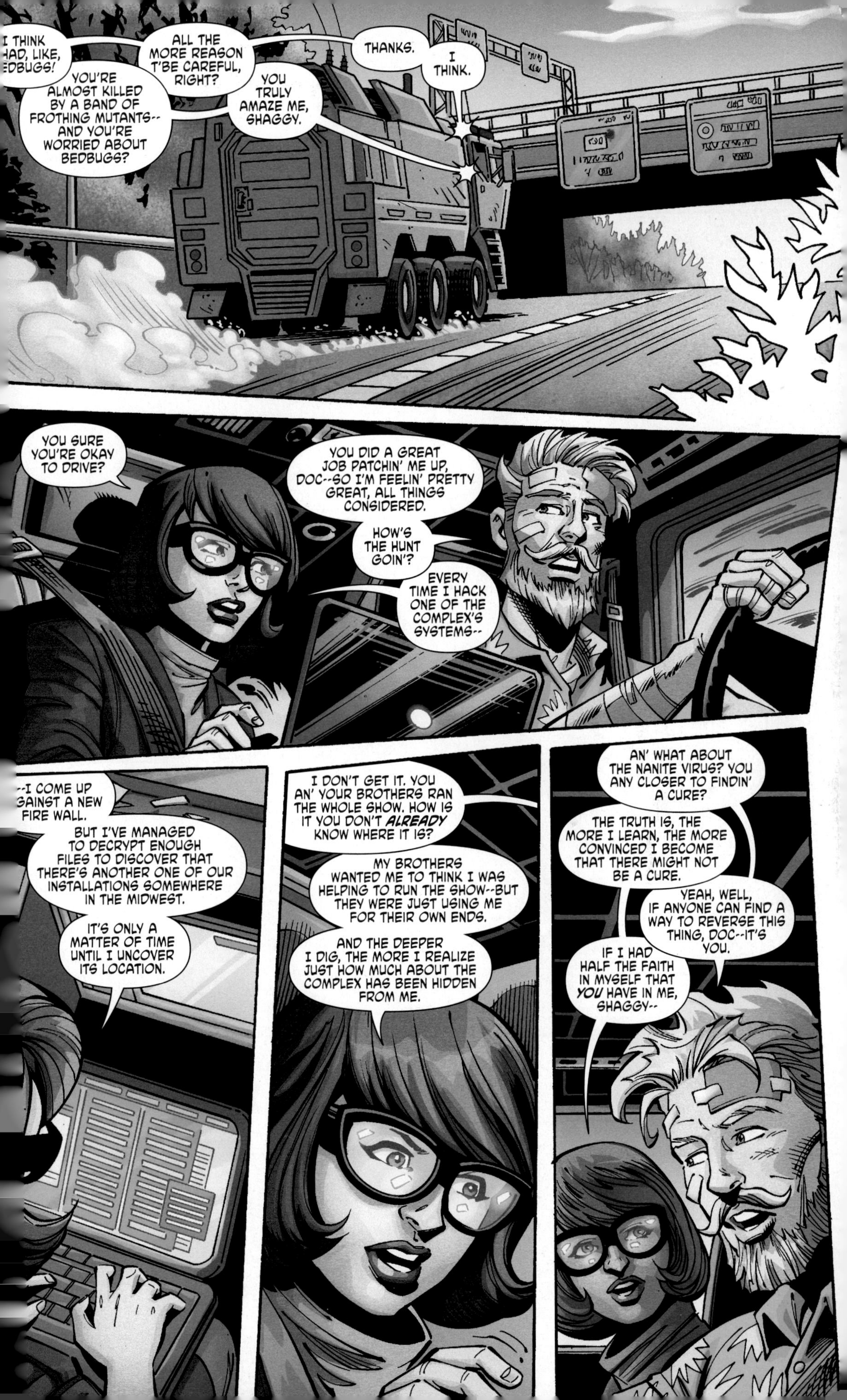
I THINK HAD, LIKE, EDBUGS!
YOU'RE ALMOST KILLED BY A BAND OF FROTHING MUTANTS-- AND YOU'RE WORRIED ABOUT BEDBUGS?
ALL THE MORE REASON T'BE CAREFUL, RIGHT?
YOU TRULY AMAZE ME, SHAGGY.
THANKS.
I THINK.
YOU SURE YOU'RE OKAY TO DRIVE?
YOU DID A GREAT JOB PATCHIN' ME UP, DOC--SO I'M FEELIN' PRETTY GREAT, ALL THINGS CONSIDERED.
HOW'S THE HUNT GOIN'?
EVERY TIME I HACK ONE OF THE COMPLEX'S SYSTEMS--
--I COME UP GAINST A NEW FIRE WALL.
BUT I'VE MANAGED TO DECRYPT ENOUGH FILES TO DISCOVER THAT THERE'S ANOTHER ONE OF OUR INSTALLATIONS SOMEWHERE IN THE MIDWEST.
IT'S ONLY A MATTER OF TIME UNTIL I UNCOVER ITS LOCATION.
I DON'T GET IT. YOU AN' YOUR BROTHERS RAN THE WHOLE SHOW. HOW IS IT YOU DON'T ALREADY KNOW WHERE IT IS?
MY BROTHERS WANTED ME TO THINK I WAS HELPING TO RUN THE SHOW--BUT THEY WERE JUST USING ME FOR THEIR OWN ENDS.
AND THE DEEPER I DIG, THE MORE I REALIZE JUST HOW MUCH ABOUT THE COMPLEX HAS BEEN HIDDEN FROM ME.
AN' WHAT ABOUT THE NANITE VIRUS? YOU ANY CLOSER TO FINDIN' A CURE?
THE TRUTH IS, THE MORE I LEARN, THE MORE CONVINCED I BECOME THAT THERE MIGHT NOT BE A CURE.
YEAH, WELL, IF ANYONE CAN FIND A WAY TO REVERSE THIS THING, DOC--IT'S YOU.
IF I HAD HALF THE FAITH IN MYSELF THAT YOU HAVE IN ME, SHAGGY--

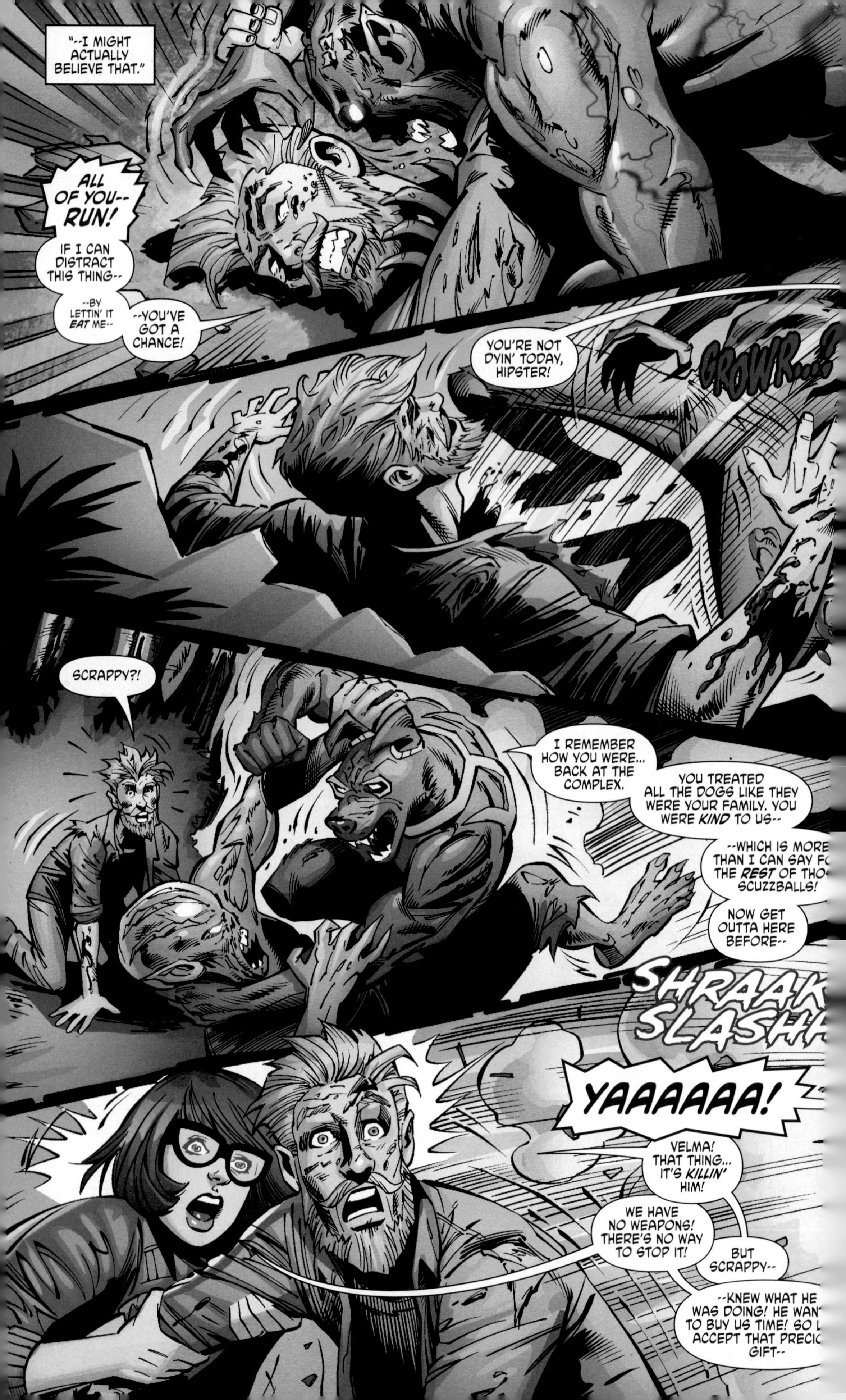
"--I MIGHT ACTUALLY BELIEVE THAT."
ALL OF YOU-- RUN!
IF I CAN DISTRACT THIS THING--
--BY LETTIN' IT EAT ME--
--YOU'VE GOT A CHANCE!
YOU'RE NOT DYIN' TODAY, HIPSTER!
GROWR...
SCRAPPY?!
I REMEMBER HOW YOU WERE... BACK AT THE COMPLEX.
YOU TREATED ALL THE DOGS LIKE THEY WERE YOUR FAMILY. YOU WERE KIND TO US--
--WHICH IS MORE THAN I CAN SAY FO THE REST OF THO SCUZZBALLS!
NOW GET OUTTA HERE BEFORE--
SHRAAK SLASH
YAAAAAA!
VELMA! THAT THING... IT'S KILLIN' HIM!
WE HAVE NO WEAPONS! THERE'S NO WAY TO STOP IT!
BUT SCRAPPY--
--KNEW WHAT HE WAS DOING! HE WAN TO BUY US TIME! SO L ACCEPT THAT PRECI GIFT--

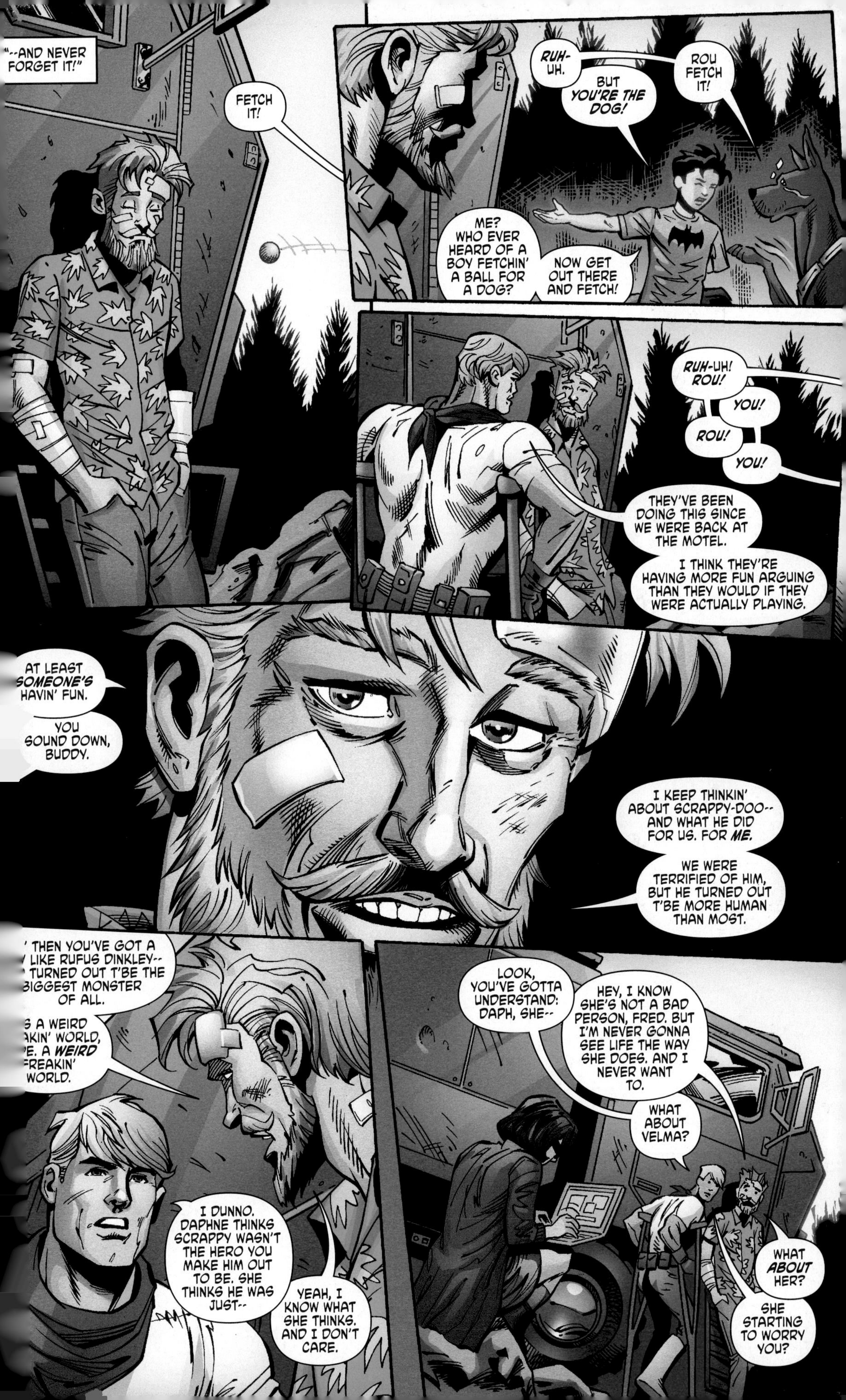
"--AND NEVER FORGET IT!"
FETCH IT!
RUH-UH.
BUT YOU'RE THE DOG!
ROU FETCH IT!
ME? WHO EVER HEARD OF A BOY FETCHIN' A BALL FOR A DOG?
NOW GET OUT THERE AND FETCH!
RUH-UH! ROU!
YOU!
ROU!
YOU!
THEY'VE BEEN DOING THIS SINCE WE WERE BACK AT THE MOTEL.
I THINK THEY'RE HAVING MORE FUN ARGUING THAN THEY WOULD IF THEY WERE ACTUALLY PLAYING.
AT LEAST SOMEONE'S HAVIN' FUN.
YOU SOUND DOWN, BUDDY.
I KEEP THINKIN' ABOUT SCRAPPY-DOO-- AND WHAT HE DID FOR US. FOR ME.
WE WERE TERRIFIED OF HIM, BUT HE TURNED OUT T'BE MORE HUMAN THAN MOST.
THEN YOU'VE GOT A LIKE RUFUS DINKLEY-- TURNED OUT T'BE THE BIGGEST MONSTER OF ALL.
A WEIRD AKIN' WORLD, E. A WEIRD FREAKIN' WORLD.
I DUNNO. DAPHNE THINKS SCRAPPY WASN'T THE HERO YOU MAKE HIM OUT TO BE. SHE THINKS HE WAS JUST--
YEAH, I KNOW WHAT SHE THINKS. AND I DON'T CARE.
LOOK, YOU'VE GOTTA UNDERSTAND: DAPH, SHE--
HEY, I KNOW SHE'S NOT A BAD PERSON, FRED. BUT I'M NEVER GONNA SEE LIFE THE WAY SHE DOES. AND I NEVER WANT TO.
WHAT ABOUT VELMA?
WHAT ABOUT HER?
SHE STARTING TO WORRY YOU?

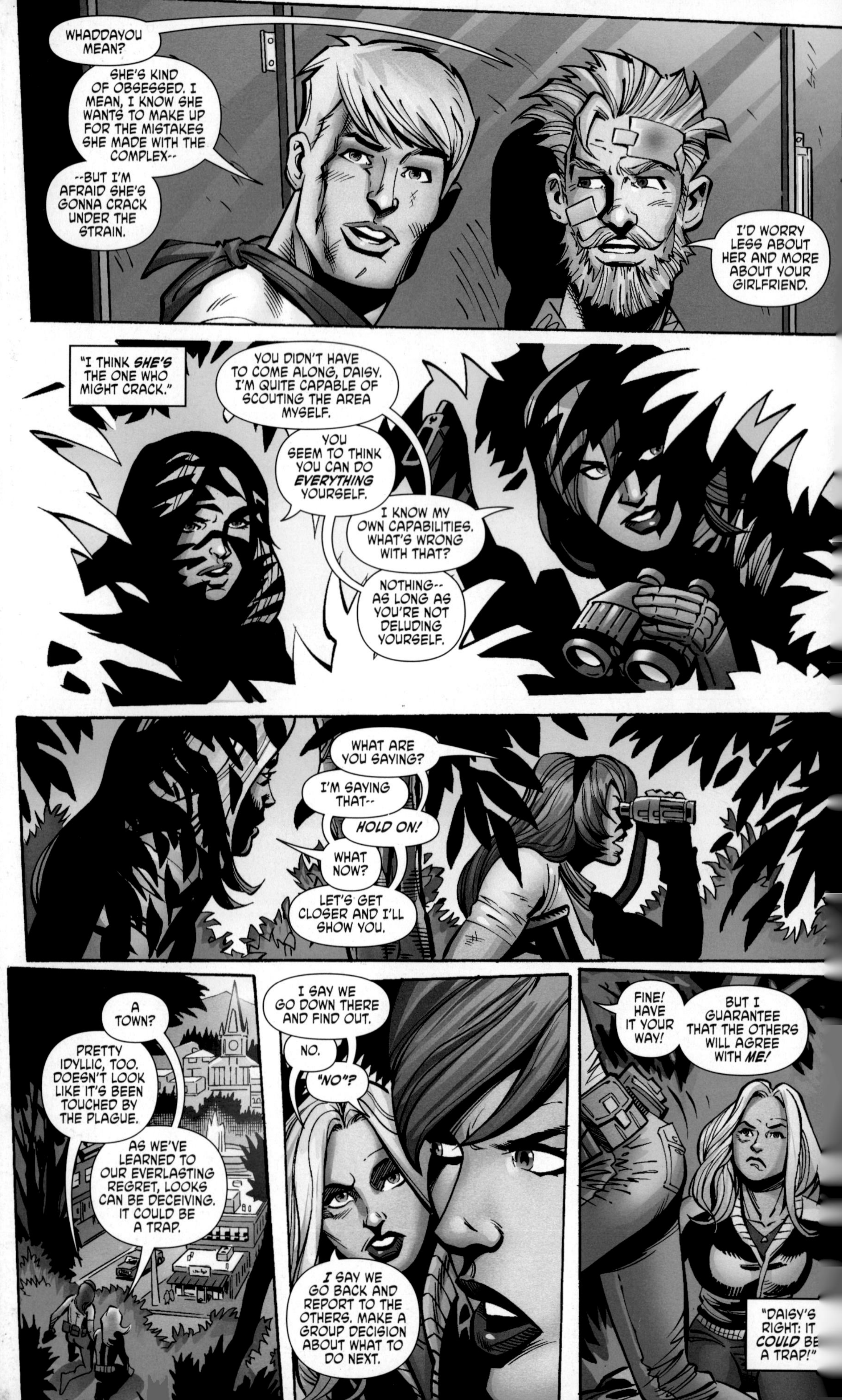
WHADDAYOU MEAN?
SHE'S KIND OF OBSESSED. I MEAN, I KNOW SHE WANTS TO MAKE UP FOR THE MISTAKES SHE MADE WITH THE COMPLEX--
--BUT I'M AFRAID SHE'S GONNA CRACK UNDER THE STRAIN.
I'D WORRY LESS ABOUT HER AND MORE ABOUT YOUR GIRLFRIEND.
"I THINK SHE'S THE ONE WHO MIGHT CRACK."
YOU DIDN'T HAVE TO COME ALONG, DAISY. I'M QUITE CAPABLE OF SCOUTING THE AREA MYSELF.
YOU SEEM TO THINK YOU CAN DO EVERYTHING YOURSELF.
I KNOW MY OWN CAPABILITIES. WHAT'S WRONG WITH THAT?
NOTHING-- AS LONG AS YOU'RE NOT DELUDING YOURSELF.
WHAT ARE YOU SAYING?
I'M SAYING THAT--
HOLD ON!
WHAT NOW?
LET'S GET CLOSER AND I'LL SHOW YOU.
A TOWN?
PRETTY IDYLLIC, TOO. DOESN'T LOOK LIKE IT'S BEEN TOUCHED BY THE PLAGUE.
AS WE'VE LEARNED TO OUR EVERLASTING REGRET, LOOKS CAN BE DECEIVING. IT COULD BE A TRAP.
I SAY WE GO DOWN THERE AND FIND OUT.
NO.
"NO"?
I SAY WE GO BACK AND REPORT TO THE OTHERS. MAKE A GROUP DECISION ABOUT WHAT TO DO NEXT.
FINE! HAVE IT YOUR WAY!
BUT I GUARANTEE THAT THE OTHERS WILL AGREE WITH ME!
"DAISY'S RIGHT: IT COULD BE A TRAP!"

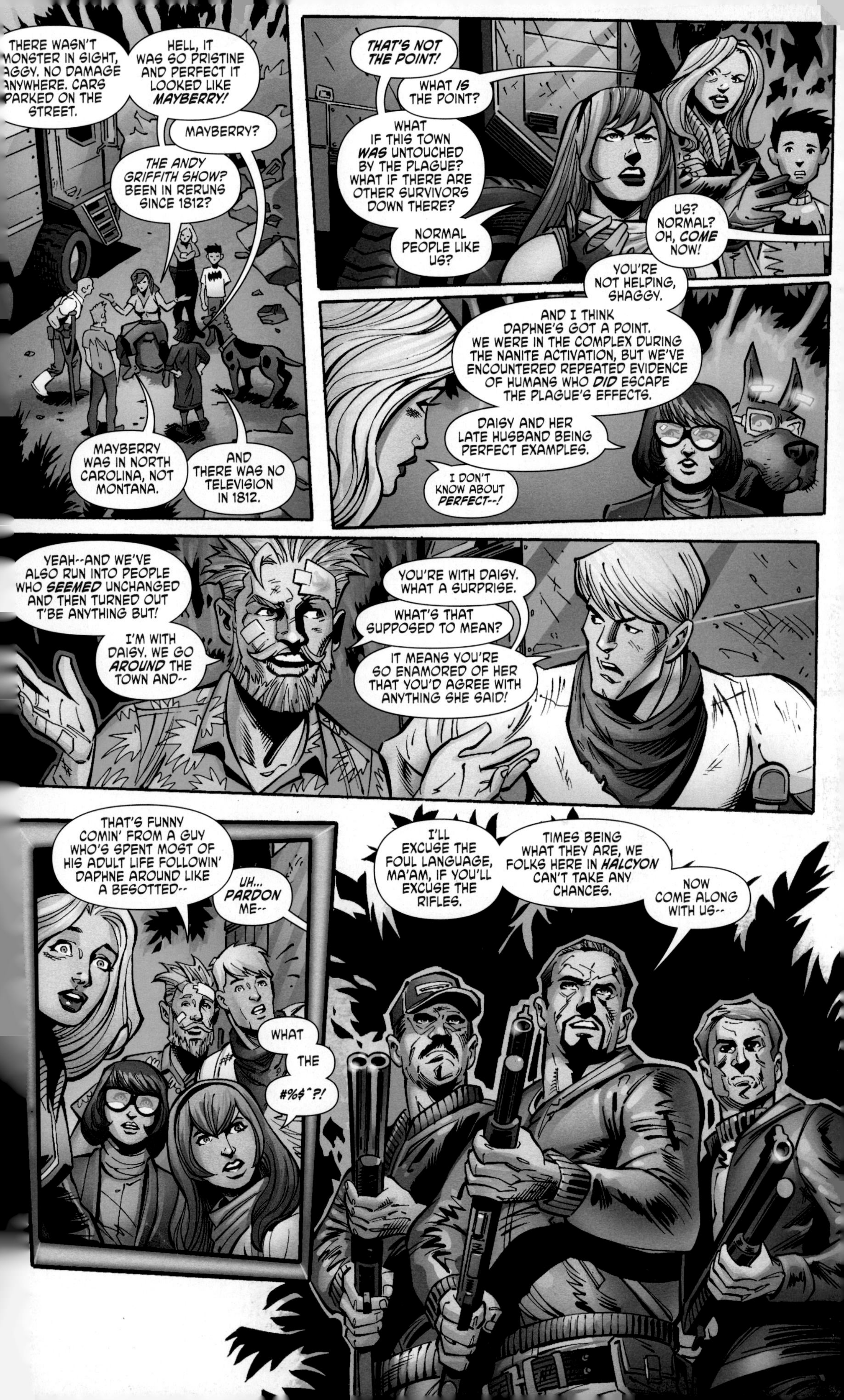
THERE WASN'T MONSTER IN SIGHT, AGGY. NO DAMAGE ANYWHERE. CARS PARKED ON THE STREET.
HELL, IT WAS SO PRISTINE AND PERFECT IT LOOKED LIKE MAYBERRY!
MAYBERRY?
THE ANDY GRIFFITH SHOW? BEEN IN RERUNS SINCE 1812?
MAYBERRY WAS IN NORTH CAROLINA, NOT MONTANA.
AND THERE WAS NO TELEVISION IN 1812.
THAT'S NOT THE POINT!
WHAT IS THE POINT?
WHAT IF THIS TOWN WAS UNTOUCHED BY THE PLAGUE? WHAT IF THERE ARE OTHER SURVIVORS DOWN THERE?
NORMAL PEOPLE LIKE US?
US? NORMAL? OH, COME NOW!
YOU'RE NOT HELPING, SHAGGY.
AND I THINK DAPHNE'S GOT A POINT. WE WERE IN THE COMPLEX DURING THE NANITE ACTIVATION, BUT WE'VE ENCOUNTERED REPEATED EVIDENCE OF HUMANS WHO DID ESCAPE THE PLAGUE'S EFFECTS.
DAISY AND HER LATE HUSBAND BEING PERFECT EXAMPLES.
I DON'T KNOW ABOUT PERFECT--!
YEAH--AND WE'VE ALSO RUN INTO PEOPLE WHO SEEMED UNCHANGED AND THEN TURNED OUT T'BE ANYTHING BUT!
I'M WITH DAISY. WE GO AROUND THE TOWN AND--
YOU'RE WITH DAISY. WHAT A SURPRISE.
WHAT'S THAT SUPPOSED TO MEAN?
IT MEANS YOU'RE SO ENAMORED OF HER THAT YOU'D AGREE WITH ANYTHING SHE SAID!
THAT'S FUNNY COMIN' FROM A GUY WHO'S SPENT MOST OF HIS ADULT LIFE FOLLOWIN' DAPHNE AROUND LIKE A BESOTTED--
UH... PARDON ME--
WHAT THE #%$^?!
I'LL EXCUSE THE FOUL LANGUAGE, MA'AM, IF YOU'LL EXCUSE THE RIFLES.
TIMES BEING WHAT THEY ARE, WE FOLKS HERE IN HALCYON CAN'T TAKE ANY CHANCES.
NOW COME ALONG WITH US--

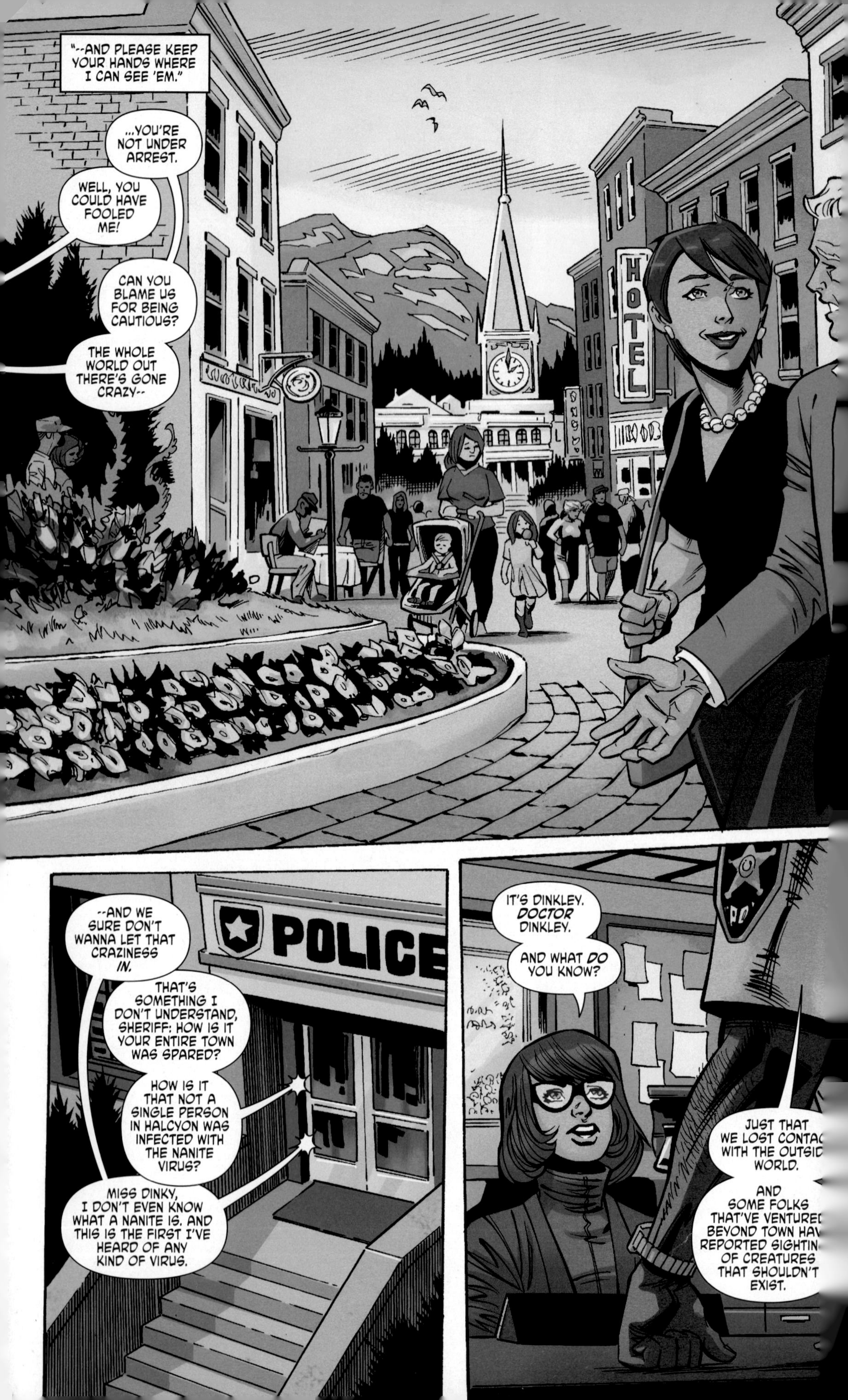
"--AND PLEASE KEEP YOUR HANDS WHERE I CAN SEE 'EM."
...YOU'RE NOT UNDER ARREST.
WELL, YOU COULD HAVE FOOLED ME!
CAN YOU BLAME US FOR BEING CAUTIOUS?
THE WHOLE WORLD OUT THERE'S GONE CRAZY--
HOTEL
--AND WE SURE DON'T WANNA LET THAT CRAZINESS *IN.*
THAT'S SOMETHING I DON'T UNDERSTAND, SHERIFF: HOW IS IT YOUR ENTIRE TOWN WAS SPARED?
HOW IS IT THAT NOT A SINGLE PERSON IN HALCYON WAS INFECTED WITH THE NANITE VIRUS?
MISS DINKY, I DON'T EVEN KNOW WHAT A NANITE IS. AND THIS IS THE FIRST I'VE HEARD OF ANY KIND OF VIRUS.
POLICE
IT'S DINKLEY. *DOCTOR* DINKLEY.
AND WHAT *DO* YOU KNOW?
JUST THAT WE LOST CONTAC WITH THE OUTSID WORLD.
AND SOME FOLKS THAT'VE VENTURED BEYOND TOWN HAV REPORTED SIGHTIN OF CREATURES THAT SHOULDN'T EXIST.

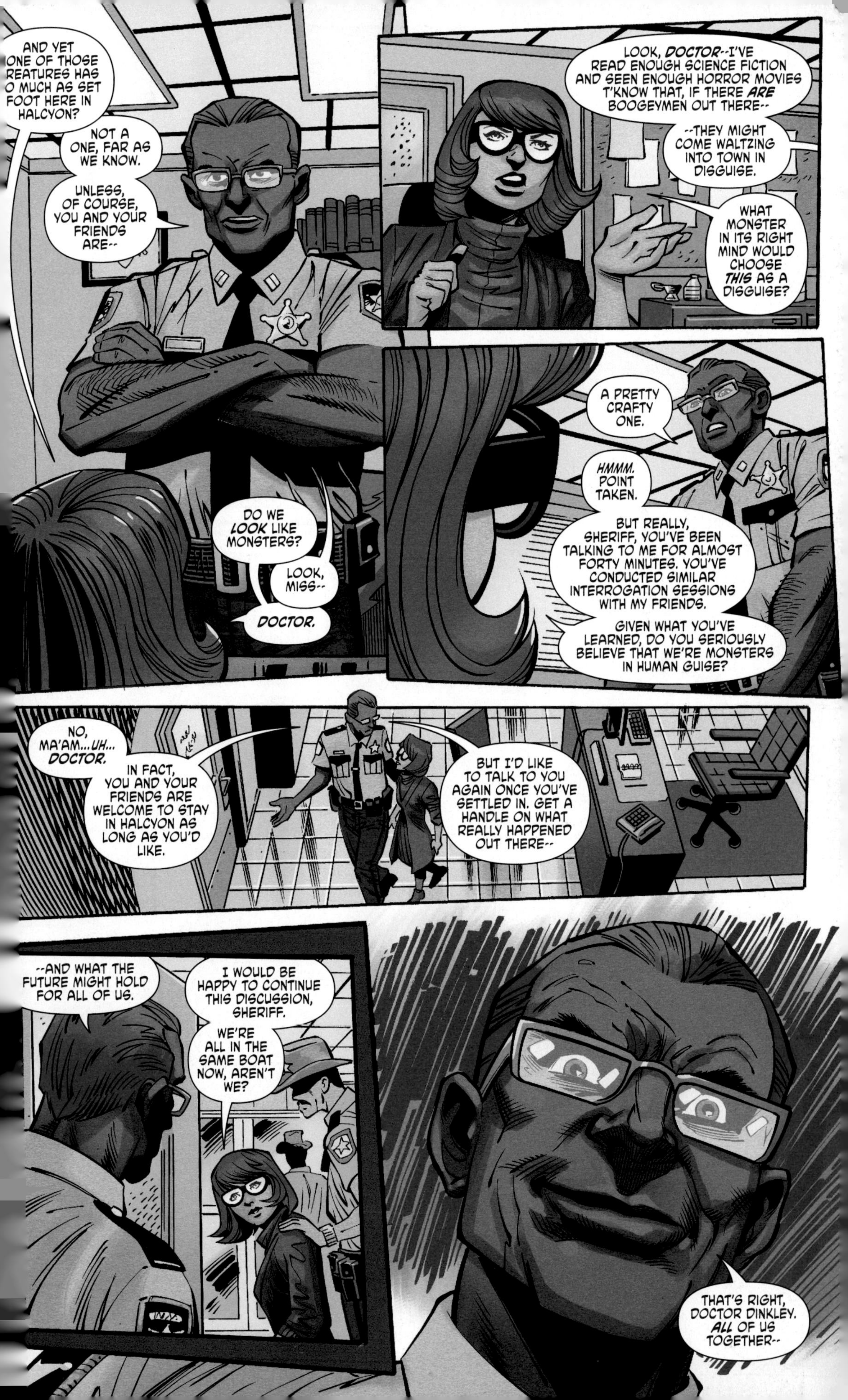
AND YET ONE OF THOSE REATURES HAS O MUCH AS SET FOOT HERE IN HALCYON?
NOT A ONE, FAR AS WE KNOW.
UNLESS, OF COURSE, YOU AND YOUR FRIENDS ARE--
LOOK, DOCTOR--I'VE READ ENOUGH SCIENCE FICTION AND SEEN ENOUGH HORROR MOVIES T'KNOW THAT, IF THERE ARE BOOGEYMEN OUT THERE--
--THEY MIGHT COME WALTZING INTO TOWN IN DISGUISE.
WHAT MONSTER IN ITS RIGHT MIND WOULD CHOOSE THIS AS A DISGUISE?
DO WE LOOK LIKE MONSTERS?
LOOK, MISS--
DOCTOR.
A PRETTY CRAFTY ONE.
HMMM. POINT TAKEN.
BUT REALLY, SHERIFF, YOU'VE BEEN TALKING TO ME FOR ALMOST FORTY MINUTES. YOU'VE CONDUCTED SIMILAR INTERROGATION SESSIONS WITH MY FRIENDS.
GIVEN WHAT YOU'VE LEARNED, DO YOU SERIOUSLY BELIEVE THAT WE'RE MONSTERS IN HUMAN GUISE?
NO, MA'AM...UH... DOCTOR.
IN FACT, YOU AND YOUR FRIENDS ARE WELCOME TO STAY IN HALCYON AS LONG AS YOU'D LIKE.
BUT I'D LIKE TO TALK TO YOU AGAIN ONCE YOU'VE SETTLED IN. GET A HANDLE ON WHAT REALLY HAPPENED OUT THERE--
--AND WHAT THE FUTURE MIGHT HOLD FOR ALL OF US.
I WOULD BE HAPPY TO CONTINUE THIS DISCUSSION, SHERIFF.
WE'RE ALL IN THE SAME BOAT NOW, AREN'T WE?
THAT'S RIGHT, DOCTOR DINKLEY. ALL OF US TOGETHER--

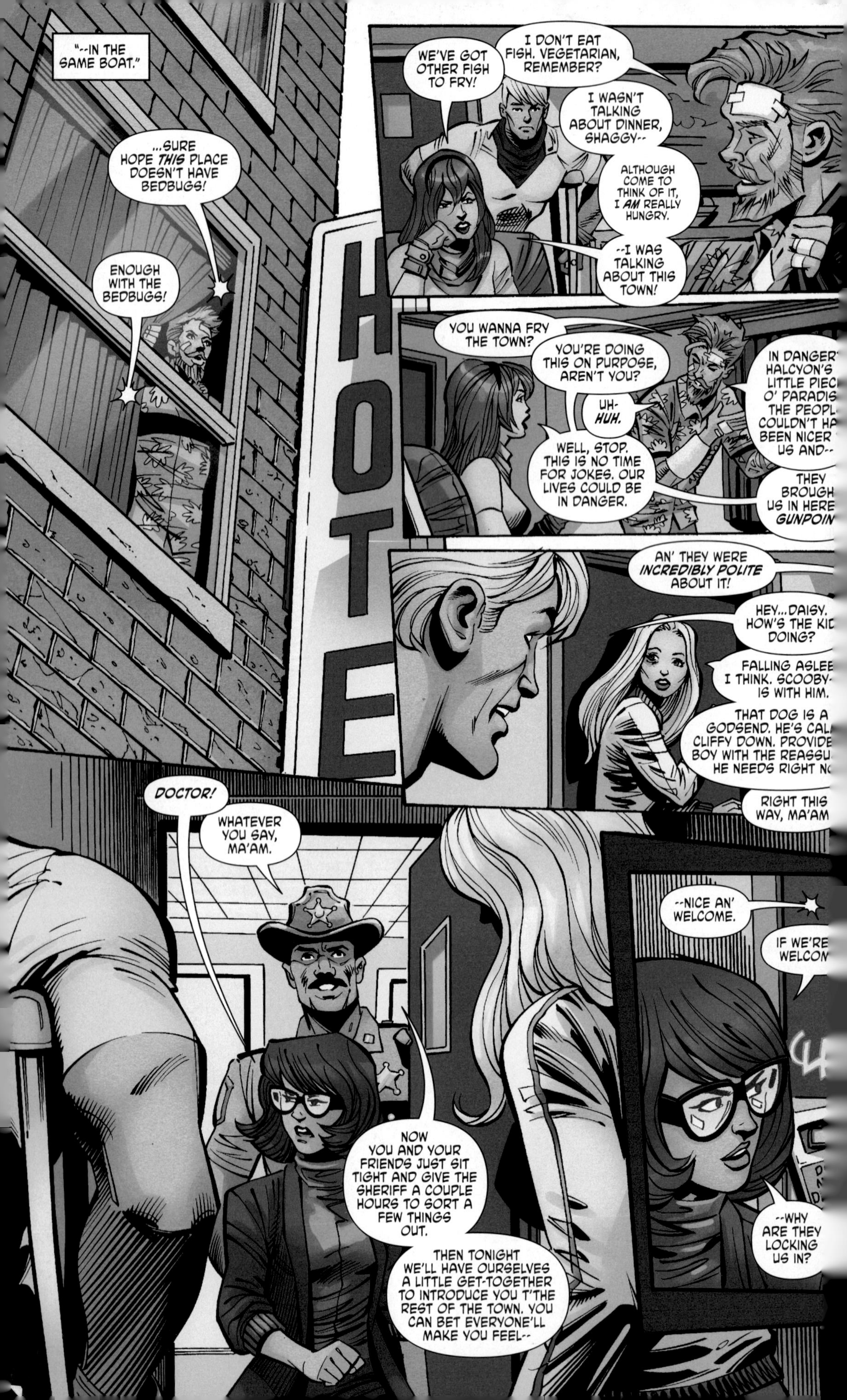

"--IN THE SAME BOAT."
...SURE HOPE *THIS* PLACE DOESN'T HAVE BEDBUGS!
ENOUGH WITH THE BEDBUGS!
HOTE
WE'VE GOT OTHER FISH TO FRY!
I DON'T EAT FISH. VEGETARIAN, REMEMBER?
I WASN'T TALKING ABOUT DINNER, SHAGGY--
ALTHOUGH COME TO THINK OF IT, I *AM* REALLY HUNGRY.
--I WAS TALKING ABOUT THIS TOWN!
YOU WANNA FRY THE TOWN?
YOU'RE DOING THIS ON PURPOSE, AREN'T YOU?
UH-*HUH.*
WELL, STOP. THIS IS NO TIME FOR JOKES. OUR LIVES COULD BE IN DANGER.
IN DANGER? HALCYON'S LITTLE PIEC O' PARADIS THE PEOPL COULDN'T HA BEEN NICER US AND--
THEY BROUGH US IN HERE *GUNPOIN*
AN' THEY WERE *INCREDIBLY POLITE* ABOUT IT!
HEY...DAISY. HOW'S THE KID DOING?
FALLING ASLEE I THINK. SCOOBY-IS WITH HIM.
THAT DOG IS A GODSEND. HE'S CAL CLIFFY DOWN. PROVIDE BOY WITH THE REASSU HE NEEDS RIGHT NO
RIGHT THIS WAY, MA'AM
DOCTOR!
WHATEVER YOU SAY, MA'AM.
NOW YOU AND YOUR FRIENDS JUST SIT TIGHT AND GIVE THE SHERIFF A COUPLE HOURS TO SORT A FEW THINGS OUT.
THEN TONIGHT WE'LL HAVE OURSELVES A LITTLE GET-TOGETHER TO INTRODUCE YOU T'THE REST OF THE TOWN. YOU CAN BET EVERYONE'LL MAKE YOU FEEL--
--NICE AN' WELCOME.
IF WE'RE WELCOM
--WHY ARE THEY LOCKING US IN?

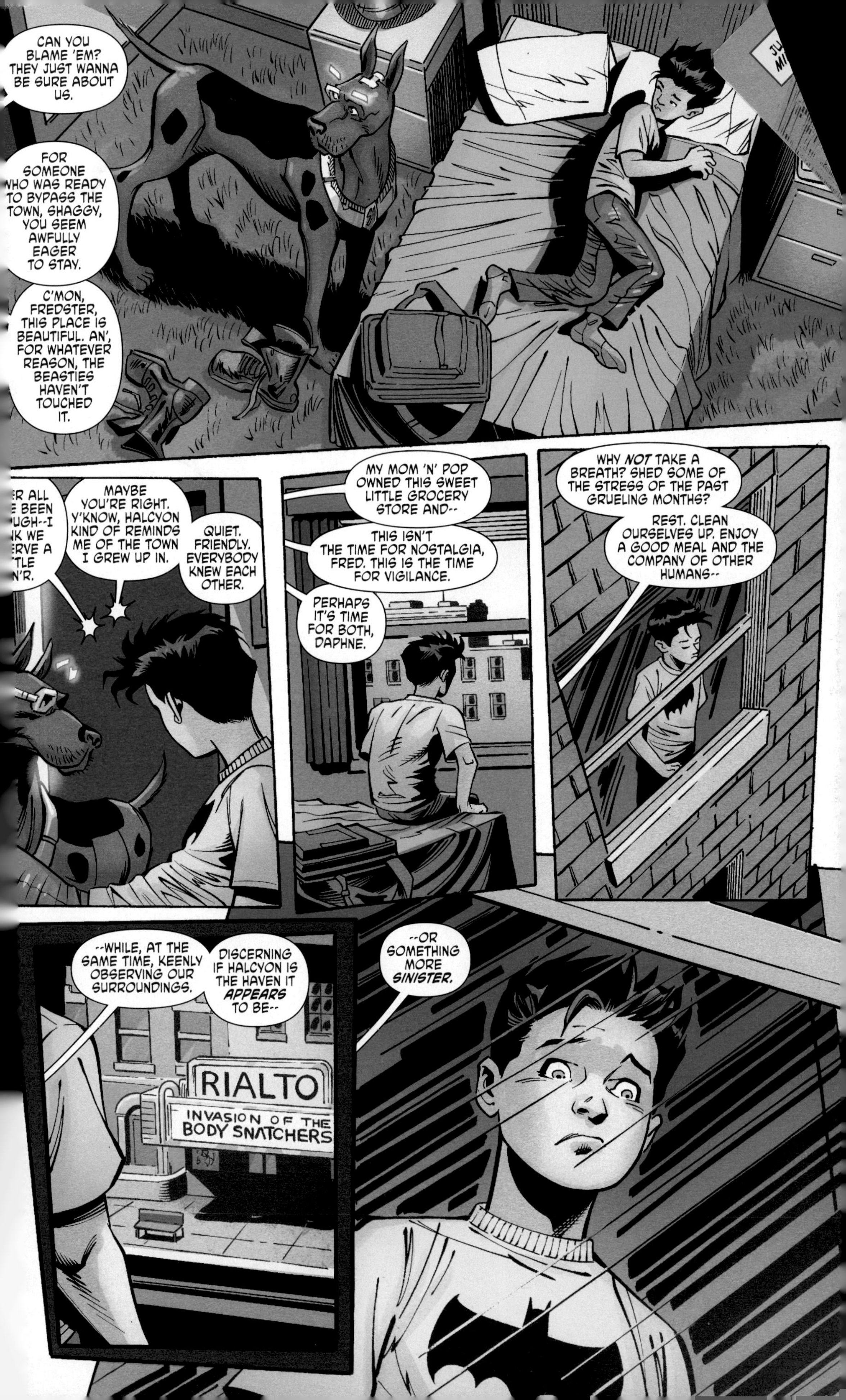
CAN YOU BLAME 'EM? THEY JUST WANNA BE SURE ABOUT US.
FOR SOMEONE WHO WAS READY TO BYPASS THE TOWN, SHAGGY, YOU SEEM AWFULLY EAGER TO STAY.
C'MON, FREDSTER, THIS PLACE IS BEAUTIFUL. AN', FOR WHATEVER REASON, THE BEASTIES HAVEN'T TOUCHED IT.
MAYBE YOU'RE RIGHT. Y'KNOW, HALCYON KIND OF REMINDS ME OF THE TOWN I GREW UP IN.
QUIET. FRIENDLY. EVERYBODY KNEW EACH OTHER.
MY MOM 'N' POP OWNED THIS SWEET LITTLE GROCERY STORE AND--
THIS ISN'T THE TIME FOR NOSTALGIA, FRED. THIS IS THE TIME FOR VIGILANCE.
PERHAPS IT'S TIME FOR BOTH, DAPHNE.
WHY *NOT* TAKE A BREATH? SHED SOME OF THE STRESS OF THE PAST GRUELING MONTHS?
REST. CLEAN OURSELVES UP. ENJOY A GOOD MEAL AND THE COMPANY OF OTHER HUMANS--
--WHILE, AT THE SAME TIME, KEENLY OBSERVING OUR SURROUNDINGS.
DISCERNING IF HALCYON IS THE HAVEN IT *APPEARS* TO BE--
RIALTO
INVASION OF THE BODY SNATCHERS
--OR SOMETHING MORE *SINISTER.*

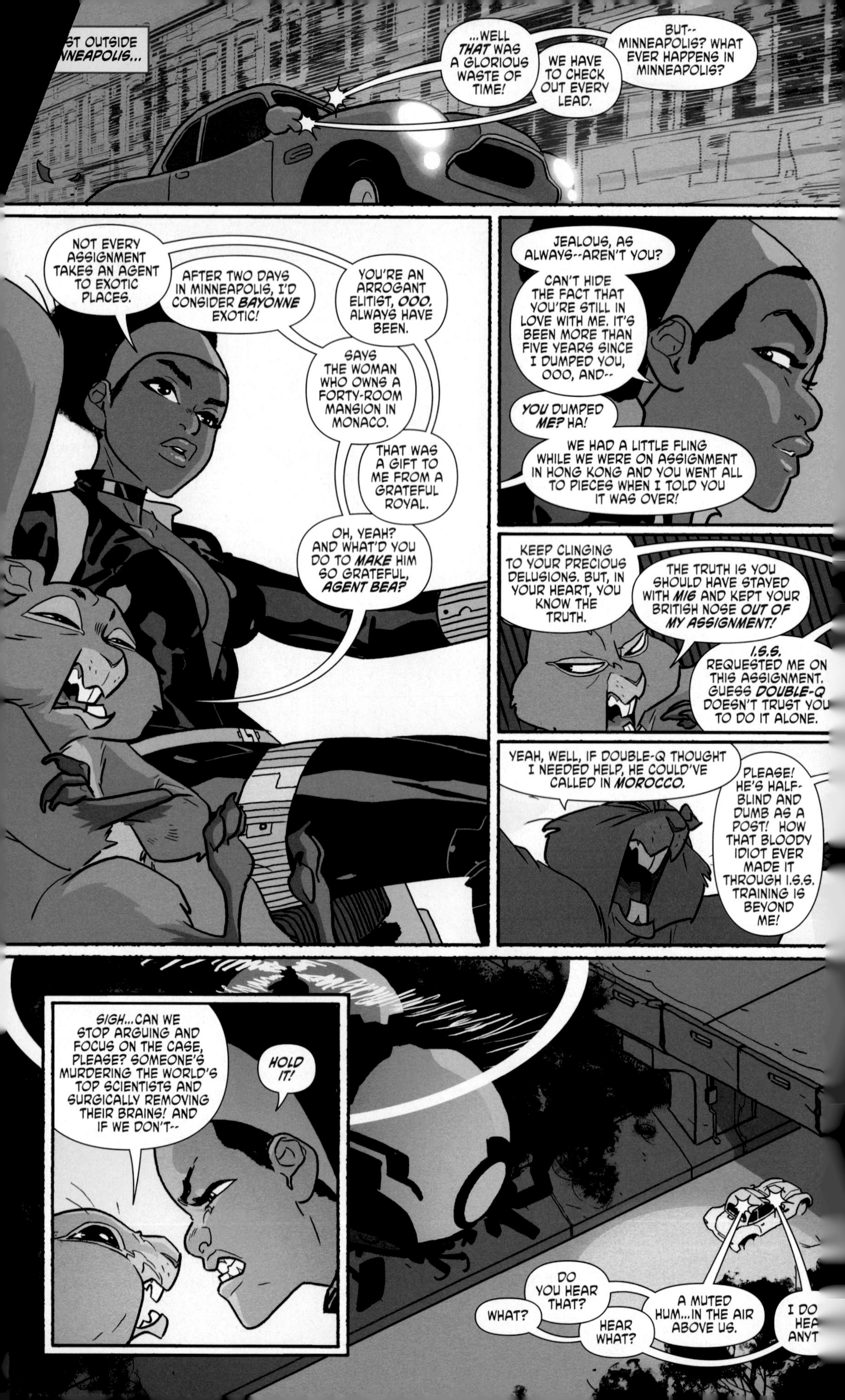
...ST OUTSIDE
...NNEAPOLIS...
...WELL THAT WAS A GLORIOUS WASTE OF TIME!
WE HAVE TO CHECK OUT EVERY LEAD.
BUT-- MINNEAPOLIS? WHAT EVER HAPPENS IN MINNEAPOLIS?
NOT EVERY ASSIGNMENT TAKES AN AGENT TO EXOTIC PLACES.
AFTER TWO DAYS IN MINNEAPOLIS, I'D CONSIDER BAYONNE EXOTIC!
YOU'RE AN ARROGANT ELITIST, OOO. ALWAYS HAVE BEEN.
SAYS THE WOMAN WHO OWNS A FORTY-ROOM MANSION IN MONACO.
THAT WAS A GIFT TO ME FROM A GRATEFUL ROYAL.
OH, YEAH? AND WHAT'D YOU DO TO MAKE HIM SO GRATEFUL, AGENT BEA?
JEALOUS, AS ALWAYS--AREN'T YOU?
CAN'T HIDE THE FACT THAT YOU'RE STILL IN LOVE WITH ME. IT'S BEEN MORE THAN FIVE YEARS SINCE I DUMPED YOU, OOO, AND--
YOU DUMPED ME? HA!
WE HAD A LITTLE FLING WHILE WE WERE ON ASSIGNMENT IN HONG KONG AND YOU WENT ALL TO PIECES WHEN I TOLD YOU IT WAS OVER!
KEEP CLINGING TO YOUR PRECIOUS DELUSIONS. BUT, IN YOUR HEART, YOU KNOW THE TRUTH.
THE TRUTH IS YOU SHOULD HAVE STAYED WITH MI6 AND KEPT YOUR BRITISH NOSE OUT OF MY ASSIGNMENT!
I.S.S. REQUESTED ME ON THIS ASSIGNMENT. GUESS DOUBLE-Q DOESN'T TRUST YOU TO DO IT ALONE.
YEAH, WELL, IF DOUBLE-Q THOUGHT I NEEDED HELP, HE COULD'VE CALLED IN MOROCCO.
PLEASE! HE'S HALF-BLIND AND DUMB AS A POST! HOW THAT BLOODY IDIOT EVER MADE IT THROUGH I.S.S. TRAINING IS BEYOND ME!
SIGH...CAN WE STOP ARGUING AND FOCUS ON THE CASE, PLEASE? SOMEONE'S MURDERING THE WORLD'S TOP SCIENTISTS AND SURGICALLY REMOVING THEIR BRAINS! AND IF WE DON'T--
HOLD IT!
DO YOU HEAR THAT?
WHAT?
HEAR WHAT?
A MUTED HUM...IN THE AIR ABOVE US.
I DO... HEA... ANYT...

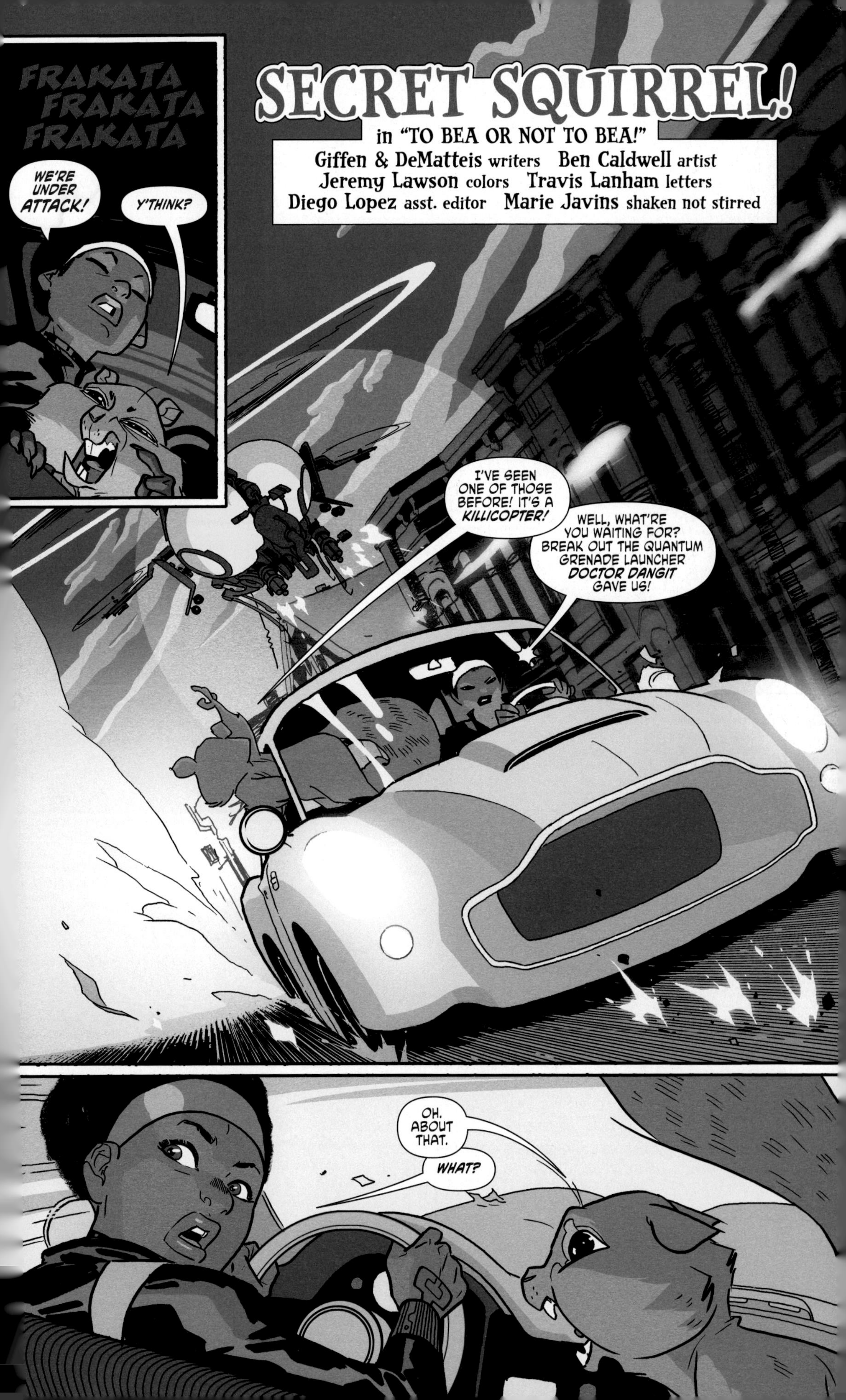
SECRET SQUIRREL!
in "TO BEA OR NOT TO BEA!"
Giffen & DeMatteis writers Ben Caldwell artist
Jeremy Lawson colors Travis Lanham letters
Diego Lopez asst. editor Marie Javins shaken not stirred
FRAKATA FRAKATA FRAKATA
WE'RE UNDER ATTACK!
Y'THINK?
I'VE SEEN ONE OF THOSE BEFORE! IT'S A KILLICOPTER!
WELL, WHAT'RE YOU WAITING FOR? BREAK OUT THE QUANTUM GRENADE LAUNCHER DOCTOR DANGIT GAVE US!
OH. ABOUT THAT.
WHAT?

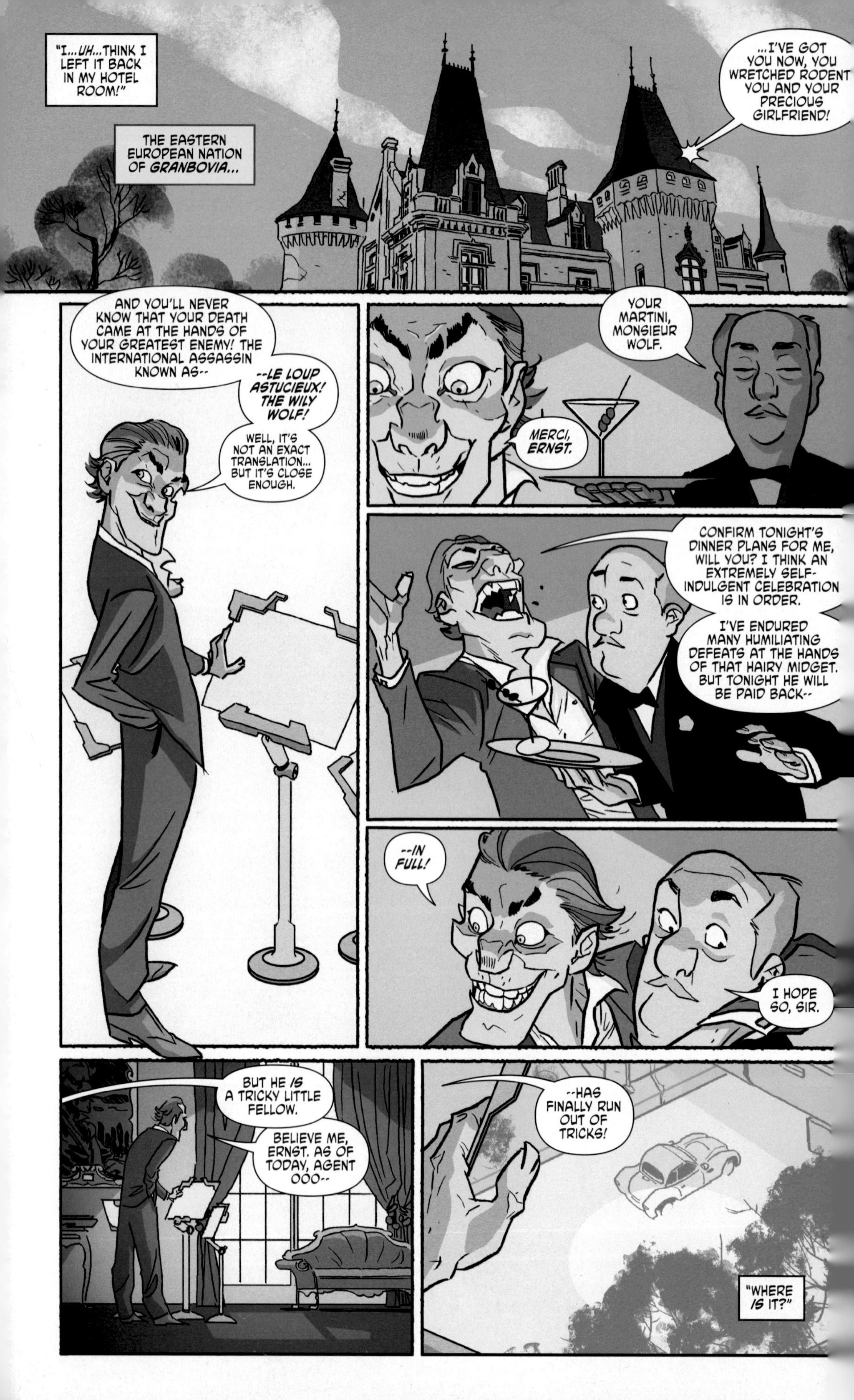
"I...UH...THINK I LEFT IT BACK IN MY HOTEL ROOM!"
THE EASTERN EUROPEAN NATION OF GRANBOVIA...
...I'VE GOT YOU NOW, YOU WRETCHED RODENT YOU AND YOUR PRECIOUS GIRLFRIEND!
AND YOU'LL NEVER KNOW THAT YOUR DEATH CAME AT THE HANDS OF YOUR GREATEST ENEMY! THE INTERNATIONAL ASSASSIN KNOWN AS--
--LE LOUP ASTUCIEUX! THE WILY WOLF!
WELL, IT'S NOT AN EXACT TRANSLATION... BUT IT'S CLOSE ENOUGH.
YOUR MARTINI, MONSIEUR WOLF.
MERCI, ERNST.
CONFIRM TONIGHT'S DINNER PLANS FOR ME, WILL YOU? I THINK AN EXTREMELY SELF-INDULGENT CELEBRATION IS IN ORDER.
I'VE ENDURED MANY HUMILIATING DEFEATS AT THE HANDS OF THAT HAIRY MIDGET. BUT TONIGHT HE WILL BE PAID BACK--
--IN FULL!
I HOPE SO, SIR.
BUT HE IS A TRICKY LITTLE FELLOW.
BELIEVE ME, ERNST. AS OF TODAY, AGENT OOO--
--HAS FINALLY RUN OUT OF TRICKS!
"WHERE IS IT?"

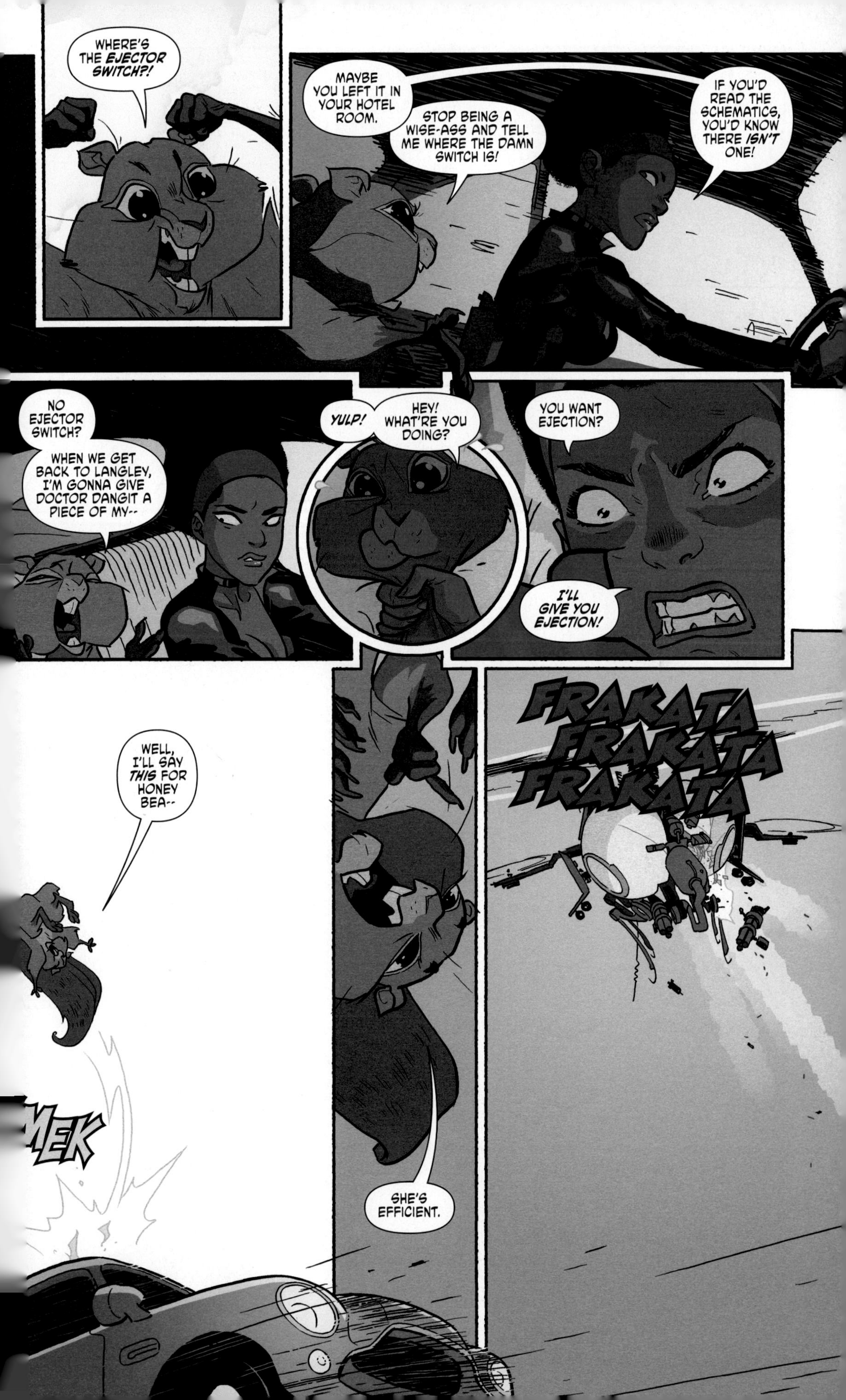

WHERE'S THE EJECTOR SWITCH?!
MAYBE YOU LEFT IT IN YOUR HOTEL ROOM.
STOP BEING A WISE-ASS AND TELL ME WHERE THE DAMN SWITCH IS!
IF YOU'D READ THE SCHEMATICS, YOU'D KNOW THERE ISN'T ONE!
NO EJECTOR SWITCH?
WHEN WE GET BACK TO LANGLEY, I'M GONNA GIVE DOCTOR DANGIT A PIECE OF MY--
YULP!
HEY! WHAT'RE YOU DOING?
YOU WANT EJECTION?
I'LL GIVE YOU EJECTION!
WELL, I'LL SAY THIS FOR HONEY BEA--
MEK
SHE'S EFFICIENT.
FRAKATA FRAKATA FRAKATA

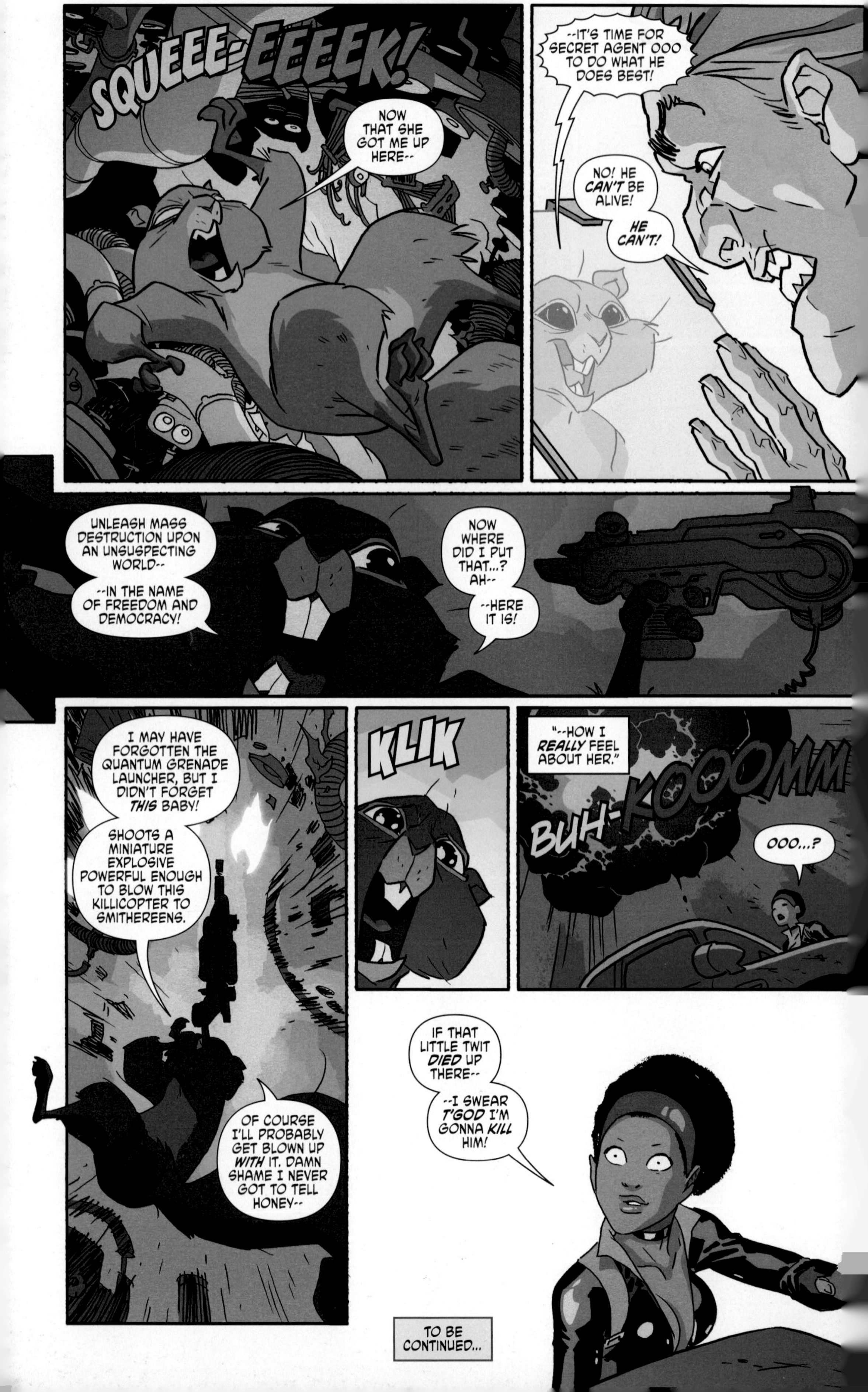
SQUEEE-EEEEK!
NOW THAT SHE GOT ME UP HERE--
--IT'S TIME FOR SECRET AGENT OOO TO DO WHAT HE DOES BEST!
NO! HE CAN'T BE ALIVE!
HE CAN'T!
UNLEASH MASS DESTRUCTION UPON AN UNSUSPECTING WORLD--
--IN THE NAME OF FREEDOM AND DEMOCRACY!
NOW WHERE DID I PUT THAT...? AH--
--HERE IT IS!
I MAY HAVE FORGOTTEN THE QUANTUM GRENADE LAUNCHER, BUT I DIDN'T FORGET THIS BABY!
SHOOTS A MINIATURE EXPLOSIVE POWERFUL ENOUGH TO BLOW THIS KILLICOPTER TO SMITHEREENS.
OF COURSE I'LL PROBABLY GET BLOWN UP WITH IT. DAMN SHAME I NEVER GOT TO TELL HONEY--
KLIK
"--HOW I REALLY FEEL ABOUT HER."
BUH-KOOOMM
OOO...?
IF THAT LITTLE TWIT DIED UP THERE--
--I SWEAR T'GOD I'M GONNA KILL HIM!
TO BE CONTINUED...

VARIANT COVER GALLERY

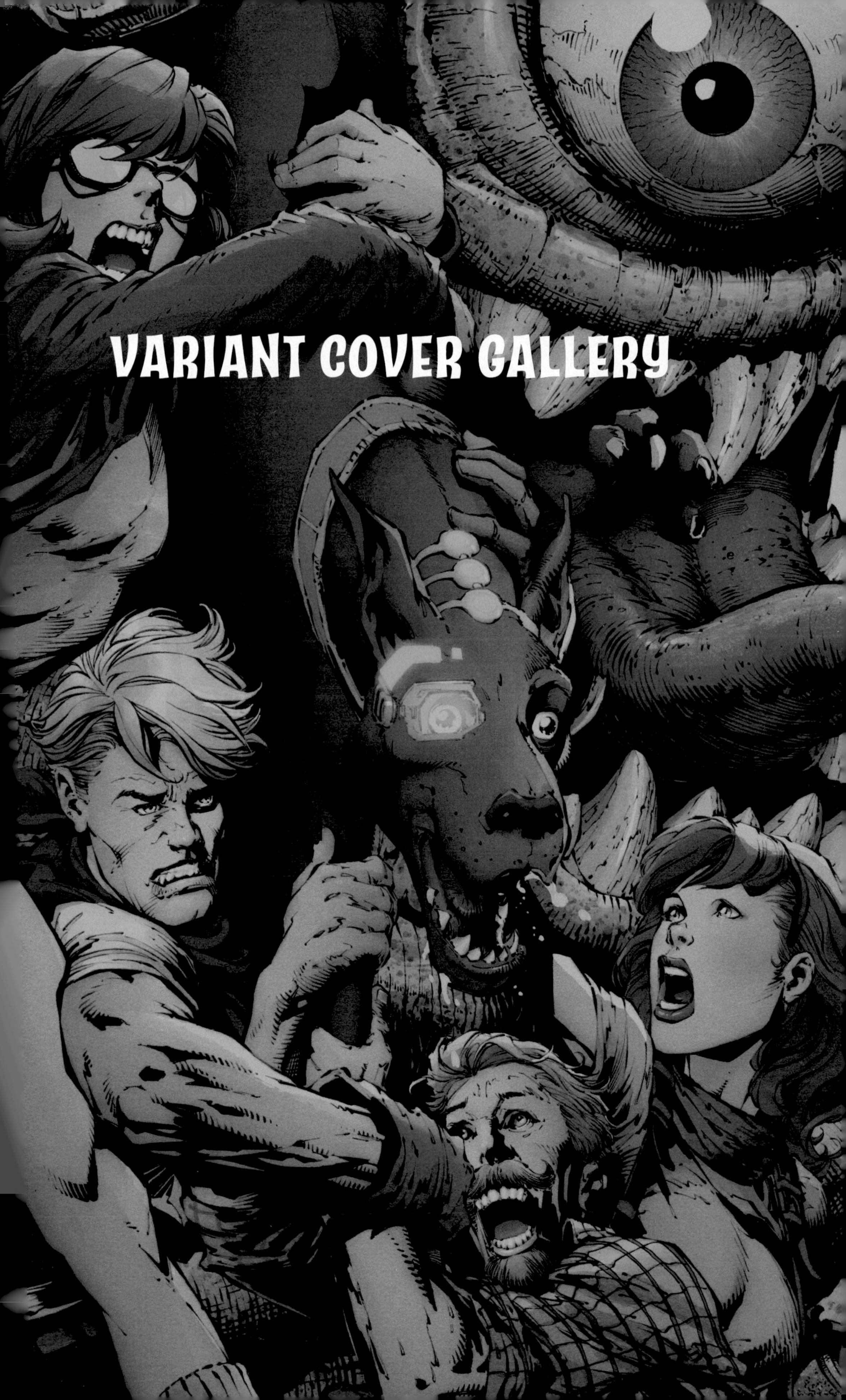

SCOOBY APOCALYPSE #13 variant cover by NICK BRADSHAW and TOMEU MOREY

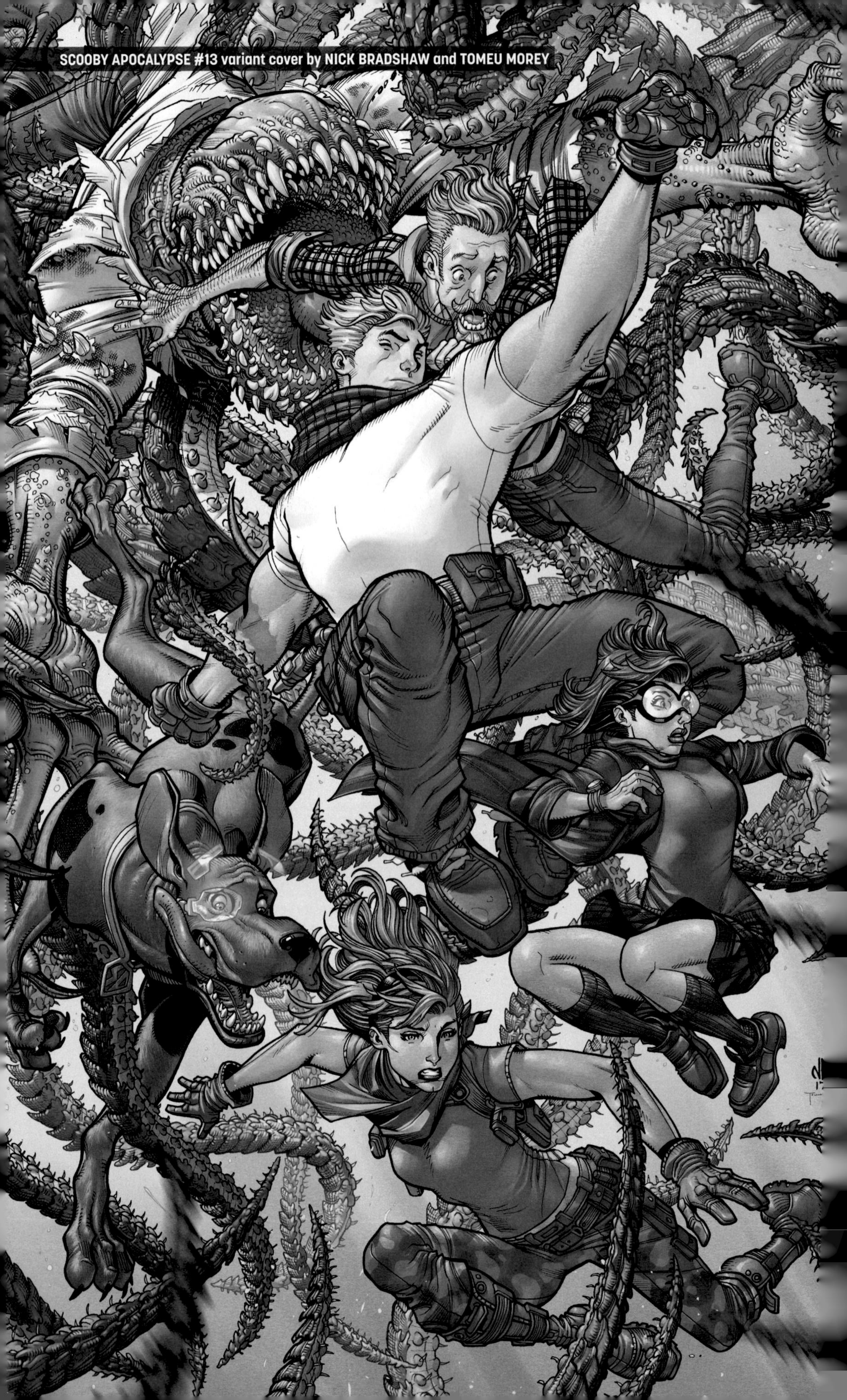

SCOOBY APOCALYPSE #14 variant cover by CULLY HAMNER

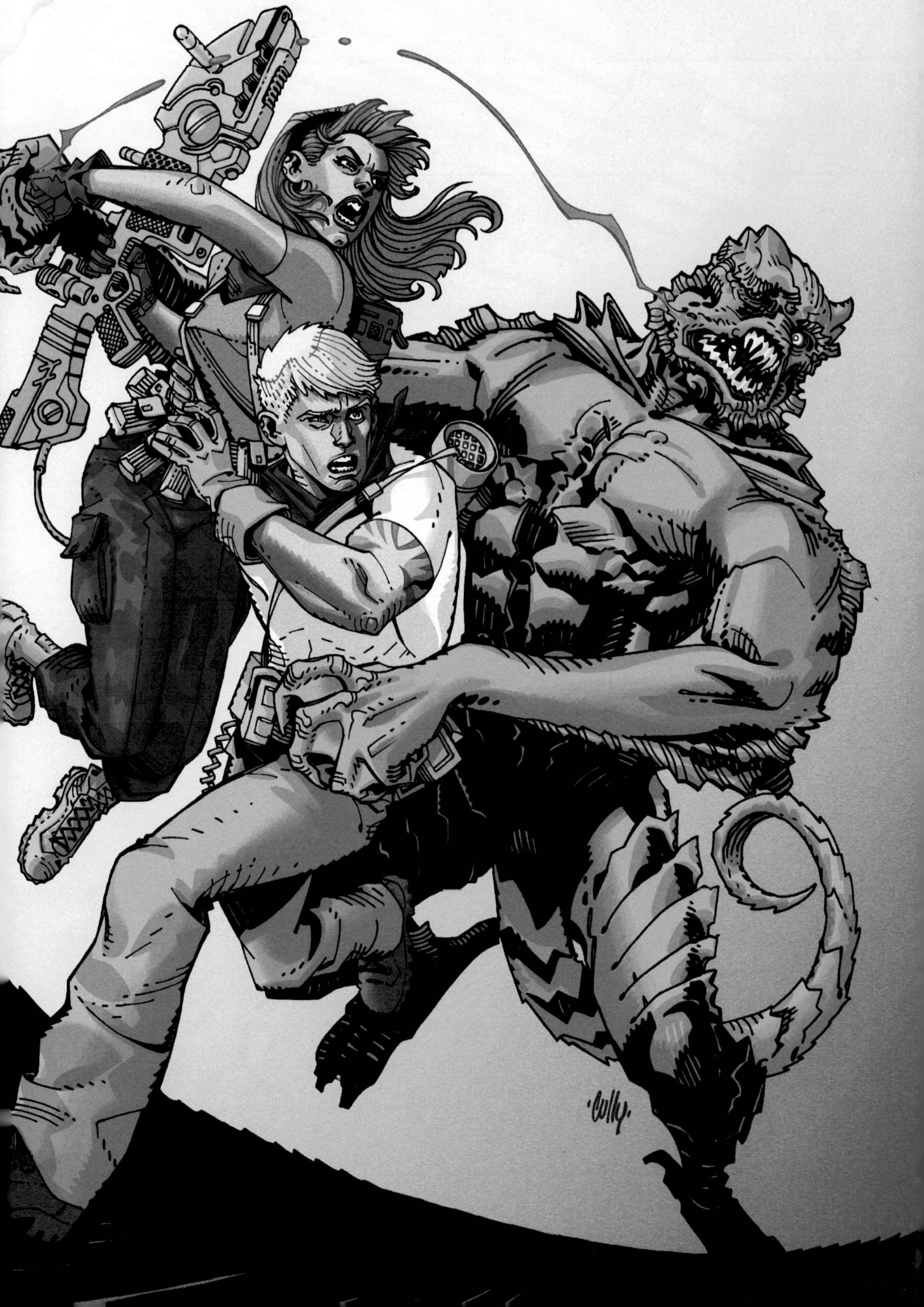

SCOOBY APOCALYPSE #15 variant cover by JILL THOMPSON

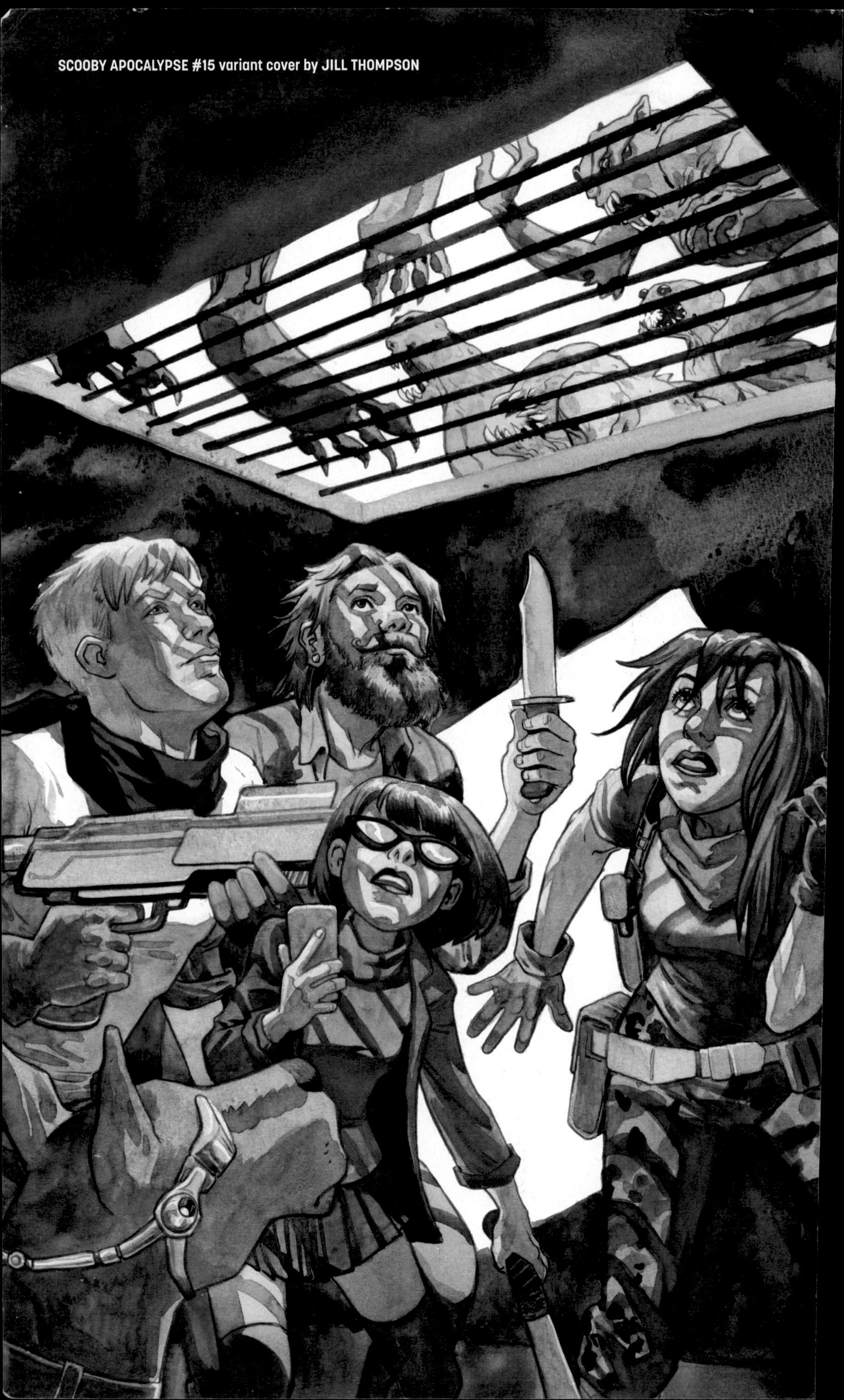

SCOOBY APOCALYPSE #16 variant cover by EMANUELA LUPACCHINO, MARK MORALES and TOMEU MOREY

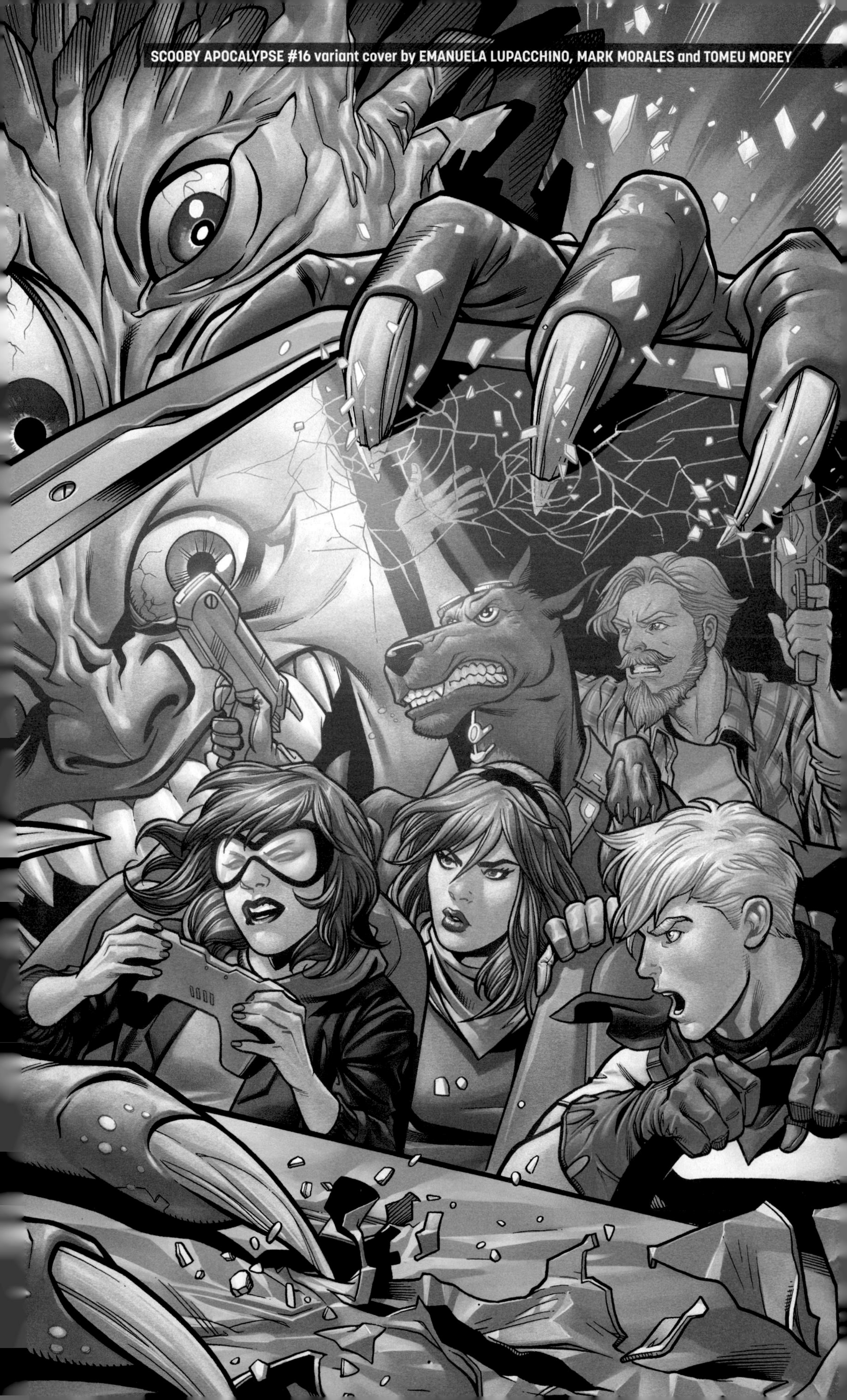

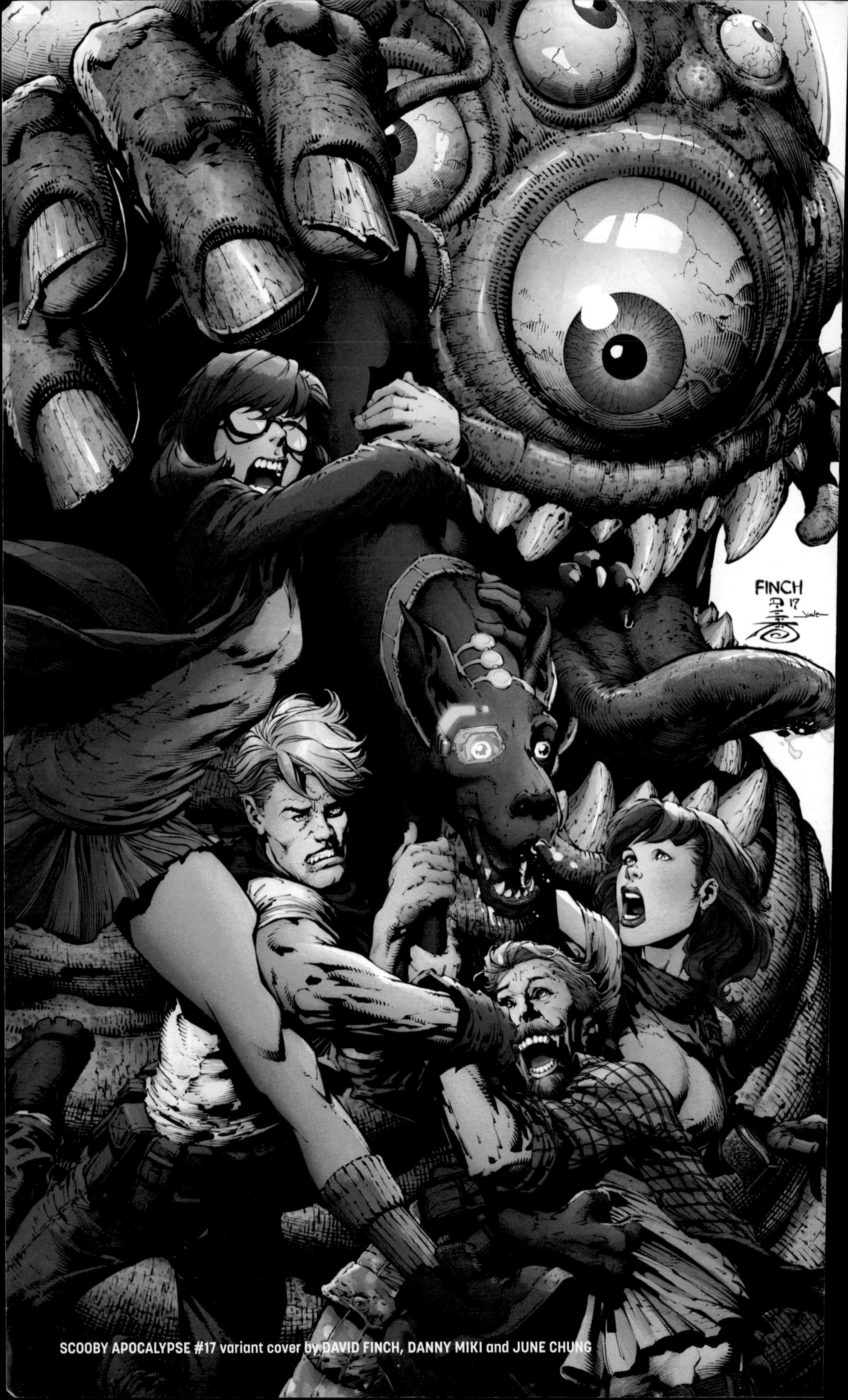
FINCH
17
June
SCOOBY APOCALYPSE #17 variant cover by DAVID FINCH, DANNY MIKI and JUNE CHUNG

SCOOBY APOCALYPSE #18 variant cover by MARK BUCKINGHAM and STEVE BUCCELLATO

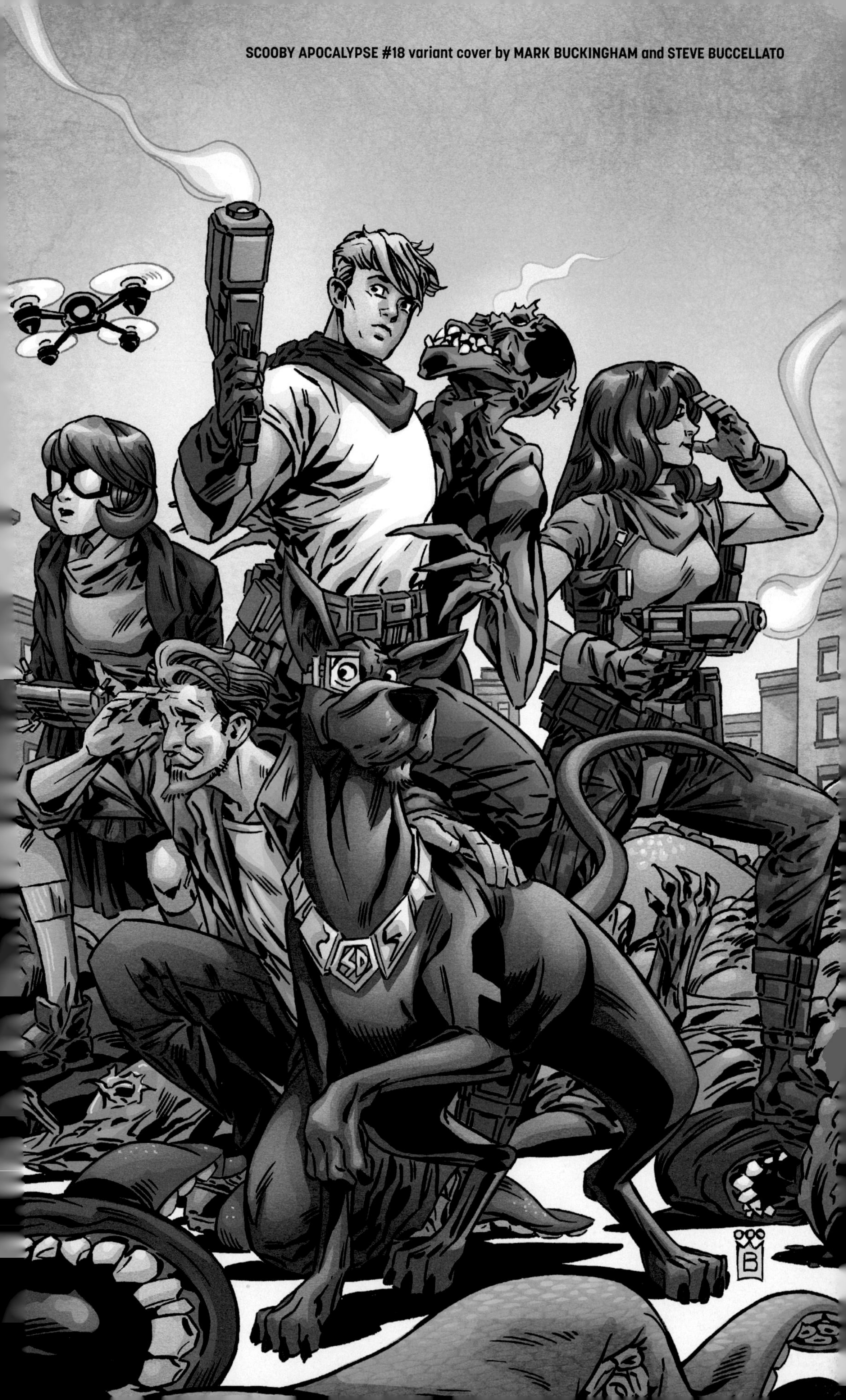
SD

SECRET SQUIRREL CHARACTER DESIGN by HOWARD PORTER

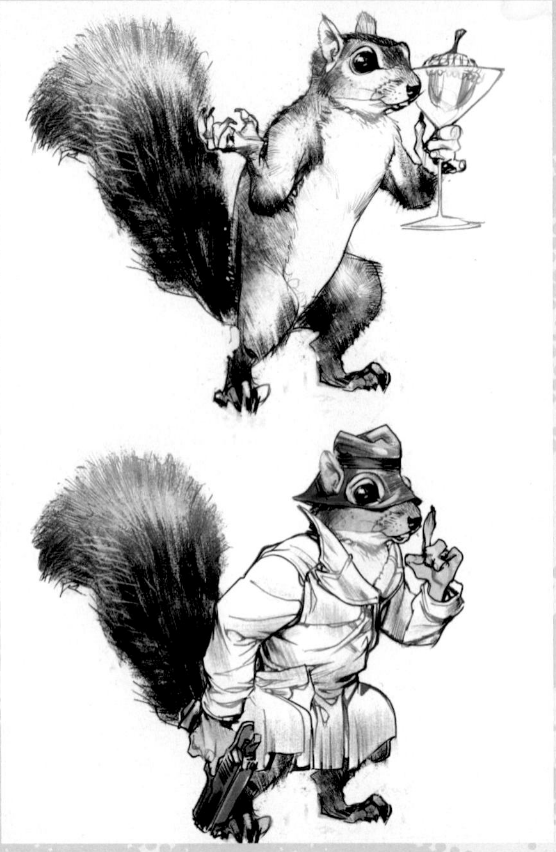

MONSTER CONCEPT by CARLOS D'ANDA

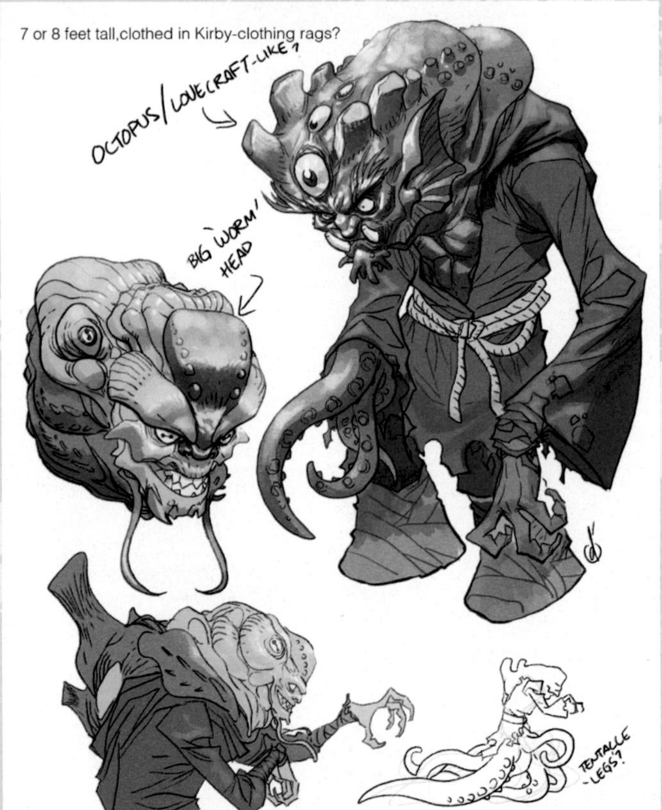
7 or 8 feet tall,clothed in Kirby-clothing rags?
OCTOPUS/LOVECRAFT-LIKE?
BIG 'WORM' HEAD
TENTALLE -LEGS?

SCOOBY APOCALYPSE #13 variant cover inks by NICK BRADSHAW

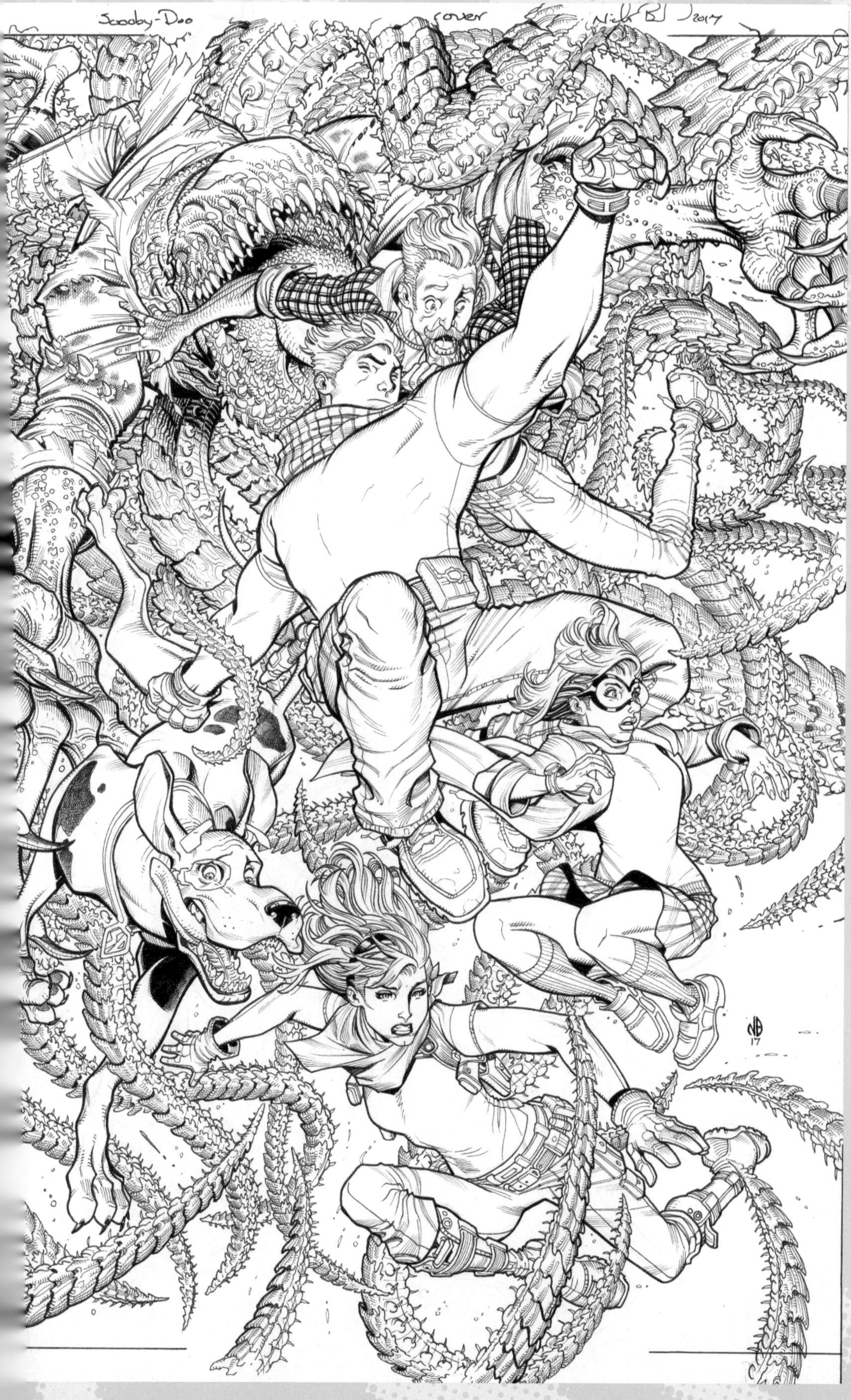
Scooby-Doo
cover

SCOOBY APOCALYPSE #14 variant cover inks by CULLY HAMNER

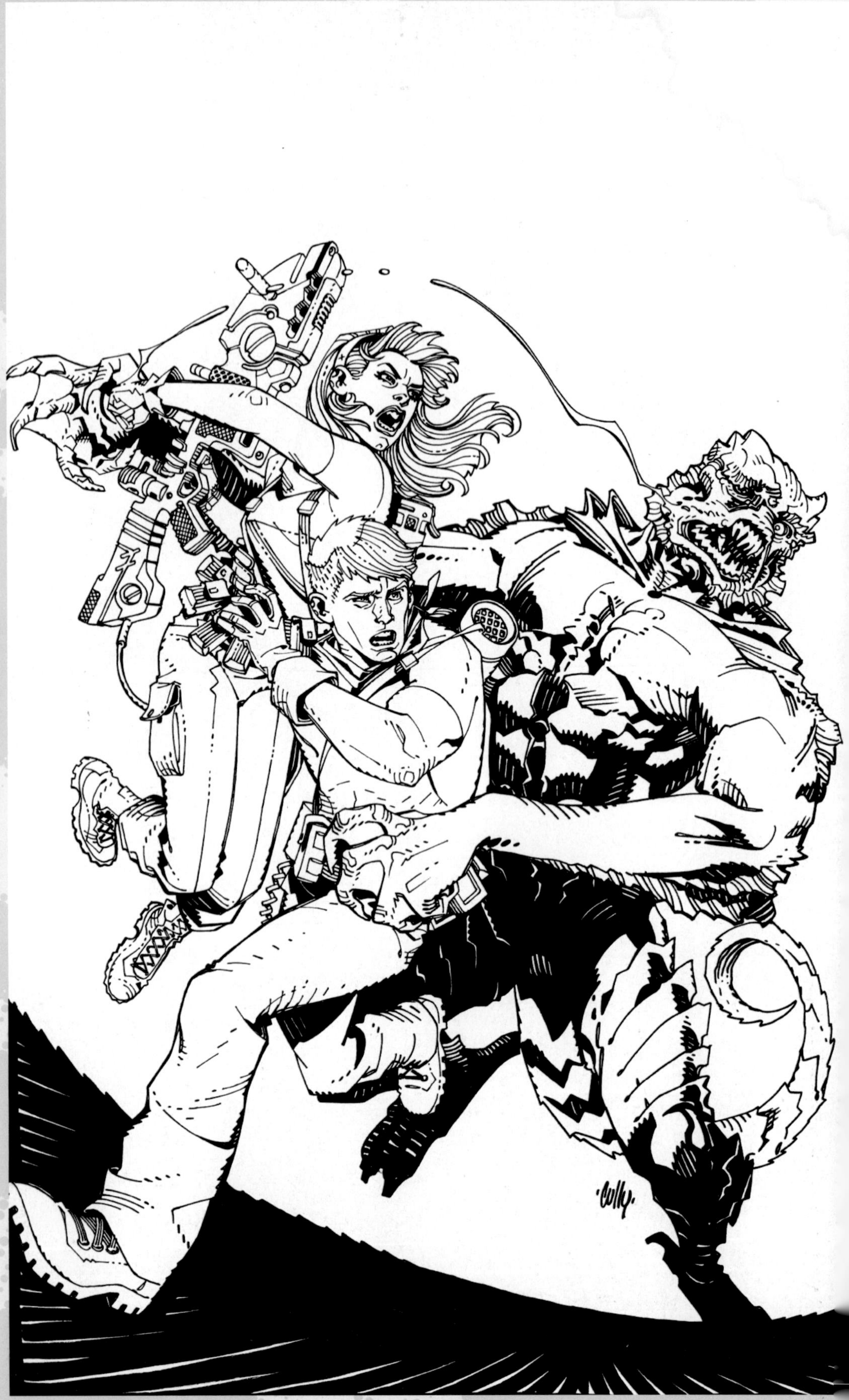

SCOOBY APOCALYPSE #14 variant cover sketches by CULLY HAMNER

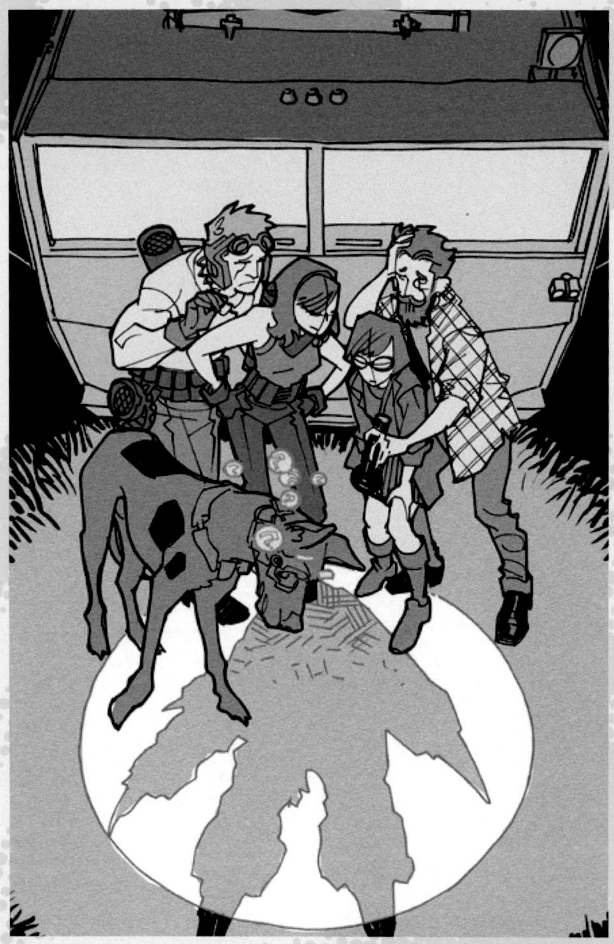

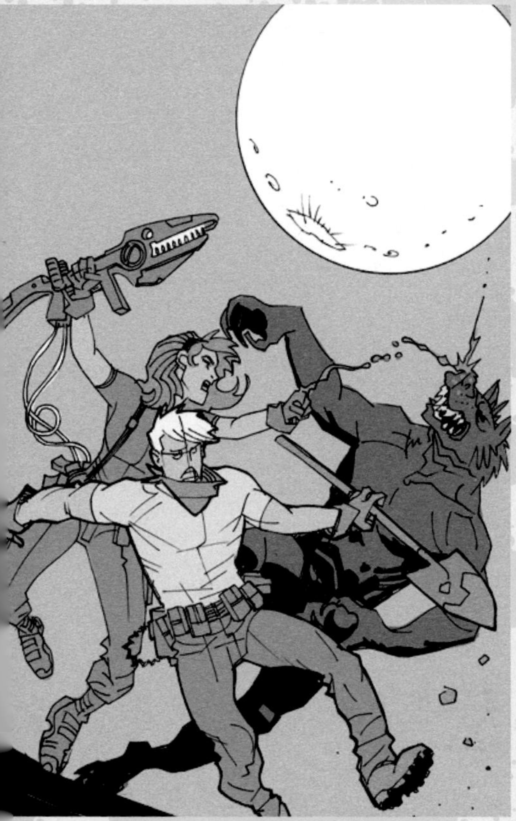

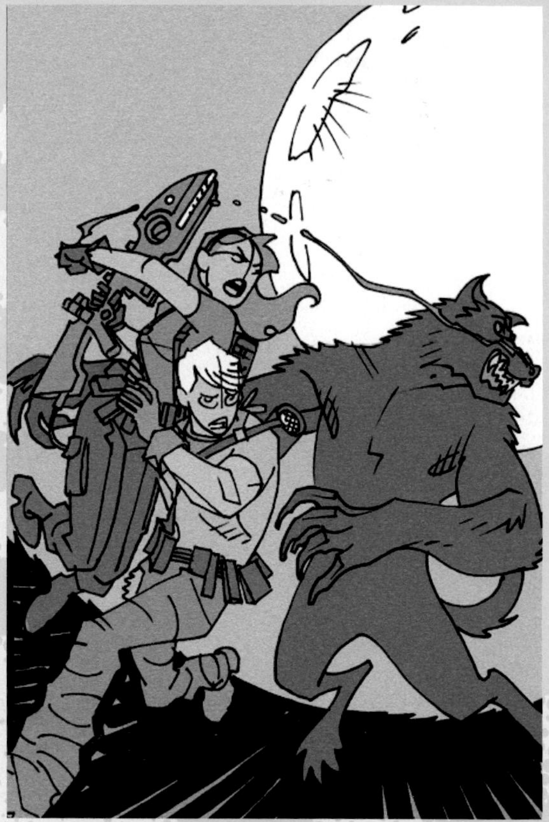

SCOOBY APOCALYPSE #16 variant cover pencils by EMANUELA LUPACCHINO

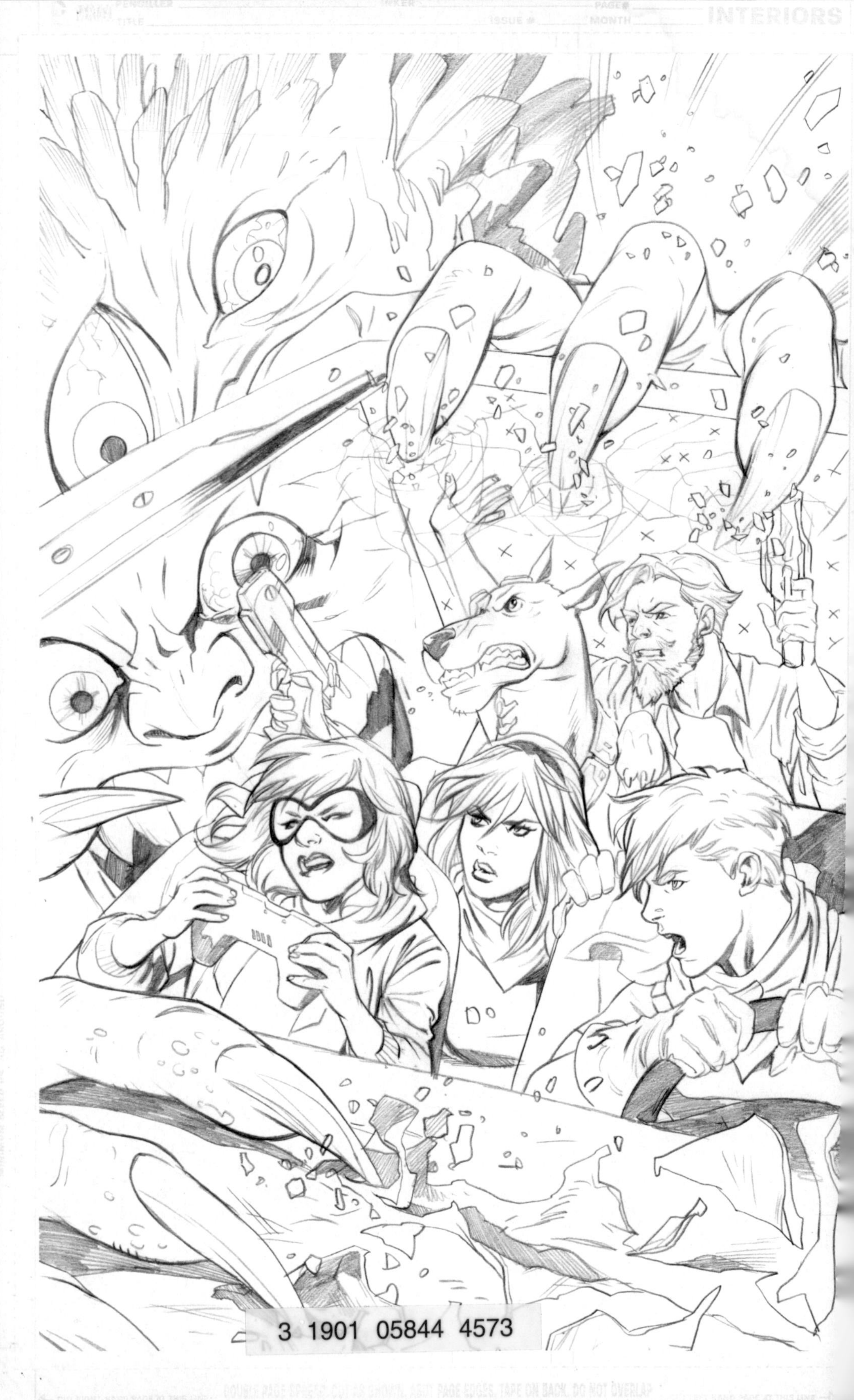